DJ Culture in the Mix

DJ Culture in the Mix

Power, Technology, and Social
Change in Electronic Dance Music

EDITED BY
BERNARDO ALEXANDER ATTIAS
ANNA GAVANAS
HILLEGONDA C. RIETVELD

BLOOMSBURY
NEW YORK • LONDON • NEW DELHI • SYDNEY

Bloomsbury Academic

An imprint of Bloomsbury Publishing Inc.

1385 Broadway	50 Bedford Square
New York	London
NY 10018	WC1B 3DP
USA	UK

www.bloomsbury.com

Bloomsbury is a registered trade mark of Bloomsbury Publishing Plc

First published 2013

© Bernardo Alexander Attias, Anna Gavanas,
Hillegonda C. Rietveld and contributors, 2013

Cover photography by Henrik Landén

Library of Congress Cataloging-in-Publication Data
DJ culture in the mix : power, technology, and social change in electronic
dance music / edited by Bernardo Alexander Attias, Anna Gavanas, and
Hillegonda C. Rietveld.
pages cm
Includes bibliographical references and index.
ISBN 978-1-62356-690-6 (hardcover : alk. paper)-- ISBN 978-1-62356-006-5
(pbk. : alk. paper) 1. Underground dance music--Social aspects. I. Attias,
Bernardo Alexander. II. Gavanas, Anna, 1971- III. Rietveld, Hillegonda C.
ML3918.U53D5 2013
781.648--dc23

ISBN: HB: 978-1-62356-690-6
PB: 978-1-62356-006-5
ePub: 978-1-62356-994-5
ePDF: 978-1-62356-437-7

Typeset by Fakenham Prepress Solutions, Fakenham, Norfolk NR21 8NN
Printed and bound in the United States of America

To Graham, international man of mystery.

CONTENTS

Acknowledgements ix

1 Introduction 1
   Hillegonda C. Rietveld

2 Subjectivity in the Groove: Phonography, Digitality and Fidelity 15
   Bernardo Alexander Attias

3 DJ Technologies, Social Networks and Gendered Trajectories in European DJ Cultures 51
   Anna Gavanas and Rosa Reitsamer

4 Journey to the Light? Immersion, Spectacle and Mediation 79
   Hillegonda C. Rietveld

5 The DJ as Electronic Deterritorializer 103
   Mirko M. Hall and Naida Zukic

6 'It's Not the Mix, It's the Selection': Music Programming in Contemporary DJ Culture 123
   Kai Fikentscher

7 Electronic Dance Music and Technological Change: Lessons from Actor-Network Theory 151
Jonathan Yu

8 DJ Culture and the Commercial Club Scene in Sydney 173
Ed Montano

9 DJs and the Aesthetic of Acceleration in Drum 'n' Bass 195
Chris Christodoulou

10 The Forging of a White Gay Aesthetic at the Saint, 1980–4 219
Tim Lawrence

11 DJs as Cultural Mediators: The Mixing Work of São Paulo's Peripheral DJs 247
Ivan Paolo de Paris Fontanari

12 War on the Dancefloor: *Synthscenen*'s Military Power Games 269
Johanna Paulsson

13 DJ-driven Literature: A Linguistic Remix 291
Simon A. Morrison

Contributors 315
Index 319

ACKNOWLEDGEMENTS

The editors thank each other for being great colleagues, working together across time zones in an ever-accelerating pace. We are thankful to each of the authors for their dedication in contributing to a multi-facetted book on the cultures of the electronic dance music DJ, patiently putting up with our endless questions. We thank editors David Barker, Kaitlin Fontana and Ally Jane Grossan at Bloomsbury Publishing for their support of this project. And we are grateful to Graham St John for his unswerving dedication to developing and maintaining the *Dancecult* network, bringing us together for an electronic dance music culture panel at the Cultural Crossroads conference of the Association of Cultural Studies at West Indies University, Jamaica, back in 2008.

Hillegonda C. Rietveld additionally wishes to acknowledge the Centre for Media and Culture Research at London South Bank University for financially supporting the research time and conference travel related to completing this project. I also thank my students in Music and Sonic Media and my PG research students for their stimulating questions and insights – you keep me young! I'm especially grateful to Chris Christodoulou, Barbara Panuzzi and Dan Fenton for stimulating conversations regarding music, technology, mediation and the senses. On a personal note, I would not be here without the musicality of my family or Max's love of food. Finally, I want to thank Will Straw, Sheila Whiteley, Graham St John, Steve Redhead, Martha Tupinambá de Ulhôa, Sean Albiez, Tim Lawrence, Lisa Blackman, Jeffrey Weeks, Janet Holland and Michal Lyons for their warm academic encouragement. Rest in peace, Michal.

Anna Gavanas sends her biggest respect to her DJ grandmasters and crew. Bigups to Mutamassik, Anaya, Aimnbreak, Paizan, Funky Tuna, Mikronesien, Hardware, Struck, D. Wattsriot and Aroma: relentless instigators, troublemakers on the musical frontline. And bigups to Graham St John, DJ Professor Ben, DJ Empress Gonnie,

Hillevi Ganetz, Ann Werner, Hasse Huss, Marie Selander and Johan Fornäs: musical troopers on the textual frontline. Massive praise also for DJ-horan for decades of carrying record bags and fetching drinks. Plus Sideshow Rodge, of the Meerkat Recordings crew, for messing with my equipment while playing, getting everyone wasted and making sure we get kicked out every once in a while. And huge respect to my musical influencers: Nuphlo, Mala, Kutterfugel, Uzul, Hab, Ombudsman, Jah Warrior and Warrior Queen – to name a few. Finally, Gavanas would like to send her thanks to her musical influences beyond life, to her grandfather Kurt Pettersson and her brother Christos Gavanas. And to Henrik Landén, keeping the legacy of Christos alive in sound and vision.

Bernardo Alexander Attias would like to acknowledge his family, colleagues and friends who have put up with his insane work hours and mood swings as this project slowly came together. Special thanks to Dean Robert Bucker and Provost Harry Hellenbrand at California State University Northridge for supporting a sabbatical that allowed me to focus on research for a semester, as well as to University colleagues and staff (particularly Don Brownlee, Daisy Lemus, Rebecca Litke and Yolanda Avila) who helped keep the Department functioning during my absence. Thanks to Henry Krips and Judy Battaglia for inviting me to present some of my early thoughts on DJ culture to their students at Claremont Graduate College and Loyola Marymount University, and to supportive collaborators Christy Brand, Fred Church, Anna Gavanas, Trademark Gunderson, Hillegonda Rietveld, Shane Martin, Randy Stearns and tobias van Veen for participating with me in public performances and think-pieces touching on the questions raised in this collection. Big love to Mieka du Franx, Karina Junker, Elizabeth A. Moore and Beatrice Neumann for sharing their passion for electronic music and constantly introducing me to fresh sounds, and to Jessica Baty-McMillan, Karyl Kicenski, Geoff Klinger, Lilah Martin, Jeanine Mingé, Gordon Mitchell and Randi Picarelli for always being fantastic and supportive sounding boards and very dear friends. Max respect to the Scratch DJ Academy family in Los Angeles for their tireless promotion of DJ culture and skills, and for the welcoming sense of community I found among them. Big shout out to the Train Wreck Crew and the teachers and students from whom I learned so much, including Denkym, Hapa, Shortee, Faust, Dynamix, Puffs, QUIX05, Lost, Just MATTER, Fade, O, James Jordan, Tosh Biko, and, of course, DJ Hideo. Rest in peace, Hideo. Live life!

CHAPTER ONE

Introduction

Hillegonda C. Rietveld

The electronic dance music DJ: party leader, sonic entertainer, auditory artist, music programmer, record mixer, beatmatcher, cultural masher, music producer, creative music archivist, record collector, sex symbol, role model, upwardly mobile brand, youth marketing tool, dancefloor parent, witch-doctor, tantric yogi, cyborgian shaman, the embodiment of studio-generated music. Mixing music recordings into a long danceable sound track, we find them at work at discos, clubs, rave parties and dance festivals; in smoky dark basements, custom-made dance spaces, squatted warehouses, damp railway arches and lofty penthouse parties; filling stadiums, seducing the beach crowds, playing the crowd. At their best, dance DJs save our nights with their music, push our dancing bodies to the limits of endurance, lull us gently to a restorative state and make us feel reborn. In short, the DJ is endowed with a hefty dose of aura, authenticity and cultural capital; and so are the tools of their trade, not least the residual disco dance single of 12-inch vinyl analogue format. Admittedly, there are plenty of dance DJs offering banal sets of inoffensive dance MP3s, at worst driving their audiences to alcoholism with dull tunes on a distorted soundsystem, as bar-owners count their drink profits. But what do we really know about the dance DJ and the cultural discourses that surround them? Can we explode the myth of the masculine, and increasingly whitewashed, millionaire DJ? How do dance DJs perceive their role, their music, their technologies and their career prospects? What does the DJ do, to make our secret fleeting moments on the dancefloor so special?

Electronic Dance Music

Dance music genres (such as techno, trance, house music, garage, drum 'n' bass, dubstep) shatter into a myriad of subgenres, known in the US under the umbrella term 'electronica' and more widely understood as electronic dance music, often abbreviated by scholars and journalists as 'EDM'. However, during 2012 in the US, the rich meanings of the term 'EDM' seem to have been narrowed in the popular media to electronic pop-dance (Sherburne, 2012), a marketable ubiquitous music format that cannibalizes globally fashionable electronic textures. The sounds of electronic dance music have been shaped over several decades by audience tastes, DJ practices, production techniques and genre formations associated with discotheques and dance clubs; post-industrial warehouse parties; post-colonial dance halls; countercultural dance festivals; and globally spreading rave parties. An arguable commonality between the diverse sounds, user-groups[1] and spaces that reside under the umbrella of electronic dance music may be a shared relationship to the alienating effects of computerized and accelerated globalization, which is articulated in local inflections (Christodoulou, 2011; Rietveld, 2004).

During the genre development of electronic dance music, the tempo on the dancefloor hardly ever dips below 120 BPM (beats per minute), keeping the pace of the heartbeat rate of a person in exercise, in excitement or even out of their mind, as

---

[1] The user-groups of electronic dance music DJ cultures are numerous, including the participating DJs and dancers; the onlookers; the dance music producers and remixers; the specialist record labels; the record and video buyers; the event promoters; the sound technicians; the set designers; the VJs; the light crews; the flyer and poster designers; the poster and flyer distributors; the music journalists; the specialist authors; the music broadcasters; the specialist internet companies; the web forum conveners; the merchandise traders; the fashion designers; the consumers; the marketing agencies; and the dedicated academics.

the accelerating pace can reach tempos to 160 BPM and above. Although acoustic instruments can be heard in the mix, as well as incidental field recordings, the dominant sounds associated with such dance events are electronic, synthesized, sometimes analogue, but mostly digital, with a distinctive dominance of the bass-line and programmed repetitive beats. Butler (2006) offers notational analyses of several drum 'n' bass and trance examples, demonstrating differences in rhythmical approaches. Of importance here, though, is the central role of the DJ in the development of such rhythmical structures. For example, breakbeats are produced from, or inspired by, the rhythm breaks that can be found in older R&B recordings, creating flow from these deconstructed, ruptured, components, a practice borrowed from hip-hop and electro DJs. In this way, the genealogy of breakbeats can be traced rhizomically through a soundsystem culture that initially developed in Jamaica (Belle-Fortune, 2004; Christodoulou, in this volume; James, 1997; Keyes, 2002; Reynolds, 1998). By contrast, programmed 'four-to-the-floor' disco beats, as can be heard in house music, techno and trance, enable DJs to produce a seamless beatmatched mix that keeps their dancers locked to the dancefloor in a hypnotized state (Gaillot, 1998; Rietveld, 1998, 2004, 2007). In addition, some trance recordings rely on washes of synthesized sounds, rather than on beats, for mixing – initially to enable the Goa-based trance DJ to segue one tape-recorded track onto the next, as the hot climatic conditions of India, where backpacking trance fans congregated during its genre formation in the early 90s, made vinyl unworkable (Rietveld, 2010).

In short, new dance genres evolve as the music is adapted for the DJ. This is mostly done by DJs, both as remixers and as electronic music producers. The specific dance genre formats help DJs to segue the recorded music components of their mix together into a kinetic musical journey. Simultaneously, genres develop in response to the musical preferences of the participants on the dancefloor, who ruthlessly vote with their feet; the more participants feel engaged with, or seduced by, the DJ during a dance event, the more likely dancers will continue dancing – in some cases for hours on end. In this way, the DJ may be regarded as a facilitator (Ferreira, 2008), a component in a network of relationships between the participants, music culture, DJ technology and entertainment business (see also Yu in this volume).

Writing the DJ

As the development of the dance DJ can be traced back over more than 30 years, there is a need for an academic collection wholly dedicated to the DJ in electronic dance music. During the 1990s, several journalistic books appeared in the English language, offering insightful DJ narratives aimed at fans and practitioners – in particular, an extensive volume penned by German journalist Poschardt (1998) and a successful tome by British writers Brewster and Broughton (1999, 2010), both offering useful histories. In addition, Haslam (2001), Phillips (2009) and Belle-Fortune (2004) made their mark in this area. The majority of factual books in which the dance DJ plays a role seem to focus on scene and genre development – important examples can be found on disco (Goldman, 1978; Shapiro, 2005); club, rave and techno music culture (Collin, 1997; Garratt, 1998; Reynolds, 1998; Sicko, 1999; Silcott, 1999); drum 'n' bass (James, 1997); reggae soundsystems (Bradley, 2000; David Katz, 2003); and hip-hop (Chang, 2005; Toop, 1984). Finally, there are plenty of technical manuals available that describe the work practices of a DJ, including Brewster and Broughton (2002) as well as Brophy and Frempong (2010).

In the academic realm, a range of research monographs has appeared, helping to constitute an emerging field of DJ studies. Particularly in the area of the electronic dance music DJ, Farrugia (2012) addresses the careers of (female) DJs in the US; Hutton (2006) investigates the role of women as DJs in a British night-time economy; Rodgers (2010) gives voice to women as DJs and music producers; and Rietveld (1998) shows how the DJ authors a fluid musical text in dialogue with dancers. Not only do these research publications define academic DJ studies in the context of electronic dance music, they also explicitly address a gender gap in what is produced in the popular press as a male-dominated occupation, in which the DJ is generally described in the masculine singular third person: 'he', 'his', 'him'. Further monographs in electronic dance music offering some reflection on related DJ practices include Anderson (2009), Buckland (2002), Butler (2006), Gaillot (1998) and Thornton (1995). In terms of other, yet related, music scenes, underground disco music DJs of downtown New York are detailed by music historian Lawrence (2003) and ethnomusicologist Fikentscher

(2000), while DJ-related histories, aesthetics and techniques in the hip-hop scene are specifically assessed by Mark Katz (2012) and also, to a lesser extent, in publications like Rose (1994) and Keyes (2002). The 'selector', as the DJ is called in the context of reggae soundsystems, is usually subsumed by their creative sound engineer and leading 'toaster' (called the 'deejay', comparable to the talking, rather than programming, radio DJ) but is given some attention by authors like Veal (2007) and Patridge (2010).

In addition, a range of research papers that are dedicated to DJ practices can be found in conference proceedings (Ferreira, 2008; Fikentscher, 1997; Straw, 1995) and particularly in academic journals (Back, 1988; Christodoulou, 2011; Fikentscher, 2001; Hadley, 1993; Herman, 2006; Langlois, 1992; Lawrence, 2011; Nye, 2011; Reitsamer, 2011; Rietveld, 2011; St John, 2011), some of which have been collected by Butler (2012). Furthermore, edited volumes in popular music studies offer a mix of journalistic and academic work in which one can find the occasional chapter or extract that engages with the role of the DJ or the practice of DJing (Gavanas, 2009; Fikentscher, 2003; Ford, 2011; Haslam, 1998; Houssee and Dar, 1996; Rietveld, 2001, 2004, 2007, 2011; Shapiro, 2002; Toop, 2000, 2004).

It is high time, therefore, to introduce an academic collection that is wholly dedicated to the DJ in electronic dance music. After meeting at Graham St John's electronic dance music panel for the ACS Crossroads conference in Jamaica, Anna Gavanas and Bernardo Attias started the process by producing a special edition on the DJ for *Dancecult: Journal of Electronic Dance Music Culture* (2011). Being part of the Crossroads panel I joined them after the journal publication for the current edited collection, which morphed into a stimulating international collaboration between a mix of established and young researchers from Australia, Austria, Brazil, Germany, the Netherlands, Sweden, the UK and the US. This was enabled by online forums, email and video-conferencing, as well as meetings and joint presentations at various international conferences that are geographically spread as far apart as Spain, Sweden, Jamaica and Hawai'i. The resultant chapters offer an engaging variety of registers in their approach to the topic, not only in their discursive and musical focus, but also conceptually, moving from sociology to media studies, and from critical theory to the use of pulp fiction as ethnographic tool.

DJ Technics

The DJ, or disc jockey, is literally a rider of the recorded music on discs, a surfer of seemingly endless sound waves, music to move to and music to be moved by. Being dependent on music recordings for their practice, the DJ personifies the product of the music studio, which is further actively embodied by the dancers (Ferreira, 2008). The music studio is the place where contemporary compositions are created and assembled from sound waves that are recorded and produced, manipulated and edited, to be polished into a repeatable musical experience, cut on analogue record or converted to a digital audio file, which is then mechanically reproduced or digitally cloned. In turn, the DJ uses the turntable as a musical instrument (Shapiro, 2002), recombining music recordings as the building blocks of the sound track of the dance event. As music for DJs by DJs, each dance recording can be understood as, 'what Umberto Eco has called an "open work"' (Gaillot, 1998, p. 49), the meaning of which is anchored in the mix.

In the opening chapter, Bernardo Attias shows that by reimagining the function of the record player beyond its intended function to consume music, and instead using it as a creative music tool, the DJ stands at a juncture of technology, performance and culture in the increasingly uncertain climate of the popular music industry, functioning both as pioneer and gatekeeper of musical taste. Together with promoters, producers and other professionals in dance music scenes, DJs have advanced music techniques and technological developments, including the creation of digital systems for emulating vinyl performance modes during the late 1990s and tablet 'apps' that remediate (Bolter and Grusin, 1999) their practices in the fluid mobile world of online cultures. Through their aesthetic practices, DJs have the potential to shake up cultural and creative industries. Walter Benjamin (1969) made a comparable optimistic point in his influential 1937 analysis of the work of art in the age of mechanical reproduction, which Middleton (1990, p. 66) draws on in relation to popular music, when he states that, '[an artist] must work towards an *Umfunktionierung*, as Brecht called it – a transformation of the apparatus – which will result in new fusions and relationships between media, genres and techniques, new, more collective production processes, and a new, more participative role for audiences'. In addition, as Mirko M. Hall and Naida Zukic show in this volume, the DJ deconstructs and recombines musical elements to produce new ways of hearing. This is achieved in dialogue with the dancing crowd, the participating audience, which is illustrated well through a considered case study by Tim Lawrence in a chapter on the smooth DJ mix-style at New York's gay club the Saint in response to its specific clientele during the late 1970s and 1980s, as well as in Kai Fikentscher's chapter on the DJ art of music programming.

DJ Contexts

De Certeau (1988, p. 170) suggests that, in contrast to governmental strategic planning, at ground level the production of cultural space is forged from contradictory and heterogeneous components, making holes in 'the constructed order', to turn it into 'a sieve order'. The practice of the dance DJ embodies such a heterogeneous existence, created through the manipulation, deconstruction and reassemblage of existing artefacts into a new, temporary, whole. By creating unique (re)combinations of musical elements in response to the dancers on the floor, the successful club and party DJ can take on a magical role in a culture of industrial reproduction and alienating globalization. As a creative performance, the DJ set has the potential to communicate new ways of being, of feeling, producing musical discourses that are nevertheless embedded in real-world, material, politics. In this way, DJ practices enable the immediate reconstitution of local cultural identity, as shown in this volume by Ivan Paolo de Paris Fontanari regarding peripheral DJs in Brazil's megacity São Paulo; in Chris Christodoulou's chapter on the British dancefloor development of drum 'n' bass in London's energetic sprawl; and in a chapter on DJ culture in Sydney, Australia, by Ed Montano. Johanna Paulsson's chapter provides additional insight into a North European party scene that embraces war and militarism as a stylistic feature, arguing that this ironically undermines hierarchical power divisions.

Further holes seem to appear in a patriarchal social order as women take to the night-time economy as public performers, taking control of the various musical soundscapes that move the

crowds (Hutton, 2006; Rodgers, 2010). In particular, Farrugia
(2012) shows there are various performative options for women in
the DJ profession, in which lesbians are most likely to be accepted
by an established DJ fraternity. And yet – in terms of career development, there is a glass ceiling for women. After the increasing
visibility of successful female DJs during the 1990s, there seems
even a backlash in the specialist media during the last five years,
whereby the othering adjective, 'female', firmly sticks in the
popular realm to differentiate women from the normalized (male)
DJ. Marketing campaigns and journalistic accounts construct the
male DJ as competing with masculine DJs while subordinating
femininized dancers with a mastering beat. By contrast, as Gavanas
and Reitsamer argue in this volume, women are subjected to visual
differentiation and, as DJs, are therefore more often judged by their
looks than by their DJ skills. In an analysis of British dancefloor
literature, Simon A. Morrison's chapter provides further evidence
that the cultural authenticity associated with the role of DJ as hero
is normalized as masculine or, at least, as androgynous.

By using an actor-network approach in his analysis of DJ
practices in Melbourne, Australia, Jonathan Yu argues that
ultimately the humanity (and by implication, I venture, the gender)
of the DJ is of little importance in understanding the assemblage
of the dance event. Instead, Yu shows that the crowd, technology
and DJ are of similar, even equal, importance in establishing the
'fact' of a dance event's existence. In the fluid context of the dance
music exchange perhaps the concept of an androgynous cyborgian
relationship between DJs and their tools could be fruitful. In
popular imagery, as Spinger (1996) shows, the cyborg is nevertheless highly gendered. In this context, some women have found a
degree of success as DJs by embracing otherness as female prerog-
ative in a male-defined world, slipping into the cyborgian role of
vamp in the techno-machine (Rietveld, 2004).

Gendered identity is therefore crucial to understanding DJ trajectories. As women are routinely exscripted as professional DJs, it is
important to establish what it means to be a 'female DJ' in a politically unequal network of male-oriented relationships. Gavanas and
Reitsamer investigate this issue further through extensive ethnographic fieldwork, demonstrating that DJ technologies are coded
as masculine tools. They further find that in response to (hetero)
sexualization of women in the DJ profession and the related gender

discrepancy in DJ employment at clubs and dance events, female networks are being established that aim to change public attitudes in a range of tactical interventions. Nevertheless, they also find that not all participating DJs seek to publicly engage in professional gender struggles, a position that could enhance gender divisions. Some women prefer to even dissociate themselves from female support networks, in fear of ghettoization, perhaps hoping that the adjective 'female' may evaporate through evasion.

Despite the democratic potential of DJs as music performers to anticipate and articulate cultural and social change, and despite the historically crucial role of women and gay men in the hetero-geneous development of DJ practices, within the mediated flow of images and stories, dance DJs are inserted into populist hegemonic gender norms, regarding public exposure, night employment, cultural authenticity and technologies of creative crowd control. Where are the participative audiences in this case? And, how are the senses involved in these relationships? By evaluating potenti-alities and contradictions in the realm of the electronic dance music DJ, this collection of essays wishes to contribute to an iridescent mix of debates. In doing so, the chapters that follow offer critical insights into DJ activities within a selection of global music and media contexts. By bringing together recent scholarly activity that specifically addresses technological and power dynamics in DJ practices and cultures, the editorial team wishes to stimulate a rich understanding of the identity politics and material cultures at play in the realm of electronic dance music DJs.

Enjoy.

References

Anderson, Tammy L. (2009) *Rave Culture: The Alteration and Decline of a Philadelphia Music Scene*. Philadelphia, PA: Temple University Press.

Back, Les (1988) ' "Coughing Up Fire": Sound systems and Cultural Politics in South East London'. *New Formations*, 5: 141–52.

Belle-Fortune, Brian (2004) *All Crews: Journeys Through Jungle / Drum 'n' Bass Culture*. London: Vision Publishing.

Benjamin, Walter (1969) 'The Work of Art in the Age of Mechanical

Reproduction'. In *Illuminations: Essays and Reflections*, trans. Harry Zohn. New York: Schochen.

Bolter, Jay David and Grusin, Richard (1999) *Remediation: Understanding New Media*, Cambridge, MA: MIT Press.

Bradley, Lloyd (2000) *Bass Culture: When Reggae Was King*. London, New York, Ringwood, Toronto, New Delhi, Auckland and Johannesburg: Viking.

Brewster, Bill and Broughton, Frank (1999) *Last Night a DJ Saved My Life: The History of the Disc Jockey*. London: Headline.

—(2002) *How to DJ Properly: The Art and Science of Playing Records*. London, New York, Toronto, Sydney and Auckland: Bantam Press.

—(2010) *The Record Players: DJ Revolutionaries*. London: DJhistory. com.

Brophy, Ben and Frempong, Jerry (2010) *Everything You Need to Know About DJ'ing & Success: Danny Rampling Shares His 20 Years Experience at the Top*. London: Aurum Press.

Buckland, Fiona (2002) *Impossible Dance: Club Culture and Queer World-Making*. Middletown, CT: Wesleyan University Press.

Butler, Mark J. (2006) *Unlocking the Groove: Rhythm, Meter, and Musical Design in Electronic Dance Music*. Bloomington and Indianapolis, IN: Indiana University Press.

—(ed.) (2012) *Electronica, Dance and Club Music*. Burlington, VT and Farnham: Ashgate.

Chang, Jeff (2005) *Can't Stop, Won't Stop: A History of the Hip-Hop Generation*. London: Edbury Press.

Christodoulou, Chris (2011) 'Rumble in the Jungle: City, Place and Uncanny Bass'. *Dancecult: Journal of Electronic Dance Music Culture*, 3(1): 44–63.

Collin, Matthew (1997) *Altered State: The Story of Ecstasy Culture and Acid House*. London: Serpent's Tail.

De Certeau, Michel (1988) *The Practice of Everyday Life*, trans. Steven F. Rendall. Berkeley and Los Angeles, CA: University of California Press.

Farrugia, Rebekah (2012) *Beyond the Dancefloor: Female DJs, Technology and Electronic Dance Music Culture*. Chicago, IL and London: Intellect/University of Chicago Press.

Ferreira, Pedro Peixoto (2008) 'When Sound Meets Movement: Performance in Electronic Dance Music'. *Leonardo Music Journal*, 18: 17–20. http://www.leonardo.info/isast/journal/toclmj18.html [accessed 19 March 2013].

Fikentscher, Kai (1997) 'The DJ as Performer'. In Helmi Järviluoma and Tarja Hautamdki (eds) *Music on Show: Issues of Performance* (70–4). Tampere, Finland: Department of Folk Tradition, University of Tampere.

—(2000) *'You Better Work!' Underground Dance Music in New York City*. Hanover, NH and London: Wesleyan University Press.

—(2001) 'The DJ as Composer, or How I Became a Composing DJ'. *Current Musicology*, 65: 93–8.

—(2003) 'There's not a problem I can't fix, 'cause I can do it in the mix.' 'On the Performative Technology of 12-inch Vinyl'. In René Lysloff and Leslie Gay (eds) *Music and Technoculture* (290–315). Hanover, NH and London: Wesleyan University Press.

Ford, Robert Jr (2011) 'B-Beats Bombarding Bronx: Mobile DJ Starts Something With Older R&B Disks'. In M. Forman and M. A. Neal (eds) *That's the Joint! The Hip-Hop Studies Reader*, 2nd edn. London and New York: Routledge.

Gaillot, Michel (1998) *Multiple Meaning. Techno: An Artistic and Political Laboratory of the Present,* trans. Warren Niesluchowski. Paris: Édtions Dis Voir.

Garratt, Sheryl (1998) *Adventures in Wonderland: A Decade of Club Culture*. London: Headline.

Gavanas, Anna (2009) ' "You Better Be Listening to My Fucking Music You Bastard!" Teknologi, Genusifiering och Andlighet Bland DJs på Elektroniska Dansmusikscener i Berlin, London och Stockholm'. In Hillevi Ganetz, Anna Gavanas, Hasse Huss and Ann Werner (eds) *Rundgång: genus och populärmusik* (83–9). Stockholm: Makadam.

Gavanas, Anna and Attias, Bernardo (eds) (2011) *Dancecult: Journal of Electronic Dance Music Culture* (Special Issue on the DJ) 3(1). http://dj.dancecult.net/index.php/journal/issue/view/4 [accessed 16 March 2013].

Goldman, Albert (1978) *Disco*. New York: Hawthorn Books.

Hadley, Daniel J. (1993) 'Ride the Rhythm: Two Approaches to DJ Practice'. *Journal of Popular Music Studies*, 5: 58–67.

Haslam, Dave (1998) 'DJ Culture'. In Steve Redhead, Derek Wynne and Justin O'Connor (eds) *The Clubcultures Reader: Readings in Popular Cultural Studies* (150–61). Malden, MA and Oxford: Blackwell.

—(2001) *Adventures on the Wheels of Steel: The Rise of the Superstar DJs*. London: Fourth Estate.

Herman, Bill D. (2006) 'Scratching Out Authorship: Representations of the Electronic Music DJ at the Turn of the 21st Century'. *Popular Communication*, 4(1): 21–38.

Houssee, Shirin and Dar, Mukhtar (1996) 'Remixing Identities: "Off" the Turntable'. In Sanya Sharam, John Hutnyk and Ashwani Sharma (eds) *Dis-orienting Rhythms: The Politics of the New Asian Dance Music* (51–104). London: Zed Books.

Hutton, Fiona (2006) *Risky Pleasures? Club Cultures and Feminine Identities*. Burlington, VT and Aldershot: Ashgate.

James, Martin (1997) *State of Bass. Jungle: The Story So Far*. London: Boxtree.

Katz, David (2003) *Solid Foundation: An Oral History of Reggae*. London: Bloomsbury.

Katz, Mark (2012) *Groove Music: The Art and Culture of the Hip-Hop DJ*. Oxford and New York: Oxford University Press.

Keyes, Cheryl L. (2002) *Rap and Street Consciousness*. Urbana and Chicago, IL: University of Illinois Press.

Langlois, Tony (1992) 'Can you feel it? DJ-s and House Music Culture in the UK'. *Popular Music*, 11(2): 229–38.

Lawrence, Tim (2003) *Love Saves the Day: A History of American Music Culture, 1970–1979*. Durham, NC and London: Duke University Press.

—(2011) 'The Forging of a White Gay Aesthetic at the Saint'. *Dancecult: Journal of Electronic Dance Music Culture*, 3(1): 4–27.

Middleton, Richard (1990) *Studying Popular Music*. Philadelphia, PA: Open University Press.

Nye, Sean (2011) 'Headphone-Headset-Jetset: DJ Culture, Mobility and Science Fictions of Listening'. *Dancult: Journal of Electronic Dance Music Culture*, 3(1). http://dj.dancecult.net/index.php/journal/article/view/90 [accessed 2 May 2013].

Partridge, Christopher (2010) *Dub in Babylon: An Understanding of the Evolution and Significance of Dub Reggae in Jamaica and Britain from King Tubby to Post-Punk*. London and Oakville, CT: Equinox.

Phillips, Dom (2009) *Superstar DJs Here We Go! The Rise and Fall of the Superstar DJ*. London: Ebury Press.

Poschardt, Ulf (1998) *DJ Culture*, trans. Shaun Whiteside. London: Quartet Books.

Reitsamer, Rosa (2011) 'The DIY Careers of Techno and Drum 'n' Bass DJs in Vienna'. *Dancecult: Journal of Electronic Dance Music Culture*, 3(1): 28–43.

Reynolds, Simon (1998) *Energy Flash: A Journey through Rave Music and Dance Culture*. London: Picador/Macmillan.

Rietveld, Hillegonda C. (1998) *This Is Our House; House Music, Cultural Spaces and Technologies*. Aldershot: Ashgate.

—(2001) 'Im Strom des Techno'. In Peter Wicke (ed.) *Handbuch der Musik im 20. Jahrhundert: Rock- und Popmusik*. Laaber, Germany: Laaber-Verlag.

—(2004) 'Ephemeral Spirit: Sacrificial Cyborg and Soulful Community'. In Graham St John (ed.) *Rave Culture and Religion* (45–60). London and New York: Routledge.

—(2007) 'The Residual Soul Sonic Force of the Vinyl 12-inch Dance

Single'. In Charles Ackland (ed.) *Residual Media* (97–114). Minneapolis, MN and London: University of Minnesota Press.

—(2010) 'Infinite Noise Spirals: The Musical Cosmopolitanism of Psytrance'. In Graham St John (ed.) *Psytrance: Local Scenes and Global Culture* (69–88). London: Routledge.

—(2011) 'Disco's Revenge: House Music's Nomadic Memory'. *Dancecult: Journal of Electronic Dance Music Culture*, 2(1): 4–23. http://dj.dancecult.net/index.php/journal/article/view/79 [accessed 16 March 2013].

Rodgers, Tara (2010) *Pink Noises: Women on Electronic Music and Sound*. Durham, NC and London: Duke University Press.

Rose, Tricia (1994) *Black Noise: Rap Music and Black Culture in Contemporary America*. Hanover, NH: Wesleyan University Press.

St John, Graham (2011) 'DJ Goa Gil: Californian Exile, Dark Yogi and Dreaded Anomaly'. *Dancecult: Journal of Electronic Dance Music Culture*, 3(1): 97–128.

Shapiro, Peter (2005) *Turn the Beat Around: The Secret History of Disco*. London: Faber and Faber.

—(2002) 'Deck Wreckers: The Turnable as Instrument'. In Ed Young (ed.) *Undercurrents: The Hidden Wiring of Modern Music*. London and New York: Continuum.

Sherburne, Philip (2012) 'Top 100 DJs Poll: Who Won, Who Lost, and What the Hell Is Hardstyle?' *Spin*, 23 October. http://www.spin.com/blogs/top-100-djs-poll-who-won-who-lost-and-what-the-hell-is-hardstyle/ [accessed 17 March 2013].

Sicko, Dan (1999) *Techno Rebels: The Renegades of Electronic Funk*. New York: Billboard.

Silcott, Mireille (1999) *Rave America: New School Dancescapes*. Toronto: ECW Press.

Springer, Claudia (1996) *Electronic Eros: Bodies and Desire in the Postindustrial Age*. London: Athlone Press.

Straw, Will (1995) 'The Booth, the Floor and the Wall: Dance Music and the Fear of Falling'. In Will Straw, Stacey Johnson, Rebecca Sullivan and Paul Friedlander (eds) *Popular Music – Style and Identity* (249–54). Conference Proceedings, International Association for the Study of Popular Music, 7th International Conference. Montreal: Centre of Research on Canadian Cultural Industries and Institutions.

Thornton, Sarah (1995) *Club Cultures, Media and Subcultural Capital*, Cambridge, MA: Polity Press.

Toop, David (1984) *The Rap Attack: African Jive to New York Hip Hop*. London: Pluto Press.

—(2000) 'Iron Needles of Death and a Piece of Wax'. In P. Shapiro (ed.)

Modulations: A History of Electronic Music, Throbbing Words on Sound. New York: Caipirinha Productions.

—(2004) 'Replicant: On Dub'. In C. Cox and D. Warner (eds) *Modulations: Reading in Modern Music*. London and New York: Continuum.

Veal, Michael E. (2007) *Dub: Soundscapes and Shattered Songs in Jamaican Reggae*. Middletown, CT: Wesleyan University Press.

Virilio, Paul and Lotringer, Sylvere (1997) *Pure War*. New York: Semiotext(e).

CHAPTER TWO

Subjectivity in the Groove: Phonography, Digitality and Fidelity

Bernardo Alexander Attias

I hate CDs, CD-records are fake,
where the fuck the DJ's gonna catch the break?
Only vinyl can make my rear shake,
yo Embee, scratch the record for old times sake.

Looptroop, 'Militant Vinylists' (1996)

In 'Militant Vinylists', Swedish hip-hop artists Looptroop fantasize about firebombing record stores and eviscerating clerks who dare to sell music in digital formats. Looptroop's vinyl terrorists' call to arms 'to preserve the wax and exterminate the compact disc', recorded in 1996, may have been one of the more extreme reactions of artists to an impending change of musical format but it was hardly the first. Music journalist Greg Milner (2009, p. 189), for example, relates the story of the birth of the compact disc in 1984 and its first public unveiling outdoors at a newly opened Sony plant in Indiana, where corporate dignitaries were handed copies of the first CD release, Bruce Springsteen's *Born in the USA* (1984), 'along with a CD containing old Edison recordings'. During the ceremony, 'a Chevy with a bad muffler' turned the corner slowly, until the noise from the car drew the attention of most of the attendees, at which point the driver shouted out the window, 'FUUUUCK YOOOU!' Milner imagines that,

> this guy … didn't want pristine [sound]. I imagine his noisy Chevy having a cheap tape deck with dirty heads …. It sounds grimy, and it sounds good. And now these douches under the tent want to take it away from him. Fuck that! Compact discs … meant the digital forces had established a beachhead in America. Maybe this dude was the first to fire back. (2009, p. 189)

While Milner's description of the driver's motives is pure speculation, the anecdote, like the Looptroop fantasy, illustrates the significant emotional investment that music-lovers associate with music formats.

This is particularly true for the professional DJ, as we have seen both in the early 2000s when the compact disc became the EDM DJ's tool of choice, and in the mid-2000s when the hip-hop DJ embraced the laptop and the Digital Vinyl System (DVS). During the late 2000s and early 2010s a similar reaction emerged against so-called 'controllerists' – DJs who performed using a portable computer and a specially designed controller. Few topics raise as much controversy and stir such passion among electronic music DJs as their preferred choice of formats. Studies, such as Farrugia and Thomas (2005), Montano (2010) or Yu (this volume), have found distinctive preferences among DJs in particular music scenes for specific music storage formats, offering specific philosophical, ideological, and audiological explanations.

I must confess that my own interest in this topic is far from dispassionate: when it comes to music, I am a format fanatic. I collect music on compact disc, cassette, vinyl records and old 78s. I even have a few wax cylinders, as well as various 'one-off' formats such as Throbbing Gristle's *Gristleism* album (2009), which was released as a self-contained, hardware 'loop playback machine'. But, above all, I love vinyl records: the feel, the sound, even the seemingly annoying care and maintenance they require. I occasionally DJ in public, playing both vinyl and CDs as well as various configurations of laptops and software. I own numerous electronic gadgets that allow me to perform, using my extensive digital collection. Yet, while I love the convenience and flexibility of a laptop setup, I find myself always returning to vinyl, which as a DJ I find the most enjoyable and rewarding.

When, in 2011, I considered the oft-declared 'death' of vinyl records in the journal *Dancecult*, I used the term *formatism* to refer to such preferences for one particular format over others: vinyl record, CD, WAV file or MP3 (Attias, 2011). I argued that anxiety over formats in DJ culture marked a 'crisis of identity' that was mediated by discourses of *virtuosity* and *authenticity*. This chapter continues that work, examining two specific manifestations of those discourses – claims about the 'sync' button and claims about digital sound quality – teasing out narratives that animate them. Jonathan Sterne's recent work on the MP3 introduces a notion of 'format theory' that 'refuses an a priori hierarchy of formations of any given medium' (Sterne, 2012, p. 11). I attempt here to evaluate the significance of these arguments about formats from such a perspective: although I have my own preferences, my goal is not to discover which arguments are correct but rather to explore whether these arguments can help us better understand a particular dynamic within DJ culture. I hope to show that formats themselves are ultimately less important than the creative discourses that contextualize them. The two arguments I focus on here are certainly not the only ones put forth in these discourses, but they seem to me to best manifest anxieties about the relationship between technology and human identity that seem bound up in these conflicts over formats. Before exploring these arguments as they appear in contemporary DJ cultures, some historical context will help situate the current debate.

The Early Format Wars

In 1877, Thomas Edison experimented with ways of recording telegraphic messages. He discovered that changing an electrical current in a stylus could change its physical impressions on a rotating cylinder made of tin foil. In the early days Edison was interested in bringing to market a machine that would record information rather than music – a dictaphone whose primary

application was in the business office, not the dancehall.[1] His first
test of the new machine was to record his voice singing a nursery
rhyme: 'Mary had a Little Lamb'. Yet despite this whimsy on
Edison's part, he rejected the idea of his 'favorite invention' being
marketed for amusement. In any case, the invention 'languished
unattended' for several years: 'From 1879 to 1887 the phonograph
went into torpid retirement' (Gelatt, 1977, pp. 36, 33). What
broke the retirement was inspiration born of conflict: Edison's rival
Alexander Graham Bell had financed a similar invention developed
by his cousin Chichester A. Bell and partner Charles Sumner
Tainter. The machine followed the same basic formula as Edison's
phonograph, but Edison's rigidly mounted needle was replaced
with a movable stylus, and the tin foil of Edison's cylinders was
replaced with wax-coated cardboard, to produce a less raspy
sound. Edison responded with a machine with a similar stylus that
etched cylinders made entirely of a 'wax-like compound' (Gelatt,
1977, p. 36). The format wars had begun.

By the 1890s, despite Edison's disdain for marketing his invention
as an entertainment novelty, various companies were experimenting
with coin-operated phonographs playing music in public areas

---

[1] See Jones (1992, p. 18), Millard (2005, p. 37) and Coleman (2003, p. 12).
Read and Welch (1959, p. 107) argue that Edison's disdain for the entertainment
possibilities of the phonograph has been exaggerated by his representative Samuel
Insull, who expressed fear that the use of phonographs as coin-operated amuse-
ments would 'discourage acceptance of the phonograph as a business machine'.
Nevertheless, in one article Edison wrote for the *North American Review*, published
in 1878, he listed some of the primary uses to which the phonograph could be put.
He devoted most of his words in this section to the two primary uses he considered,
letter-writing and dictation. Music is mentioned, but only in terms of individual,
nonprofessional, recordings – 'thus a friend may in a morning-call sing us a song
which shall delight an evening company' – and in terms of music education. The
notion of producing musical recordings of recognized artists does not seem to have
occurred to him at this time (Edison, 1878, p. 533). Ten years later, he seems to have
come to this realization, and seems more enthusiastic about the musical potential
of the device (Edison, 1888, pp. 646–7). Interestingly, the phonograph's technological shortcomings in terms of playback fidelity made it ultimately inadequate to
the business dictation tasks Edison had envisioned for it; as Morton (2000, p. 17)
notes, 'Music, ironically, was in some ways well-suited to the phonograph's limited
sonic range and high levels of noise and distortion. Listeners often knew the words
to popular songs already, or could recognize the melody of even a badly recorded
song. Then as now, it was not usually necessary for the recording of a song to be
perfectly free of scratches, hissing, or distortion for it to be thoroughly enjoyable.'

(Morton, 2000, p. 17). Oliver Read and Walter Welch (1959, p. 165) note that 'there was a genuine hobby interest in phonographs and records ... illustrated by the fact that phonograph and talking machine parties were popular in the late 1890s and early 1900s'. The next stage in the format wars emerged as wax cylinders gave way to the flat discs we have since called 'records'. The cylinder did not go quietly, however; format wars were fought extensively, both in the courtroom and in the advertising pages. Edison insisted, probably quite reasonably, that the sound quality of the cylinder was far superior to the disc (Read and Welch, 1959, pp. 151–75). The inherent physical properties of a flat disc spinning at a constant speed creates 'That Fearful Grating Sound' (Read and Welch, 1959, p. 165) that audiophiles would eventually call 'inner groove distortion' (Gelatt, 1977, p. 166), created as the stylus is challenged to continue pulling the same amount of information from an ever-tightening circular groove. Cylinders have no inner groove – the stylus travels the same distance per revolution at the end of a song that it does near the beginning. But after a series of patent disputes, the economics of convenience (such as flat storage and portability) as well as clever marketing won out over sound quality; by 1912 Edison had accepted the new format. Read and Welch note, 'the ultimate doom of the cylinder had been sounded with the announcement of the Edison Diamond Disc Phonograph in 1912' (1959, p. 175).

The phonograph was widely embraced by American and European consumers early on, but its acceptance was not without controversy among musicians. One of recorded music's first great economic beneficiaries, American composer John Philip Sousa launched a 'jeremiad' (Gelatt, 1977, p. 148) against what he called 'the menace of mechanical music' that was '[s]weeping across the country with the speed of a transient fashion', offering to play music 'in substitute for human skill, intelligence, and soul' (Sousa, 1993, p. 14). Sousa (1993, p. 14) predicted in 1906 'a marked deterioration in American music and musical taste': the phonograph would lead to a decline in musical virtuosity; its performance could never 'inspire embryotic Mendelssohns, Beethovens, Mozarts and Wagners to the acquirement of technical skill, or the grasp of human possibilities of art'.

Sousa's complaints ultimately betrayed his fears about political participation generally and democratization more specifically: for

Sousa, the phonograph put musical pleasure in the hands of people who had not perfected musical skills. It was a technological shortcut that replaced 'human skill, intelligence, and soul' with the soul of a machine (Sousa, 1993, p. 14). This notion of the loss of humanity to the machine – a fear of robotic automation – is a common theme in popular literature during times of technological change generally, but it takes on special significance for musicians. Sousa saw the phonograph as the return of the mechanical *in* music; long before automatons made music, he reminded readers, some insufferable musicians simply composed like automatons:

> From the days when the mathematical and mechanical were paramount in music, the struggle has been bitter and incessant for the sway of the emotional and the soulful. And now ... come these talking and playing machines, and offer again to reduce the expression of music to a mathematical system of megaphones, wheels, cogs, disks, cylinders, and all manner of revolving things .... (Sousa, 1993, p. 14)

Sousa's pronouncements 'provoked a storm of debate' (Gelatt, 1977, p. 147) about the artistic merits of the phonograph, with Henry T. Finck replying that the decline of American musical taste was hardly caused by the phonograph: 'it is a little difficult to see what there is to blunt in the musical sense of a nation which makes a hero of Sousa, paying him $50,000 for a mediocre march not worth $50' (Gelatt, 1977, p. 147). Yet Sousa was not alone in his condemnation of the phonograph; Alice Clark Cook, for example, expressed concern in 1916 that 'mere listening to a machine' was a poor substitute for musical training, encouraging 'mental muscles [to] become flabby' (Kenney, 1999, p. 57). The phonograph industry responded to such concerns with an advertising campaign in the 1910s, defending the phonograph as a boon to musical education (Kenney, 1999, pp. 58–64; Siefert, 1995), and indeed the entire field of 'music appreciation' (not to mention musical practices built around learning from recordings) was a product of the phonographic revolution (Katz, 2010, pp. 56–79). Right or wrong, however, these claims are historical antecedents to key arguments about technology in contemporary DJ culture.

The earliest popular discourses about the phonograph and its formats, it seems, were already rife with expressions of two anxieties that continue to animate current controversies in DJ culture as well as popular music listening cultures more generally: a concern that the new technologies degrade the fidelity of musical recordings and a concern that they threaten to undermine the development of musical technique. These concerns are manifestations of specific philosophical perspectives that reappear throughout the history of music formats, reaching a crescendo in the digital era: a concern on the one hand for the authenticity of musical representation, and on the other for the virtuosity of musical performance. In contemporary debates about digital DJing, arguments about virtuosity and authenticity appear in many forms, but I focus here on two disputes in particular: one regarding the use of the 'sync' button by laptop DJs and the other regarding the implications of digital formats for 'high fidelity' sound quality.

Virtuosity: Keeping the Beat

> Who gives a fuck? I don't have any shame in admitting that for 'unhooked' sets .... I just roll up with a laptop and a MIDI controller and 'select' tracks and hit a spacebar. Ableton syncs the shit up for me ... so no beatmatching skill required. 'Beatmatching' isn't even a fucking skill as far as I'm concerned anyway. So what, you can count to 4. Cool. I had that skill down when I was 3, so don't give me that argument please. (Deadmau5, 2012)

This post on the blog of Canadian EDM producer Joel T. Zimmerman, a.k.a. Deadmau5, quickly and predictably touched off a firestorm of controversy among DJs and music fans across the internet. Some applauded the honesty of this internationally famous DJ, while others bemoaned the increasing popularity of EDM and the rise of the 'superstar DJ' that has accompanied it. Zimmerman's comments followed on the heels of an interview published in *Rolling Stone* in which he took several pot shots at fellow DJ superstars, characterizing them as 'button-pushers getting paid half a million' while admitting that he too was a button-pusher, the difference being that 'I'm just pushing a lot more buttons' (Eells, 2012, p. 48). The hypocrisy that appeared to be

animating these comments confused fans while feeding the indig-
nation of detractors, and his blog post was an attempt to 'clear up'
what he had said in the interview. Needless to say, things remained
far from clear following his post.

Discussion boards on websites such as *DJ Tech Tools* (2012a) and
DJ Forums (2012) raged with debates over DJ skills and technologies, with some dismissing contemporary DJs as 'knob jockeys' and
others attacking Deadmau5 as himself devoid of talent and, indeed,
'dead'. Music blogger Jacob Schulman (2012), for example, mused
about Zimmerman's 'honesty and level-headedness'; meanwhile,
British musician and DJ Richard West (a.k.a. Mr.C) denounced
Deadmau5 as 'a complete and utter wanker' on his Facebook page
(West, 2012) and electronic musician and author Peter Kirn (2012)
suggested that 'Deadmau5 might want to take off that mouse head
and look around a bit more often.' Many electronic music fans
dismissed Deadmau5 as a shameless hypocrite: Just as Sousa, one
of America's first musical superstars, profited handsomely from
the technology he critiqued at the turn of the twentieth century,
Zimmerman, as Deadmau5 the DJ, makes millions from the very
button-pushing he derisively dismisses. I think there is more to
these reactions, however: the passion these provocations elicited
on both sides suggests that the preposterously outfitted producer
and performer struck a certain nerve in DJ culture that lies at the
intersection of technology and identity. His comments stirred up
so much anger because he touched upon a problematic that lies at
the heart of the DJ's understanding of their role as a DJ – their very
sense of self.

Deadmau5 created a similar stir over these issues a few years
earlier in 2008, when he wrote, in another incendiary blog post, 'I
don't really see the technical merit in playing two songs at the same
speed together and it bores me to fucking tears …. It's so middle
man, [DJs are] like fucking lawyers: you need them but they're all
fucking cunts' (cited in Thiessen, 2008). In 2012, these comments
probably had more impact due both to Deadmau5's dramatic
rise in popularity since 2008 and to the perceived mainstreaming
of electronic dance music culture more generally (see Petridis,
2012). There is little question that there has been unprecedented
mass media coverage of superstar DJ acts and multimillion-dollar
festivals. This perceived mainstreaming has provoked a visible
backlash, with even the *Wall Street Journal* (Fusilli, 2012) and the

New York Times (Sisario, 2012) – hardly bastions of underground dance music media – publishing handwringing editorials wondering if DJ culture was 'dumbing down' its underground edge.

Controversy over beatmatching has gained particular currency since 2010 due to the increasing appearance of automatic beat syncing features (the 'sync' button) on newer DJ software and hardware, combined with an increasing perception among many DJs that talentless hacks have been rising to superstar fame in the industry. Frequent commenters on DJ weblogs gleefully post links to photos and YouTube videos of big-name DJs such as Guetta and Skrillex performing 'live' with disconnected equipment or faders in the wrong positions, purportedly catching these stars in the act of falsifying their mixing prowess, possibly playing pre-recorded CDs to oblivious crowds (Abbott, 2012; Daverh, 2009), and hard-working DJs roar indignantly when celebrities without DJ training or experience (like *Jersey Shore* actor Pauly D or wealthy socialite Paris Hilton) hop on the DJ bandwagon, packing enormous crowds at top venues (Romero, 2011; *Daily Mail*, 2012).

It is possible that the vitriol reserved for such DJs, who are perceived as making a mockery of the DJ's virtuosity, manifests an underlying anxiety about a question that has plagued working DJs since Jam Master Jay: just what are these people who get rich playing other people's records actually *doing* anyway? The recent popularity of EDM DJs, alongside revelations about how lucrative it can be for superstars (Greenburg, 2012), has brought this question to the forefront of public representations of DJ culture, and Deadmau5's perhaps flippant remarks seemed to pull the rug out from one of the main answers DJs might give: a key skill of the EDM DJ, a skill that takes many months of practice to perfect, is to sync two tracks playing simultaneously by adjusting the speed of one record until the tempo of the music matches that of the other record. For the DJ who spins vinyl records, this technique requires physical training; the DJ must learn to listen simultaneously to two (or sometimes more) tracks playing at once, distinguish subtle tempo differences between the two records, and adjust the pitch control, a variable (and in most cases imprecise) slider on the DJ turntable. The skilled vinyl DJ can have two records playing simultaneously at matched tempos, sometimes for minutes at a time, while adjusting the volume and equalization of the tracks to blend them together seamlessly. Weheliye (2005, p. 90) argues that the DJ learning to sync tempos manually develops 'a sonorous double consciousness wherein his/her hearing capacities are utterly reconfigured'. As tobias van Veen (van Veen and Attias, 2011) points out, this makes beatmatching a kind of musical virtuosity, defined as such because the performer in a live situation runs the risk of failure: 'this latter path is implicitly what is at stake, I believe, with the commodification of "DJ culture" as it loses touch not with the vinyl format, but with what constitutes the virtuosity of playing an inventive instrument – RISK. Without risk of fucking-up (train-wrecking, skipping the needle, a bad mix, etc.), there is no need for the human whatsoever.' From this perspective, the essentially *human* component of musical virtuosity, defined here by the risk of failure in live performance, is ultimately threatened by a relentless, beatmatching automaton: the robots are taking over.

Deadmau5's comments equating beatmatching with 'counting to four' raised so much ire because, I argue, they pulled the curtain back for a moment to reveal a seldom-acknowledged truth: beatmatching is, at its root, a simple matter of mathematics. Vinyl DJs who first reacted negatively to the spread of CD players in DJ booths, many with LED displays indicating tempo values in beats per minute (BPM), may have acknowledged as much by denigrating the CD player as 'cheating' (see for example *DJ Tech Tools Forum*, 2012c). The CD player was seen by some as a cheat because it reduced the 'risk of failure' so essential to perceived virtuosity. Whereas the vinyl turntable most favoured by DJs, the Technics SL–1200 from Panasonic, had no digital displays to speak of, the CDJ–1000 developed by Pioneer (which quickly became the CD DJ's player of choice) provided the user a visual representation of the tempo of the music, as well as a precise readout of the percentage by which the user is changing the tempo with the pitch slider. A quick look at the numbers greatly simplifies the task of syncing beats, allowing the DJ to 'cheat' by relying on visual analysis rather than on the musical skill of close listening.

CD players have also taken 'wow and flutter' out of the DJ mix equation: CD playback occurs via a digital buffer, meaning minor fluctuations in the rotation speed of the disc will not affect the speed at which the music is played back. In an analogue system such as a turntable, these tiny fluctuations register during playback. Such fluctuations, if audible at all, would likely only be noticed by the most discriminating of listeners, but they make the beatmatching process a far less precise affair than it is for CD DJs. Two CDs properly beatmatched should stay synced until the end of the tracks, whereas two vinyl records playing songs at the same tempo will still require the DJ's attention to make minor adjustments if they are to stay matched for more than a few bars. Some DJs, like Richie Hawtin, earned reputations for their aptitude for long, drawn-out blends, sometimes of three or four vinyl records at a time; with CDs, keeping such long mixes in sync for longer periods of time is far less impressive.

Although not addressing beatmatching per se, Montano (2010) suggests that with CD players, there is 'less of an emphasis on skill, and more of an emphasis on being able to operate the machines properly' (p. 405). The argument itself is probably a weak one – after all, turntables are also machines, and 'operating them properly' is certainly a 'skill' – but its implications manifest a concern that seems to arise whenever new technologies are introduced into musical practice. The DJ who performs with CDs is seen here as an engineer rather than a performer, a technician rather than an artist. The DJ, in essence, *becomes machinic* in such discourses; his/her very soul is at issue. As Marx (1993, pp. 690–706) warned long ago about workers on the assembly line, the DJ becomes a cog in the machine; rather than the DJ exercising agency with the help of a machine, the machine exercises agency through the DJ.

While some vinyl DJs still complain loudly about the CDJ, most had by 2005 at least begrudgingly accepted its domination of the club and festival scene. By this time the Pioneer CDJ–1000 had become industry standard (Osborne, 2009); its use had been 'authenticated' in most electronic dance club scenes, although by no means all; certain music scenes remain entirely and adamantly vinylist. Around 2000, a new threat to DJ virtuosity had appeared on the scene: the laptop computer. The laptop crept into mainstream DJ culture almost surreptitiously through the hip-hop scene thanks to the advent of the Digital Vinyl System (DVS), which allowed DJs to access music libraries from laptop computers connected to vinyl turntables.[2] The

---

[2] Laptops also emerged in minimal techno and electronica scenes in the US and Europe around the same time; rather than DVS, however, these performers generally utilized digital audio workstation and sequencing software such as Ableton Live.

DVS preserved the physical interaction with records preferred by vinylists; it used specialist vinyl records pressed with a 'time code' – a high-pitched sound that conveys information to the computer. A computer program uses the time code to ascertain the position of the stylus in the groove as well as its velocity and direction. This allows the DJ to play digital files directly from the computer, yet manipulate the sounds physically using the turntables and vinyl records, almost exactly as if the sounds were recorded on the records.[3] The DJ's skillset and physical conditioning transferred over to DVS quite seamlessly; as Katz (2012, p. 220) argues, 'DVS allows DJs to keep what they love about vinyl – its feel, look, and authenticity – and avoid what they don't love about it – its weight, cost, and inconvenience'.

DVS is ultimately independent of format selection: the time code can be recorded to CDs and then just as easily be manipulated with CDJs. Although mostly vinyl-oriented hip-hop DJs may have taken to DVS earliest thanks to Serato Scratch Live software, released in 2004, Native Instruments' Traktor Scratch (based on the earlier Final Scratch) quickly became the DVS of choice among EDM DJs.[4] Time code DJs, at first criticized for 'pretending' to play records or CDs, still needed beatmatching skills: their record libraries may

---

[3] The sound file is processed according to computer algorithms to mimic the sound of a record moving forward, backward, and at different speeds, emulating the 'scratch' sound of a record being manipulated by the DJ. This processing, while quick, still takes some time, so there is a delay – measurable in microseconds – known as 'latency' that a vinyl DJ must get accustomed to the first time they use DVS.

[4] There is some debate about who 'invented' DVS; in a bizarre replay of some of the earliest patent disputes over the phonograph, various companies have faced off over this issue. In 1998, the company N2IT announced the first edition of 'FinalScratch' for the discontinued operating system BeOS. The company was bought by Stanton Magnetics, which released the first FinalScratch product in 2002. Native Instruments collaborated with Stanton to release version 2 of the software, but the collaboration between the two companies ended poorly (and with legal action). By 2007 Native Instruments released Traktor, a competing product that is now one of the market leaders (Kirn, 2008). However, there are competing stories about the birth of DVS. As early as 1996, Andre Rickli filed an international patent for a 'Digital Processing Device for Audio Signal' (Patent WO/1997/001168) that some claim invalidates N2IT's 2002 patents (Carroll, 2010). And rapper RZA of the group Wu Tang Clan claims to have been the first to apply time code to Rickli's invention in 1997 (Carroll, 2010). Yet another claim comes from Serato's Steve West, who claims that Serato Scratch Live was based on a prototype developed from a research paper by James Russell in 1996 (Carroll, 2010).

have resided on laptops rather than in heavy crates, but they faced the same limitations of technology as their physical media-playing peers, and needed to develop similar skills. But the computer made the task seem easier to some: tempos were calculated and displayed on the screen, and waveforms provided visual cues unavailable to the vinyl DJ. One could now learn to beatmatch without using their ears, relying primarily (or even completely) on the laptop display. DJs 'risk getting lost in their screens', Katz argues, 'focusing more on what they see than what they hear' (2012, p. 226).

The laptop also offers DJs a new approach beyond DVS and time code, however: liberated from spinning platters and physical media formats completely, DJs can mix songs internally on the computer, generally using physical controllers to manipulate virtual controls on a screen via the MIDI protocol.[5] The *controllerist*, as this type of DJ is currently known, may have started as a hobbyist, jury-rigging MIDI keyboards and gamepads for use as DJ controllers, but an entire industry of gadgets has since emerged, bringing to market a dizzying array of tools to give the DJ tactile interaction with computer programs. Most frustrating for many DJs who learned to beatmatch by ear, many of these computer programs included the dreaded 'sync' button, which allows users to bypass months of musical training with a mouse click. The CDJ and DVS had annoyed vinyl DJs by turning the aural and tactile exercise of beatmatching into a mostly visual exercise, but at least some aural skills were required to drop a track on cue and keep the beats matched. Now DJs using computer software such as Ableton Live, Virtual DJ, Traktor DJ, and Serato Itch could dispense with even that, letting the computer do the beatmatching math and produce a perfect blend (almost) every time, at least as

---

[5] Technically, such computer software was developed long before DVS; as early as 1991, Professor Jam, one of the pioneers of 'Computerized Performance Systems' predicted, 'it's no longer a question of if you will use a computer to DJ ... but rather when' (*Start Mobile Beat*, 2008). Programs such as PCDJ and Virtual DJ allowed users to DJ completely on a computer screen, but until such programs allowed users to physically interact with the software via MIDI controllers, they were impractical for most DJs (see Taylor, 2001, pp. 20–1). There were notable early exceptions, but it really wasn't until after DVS had opened the door to the laptop DJ that the 'controllerist' was born, DJing with laptops and gadgets rather than vinyl or CDs.

far as tempo was concerned.[6] More recently, some older DJs have been up in arms over the appearance of a 'sync' button even on hardware designed to be used without laptop computers, notably the soon-to-be industry standard Pioneer CDJ–2000 Nexus (ubbs, 2012; Cunningham, 2012; Ray, 2012).[7] For a younger generation of DJs, 'sync' is now accepted as normal practice.

Working within a more fluid digital framework, controllerists contend that the 'sync' button frees them up to, for example, focus on sound sculpting with filters and EQ; remix songs live using pre-assigned cue points; mix 3 or four songs at once; or turn their attention to song selection and crowd interaction. Yet for some older DJs, such activities are a mere sideshow; they argue that a DJ who does not manually beatmatch does not risk anything when performing publicly. When a DJ blends songs live for a crowded dance floor, s/he runs the risk of 'trainwrecking' – playing records with clashing tempos and thereby losing the energy of the dancers. That risk of failure gives the performance its palpable edge, and some would argue that whatever musicianship can be said to inhabit the DJ must come from that risk. tobias van Veen (van Veen and Attias, 2011) argues that that the risk functions as a 'feedback loop', enhancing and humanizing the performance by making it a communicative and transformative experience: 'When the mix is riding through a beatmatch, even if seamless, the risk of failure is transferred as tension-affect through the soundsystem's relays.

---

[6] Each of these programs relies on a 'beat grid', usually mapped to a fixed tempo based on transients in the song. Computer analysis of tracks generally works well with most flavours of electronic dance music (which is always in 4/4 time with a fixed tempo), but the resulting grid can be incorrect if a track's tempo is not completely fixed (as in tracks with live drumming). In some cases even perfectly quantized tracks will be analysed incorrectly due to unusual syncopation that throws off the software's gridding algorithm; in such cases the analysed tempo is generally a harmonic of the song's actual tempo. Such software usually allows the user to correct the grid manually. And perhaps this is obvious, but I should add that matching tempo is only part of the labour of the DJ mix. Tracks in incompatible musical keys or with diverging rhythm patterns can sound awful blended together no matter how perfectly matched their tempos.

[7] The Nexus not only included automatic beat synchronization features but also a key-detection algorithm that will suggest track choices to the DJ based on the musical key of the currently playing track. It's not difficult to see why some find this additional step even more worrisome: if both beatmatching *and* song selection are now handled by the machine, what is there left for its human operator?

This tension in turn generates feedback for the DJ who feels it from the dancefloor as the intensity of the room increases, leading to heightened mixing, etc.' At stake in such arguments is not just musicianship but the very humanity of the DJ; as one DJ put it, 'Automating this process removes the human element and creates a more sterile feel and experience' (Ray, 2012).

The problem with this argument from a logical perspective is that it privileges one particular technical skill, matching tempos, over other skills that have been developed by CD DJs and controllerists. So-called 'buttonistas' may not be matching beats by ear, but they have demonstrated an impressive array of new skills and tricks that are simply not possible using traditional DJ gear, and some have practiced and refined these skills to the point where it is difficult to deny the musicianship at work. If the litmus test for musical virtuosity is running the risk of failure in public performance, controllerists certainly fit the bill; they just run the risk of failing at something other than syncing beats. In addition, high-profile collaborations between controllerists and well-known vinyl masterminds (such as 'MIDI Fighter' inventor Ean Golden's collaboration with hip-hop turntablist DJ Qbert, or Deadmau5's work with techno superstar Richie Hawtin at the 2013 South by Southwest festival – see Golden, 2011; Rayner, 2013) suggest that the skills of the digital DJ are taken seriously and accepted by at least some more traditional virtuosos.

My point is neither to endorse nor to refute these arguments; I'm exploring them instead to tease out what I see as a fundamental paradox at their heart. For essential to such arguments is an unstated warrant: musicianship is a matter of human skill, a *techne* in the classical Greek sense, a creative practice, that nevertheless seems corrupted by the influence of technology. This warrant presumes a clear opposition between a human *techne* and an inhuman *technology*; ultimately, its advocates assume that it is acceptable for humans to enlist the assistance of technology to achieve some goals but not others. The argument takes different forms in the hands of different advocates, but this paradox remains at its heart. For the vinyl formatist, for example, it is acceptable to use turntables and vinyl records but not CDs; for others, it might be acceptable to use turntables or CDs but not computers. For still others, computers might be fine as long as the DJ avoids the 'sync' button. The question of when is it acceptable to hand off tasks to machines and which tasks must be done by hand (or ear) – why is it acceptable to play songs that use drum machines instead of live drummers, for example; more to the point, why is it acceptable to play pre-recorded songs in the first place? – is really at the heart of the DJ's sense of self as creative and performing artist.[8] Before exploring the implications of this paradox, let us turn to another set of arguments: those about the sound quality of the DJ's preferred audio format.

Authenticity: Sound Arguments

A frequently encountered argument in debates over tools and formats in DJ culture concerns the quality of the sound repro-duced by the format; indeed, this argument is relatively common outside of DJ culture as well. The CD's promise of 'Perfect Sound Forever' – the slogan used by Sony to promote CDs when they were first introduced in 1984 – was both threatening and disturbing to musicians in the 1980s, some of whom called out digital sound as a dangerous deception. Punk rock musician and analogue sound engineer Steve Albini wrote in the liner notes to Big Black's *Songs About Fucking* (1987): 'The future belongs to the analog loyalists. Fuck digital.' And recording artist Neil Young, who would eventually work with Steve Jobs, the concept developer for Apple computers, on a new digital musical format, infamously penned an anti-digital polemic in *Guitar Player*:

> Digital, CDs – I hate them. Digital is a disaster. This is the darkest age of musical sound .... Digital is a huge rip-off. It's completely premature and completely wrong. It's a farce ... [This] is the darkest time for recorded music ever. We'll ... look back and go, 'Wow, that was the digital age. I wonder what it really sounded like? They were so carried away that they didn't

---

[8] Anxiety surrounding this question is perhaps particularly acute for the DJ because there is already resistance among some more traditionally skilled musicians – particularly in the rock 'n' roll world – to consider the DJ an artist in any capacity at all.

really record it. They just made digital records of it.' That's what people will say – MARK MY WORDS. (1992, p. 14)

This is not the place to rehash all of the arguments over analogue vs. digital, some of which are overly technical and some more properly philosophical/theoretical. I do however wish to tease out one thread of discourse that seems to manifest most clearly the opposition between human and machine that resonates so fiercely in the discourse about beatmatching. Running parallel to the arguments regarding the skills necessary to spin first vinyl, CDs and then laptop-based systems, is a similar set of arguments about sound quality that are made about vinyl vs. CD, then CD vs. MP3, and finally between MP3 and 'lossless' file formats such as WAV and FLAC.[9]

There is much to be said about the cultural politics of the notion of 'fidelity' that animates discussions of sound quality: in popular music, for example, there is a suggestion of 'fidelity' to an original musical event that never actually took place in one take. The sounds stored on a recording in *any* format were generally recorded in a controlled studio environment, during different takes at different times and even places, edited and mixed in different versions for different contexts. Whatever 'hi-fi' may mean, there are some basic limitations in the recording process that give analogue recording a higher 'noise floor' than digital, as well as a much smaller dynamic range.[10] Simply put, the digital format allows the recording and storage of a much larger range of sounds from quietest to loudest without distortion. But where a digital format has the advantage in dynamic range, analogue has finer resolution. Analogue formats store continuous waveforms with a theoretically

---

[9] To the extent that the audiophile press can be taken seriously at all as indications of such things, we may soon witness a similar debate over sound quality distinctions between different lossless formats. That such debates are preposterous from the perspective of the basic computer science has not seemed to make an iota of difference those involved in them; see Zeilig and Clawson (2012).

[10] The 'noise floor' is the level of background noise in a signal; in the context of recording formats, the term refers to the noise added to the signal by the recording apparatus (the 'hum' or 'hiss' that can be sometimes be heard on analogue recordings during the silent spaces between songs, for example). The 'dynamic range' is the difference between the noise floor and the loudness ceiling (the volume at which a signal becomes audibly distorted), as expressed in decibels.

infinite resolution, while the digital storage medium – at least in the CD format – is arbitrarily limited to a fixed resolution agreed upon by the corporate interests involved.[11] While some who prefer the sound of analogue make much of these limits – Francis Fukuyama (2011), for example, bemoans the 'loss of information' in the digital waveform while Neil Young (1992) compares the digital waveform to a window screen filtering the scenery through a grid – double blind studies such as Geringer and Dunnigan (2000) tend to confirm that there is no audible waveform distortion in digital storage/playback formats.[12] And vinyl in particular suffers an additional limitation: lower bass frequencies may cause the needle to jump out of the groove, so much of that information is attenuated before the recording is made and then restored to the signal by the playback equipment according to the industry standard 'RIAA equalization curve'. Finally, there are numerous sources of distortion of the analogue signal that don't exist with digital, including 'wow and flutter' on the playback equipment as well as simple dust, scratches, and wear on the grooves of the record.

---

[11] Milner (2009, p. 224) describes the 16-bit resolution and 44.1 kHz sampling rate figures of the CD standard as 'a combination of science, habit, and expediency'.

[12] Indeed, the Nyquist–Shannon sampling theorem, which is the 'science' Milner (2009) refers to behind the CD standard's sampling rate, suggests that 44.1 kHz is more than enough (if only slightly so) to perfectly reconstruct a sound sample for human hearing. There are those who advocate for analogue storage media based on the claim that 'hypersonic' frequencies – those above 20,000 Hz and thus outside the range of human hearing – affect sound quality in less obvious ways. This argument is popular in the audiophile press, as it is driving interest in digital formats that store music at 96 kHz and higher, but it has little if any basis in empirical research. Oohashi et al. (2000) did a study that seemed to lend credence to the notion, finding some impact of hypersonic frequencies on brain activity, but he was unable to reproduce these results in headphone speakers (Oohashi et al., 2006), and studies by several other researchers found subjects unable to detect hypersonic frequencies at all under various circumstances (see Kiryu and Ashihara, 2001; Nishiguchi, 2004; Colloms, 2006; Meyer and Moran, 2007). Winer (2012, pp. 78–9) suggests that the Oohashi et al. studies measured not responses to hypersonic frequencies but rather responses to intermodulation distortion created within the *audible* frequency range as a by-product of the attempt to drive speakers beyond the frequency ranges they are capable of reproducing. And this last point suggests another problem with the argument more generally: analogue recording and reproduction equipment, from microphones to speakers, are generally not capable of either recording or reproducing frequencies much outside of the range of human hearing in the first place.

The CD may not have lived up to its promise of 'perfect sound forever', but there is little question that, at least at the very limited task of distorting the recorded audio signal as little as possible in translation and incorporating a much larger dynamic range, the CD seems to have out-performed vinyl. The CD signal is distorted in its own way, of course: a sound wave is translated (or represented) as a series of discrete locations rather than as a single continuous curve. But this digital signal is translated back into an analogue signal before it is possible for anyone to actually listen to it: while the *representation* of sound waves can be digital or analogue, sound itself is always analogue. At a high enough resolution, the digitally stored representation will produce a sound wave that is audibly indistinguishable from the 'original' sound wave. But if CDs won a victory in the format wars, it was Pyrrhic at best: the steady upswing of vinyl purchases over the period 2008–13 suggests that vinyl enthusiasts remain committed to the analogue sound (Farber, 2013). And, indeed, if CDs have an edge over vinyl as a medium for accurate sound reproduction, it is a tiny edge at best. In any realistic listening situation, and certainly for dance music audiences in clubs, the storage format of the recorded music will be one of the least significant factors affecting the quality of the sound experienced by the listener.

The compact disc was not the last word in digital sound, and many fear that we've since 'progressed' in the wrong direction. The popularity of DVS after 2004 saw vinyl and CD DJs joining forces to dispute the authenticity of the newest format on the block: the MP3. If the arguments between vinyl and CD are ultimately inconclusive, those against MP3 seem definitive: the MP3 format is by definition 'lossy'. In order to make MP3 files so economical in terms of computer disc space, a significant amount (up to 90 per cent) of the digital information in the sound recording is sacrificed. MP3s represent a mere shell of the uncompressed digital file, with much of the information discarded. If the MP3 conversion process does what it should, the discarded information should have little effect on the sound – the algorithm by which information is discarded is based on the physical characteristics of human hearing (Anonymous, 2000). The compression process, however, can also create tiny but occasionally audible 'artefacts' – 'changes or additions to the sound' (Winer, 2012, p. 67) – in the recording. Listeners also complain that the sound is 'tinny', 'harsh', or 'canned'; DJ Andrew Weatherall, for example, asserts that 'to my ears the sound is a little bit harsh in the upper-midrange area' (Taylor, 2012). However, with high-bitrate encoding these issues are generally not likely to be noticed by anyone on the dancefloor, and numerous studies have demonstrated that even critical listeners have trouble noticing differences among formats in controlled experiments on audiophile-grade equipment (see Meyer, 2000; Baguley, 2001; Adamlau, 2012; Atwood, 2012).

Many DJs and sound technicians disagree, however, despite the evidence of such studies. Tony Andrews, cofounder of the loudspeaker company Funktion One, for example, contends that if the listener cannot tell the difference between MP3 and lossless sound it is the fault of the soundsystem. MP3 is a 'toy', he says, a 'very big insult' to the listener. Andrews' comments are quite influential among DJs because of his reputation as a master engineer; his loudspeaker designs are the most highly regarded among electronic dance music DJs and fans for their unparalleled reproduction of sound across the frequency spectrum. Lower bass frequencies in particular, so incredibly important in dance music, tend to be reproduced even at very high volumes without the 'muddiness' often associated with nightclub sound, making Funktion One installations highly prized. While I'm not aware of any listening experiments specifically using Funktion One soundsystems, several studies were conducted among audiophiles using high end systems in optimal 'critical listening' environments – a far cry from the noisy and crowded nightclubs where most DJs play. On those few occasions when listeners actually were able to reliably notice a difference in sound, they tended to comment on how difficult it was to pick out the differences, which required careful and repeated listening over extended periods of time (see Meyer, 2000; Adamlau, 2012).[13]

Some listeners may argue that the problem is with a younger generation who prefers poor sound quality. Much has been made

---

[13] It's also worth noting that Andrews makes a similar claim about CD sound quality, suggesting that while not as bad as MP3, it is still an insult: 'In terms of digital, if you want to talk numbers, the minimum we would need, I would say, would be 24-bit depth at 96 kilohertz' (TIGERB3AT, 2010). Suffice to say that such resolution and frequency range is well beyond the measurable range of human hearing.

of Jonathan Berger's unpublished study of listening preferences of Stanford students, which found that students preferred what he called the 'sizzle' of low-bitrate MP3s over higher-quality digital recordings (Ahmed, 2009), but his conclusions were actually far more limited than media accounts suggested and they have not been borne out by other studies, such as Olive (2012), that indicate that users actually do prefer higher-bitrate MP3s and uncompressed sounds to lower-bitrate files. When higher-bitrate MP3s have been compared to CD-quality recordings in blind listening tests, however, listeners tend either not to be able to tell them apart, or to only notice a difference when listening extremely carefully for specific known artefacts of the MP3 conversion process – artefacts that are hardly likely to make any difference to anyone in a club full of noisy patrons, even on the best of club soundsystems.[14] The quality of the speakers, the size of the room, the placement of speakers, the number of people in the room, how loud they are talking, how much they are moving – such factors will each play a far greater and more noticeable role in how things sound than whether the DJ is using vinyl, CDs, or MP3s.

It appears to me that, at least when high-bitrate MP3s are at issue, the arguments against MP3 and in favour of any of a variety of 'lossless' formats – from vinyl to CD to WAV and FLAC – are ultimately not about sound quality so much as they are about the dialectic between human and machine in creative musical practice. While some differences in all of these circumstances can be audible, my point is that these differences alone hardly account for the passion with which arguments about format are invested. This tends to be the case, by the way, for those who prefer the sound of digital over vinyl as much as the reverse. Mostapha, for example, a participant on the *DJ Tech Tools* forum (2012b) wrote, 'vinyl is a crap medium. Its limited dynamic range and the RIAA EQ curve mean that your bass has to be compressed to all hell and shows basically no life ... it barely counts as music anymore. Highs can sound dull and lifeless compared to a pristine, well-mastered digital file.'

---

[14] Indeed it doesn't seem to make a difference to most people in the overwhelming majority of listening situations. Sterne (2012) points out: 'The MP3 format works surprisingly often and well for something so limited and so imperfect by audiophile standards' (p. 181).

These arguments, I contend, reflect something deeper than a measurable signal-to-noise ratio. The vinylist perspective, indeed, is usually expressed in quite subjective terms – the vinyl sound is said to be 'richer', 'warmer', 'fuller', for example (see Ahmed, 2013; Van Buskirk, 2007; della Cava, 2013; Ruehl, 2009; Purnell, 2010). While other issues, such as the recording and mastering process itself, can play an important role in whether a particular vinyl recording will sound 'better' than the digital recording, the more general claim about vinyl's 'richness' seems to me to be a manifestation of similar ideas to those explored above in the virtuosity debate. It would be picayune pedantry to point out that the 'warmth' one associates with the sound of vinyl records is actually noise; my contention is, however, that what the vinylist finds inadequate about digital sound is not a lack of clarity so much as the *living soul* of the music. From that perspective, every imperfection, every scratch, pop, or hiss, is a manifestation of (human) fallibility and, perhaps paradoxically, its sublimity. Digital sound is sometimes dismissed as being too 'clinical', too 'cold' (see Tatz, 2012; della Cava, 2013; Marchand, 2010); in short, for sounding too much like a clean, lean, machine. It doesn't matter that, as noted above, nobody in the crowd is likely to even notice (or care about) the difference. Here, the perceived difference is that a fundamental line has been crossed – that we have left the human behind.

DJ Subjectivity and the Ghost in the Machine

Rothenbuhler and Peters (1997) argue that the physical process of vinyl reproduction – by which real-world sound waves move a stylus that cuts the groove of a record, and that groove can later move a stylus linked to an amplifier – brings the sound much closer ontologically to its source than CD, because the patterns of grooves on a record have a direct and non-arbitrary physical relationship with the sounds thus reproduced. This relationship functions in a manner similar to what Benjamin (1969) described as the 'aura' of the work of art: the physical presence of the 'original' inhabits the reproduction as a kind of spirit. The information stored on a CD, by contrast, has a much less direct relationship to the original sounds recorded. Digital recording does not literally store sound waves; it measures their effects and it stores those measurements in a fashion that allows them to be reproduced with electrical impulses that produce physical vibrations. The relationship between the storage medium and the sounds the medium can reproduce is indirect, while the relationship with vinyl is more direct: the groove etched in the vinyl record is a topographical reproduction of the waveform in three-dimensional space. It is a physical analogue of the recorded sound, and it was etched into the vinyl 'under the rule of cause and effect in a physical world – not, as is the case with digital recording and CD playback, the rule of Sony and Phillips [sic.] in an institutional world. When we buy a record we buy music, and when we buy a CD we buy data' (Rothenbuhler and Peters 1997, p. 246). And while Rothenbuhler and Peters wrote before the advent of the MP3, their argument neatly reproduces itself in the CD vs. MP3 debate, except it is ironically now the CD that inhabits a privileged relationship to the natural world, because it stores a more complete set of data about the sounds to be reproduced. Real or imagined, the 'tinnier' sound of the MP3 is the physical manifestation of a process moving music one step further from its artistic aura.

For me, these arguments are quite compelling, but not particularly convincing. They are not convincing because the physical relationship described between the analogue format and the sound that is reproduced with it is nevertheless a relationship of analogy. The claim that 'when we buy a record we buy music' (Rothenbuhler and Peters, 1997, p. 246) is no more accurate for the vinyl record than it is for the CD or MP3. What we buy is a mass-produced etching whose valleys will make a stylus wobble, and those movements will be translated into electrical impulses to produce further vibrations, which then move air through space. The etchings themselves are not sound waves; they are analogous to sound waves. The argument is even further complicated – and less convincing – when one considers that much of the recording process itself that results in the mass produced etching is digital, making the notion of a single physical chain of cause and effect between original sound and its stored representation fanciful at best: most vinyl records are mastered from digital recordings anyway. The choice between analogue and digital is not a choice between reality and illusion; it is really a question of which illusion one prefers.

The argument is nevertheless *compelling* because of the way in which it invests the vinyl format with a kind of human subjectivity, a ghostly trace of the artist at work. As Goodwin (1988) observes, the triumph of the so-called postmodern condition has done little to stem the demand for (signifiers of) authenticity and virtuosity in popular music cultures. It doesn't matter that popular culture has been aware of the death of authenticity for the better part of a century; audiences still crave truth and meaning in artistic practices. 'If the aura is now produced on a mass scale', wrote Goodwin (1988, p. 48), 'this has not led to its demystification .... Pop fans generally appear to want their stars clad in denim, leather and spandex, not ironic quotation marks.' One might expect a subculture so steeped in – and, indeed, based on – practices of cultural appropriation and recycling as well as repurposing technology as DJ culture to be less reluctant to embrace techno- logical change, but as we have seen, every new format for sound reproduction has faced obstacles to authentication.

The format wars in DJ culture replayed a series of arguments that remains remarkably consistent within the history of recorded music. Throughout the history of these arguments, a common theme is the replacement of human soul and agency with the soul of the machine. The tools and formats are changing increasingly quickly. As recently as the late 1980s, vinyl DJs were widely scorned by rock 'n' roll musicians for playing records rather than learning instruments (indeed, that scorn continues in some quarters today). Since then, DJs have experienced several crises of professional identity regarding changes in media formats, and such crises appear to be occurring at an accelerated pace. With new format shifts came new resistances; DVS appeared and both CD and vinyl DJs complained that digital jockeys were getting lost in their computer screens, playing video games rather than blending music. Together they mourned the loss of human qualities of DJ culture, magnified by the DVS DJ's preference for lossy MP3 files and their 'perceptual coding' algorithms, whose sound they found cold and inhuman. But these algorithms, ironically, complicated their argument further: while the CD's 'perfect sound forever' is based on a purely mechanical process of storing all of the sound information recorded within a given frequency range, the MP3 coding process stores information according to a process based on the physical properties of the human ear. In other words, in this context one could just as credibly argue that MP3 is the far more 'human' format.

Ultimately, the formats themselves are less important than the creative discourses that surround them; DJs will regardless continue to develop new modes of performance, new criteria for authenticity, and new styles of virtuosity as they adapt to new tools and formats. In many cases, generational music scenes develop around the new practices that authenticate these modes of performance and the tools that they employ. However, DJ cultures are likely to remain resolutely committed to the notion that certain formats are more 'truthful' than others, and consequently, perhaps more 'human'. That the specific 'threat' to the humanity of the performer changes dramatically from year to year is of little consequence. What is to be avoided above all, in anxious debates against technological change, is domination by the mechanical, the mathematical, and the robotic: in short, the soul of the machine. Machines, paradoxically, are granted agency in this argument; human beings become empty vessels through which a mechanical consciousness is exercised.

The human-machine opposition at the heart of this formula, however, is precisely what electronic dance music interrogates and, perhaps, deconstructs. Farrugia and Swiss (2005, p. 30) comment in passing on the fundamental irony that inhabits the insistence on vinyl among some Detroit techno DJs: these are, after all, *electronic* music communities in the first place. The synthesizer and the digital sampler changed the face of popular music dramatically, and the overwhelming majority of this music is relentlessly mechanical and formulaic. Based on repetitive (and frequently quantized) percussion patterns generated by computers and incorporating entirely predictable instrumentation and heavily processed vocal arrangements, much dance music is based on particular, gendered, machine aesthetics (Bradby, 1993; Gavanas, 2009; Rietveld, 2004). Techno and house music in all their varieties, alongside synth pop, electro, drum 'n' bass, dubstep, as well as the instrumental elements of much of today's reggae, hip-hop and R&B are aesthetically constructed around continuity, rather than opposition, between the human and the machine.

The slogan 'drum machines have no soul', possibly coined by John Wood and distributed on bumper stickers and T-shirts since the early 2000s (Chamberlin, 2004; Kohlasse, 1995), expresses in a nutshell the anxieties shared by some music fans regarding technology versus human feeling. But Goodwin (1998, p. 42), describing the impact of the Roland TR–808 'handclap' sound on dance music, suggests that 'pop musicians and audiences have grown increasingly accustomed to making an association between synthetic/automated music and the communal (dance floor) connection to nature (via the body). We have grown used to connecting *machines* and *funkiness*' (p. 39). Drum machines may have no soul, but their programmers do, and that soul manifests in the beats and riffs that we shake our butts to. John Savage (1993, p. 19) writes, 'If there is one central idea in techno, it is of the harmony between man and machine'. And Kraftwerk's Ralf Hütter put it more simply: 'It's in the nature of machines. Machines are funky' (quoted in Rubin, 2009).

For the philosopher Gilbert Ryle (1949), the figure of the 'ghost in the machine' was a condescending caricature of the 'mind' under Cartesian dualism: a kind of invisible pilot that inhabits the body and operates it like a giant robot. For Ryle (1949, p. 140), in fact, the very ability of a human being to play a musical instrument – musical virtuosity – was one example that helped demonstrate that mind and body are inextricably interconnected; playing an instrument is a task that requires both mental preparation and physical coordination and training. The 'ghost in the machine' was a parody; Ryle's point is that Descartes' separation of mind and body was completely artificial. In some ways, we re-encounter this parodic figure in the creative discourses surrounding contemporary DJ culture, but instead of a human soul/ghost inhabiting and driving an otherwise inanimate robot, we have a *machine* soul inhabiting and driving the human body. Like Cartesian dualism, the notion of pure human soul that is uncontaminated by technology (yet paradoxically expressed through technology) is a category error, but it is one that inhabits the entire enterprise.

Taking the argument further, Ferreira (2008, p. 19) employs Gilles Deleuze and Félix Guattari's concept of 'machinism' to explain performance in electronic dance music as an interaction among various elements – the DJ, the sounds, the technologies that reproduce those sounds, the audience, and the dancefloor – rather than something located in specific subject positions. 'Humans and machines', he writes, 'function together in social/desiring machinisms, and the human-machine relation is one of mediation, not opposition' (p. 19). The musical experience, in other words, 'is not a kind of creative message sent by a performer to his audience, but the sonorous dimension of a particular collective movement' (p. 18). The problem with both sides of these arguments over virtuosity and authenticity is that they are marked by a kind of nostalgia for a 'real experience' that will always remain elusive. Sound quality enthusiasts long for an undistorted recording of an original sound, forgetting that a recording is distorted by definition, while disciples of musical virtuosity yearn for a display of pure human talent unmediated by tools that make things easier. The ideal DJ, in turn, is presumed to be a romantic artist – a 'musical author-god' (Herman, 2006, p. 21) – who is the creative source of (and the gatekeeper to) an authentic musical experience. Agency must be located somewhere – these discourses are threatened when agency appears to rest not with the human musician but with a machine. But Ferreira's description is far more accurate – the DJ is not the source of the experience but one among several nodes in a cluster of sounds, technologies, and bodies moving through space. The creative subjectivity at work comes not from the human agent alone (nor the machines, nor the dancing audience) but from the interactions among them all.

Conclusion

The line between the human and the machine, it turns out, while absolutely integral to our understanding of musical experience both at the level of performance and sound, is actually quite elusive. And this should perhaps not surprise us – we are playing out the artistic version of a kind of partnership that computer science has explored since the invention of cybernetics (Licklider, 1960). This musical partnership between human and machine is in no way bound to computers or to the digital age. As we have seen, new musical formats since the wax cylinder have raised concerns and provoked outrage that human musical technique and sound would fall victim to our embrace of machines. Each time it has been through a set of specific processes of authentication – thanks to users of the formats but largely led by the industries who stand to profit most directly from acceptance of the new format

– that these elusive human qualities have returned to the musical adventure. In electronic dance music DJ culture we have witnessed these processes repeating at an accelerated pace, accompanied by an eternal return of the anxieties surrounding the machine.

Debates in DJ culture over various formats have consistently clung to the notion of the DJ as a human artist creating an original text (albeit composed of previously recorded material) that audiences consume, but the creative activity that actually takes place at electronic music dance clubs and festivals is far more complex and interactive. Body movements of DJs (whether handling vinyl or twiddling knobs) and body movements of dancers interact with pre-recorded sounds that are reproduced in live contexts according to pre-arranged but infinitely variable patterns. Discourses of authenticity and virtuosity will continue to insist on a kind of purity to the dynamic in which machines must be subordinate to human expression, but such insistences will invariably miss the point.

References

Abbott, Jeremy (2012) 'Has David Guetta Been Caught Faking It?' *MixMag*, 13 August. http://www.mixmag.net/words/news/has-david-guetta-been-caught-faking-it [accessed 15 August 2012].

Adamlau (2012) 'Blind Test: Lossless vs. MP3 320'. *Head-Fi.org*, 18 February. http://www.head-fi.org/t/594934/blind-test-lossless-vs-mp3-320 [accessed 14 September 2012].

Ahmed, Murad (2009) 'MP3 Generation Prefer the Tinnier Sound of Digital to the Old-school High Fidelity'. *The Times*, 5 March: 16.

—(2013) 'Vinyl "Richer Sounds" Appeal to Young Ears'. *The Times*, 3 January. http://www.thetimes.co.uk/tto/arts/music/article3646478.ece [accessed 24 March 2013].

Anonymous (2000) 'Perceptual Coding: How MP3 Compression Works'. *Sound on Sound*, May. http://www.soundonsound.com/sos/may00/articles/mp3.htm [accessed 4 March 2013].

Attias, Bernardo Alexander (2011) 'Meditations on the Death of Vinyl'. *Dancecult: Journal of Electronic Dance Music Culture*, 3(1). http://dj.dancecult.net/index.php/journal/article/view/96/138 [accessed 23 May 2012].

Atwood, Jeff (2012) 'Concluding the Great MP3 Bitrate Experiment'. *Coding Horror*, 27 June. http://www.codinghorror.com/blog/2012/06/

concluding-the-great-mp3-bitrate-experiment.html [accessed 11 September 2012].

Baguley, Richard (2001) 'Compressed Audio vs. CDs: Can You Tell the Difference?' *PC World*, 2 October. http://pcworld.about.net/news/Oct022001id64123.htm [accessed 14 September 2012].

Benjamin, Walter (1969) 'The Work of Art in the Age of Mechanical Reproduction'. In *Illuminations: Essays and Reflections*. New York: Schochen.

Bradby, Barbara (1993) 'Sampling Sexuality: Gender, Technology and the Body in Dance Music'. *Popular Music*, 12(2), May: 155–76.

Carroll, Steven (2010) 'Who Invented Digital Vinyl?', 20 September. http://who-invented-digital-vinyl.co.uk/ [accessed 19 March 2011].

della Cava, Marco R. (2013) 'Vinyl's Sonic Splendor Draws in New Fans'. *USA Today*, 23 January: 1D.

Chamberlin, Daniel (2004) 'Ghost in the Drum Machine'. *LA Weekly*, 27 May. http://www.laweekly.com/2004-05-27/columns/the-revolution-will-be-posterized/ [accessed 8 March 2013].

Coleman, Mark (2003) *Playback: From the Victrola to the MP3, 100 Years of Music, Machines, and Money*. Cambridge, MA: Da Capo.

Colloms, Martin (2006) 'Do We Need an Ultrasonic Bandwidth for Higher Fidelity Sound Reproduction?' *Proceedings of the Institute of Acoustics*, 28(8). http://www.hificritic.com/downloads/Archive_A10.pdf [accessed 8 March 2013].

Cunningham, Katie (2012) 'The CD2000 Debate: To Sync or Not to Sync'. *Inthemix*, 7 September. http://www.inthemix.com.au/features/53689/The_CDJ2000_debate_To_sync_or_not_to_sync [accessed 25 September 2012].

Daily Mail (2012) 'Never Giving Up! Paris Hilton Makes Another Attempt at a Career Behind the Turntables after a Disastrous Debut Last Month'. *Daily Mail Online*, 18 August. http://www.dailymail.co.uk/tvshowbiz/article-2190396/Paris-Hilton-makes-attempt-DJ-career-disastrous-debut-month.html [accessed 21 September 2012].

Daverh (2009) 'Mistabishi Caught Faking a DJ Set?' *Inthemix*, 29 October. http://www.inthemix.com.au/news/intl/44729/Mistabishi_caught_faking_a_DJ_set [accessed 20 September 2012].

Deadmau5 (2012) 'All DJs Are Glorified Button Pushers'. *Gizmodo*, 25 June. http://gizmodo.com/deadmau5/ [accessed 25 June 2012].

DJ Forums (2012) 'We All Hit Play Deadmau5 (Knob Jockeys)', 25 June. http://www.djforums.com/forums/showthread.php?9804-we-all-hit-play-deadmau5-(knob-jockeys) [accessed 27 June 2012].

DJ Tech Tools Forum (2012a) 'Clearing up the Deadmau5 DJ Thing', 23 June. http://forum.djtechtools.com/showthread.php?t=54010 [accessed 24 June 2012].

—(2012b) 'So Does Anyone Spin Just Vinyl Anymore?', 18 January. http://forum.djtechtools.com/showthread.php?t=44916&page=3 [accessed 19 January 2012].

—(2012c) 'Using the BPM Counter: Would You Call It Cheating?', 28 February. http://forum.djtechtools.com/showthread.php?t=47608 [accessed 20 September 2012].

Edison, Thomas A. (1878) 'The Phonograph and Its Future'. *North American Review*, 126(262): 527–36.

—(1888) 'The Perfected Phonograph'. *North American Review*, 146(379): 641–50.

Eells, Josh (2012) 'Dance Madness: The Rise of the Mau5'. *Rolling Stone*, 5–19 July: 44–52.

Farber, Jim (2013) 'Vinyl Love: Not Only Are Sales of Old-Fashioned Albums Booming, It's the Young Who Are Buying'. *New York Daily News*, 3 February. http://www.nydailynews.com/entertainment/music-arts/vinyl-album-sales-booming-article-1.1251477 [accessed 4 March 2013].

Farrugia, Rebekah and Swiss, Thomas (2005) 'Tracking the DJs: Vinyl Records, Work, and the Debate over New Technologies'. *Journal of Popular Music Studies*, 17(1): 30–44.

Ferreira, Pedro Peixoto (2008) 'When Sound Meets Movement: Performance in Electronic Dance Music'. *Leonardo Music Journal*, 18: 17–20.

Fukuyama, Francis (2011) 'All Hail ... Analog?' *Wall Street Journal*, 26 February. http://online.wsj.com/article/SB10001424052748703529004576160300649048270.html [accessed 8 September 2012].

Fusilli, Jim (2012) 'The Dumbing Down of Electronic Music'. *Wall Street Journal*, 6 June. http://online.wsj.com/article/SB100014240527023038302045774468421347076 10.html [accessed 7 June 2012].

Gavanas, Anna (2009) ' "You Better Be Listening to My Fucking Music You Bastard!" Teknologi, Genusifiering och Andlighet Bland DJs på Elektroniska Dansmusikscener i Berlin, London och Stockholm'. In Hillevi Ganetz, Anna Gavanas, Hasse Huss and Ann Werner (eds) *Rundgång: genus och populärmusik* (77–122). Stockholm: Makadam.

Gelatt, Roland (1977) *The Fabulous Phonograph 1877–1977*, 2nd rev. edn. New York: Collier Books.

Geringer, John M. and Dunnigan, Patrick (2000) 'Listener Preferences and Perception of Digital versus Analog Live Concert Recordings'. *Bulletin of the Council for Research in Music Education*, 145, Summer: 1–13.

Golden, Ean (2011) 'Q-Bert Visits DJ TechTools: Live Jam with Ean Golden'. *DJ Tech Tools*, 1 February. http://www.djtechtools.com/2011/02/01/q-bert-visits-dj-techtools-live-jam-with-ean-golden/ [accessed 12 March 2013].

Goodwin, Andrew (1988) 'Sample and Hold: Pop Music in the Digital Age of Reproduction'. *Critical Quarterly*, 30(3): 34–49.

Greenburg, Zack O'Malley (2012) 'Electronic Cash Kings: The World's Highest-Paid DJs'. *Forbes*, 2 August. http://www.forbes.com/special-report/2012/0802_top-djs.html [accessed 8 August 2012].

Herman, Bill D. (2006) 'Scratching Out Authorship: Representations of the Electronic Music DJ at the Turn of the 21st Century'. *Popular Communication*, 4(1): 21–38.

Jones, Steve (1992) *Rock Formation: Music, Technology, and Mass Communication*. Newbury Park, CA, London and New Delhi: Sage Publications.

Katz, Mark (2010) *Capturing Sound: How Technology Has Changed Music*, rev. edn. Berkeley, CA: University of California Press.

—(2012) *Groove Music: The Art and Culture of the Hip Hop DJ*. New York: Oxford University Press.

Kenney, William Howland (1999) *Recorded Music in American Life: The Phonograph and Popular Memory, 1890–1945*. New York: Oxford University Press.

Kirn, Peter (2008) 'NI Ends Legal Dispute Over Traktor Scratch; Digital Vinyl's Twisty, Turny History'. *Create Digital Music*, 28 April. http://createdigitalmusic.com/2008/04/ni-ends-legal-dispute-over-traktor-scratch-digital-vinyls-twisty-turny-history/ [accessed 1 May 2008].

—(2012) 'Deadmau5, Honest About His Own Press-Play Sets, Misses Out On Scene'. *Create Digital Music*, 25 June. http://createdigitalmusic.com/2012/06/deadmau5-honest-about-his-own-press-play-sets-misses-out-on-scene/ [accessed 27 June 2012].

Kiryu, Shogo and Ashihara, Kaoru (2001) 'Detection Threshold for Tones Above 22Hz'. *Proceedings of the Audio Engineering Society 110th Convention*, Amsterdam, May. http://www.aes.org/e-lib/browse.cfm?elib=10005 [accessed 7 November 2012].

Kohlhaase, Bill (1995) 'He Knows the Day the Music Died'. *Los Angeles Times*, 6 September. http://articles.latimes.com/1995-09-06/entertainment/ca-42642_1_john-wood [accessed 8 March 2013].

Licklider, J. C. R. (1960) 'Man-Computer Symbiosis'. *IRE Transactions on Human Factors in Electronics*, HFE–1, March: 4–11. http://groups.csail.mit.edu/medg/people/psz/Licklider.html [accessed 1 October 2012].

Marchand, Philip (2010) 'The Year of the Printerruption: Can Beautiful Tactility Ever Trump Digital Convenience?' *National Post* (Canada), 31 December: WP15.

Marx, Karl (1993), *Grundrisse*, trans. Martin Nicolaus. New York, NY: Penguin.

Meyer, Carsten (2000) 'Kreuzverhörtest – Der c't-Leser-Hörtest: MP3 gegen CD'. *c't – Magazin für Computertechnik*, June. http://www.

heise.de/artikel-archiv/ct/2000/06/092 [Machine translation archive
  at http://web.archive.org/web/20091026193142/http://geocities.com/
  altbinariessoundsmusicclassical/mp3test.html [accessed 14 September
  2012].

Meyer, E. Brad and Moran, David R. (2007) 'Audibility of a CD-standard
  A/DA/A Loop Inserted into High-resolution Audio Playback'. *Journal
  of the Audio Engineering Society*, 55(9), September: 775–9.

Millard, Andre (2005) *America on Record: A History of Recorded
  Sound*, 2nd edn. New York: Cambridge University Press.

Milner, Greg (2009) *Perfecting Sound Forever: An Aural History of
  Recorded Music*. New York: Faber and Faber.

Montano, Ed (2010) ' "How Do You Know He's Not Playing Pac-Man
  while He's Supposed to be DJing?": Technology, Formats and the
  Digital Future of DJ Culture'. *Popular Music*, 29(3): 397–416.

Morton, David (2000) *Off the Record: The Technology and Culture of
  Sound Recording in America*. New York: Rutger's University.

Nishiguchi, Toshiyuki (2004) 'Perceptual Discrimination between
  Musical Sounds with and without Very High Frequency Components'.
  NHK Laboratories Note, 486. http://www.nhk.or.jp/strl/publica/
  labnote/lab486.html [accessed 8 March 2013].

Olive, Sean (2012) 'Some New Evidence that Teenagers and College
  Students May Prefer Accurate Sound Reproduction'. *Journal of the
  Audio Engineering Society*, 132, April. http://www.aes.org/e-lib/
  browse.cfm?elib=16321 [accessed 26 April 2013].

Oohashi, Tsutomu, Kawai, Norie, Nishina, Emi, Honda, Manabu, Yagi,
  Reiko, Nakamura, Satoshi, Morimoto, Masako, Maekawa, Tadao,
  Yonekura, Yoshiharu and Shibasaki, Hiroshi (2006) 'The Role of
  Biological System other than Auditory Air-conduction in the Emergence
  of the Hypersonic Effect'. *Brain Research*, 1073, February: 339–47.

Oohashi, Tsutomu, Nishina, Emi, Honda, Manabu, Yonekura,
  Yoshiharu, Fuwamoto, Yoshitaka, Kawai, Norie, Maekawa, Tadao,
  Nakamura, Satoshi, Fukuyama, Hidenao and Shibasaki, Hiroshi
  (2000) 'Inaudible High-frequency Sounds Affect Brain Activity:
  Hypersonic Effect'. *Journal of Neurophysiology*, 83(6): 3548–58.

Osborne, Ben (2009) 'Put the Needle on the Sound File'. *Music Week*,
  4 April: 16.

Petridis, Alexis (2012) 'Deadmau5: Album Title Goes Here – Review'.
  The Guardian, 20 September. http://www.guardian.co.uk/music/2012/
  sep/20/deadmau5-album-title-goes-here-review [accessed 27 September
  2012].

Purnell, Charles (2010) 'The Survival of Vinyl Records'. *The Daily Titan*,
  24 January. http://www.dailytitan.com/2010/01/the-survival-of-vinyl-
  records/ [accessed 24 March 2013].

Ray, Sean (2012) 'The Sync Button Strikes Again'. *Not Your Jukebox*, 6 September. http://notyourjukebox.com/2012/09/06/the-sync-button-strikes-again/ [accessed 25 September 2012].

Rayner, Ben (2013) 'SXSW: Deadmau5, Richie Hawtin Team Up for Techno Talk'. *Toronto Star*, 12 March. http://www.thestar.com/entertainment/music/2013/03/12/sxsw_deadmau5_richie_hawtin_team_up_for_techno_talk.html [accessed 12 March 2013].

Read, Oliver and Welch, Walter L. (1959) *From Tin Foil to Stereo: Evolution of the Phonograph*. Indianapolis, IN: Howard W. Sams.

Rietveld, Hillegonda C. (2004) 'Ephemeral Spirit: Sacrificial Cyborg and Communal Soul'. In Graham St John (ed.) *Rave Culture and Religion* (45–60). London and New York: Routledge.

Romero, Dennis (2011) 'World's Douchiest DJs: The Top Five'. *LA Weekly*, 16 November. http://blogs.laweekly.com/westcoastsound/2011/11/worlds_douchiest_djs_the_top_5.php [accessed 12 June 2012].

Rothenbuhler, Eric W. and Peters, John Durham (1997) 'Defining Phonography: An Experiment in Theory'. *Musical Quarterly*, 81(2): 242–64.

Rubin, Mike (2009) 'Who Knew that Robots were Funky?' *New York Times*, 4 December. http://www.nytimes.com/2009/12/06/arts/music/06kraftwerk.html [accessed 18 March 2013].

Ruehl, Peter (2009) 'Vinyl's Groovy, But Then There's the Turntable Work'. *Australian Financial Review*, 1 August: 64.

Ryle, Gilbert (1949) *The Concept of Mind*. London: Hutchinson.

Savage, John (1993) 'Machine Soul: A History of Techno'. *Village Voice*, 20 July: SS18.

Schulman, Jacob (2012) 'Dance Music Has Gone Mainstream, but it Doesn't Have to Sell Out'. *Dancing Astronaut*, 24 June. http://www.dancingastronaut.com/2012/06/editorial-dance-music-has-gone-mainstream-but-it-doesnt-have-to-sell-out [accessed 27 June 2012].

Siefert, Marsha (1995) 'Aesthetics, Technology, and the Capitalization of Culture: How the Talking Machine Became a Musical Instrument'. *Science in Context*, 8(2): 417–49.

Sisario, Ben (2012) 'Electronic Dance Concerts Turn Up Volume, Tempting Investors'. *New York Times*, 4 April. http://www.nytimes.com/2012/04/05/business/media/electronic-dance-genre-tempts-investors.html [accessed 27 June 2012].

Sousa, John Philip (1993) 'Machine Songs IV: The Menace of Mechanical Music'. *Computer Music Journal*, 17(1): 14–18, reprinted from *Appleton's Magazine* 8 (September 1906).

Start Mobile Beat (2008) 'Song Transferring Good or Bad?', 3 March. http://start.mobilebeat.com/archive/index.php/t-43309.html [accessed 20 September 2012].

Sterne, Jonathan (2012) *MP3: The Meaning of a Format*. Durham, NC: Duke University Press.

Tatz, Simon (2012) 'Vinyl Cool Turns Tables on Digital Rivals'. *Canberra Times*, 22 November: A5.

Taylor, Ken (2012) 'Weatherall, Magda, Sander Van Doorn, and Loco Dice on the Benefits of Lossless Files'. *Beatport News*, 30 May. http://news.beatport.com/blog/2012/05/30/weatherall-magda-sander-van-doorn-and-loco-dice-on-the-benefits-of-lossless/ [accessed 16 September 2012].

Taylor, Timothy D. (2001) *Strange Sounds: Music, Technology & Culture*. New York: Routledge.

Thiessen, Brock (2008) 'Deadmau5 Proclaims DJs Are "Fucking Cunts"'. *Exclaim.ca*, 8 November. http://exclaim.ca/News/deadmau5_proclaims_djs_are_fucking_cunts [accessed 4 February 2009].

Thornton, Sarah (1996) *Club Cultures: Music, Media, and Subcultural Capital*. Middletown: Wesleyan University Press.

TIGERB3AT (2010) 'Slices Tech Talk – Funktion One'. *Tech Talk*, *YouTube* video, 18 October. http://www.youtube.com/watch?v=MxhtIbK-Dqc [accessed 11 September 2012].

ubbs (2012) 'First Thoughts: Pioneer CDJ2000 Nexus'. *Stoney Roads*, 6 September. http://stoneyroads.com/first-thoughts-pioneer-cdj2000-nexus/ [accessed 25 September 2012].

Van Buskirk, Eliot (2007) 'Vinyl May be Final Nail in CD's Coffin'. *Wired*, 29 October. http://www.wired.com/entertainment/music/commentary/listeningpost/2007/10/listeningpost_1029 [accessed 24 March 2013].

van Veen, tobias and Attias, Bernardo (2011), 'Off the Record: Turntablism and Controllerism in the Twenty-first Century. Part I'. *Dancecult: Journal of Electronic Dance Music Culture*, 3(1). http://dj.dancecult.net/index.php/journal/article/view/104/131 [accessed 23 May 2012].

—(2012) 'Off the Record: Turntablism and Controllerism in the Twenty-first Century. Part II'. *Dancecult: Journal of Electronic Dance Music Culture*, 4(1). http://dj.dancecult.net/index.php/journal/article/view/121/144 [accessed 4 June 2012].

Weheliye, Alexander G. (2005) *Phonographies: Grooves in Sonic Afro-Modernity*. Durham, NC: Duke University Press.

West, Richard (2012), *Facebook*, 25 June. http://www.facebook.com/richardwestmrc/posts/324548870959603 [accessed 27 June 2012].

Winer, Ethan (2012) *The Audio Expert: Everything You Need to Know about Audio*. Burlington, MA: Focal Press.

Young, Neil (1992) 'Digital is a Huge Rip-Off'. *Guitar Player*, May: 14.

Zeilig, Charles, and Clawson, Jay (2012) 'Computer Music Audio Quality, Part 3'. *The Absolute Sound*, 220, February: 34–9.

Discography

Big Black (1987) *Songs About Fucking*. Touch & Go: United States, [T&G #24 / LP].

Looptroop (1996) 'Militant Vinylists', *From the Wax Cabinet*, not on label (self-released). Sweden [FTW01 /12"].

Springsteen, Bruce (1984) *Born in the USA*. CBS: United States [CDCBS 86304 / CD].

Throbbing Gristle (2009) *Gristleism*. Industrial Records: United Kingdom [IR2009005C / 13 x File, EPROM].

CHAPTER THREE

DJ Technologies, Social Networks and Gendered Trajectories in European DJ Cultures

Anna Gavanas and Rosa Reitsamer

Across historical, local and cultural contexts, DJ cultures have been, and continue to be, overwhelmingly male dominated (see for example, Brewster and Broughton, 1999; Farrugia, 2012; Rose, 1994).[1] This male dominance is reconfirmed by the rest of the chapters in the book you are reading right now; see, for instance, chapters by Fontanari, Montano, Paulsson and Yu. Between 2005 and 2011, while we did our fieldwork among DJs in Berlin,

---

[1] For instance, when Attias and Gavanas guest edited the special issue on the DJ for *Dancecult*, the international journal on electronic dance music cultures (vol. 3, no. 1, 2011), all ten contributions – regardless of geographic, historical and genre context – wrote of DJs and DJ culture as overwhelmingly male: see Gavanas and Attias (2011). These contributions were solicited through open public calls on international forums for popular music scholars. These accounts of DJ culture – despite differing temporal and geographic contexts – describe DJ culture as primarily a 'masculine' pursuit, reminding us that certain gendered power relations may resist change across time, space, format and technology (Gavanas and Attias, 2011).

Stockholm, London and Vienna, male DJs constituted the majority of DJs in the electronic music scenes under study: from house to techno and the various related local genres, around and in between. The majority of the 'big names' among international and local DJs remain male, scoring the top positions on DJ lists and representing music genres despite the growing presence of female DJs (Rodgers, 2010; Öström, 2011a, 2011b). Thus, although the proportion[2] of female DJs in Stockholm increased from a marginal handful in the early 2000s to between 21–38 per cent in 2011 (Öström, 2011b), and Berlin was celebrated by the *Guardian* as a haven for female techno DJs in 2008 (Naylor, 2008), the UK-based *DJ Mag* listed zero (0!) female DJs in its yearly 'Top 100 DJs' in 2011. In 2010 there was only one female DJ listed, at number 93 (*DJ Mag*, 2012).

What does this overwhelming male dominance say about DJ culture and the conditions for women DJs and music producers? We argue, in line with Rodgers (2010) regarding electronic music production, that it is not sufficient to simply and matter-of-factly conclude that there is (and always has been) a gender imbalance in electronic dance music culture without analysing what this fact means to DJ culture as a whole, within and across music genres. Furthermore, it is important to analyse the (self-) representations of women in electronic dance music culture in relation to the specific characteristics of male bias within that culture. In practice, youth cultural and subcultural studies have tended to mainly constitute explorations of masculinity (Holland, 2004, p. 21). With a few exceptions (for example: Farrugia, 2012; Hutton, 2006; McRobbie, 1994; Pini, 2001), electronic dance music studies follow this male-oriented approach. As Rodgers (2010, p. 11) reminds us, some of the most important contributions to the study of electronic dance music position women outside the scope of study (as she exemplifies with Kahn, 1999) and define DJ cultures as 'distinctly masculine' with relative inattention paid to women's participation in these cultures (as she exemplifies with Reynolds, 1998); alternatively, they use observational statistics that show that fewer than one in ten DJs are female (as she

[2] Unfortunately no comparable statistics are available over time as to the proportion of male and female DJs in the locations under study: for a recent summary, see http://www.femalepressure.net, female pressure report 03/2013.

exemplifies with Fikentscher, 2000), as though this somehow explains the absence of women from study.

This chapter discusses the ways in which notions of technology and masculinity are crucial to values in electronic dance music culture, from the position that both technology and gender are socially constructed and the relationship between technology and society are mutually constituted (Cockburn and Ormrod, 1993; Wacjam, 2004). This approach allows for an analysis that conceives a relationship of mutual formation between gender and technology, in which technology is both a source and a consequence of gendered relations – homosocial as well as heterosocial (Wacjman, 2004, p. 107). The association between masculinity and technology is at the heart of gendered dynamics in EDM culture in general and its social networks in particular. Additionally, feminist sociology, media and cultural studies (Buszek, 2006; Gill, 2011; Hutton, 2006; McRobbie, 2009; Puwar, 2004) provide us with helpful theoretical tools for analysing the gendered dynamics of (self-) representation by female DJs in what Thornton (1996) calls 'scene media'. Finally, we apply Bourdieu's (1993) concept of social, symbolic and cultural capital to explore the social networks in specific EDM scenes, which are made up of associations between DJs, musicians, producers, event organizers and promoters, as well as the accumulation of credibility and social capital that are necessary preconditions to gain appearances at club nights.

The core of our research insights emerged from interviews that were collected between 2005 and 2011, complemented by an analysis of discussions on an international internet forum[3] for female DJs, from 2009 to 2011. Internet networks such as Female Pressure, Shejay and SisterDJs have become increasingly common networking strategies among female DJs, which is why we combine the study of our face-to-face interviews with such forum discussions. A total of 75 face-to-face interviews were conducted with mostly female DJs based in Berlin (15 female DJs), London (15 female DJs), Stockholm (15 DJs: 12 female; three male) and Vienna (30 DJs: 18 female; 12 male). The interviews were in-depth and lasted between 30 and 90 minutes. The majority of the interviewees were white, middle class and between 17 and 45 years old. They

---

[3] The name of this forum will remain anonymous to ensure the anonymity of its participants and organizers.

were selected on the basis of being well-established DJs in their scenes and representing a variety of subgenres within the scope of electronic dance music culture in the cities under study.

Reasons for the Underrepresentation of Female DJs

If we look, for example, at the *The Encyclopedia of Record Producers* (Olsen et al., 1993), at video documentaries on electronic music in the twentieth century, such as *Modulations: Cinema for the Ear* (1998), or the majority of studies on electronic dance music cultures (Brewster and Broughton, 1999; Collin, 1997; Kirn, 2011; Poschardt, 1997; St John, 2009) we learn that female DJs and music producers are rare exceptions. But this only shows the result, not the causes for the underrepresentation of female artists in electronic dance music scenes – and possibly reflects the social networks and orientations of the (male) researchers themselves. We argue that this scarcity of women artists originates partly in the gendered social construction of technology and partly in the informal character of working environments and social networks in electronic dance music cultures, dominated by images of male artist/musician/producer/ entrepreneur and the sexualized images of (young) women.

The history of music, regardless of genre, has been shaped by a mutually constituting relationship between technology and mascu-linity, with exclusionary effects for women who wish to become musicians, DJs and/or music producers. Mavis Bayton (2011), for example, shows how the arrival of the electric guitar in the 1960s significantly contributed to the image of the male rock star. At that time, many girls played the acoustic guitar and sang, inspired by Joan Baez and Joni Mitchell, but the idea of playing the electric guitar was alien to them because the electric guitar itself and the technical skills involved in playing the instrument as well as the guitar pose perfected by the earliest guitar 'heroes' are generally perceived as masculine. Thus, technological mastery, for boys and young men playing the guitar in a band or producing electronic music in their bedrooms means enhancing their masculinity, while for girls and young women the same activities mean breaking the gender code (Bayton, 2011; Cohen, 1997; Ganetz, 1997).

Similarly, in electronic dance music scenes, which evolved in the early 1980s, the use of machines and digital music technologies has become an essential precondition for DJing and music making. Since the computer is used in all kinds of mixed gendered contexts and not a technology associated with muscles, manual skills and all-male environments, one might think this would mean an end to men's hegemony in DJ culture. Especially due to the similarity between computers and typewriters, which was accorded to female secretaries (Lie, 1995, p. 392). Furthermore, digital technology and computers have been ambiguously gendered as the design of computers has not been straightforwardly associated with male or female attributes, but rather representing a bland and asexual surface (Springer, 1993, p. 9). However, as we are arguing in this chapter, technology does not only apply to technological objects but the knowledge and social relations they are part of, as well as the gendered imagery around associated products.

Moreover, technological mastery has become central to the values and social interactions as well as to the ideals and passions related to DJing and music making (Rietveld, 2004). For instance, the work and aesthetics of Kraftwerk (one of the seminal artists of electronic dance music music) exemplify the association technology and masculinity, men and machines. Likewise, in writings about electronic dance music culture, men and their machines are featured as foundational (see, Eshun, 1998; Goodman, 2010; Taylor, 2001). Correspondingly, as Walser argues in Negus (1999, p. 126), within DJ culture as well as other genres such as rock, music styles and DJ/producer/musician practices are actively *made* as male (or female). In other words, DJs, producers and musicians are involved in strategies of 'forging masculinity' (Negus, 1999, p. 126). As quoted in Negus (1999, p. 126) Walser identifies 'excription' as one such strategy, meaning straightforward exclusion of women from the world of male bonding.

To obtain the status of a 'good' DJ and/or music producer importantly includes competence in the latest music production equipment and software. The significance of technical knowledge has even increased as a successful DJ career has come to require competence in both DJing and music production. DJs have to make a name for themselves not only by winning over club audiences with good performances, but also by releasing recordings (Reitsamer, 2011a). However, achieving such technological mastery does not appear as 'natural' when it comes to female DJs. For example, one Stockholm-based DJ said:

> I like to work with technology, I have always messed about with cassette decks and recording sounds on different channels and [that is] not normal. Perhaps it is normal for a guy who builds loudspeakers [...] it is more natural for them to do that. But I think I am probably the third sex (laughs). Perhaps not very feminine ... (DJ, female, Stockholm 2006)

This DJ addresses the symbolic association between masculinity and technology in society in general and in electronic dance music scenes in particular, such that technical competence has come to constitute an integral part of masculine gender identity, and, vice versa, a specific notion of masculinity has become central to our very definition of technology (Cockburn and Ormrod, 1993). As Wajcam (2004, p. 106) puts it, 'technology must be understood as part of the social fabric that holds society together; it is never merely technical or social. Rather technology is always a socio-material product – a seamless web or network combining artefacts, people, organizations, cultural meanings and knowledge.'

The values associated with various music technologies are inter-connected with discursive gatekeeping practices that define who counts as a 'real DJ' and who does not, and according to what logic (Attias, 2011; Gavanas, 2009; Farrugia and Swiss, 2005). These cultural processes are, in their various configurations, encountered by women and racialized minorities occupying tenuous positions as both insiders and outsiders (Puwar, 2004, p. 10). A central assumption in some electronic dance music scenes about 'real DJs' is that they are intensive record collectors who visit record stores a few times a week (Reitsamer, 2011b). A Berlin-based DJ addresses the behaviour of young men in record stores as follows:

> Normally when you go into the record store, there were only boys standing in there. If you entered the record store, all heads were turning around staring at you, and nobody was talking anymore. And if you're twenty years old, it's somehow scary, you know. I mean it's doesn't feel comfortable. (DJ, female, Berlin 2006)

In his study of record collectors, Will Straw (1997) describes record collecting as a social practice associated with masculinity. He identifies several characteristics of record collecting such as hipness, connoisseurship, bohemianism and the adventurous hunter, all of which revolve around the accumulation of material objects that prove hunting skills, provide opportunities for adventure and conquest, and allow for the display of authority and knowledge. The behaviour of the men in the record store, as the female DJs described above, aims to display authority and knowledge, through which the record store becomes coded as a male space. Like women in other male-coded spaces, female DJs do not have an undisputed right to occupy this space; 'their arrival brings into clear relief what has been able to pass as the invisible, unmarked and undeclared somatic norm' (Puwar, 2004, p. 8). However, some DJs argue that digitalization and the increasing purchase of music on the internet (as compared to physical record stores) has democratizing effects to the advantage of female DJs (Gavanas, 2009, p. 92). In other words, as record stores are dwindling and internet-based shopping (of physical as well as digital formats) becomes the norm in DJ cultures, female DJs are no longer gendered as customers and do not need to interact with potentially problematic male gate keepers to access crucial professional information and DJ tools.

Another example of gatekeeping practices with regards to the importance of networks in electronic dance music scenes is conveyed by a female DJ in Vienna, regarding her early experience as a DJ:

> The guys don't want to have anything to do with you as a woman, and certainly not when you're starting out. They mutually invite one another, regardless of whether they have a good selection and can mix or not, and they sit and talk about music as if it were a science, and make collaborative music. (DJ, female, Vienna 2008)

Similarly, a Berlin-based DJ addresses the male dominance at the level of cultural production: 'There are a lot of girl DJs [...] [but] the thing is that there are still a lot of men in this business [...] most of the party organizers, the club owners, promotion people are guys' (DJ, female, Berlin 2006). There are no comparable statistics available over time on the proportion of female DJs in the sites under study, but among interviewees in Stockholm, Berlin, London, as well as Vienna there seemed to be a general impression that gender equality is improving. In the electronic dance music scenes under study, the various scene networks are organized informally, and still mostly dominated by (young) men. Scene networks acquire a gatekeeping function, regulating the accumulation of social, economic, cultural and symbolic capital (Bourdieu, 1993) as well as subcultural capital (Thornton, 1996), which refer to such assets of DJs and producers as musical taste, dance style, fashion attributes, record collections and technical equipment. As the comments above indicate, female DJs and music producers are often excluded from these networks, and these exclusions are naturalized by certain images, perceptions and prejudices – for example, that women would not be interested in technology, not competitive enough, not intensive record collectors (Straw, 1997), or that they would not take active roles in music scenes as DJs, musicians, producers and event organizers. Participating as anomalies in contexts where they are not seen as the normative figure of authority, the capacities of female DJs are viewed with suspicion; there is a significant burden of doubt as to whether female DJs possess the required competencies and capabilities to measure up to the job (Puwar, 2004, p. 59; Wahl et al., 2011). However, these prejudices tend to be shared by men and women alike, as the following statement by a female interviewee indicates: 'This is going to be a sexist comment really, but I find that musically, women are less interested in really being like train-spotters, like really being interested in DJing and really getting to know who produced this track? […] I find that women are probably […] not interested in […] studying it' (DJ, female, London 2006).

As a result of such prejudices, women artists are assumed to lack the assertiveness and drive for success – a view that is reinforced by a male interviewee from Vienna:

Women are more modest, which makes it harder for them to establish themselves in the scene. At the beginning […] as unknown DJ, you have to be really pushy to make it, because it doesn't work with good looks alone. (laughs) There are a few female DJs, but much less than men, of course. Male DJs have a bigger hunger for fame, and they stick around, while many women give up. But if a woman really wants [to become a DJ] and has a good [music] style, I am sure she can make it. (DJ, male, Vienna 2008)

This DJ assumes that a 'good' DJ style and 'good' performances at club nights can lead to recognition and success. Women do not seem to measure up to this achievement principle, because the attributes necessary to access DJ performances, namely perseverance, tenacity, persistence, and the desire for recognition, are attributed to men. This association of specific attributes with masculinity, coupled with the social association of technical competence with masculine gender identity, produces the idea that only men can be 'good' DJs and are thus likely to be successful (Reitsamer, 2011b). In order to combat under-expectations and doubt, female DJs constantly have to prove themselves (Puwar, 2004, p. 59).

However, as new and old technologies are developed, negotiated and adopted, claims for authenticity and knowledge are shifting in electronic dance music culture (Attias, 2011). The digitalization of DJing, production and consumption has been discussed in terms of democratization and new possibilities for gender equality as it allowed access to relatively (compared to hardware alternatives) inexpensive music production techniques and tools for (self-) promotion, while at the same time the internet has enabled social networking sites and instant access to music collection, promotion and distribution regardless of location (Gavanas, 2009; Farrugia, 2004; Lin, 2002). However, digitalization and the internet have not necessarily brought about change in gendered constructions in electronic dance music scenes. Genre-based notions of authenticity and socio-technical practices are inseparable (Rietveld, 2004; Farrugia, 2012; Farrugia and Swiss, 2005). Interestingly, technology fetishism, and the interest, knowledge and mastery of creative and performance music technologies tend to be coded by our interviewees in terms of maleness: as 'boyishness', 'nerdishness' and 'cockiness'. Thus, the interest and passion for music technology and production may reinforce normative masculinity, while simultaneously being perceived as un-feminine, which challenges the position of female DJs and negatively impacts their career trajectories. In the words of a Stockholm-based DJ:

> It feels like many presume that the best compliment one can give to a woman is to recognize her based on her looks. And if one would rebel against the given 'female' image, they call you 'tomboy' or [nerd], 'not a real girl,' etc. …. I would prefer 'real girls' to have the freedom to work with technology and not be reduced or questioned. (DJ, female, Stockholm 2006)

This interviewee echoes sociologist Nirmal Puwar's analysis that women in male-dominated professions cannot simply mimic male performances because they will be charged with lacking femininity (Puwar, 2004, p. 148). In other words, because the knowledge, skills and symbolism relating to music technology are gendered, relationships to both new and old DJ technologies may well be different for male and female DJs. However, female DJs and music producers do appropriate and take advantage of recent technological developments in the wake of digitalization and the possibilities of the internet – for instance by means of translocal mobilization and the exchange of knowledge in internet forums and platforms such as Female Pressure, Pink Noises, Shejay and Rubina DJanes (Farrugia, 2004, 2012; Reitsamer, 2012).

Commercial Strategies, Representation and Credibility

Hutton (2006) shows that there is a close relationship between a lack of female club DJs and the lack of women elsewhere in the production of dance events. In particular, increasing commercialization seems to reinforce gender difference. In this context, Hutton importantly points out that, 'The performance of femininities and sexualities is therefore significant for female DJs just as they are for female clubbers who participate in the consumption of these spaces' (Hutton, 2006, p. 57). In contemporary popular culture generally, there is an overwhelming focus on the visual appearance of women and femininity, along with sexualization according to heterosexual ideals (Buszek, 2006; Holland, 2004; Puwar, 2004). Angela McRobbie (2009) addresses the recent pervasive sexualization of contemporary popular culture within the wider context of neoliberalism. She argues that this dominant economic and cultural mode of Western societies encourages girls and young women to turn their bodies into vehicles for individual achievement. Such an aspirational model of equal opportunities and advancement pervades the current 'postfeminist' popular culture. Rosalind Gill suggests that to understand 'postfeminism ... as a sensibility' as such a construct, allows for an emphasis on 'the contradictory nature of postfeminist discourses and the entanglement of both feminist and anti-feminist themes within them' (Gill, 2011, p. 137). A defining aspect of postfeminist popular culture seems to be a preoccupation with the female body, which is constructed as a tool for female choice and empowerment. With the bodies and sexuality of women under super-exposure, how women style their bodies seems to be of immense importance (Puwar, 2004, p. 148). In addition, hyper-sexualized images of (young) women are currently a dominant marketing technique in advertising, magazines, internet sites and cable television, whereby many of the images contribute to what Gill (2011, p. 138) calls 'porno chic' – the blurring of the boundaries between pornography and other visually mediated genres.

In this section we will analyse how our interviewees understand the sexualization of contemporary popular culture in general and electronic dance music cultures in particular and, as a result, how they place themselves in relation to it. Hereby we focus on the contradiction and tensions experienced and negotiated by the inter-viewees, in relation to their appearance behind the DJ desk and in various scene-specific media, such as web-based promotional material, flyers, posters and magazines. We will also explore how our interviewees articulate their resistance to pressures for (young) women to cultivate their appearance and which alternatives modes of (self-) representation they develop.

Female DJs and music producers experience not only exclusion from male-dominated scene networks; they also experience ambiv-alent inclusions by media that are specific to electronic dance music scenes. As the media place more surveillance on the appearance of women, female DJs have to manage their femininity both in terms of the connotations and issues they raise as well as their physical appearance (Puwar, 2004, p. 95). According to feminist musicolo-gists such as McClary (1991) and Rodgers (2010), historically we can identify three types of gendered representations particular for female music producers. First, the work of women music producers is often perceived as representing an essentially 'feminine' aesthetic (McClary, 1991). For instance, DJ and writer Anna Öström describes how female DJs in Stockholm are portrayed by journalists as sensual, having a feel for melodies and 'adding a touch of female finesse' (2011b). Second, music journalists tend to compare the work of female DJs and music producers reductively to other female artists simply because they are women. The experiences of many female DJs reconfirm Puwar's analysis of the 'burden of representation' that befalls on women in male dominated professions (2004, p. 58). This means that female DJs are seen as representing the capacities of women as a group, for which they are marked and visible per se (2004, p. 62). These patterns of representation enact a double reinforcement of electronic music's male domain by gendering important stylistic developments as male, and grouping women together as the ghettoized counterpart of this master narrative (Rodgers, 2010). Thirdly, the recent pervasive hyper-sexualisation of contemporary culture also manifests in representations of female DJs and music producers in music magazines (for example, *URB*, *DJ*, *IDJ*, *Mixmag*), posters and flyers, as music journalists and club hosts can pay more attention to their appearances than to their musical skills and their work. The sexualized representations of women artists correspond to the invitation politics of certain club hosts – as a female DJ from Berlin notes:

> You always had kind of waves that focus on female DJs ..., always from the exotic way of looking at it .... Like girls in men's professions or so which sucked ..., because you're always feeling like an example, not like an artist, an example of something which is so untypical. And ... it also had this aspect, that organizers were organising parties with female DJs ... like stupid ones and more interesting ones. .... It also had parties where there would be housewives from the 50s on the flyer ... and champagne was 2.50 for girls coming before midnight .... Like this kind of thing ..., which we agreed that we should stop that, you know (laughs). (DJ, female, Berlin 2006)

This interviewee speaks of 'tokenism' (Kanter, 1977) by club organ-izers and music journalists as an established strategy in Berlin's techno, minimal and house music scenes. According to a number of women we interviewed, they also experience the ambivalent advantages of such tokenism, paradoxically changing the minority status of female DJs in club culture. For example, an interviewee from London said:

> When I first started DJing it was extremely male dominated and there were not many women DJing – only a few. You would get a lot of attention, but I used to hate it when a promoter would decide to have an all-girl DJs night as a novelty. I especially hate

it when that is the only time you get asked to play! Nowadays, there are a lot more women DJs and I can see that the ratio of male and female DJs is now slowly starting to balance out. I am happy that I have been part of this progression. (DJ, female, London 2006)

Playing along with problematic representations in DJ culture may increase chances for gigs and media attention even though this decreases chances of recognition in peer networks, such as informal social networks among male and female DJ colleagues as well as scene-based internet forums (Gavanas, 2009). Not only do a number of interviewees mention that promoters book female DJs because of their novelty value, but also because they are more marketable than male DJs due to the possibility of promoting them with appealing sexualized images (Farrugia, 2012). This ambivalent inclusion of female DJs in the line-up of club nights is illustrated by a London DJ, saying that she gained gigs because of her looks – yet this was a main criterion for promoters to book her. She DJ-ed in hotpants and high heels and used sexualized images to promote herself, concluding that this has proven to be a successful marketing strategy. Likewise, a different London-based DJ states on a forum for female DJs that

> THE FACT IS: 99% of the people that book female DJs are male. So therefore [my] website is targeted at men. That's what's called 'marketing'. If any of you are female artists in an industry and haven't grasped this simple fact yet then you aren't pushing yourselves to your full potential. (DJ, female, London – website forum 2011)

Paradoxically, the more women achieve in male-dominated professional hierarchies, the more their looks, image, styles and size carry significance (Puwar, 2004, p. 96). Apart from that some female DJs might increase their appearances at club nights, the stereotypical, tokenistic and sexualized representations of female DJs contradict what seems an all-encompassing norm in electronic dance music culture that 'real' DJs should be 'all about the music' (Farrugia, 2004, p. 245; Gavanas, 2009). Thus, in a long and controversial discussion on a website forum for female DJs in 2011, participants debated whether (hetero)sexualized representation ought to be relevant to female DJs. There was one thing all participants seemed to agree upon: musical skills and talent should be the main criteria to get ahead. As one DJ finished her argument: 'Anyhow, back to making music, undeniably, that is the most important thing.' Male and female DJs tend to agree that their musical contributions can, and should, be measured according to 'objective' criteria, such as whether they master certain mixing techniques, or possess enough musical knowledge. For example, as one interviewee told us: 'It takes me five minutes to put on makeup but it took me ten years to learn the trade of DJing and that's what I want to be appreciated for' (DJ, female, Berlin 2006).

However, due to the practice of 'booking ladies for their looks', such a notion of 'real DJs' leads to a socially constructed opposition between music and gender (Gavanas, 2009). In other words, an overt focus on appearances may detract from the perceived 'seriousness' of the DJ's music, as stated here by one of our female DJ respondents:

It's not about me going up there with my pretty face and my pretty dress, it's something else. I mean I give my show and what I do give when I'm on the turntables is like 'listen to the music'. .... This is what I'm trying to say .... So I don't think ... a flashy dress will do the job. (DJ, female, Berlin 2006)

Attributes that are discursively associated with men and masculinity (aggressiveness, risk taking, seriousness, confidence) are considered more serious and worthy of respect, in contrast to attributes projected on women and femininity (superficiality, commercialism, sexiness, handbags, populist vocals and melodies) (Ganetz et al., 2009; Gavanas, 2009). We argue here that criteria for the authenticity of musical skills are actually gendered by unrelated 'masculine' features in and by themselves (McClary, 1991; Ganetz et al., 2009). As a result, when femininity is highlighted in controversial ways it becomes heavily debated among female and male DJs alike. According to a Berlin-based DJ, one of the worst aspects of club culture is that 'tits are worth more than ten years of experience and skill' and that DJs who capitalize on sexualized marketing are a 'kick in the face for us who do it with quality for years'. She elaborates on her view:

I just DJed with two girlie-DJs a couple of weeks ago, they're called Female DJs .... They have a management that's really pushing them very hard ... and I didn't know it, because if I had known it, I would have rejected the gig .... They played commercial music that was very, very predictable. And they were like the tit-DJs. The one served the picture of the exotic woman, and the other one was a blonde girl that was very much into her make up all the time .... It's not a coincidence that they're called Female DJs because ... they could just as well work in a striptease bar. (DJ, female, Berlin 2006)

In other words, there are interviewees who stress that they despise, and wish to disassociate themselves from, female DJs who blatantly market themselves through either 'sexiness' or 'fluffy' 'girlishness,' rather than through focus on musical DJ skills. Similarly, a DJ from London states: 'I also do not like women DJs who use their sexuality to get to the top. I know it has happened throughout history, but it gets on my nerves and sometimes, I think, it's a little boring. This is all about music, not who looks sexy behind the decks' (DJ, female, London 2006).

A discussion at the internet forum for female DJs/producers we studied further illustrates the controversies and dilemmas of navigating between sexualization and autonomous self-expression. Over the course of the discussion, the participants reconfirm their common denominator as music professionals but disagree over strategies to get ahead in male dominated music scenes. Some DJs argue, in line with post- and liberal-feminist perspectives, that one needs to be realistic and adapt one's strategies to sexist conditions in order to get ahead; for example, 'I have seen in all areas of life that the best way to fight the system is through the system! ... not much can come out from marginalizing yourself as a principle.' Another DJ refutes the idea that one needs to 'tone down' feminine attributes in order to get respected:

If I'm about to make photos then surely I want to 'stage' myself as strong and desirable!!! I want to get booked, halloooooo! In the club, dressed in baggys and tee I get the same respect from fellow DJs and clubbers as in a short, tight skirt. btw, I'm often the only girl in sneakers in the club when I'm DJing. Neither an issue. Dressed in burlaps doesn't automatically turn you into a 'more real' DJ, ladies. (DJ, female, website forum 2011)

In contrast, other DJs in the same forum discussion refuse, in line with more radical feminist perspectives, to buy into a sexist system in DJ culture:

> We all have choices in how we want to be represented as females and as DJs. And I'm sure there are people who buy in to the aesthetic on your site. But there are also some of us who don't wish to further sexism by marketing to what you think men want to see. Anyhow, back to making music. (DJ, female, website forum 2011)

Some interviewees, however, do take advantage of the market value in (certain idealized types of) 'feminine' (self-) representation:

> You may as well make the best of what you've got, and being female is really different: it puts you in a niche and you may as well really embrace that. (DJ, female, London 2006)

Other interviewees choose to disassociate themselves with attributes and presentation coded as 'feminine', given that this option would be available to them according to the contextual ideals in play in their specific music scene. These DJs/producers articulate their resistance to sexualization of electronic dance music culture and as a result develop alternative modes of femininities. Although female DJs may defend the view that electronic dance music scenes should focus on music and not on 'sexiness' according to heteronormative ideals, it is very difficult for women artists to get assessed purely on the basis of their music-technical skills and contributions. It therefore is a concern among some female DJs, that to be taken seriously – and to prevent suspicions among male and female peers that one has progressed one's career through looks alone – it is crucial to anticipate accusations that one might have been 'cheating' (see also Farrugia, 2012). In other words, female DJs may here run into a 'damned if you do, damned if you don't' situation when it comes to femininity and (self-) representation. One Stockholm-based DJ described potential accusations of unfair female advantage as an important issue:

> My absolute nightmare is to become one of those ... or if one would be the type of person that people question, like (saying) that one is not able to mix .... I don't want to name any names

but just this type of bullshit 'yes but the only reason that she gets any gigs is because she has slept with so and so' or 'she only gets gigs because she is a woman or because of her looks' or if one wouldn't be taken seriously based on one's music. (DJ, female, Stockholm 2006)

In line with Gill's understanding of postfeminism (2011), as mentioned above, feminist and anti-feminist themes are entangled in approaches by female DJs to the sexualization of women artists. In contrasting and conflicting ways, our interviewees may both critique and reinforce sexist stereotypes.

Given the masculinized mainstream norms in DJ cultures, female DJs deviate from traditional notions of femininity in the first place (Ganetz, 1997). In the following comment, one DJ describes how s/he performs a kind of 'queer feminist femininity' in the context of queer electronic dance music scenes:

My appearance is quite sexualized, but not in a heterosexual way. I like to mix all kinds of female styling, heavy lipstick, make up, sometimes I wear a wig with long black or blond hair, a tight red dress and big glasses and a beard, or I come to my gigs with a very lady-like handbag (laughs). I combine all these things to make it look very queer and it works for my club audience. I try to challenge the stereotypes of conventional femininity and masculinity and I guess my audience understands these codes. (DJ, female, Vienna 2010)

The DJ creates a performance of femininity and sexuality to confuse and subvert a binary gender system and heternormative expectations of the club audience. She makes use of what we could call a 'politics of ambiguity' (Genz and Brabon, 2009, p. 158) in which identity is 'under construction' and 'a site of permanent becoming' (Jagose, 1996, p. 131). This queer (self-) representation challenges the sexualized representations of female DJs in heteronormative electronic dance music scenes, but it also calls into question the identity politics of second wave feminism. This identity politics understands sexualized (self-) representations of women as a form of misogyny and an 'objectification' of female bodies.

However, we did not find a complete resistance to femininity among interviewees. Thus the strategies of female DJs partly correspond to the analysis of alternative femininities, suggested by Holland (2004) as they negotiate between ideals of femininity and remain comfortably alternative to existing norms. Resisting certain caricatures, such as 'tit-DJs', 'fluffiness' and 'girlishness', does not mean that interviewees see themselves as unfeminine. Some interviewees raised age (or youth) as an important precondition for sexualized strategies; sexualized femininity strategies are inseparable from age norms (Holland, 2004). Thus, some interviewees pointed out that as they aged they could no longer rely on their looks as marketing strategy. In the words of a participant in a forum for female DJs: 'Now I'm nearing 40 I feel the bookings based purely on my looks are dwindling, and that is fine by me as those kind of bookings weren't ever really that enjoyable because the people didn't appreciate my music as much as they do now' (DJ, female, website forum 2011).

Importantly, the processes by which female DJs/producers relate to norms for (self-) representation in their scenes intersect not only with age specific norms, but also with scene specific classifications according to ethnicity and sexual orientation. One of our London based DJs underlines this issue:

Most DJs are men; 90 per cent at least are male, boys, guys. And out of the female DJs there are only a few black women actually. Most of female DJs are white. And there are a couple of Asian[s] that I could name. I think when people see a black woman in the DJ box, they definitely notice me. (DJ, female, London 2006)

This interviewee illustrates the intersectional ways in which female DJs may challenge invisible gendered and racialized norms, where some bodies are deemed as having the right to belong while others are marked out as 'trespassers' and circumscribed as being 'out of place' (Puwar, 2004, p. 8). In line with Puwar's analysis of 'space invaders', this interviewee illustrates how a specific masculinized and white space can be disturbed by the arrival of black and Asian bodies in occupations which are not historically and normatively marked out as their 'natural' domain (2004, p. 32). Since most of the interviewed DJs in the EDM scenes of Berlin, London, Stockholm and Vienna corresponded to unmarked white norms in their scenes, interviewees rarely brought up issues of race or ethnicity as significant to career prospects and social dynamics.

However, one Turkish DJ interviewed in London in 2006, brought up whiteness in terms of 'blondness' as a factor, framing the ways in which she was being gendered as a DJ, being blond and considered 'pretty'. In the experience of this DJ, promoters have a hard time understanding that a blond female DJ could possibly have anything to contribute musically, especially if she is pretty. For this reason, this interviewee had a difficult time getting taken seriously for her musical skills even though she could get bookings and concludes, 'it's nice being a female DJ as long as you keep it modest'. As these examples indicate, it is crucial in this type of analysis to investigate various contexts and club scenes in order to ascertain which specific type of gendered or ethnic strategy is effective amongst peers and audience, whether it be whiteness, blondness, youthfulness, hetero-sexually, 'respectable' sexiness/prettiness and so on.

Regardless of their feminist, queer or anti-feminist approach or gendered/ethnic/commercial strategy, we found that the majority of the interviewed female DJs resist the tendency to be judged by their appearance instead of their musical abilities. By rejecting a main focus on appearance, these DJs are first and foremost resisting fundamental assumptions about femininity: 'I want to be treated with respect ... for my mixing ... I want to be respected ... solely for what I do musically ... and this bullshit about looks and stuff like that, it is IRRELEVANT, I don't want to HEAR it! It is not what I'm doing or want to be appreciated for ...' (DJ, female, Stockholm 2006).

Female Networking Strategies

As we have shown, female DJs and music producers are forced to consciously employ strategies to gain recognition in relevant social networks in contrast to male DJs and producers who may have an easier time in receiving recognition in their scene networks because they are already expected to correspond to masculinized norms and ideals (Gavanas, 2009; Reitsamer, 2011a). The very real exclusion from scene networks is the central motivation for women to launch their own forms of local, translocal and virtual networking, separate from the existing male-dominated scene networks. Examples of networks for women artists are Women on Wax (US), Pink Noises (US), Female Pressure (Austria), Shejay (UK), SisterDJs (US), Sister Sthlm (SWE), and Rubina DJanes (Switzerland). These networks are effective in introducing female role models; sharing technical knowledge; increasing invitations to DJ performances; receiving feedback on DJ sets; producing tracks; and so on. In line with tendencies in electronic dance music culture to compare female DJs to other female DJs (as opposed to DJs in general, including male DJs), interviewees tend to relate to other women DJs and music producers in various ways. Some interviewees stress that they admire and associate themselves with strong female DJs who have 'made it' in spite of male dominance, especially those who have made it independently.

> I'd like to put something here for the networks and sites that were particularly significant to my development. Let's say it's only the start with DJing, I've had a process where a lot of people have influenced me over the years. And for sure it's also the (name of the network), and I really mean that, especially (name of a female DJ), who was very much influencing me for her ... When I started out as a DJ, I found her so uncompromising, and I was really fascinated by that fact .... She shaved her head at the beginning of the 90s, and so she looked heavy. And she was always wearing camouflage clothes, she was said ... to be the hardest female DJ ... because she was playing fast or hard techno. I think she always had a unique style for rhythmical patterns, and I was really ... so fascinated when I first heard her, because I was really wondering where she found all those tracks! (DJ, female, Berlin 2006)

Quite a few female DJs we interviewed say that networks such as Female Pressure were very useful when they started out DJing because they get access to DJ performances and to female DJs who have been in the business longer and can therefore support the female newcomers. However, such homosocial strategies may lead to tensions and dilemmas. A few DJs address the difficulties of developing effective networking strategies on mailing lists to protest exclusions of female DJs from club nights and international music festivals because time-consuming discussions are a necessary precondition to negotiate the political standpoint of each DJs involved in order to build a basis for collective activism.

As a result of a lack of time and commitment as well as political disagreements in which the initial idea often gets lost, the development of collective activism tends to disintegrate on the internet. Ultimately, what remains are the actions of individuals and local groups such as the call to protest against the invitation policy of the German music magazine *Groove* on its twentieth anniversary parties in several German cities, where exclusively male DJs were invited (Reitsamer, 2012).

Additionally, once newcomers are settled, they tend to withdraw themselves from female networks because, for example,

> The [name of the network] was very good at the beginning because nobody invited me at the beginning and nobody recommended me as a DJ. But now I consider the network as a blockade and a burden. I play a lot at parties with female DJs only, but it gets on my nerves. The people and the club promoters love these kinds of events, but for me it means that I don't find access to the real market and that's actually where I want to be part of. There I am permanently excluded because of this ghettoisation, which is celebrated by female DJs, club promoters and the audience alike. Once you achieved success, you have to network with men. (DJ, female, Vienna 2008)

A female DJ in Stockholm said that she did not want to associate herself with her female network publicly, because that would make her skills and knowledge appear suspect. Another female DJ in Stockholm wanted to disassociate herself from her (previous) female DJ network when she became more established professionally because she felt that public association with the female network reduced her popularity among promoters and fellow (male) DJs.

Female networks are confronted with the problem of possibly reinforcing hierarchical gender differences and as a result, the binary structure of male/female social network segregation, as well as self-presentation in terms of masculinity and femininity, is not altered (Gildemeister and Wetterer, 1995). In the internet forum we studied, reinforcement of hierarchical gender differences is heavily debated and female DJs develop two main strategies to escape the dilemmas of career progress for women. The first strategy could be described as a 'programmatic politics' which suggest to increase the visibility of female DJs and producers by inviting them to club appearances without directly addressing the advancement of women or feminism; the second strategy refers to a 'feminist-queer politics' whereby 'queer' is understood as a strategic term for alliance-building with cultural producers in electronic dance music cultures who identify as transgender or refuse membership in the heteronormative and male dominated electronic dance music scenes (Reitsamer, 2012). This feminist–queer strategy manifests itself in the organization of club events that include the terms 'queer', 'trans' and 'drag' on the flyer, but the DJs and organizers welcome anyone interested in these events regardless of their gender. In the internet forum, the strategies to avoid a reinforcement of hierarchical gender differences are often supported by the advice to ignore sexist and racist comments and to carry on DJing and music-making as male colleagues will sooner or later show respect for the activities of female DJs/producers. However, how effective the strategies are depends upon the heteronormative or queer context of the club scene as well as on various other factors such as race, ethnicity or locality, as they each function in relation to specific norms for normality.

Whether they want to or not, female DJs are forced to deal with gendered concerns as part of their social network strategies. Net-based female social networks (such as Female Pressure, Shejay and SisterDJs) may be analysed in terms of liberal feminist responses to exclusion from male homosocial networks, promoting equal opportunities for individual careers. However, there are conflicting feminist and non-feminist approaches among female DJs in these and other networks, which can cause tensions. It may become counterproductive in terms of the social capital and peer recognition to be publicly associated with feminism, or any type of self-conscious gender politics. Furthermore, explicitly employing such social network strategies may leave a female DJ open to accusations of relying on gendered quota tokenism instead of their actual musical skills. This dilemma may result in tensions between individual career interests in line with market/ capitalist conditions, and critiquing those conditions out of collective concerns. Female DJs may maximize their social networks and simultaneously be part of mixed as well as male and female dominated networks. However, there may occur situations where multiple network strategies are mutually conflicting. On the other hand, it may be difficult for female DJs to navigate relations with male colleagues, risking the accusation of taking unfair advantage of femininity and (hetero)sexuality in order to get ahead. As shown elsewhere by Gavanas (2009), many female DJ interviewees make a point of disassociating themselves from suspicions that they have received any kind of help from boyfriends (in cases where they have any boyfriends in the DJ business and/or are presumed to be hetero- or bisexual). Importantly, though, male DJs are rarely made suspect of cheating due to support from, or association with, DJing girlfriends or women – or their male colleagues for that matter.

Conclusion

This chapter explored the scarcity of big name female DJs and music producers that originates partly in the gendered social construction of technology and partly in the informal character of working environments and social networks in electronic dance music cultures, which are dominated by a combination of gendered images that present men as music technicians and women as sexualized 'objects'. However, our analysis also pointed out the contradiction and dilemmas regarding technology, sex and gender as well as sexuality, identity and (self-) representation through which the positions of female DJs and producers are characterized. The overwhelming majority of our female interviewees challenge the socially constructed association of technological competence with masculinity by describing at length how they use their hardware and software for music-making and by portraying themselves as 'nerds' who enjoy spending time with their technical equipment. This interest in technology is a necessary precondition for becoming a successful DJ or music producer; for female DJs and producers, however, this interest is a means to obtaining the status as 'exceptional women' in society in general and in electronic dance music cultures in particular. Additionally, attributes such as perseverance and persistence, which are regarded as necessary for a successful DJ career, are ascribed to men. The combination of these gender-specific attribution practices ultimately gives rise to the idea that only men can be 'good' DJs and place burdens of representation and doubt on those who deviate from unmarked masculine norms (Puwar, 2004). This idea corresponds to the idealized notion of successful and assertive masculinity in the cultural contexts under study (Reitsamer, 2011b).

However, the development of new technologies also brings about shifts in the discussions on authenticity and the accumulation of social capital in electronic dance music cultures, and has opened new possibilities for translocal and virtual networking through Web 2.0, mailing lists and databases. Our analysis has shown how networks for female artists such as Female Pressure, Pink Noises or Shejay offer various advantages for female DJs and producers to advance their careers, as well as how networking and collective activism have become a means for protesting exclusions from club nights, harassment and tokenism in electronic dance music cultures. But the interviewees also realize that female networks remain marginalized in male-dominated electronic dance music cultures and a reification of the hierarchical gender differences can hardly be avoided. As a result of their experiences, many of the female DJs and producers we interviewed in the course of our study distance themselves from female-oriented networking strategies, while only a tiny minority involve themselves in these networks for long periods of time. The former may seek to blend in with the norm, concentrate on the job and avoid publicly associating themselves with gender issues as a strategy of survival (Puwar, 2004, p. 154). The latter try to struggle meaningfully against discrimination and to break heteronormative notions of gender and sexuality in their interplay with other categories of social differentiation such as race, age or class.

References

Attias, Bernardo (2011) 'Meditations on the Death of Vinyl'. *Dancecult: Journal of Electronic Dance Music Culture*, 3(1).

Bayton, Mavis (2011) 'Women and the Electric Guitar'. In Mary Celeste Kearney (ed.) *The Gender and Media Reader* (265–72). London: Routledge.

Bourdieu, Pierre (1993) *The Field of Cultural Production: Essays on Art and Literature*. Cambridge: Polity Press.

Brewster, Bill and Broughton, Frank (1999) *Last Night a DJ Saved My Life: The History of the Disc Jockey*. New York: Headline.

Buszek, Maria Elena (2006) *Pin-up Grrrls: Feminism, Sexuality, Popular Culture*. Durham, NC: Duke University Press.

Christodoulou, Christodoulos (2011) 'Rumble in the Jungle: City, Place and Uncanny Bass'. *Dancecult: Journal of Electronic Dance Music Culture*, 3(1): 44–63.

Cockburn, Cynthia and Ormrod, Susan (1993) *Gender and Technology in the Making*. London and New Delhi: Sage.

Cohen, Sara (1997) 'Men Making a Scene: Rock Music and the Production of Gender'. In Sheila Whitley (ed.) *Sexing the Groove: Popular Music and Gender* (17–36). New York: Routledge.

Collin, Matthew (1997) *Altered State: The Story of Ecstasy Culture and Acid House*. London: Serpent's Tail.

DJ Mag (2012) 'Top 100'. http://www.djmag.com/top100 [accessed 8 November 2012].

Eshun, Kodwo (1998) *More Brilliant than the Sun*. London: Quartet Books.

Farrugia, Rebekah (2004) 'Sisterdjs in the House: Electronic/Dance Music and Women-Centred Spaces in the Net'. *Women's Studies in Communication*, 27(2): 236–62.

—(2012) *Beyond the Dance Floor. Female DJs, Technology and Electronic Dance Music Culture*. Bristol and Chicago: intellect.

Farrugia, Rebekah and Swiss, Thomas (2005) 'Tracking the DJs: Vinyl Records, Work, and the Debate over New Technologies'. *Journal of Popular Music Studies*, 17(1): 30–44.

Fikentscher, Kai (2000) *'You Better Work!' Underground Dance Music in New York City*. Hanover, NH: Wesleyan University Press.

Ganetz, Hillevi (1997) *Hennes Röster*. Stockholm: Symposium.

Ganetz, Hillevi, Gavanas, Anna, Huss, Hasse and Werner, Ann (eds) (2009) *Rundgång: genus och populärmusik*. Stockholm: Makadam.

Gavanas, Anna (2009) ' "You Better Be Listening to My Fucking Music You Bastard!" Teknologi, Genusifiering och Andlighet Bland DJs på Elektroniska Dansmusikscener i Berlin, London och Stockholm'. In Hillevi Ganetz, Anna Gavanas, Hasse Huss and Ann Werner (eds) *Rundgång: genus och populärmusik* (77–122). Stockholm: Makadam.

Gavanas, Anna and Attias, Bernardo (2011) 'Guest Editor's Introduction to *Dancecult* Special Issue on the DJ'. *Dancecult: Journal of Electronic Dance Music Culture*, 3(1): 1–3.

Genz, Stephanie and Brabon, Benjamin A. (2009) *Postfeminism: Cultural Texts and Theories*. Edinburgh: Edinburgh University Press.

Gildemeister, Regina and Wetterer, Angelika (1995) 'Wie Geschlechter gemacht warden. Die soziale Konstruktion der Zweigeschlechtlichkeit und ihre Reifizierung in der Frauenforschung'. In Gudrun-Axeli Knapp and Angelika Wetterer (eds) *Traditionen Brüche. Entwicklungen feministischer Theorie* (201–50). Freiburg: Kore.

Gill, Rosalind (2011) 'Postfeminist Media Culture: Elements of a
    Sensibility'. In Mary Celeste Kearney (ed.) *The Gender and Media
    Reader* (136–48). New York, London: Routledge.
Goodman, Steve (2010) *Sonic Warfare. Sound, Affect and the Ecology of
    Fear*. Cambridge, MA: MIT Press.
Holland, Samantha (2004) *Alternative Femininities. Body, Age and
    Identity*. New York: Berg.
Hutton, Fiona (2006) *Risky Pleasures? Club Cultures and Feminine
    Identities*. Burlington, VT and Aldershot: Ashgate.
Jagose, Annamarie (1996) *Queer Theory*. New York: New York
    University Press.
Kahn, Douglas (1999) *Noise Water Meat: A History of Sound in the
    Arts*. Cambridge, MA: MIT Press.
Kanter, Rosabeth M. (1977) *Men and Women of the Corporation*. New
    York: Basic Books.
Kirn, Peter (2011) *The Evolution of Electronic Dance Music*. London:
    Backbeat Books.
Lawrence, Tim (2011) 'The Forging of a White Male Gay Aesthetic at
    the Saint, 1980–84'. *Dancecult: Journal of Electronic Dance Music
    Culture*, 3(1): 4–27.
Lie, Merete (1995) 'Technology and Masculinity: The Case of the
    Computer'. *European Journal of Women's Studies*, 2: 379–94.
Lin, Nan (2002) *Social Capital: A Theory of Social Structure and Action*.
    Cambridge: Cambridge University Press.
McClary, Susan (1991) *Feminine Endings; Music, Gender and Sexuality*.
    Minneapolis, MN: University of Minnesota Press.
McRobbie, Angela (1994) 'Shut Up and Dance: Youth Culture
    and Changing Modes of Femininity'. In Angela McRobbie (ed.)
    Postmodernism and Popular Culture (155–76). New York:
    Routledge.
—(2009) *The Aftermath of Feminism. Gender, Culture and Social
    Change*. London, New Delhi and Singapore: Sage.
Naylor, Tony (2008) 'The Female Techno Takeover: Women Tastemakers
    on Top and No Leering Blokes: Tony Naylor Digs Berlin'. *The
    Guardian*, 24 May. http://www.guardian.co.uk/music/2008/may/24/
    features16.theguide [accessed 10 November 2012].
Negus, Keith (1999) *Popular Music in Theory: An Introduction*.
    Cambridge: Polity Press.
Olsen, Eric, Verna, Paul and Wolff, Carlo (1993) *The Encyclopedia of
    Record Producers*. New York: Watson-Guptill.
Öström, Anna (2011a) 'We call it Swedish Techno'. *Dancecult: Journal
    of Electronic Dance Music Culture*, 3(1).
—(2011b) 'Testosterontechno'. *Bang*, 14 September. http://www.bang.se/

artiklar/2011/testosterontechno–2011–09–13 [accessed 10 November 2012].

Pini, Maria (2001) *Club Cultures and Female Subjectivity: The Move from House to House.* Basingstoke: Palgrave.

Poschardt, Ulf (1997), *DJ Culture. Diskjockeys und Popkultur.* Hamburg: Rowohlt.

Puwar, Nirmal (2004) *Space Invaders. Race, Gender and Bodies Out of Place.* Oxford: Berg.

Reitsamer, Rosa (2011a) 'The DIY Careers of Techno and Drum'n'Bass DJs in Vienna'. *Dancecult: Journal of Electronic Dance Music Culture,* 3(1): 28–43.

—(2011b) 'Leistung, Anerkennung und Geschlecht im kulturellen Feld: Zur Unterrepräsentanz von DJ-Frauen in elektronischen Musikszenen'. *Österreichische Zeitschrift für Soziologie,* 36(3): 39–48.

—(2012) 'Female Pressure: A Translocal Feminist Youth-centred Cultural Network'. *Continuum: Journal for Media & Cultural Studies,* 26(3): 399–408.

Reynolds, Simon (1998) *Generation Ecstasy: Into the World of Techno and Rave Culture.* Boston, MA: Little, Brown.

Rietveld, Hillegonda C. (2004) 'Ephemeral Spirit: Sacrificial Cyborg and Communal Soul'. In Graham St John (ed.) *Rave Culture and Religion* (45–60). New York: Routledge.

Rodgers, Tara (2010) *Pink Noises: Women on Electronic Music and Sound.* Durham, NC: Duke University Press.

Rose, Tricia (1994) *Black Noise: Rap Music and Black Culture in Contemporary America.* Hanover, NH: Wesleyan University Press.

Springer, Claudia (1993) *Electronic Eros: Bodies and Desire in the Postindustrial Age.* Austin, TX: University of Texas Press.

St John, Graham (2009) *Technomad: Global Raving Countercultures.* London: Equinox.

Straw, Will (1997) 'Sizing Up Record Collections: Gender and Connoisseurship in Rock Music Culture'. In Sheila Whitley (ed.) *Sexing the Groove: Popular Music and Gender* (3–16). New York, NY: Routledge.

Taylor, Timothy (2001) *Strange Sounds: Music, Technology and Culture.* London: Routledge.

Thornton, Sarah (1996) *Club Cultures: Music, Media and Subcultural Capital.* London: Wesleyan University Press.

Wacjam, Judy (2004) *TechnoFeminism.* Cambridge, MA: Polity Press.

Wahl, Anna, Holgersson, Charlotte, Höök, Pia and Linghag, Sophie (2011) *Det ordnar sig. Teorier om Organisation och kön.* Lund: Studentlitteratur.

CHAPTER FOUR

Journey to the Light? Immersion, Spectacle and Mediation

Hillegonda C. Rietveld

EDM today has come a long way from the early days of house and techno, when sound was privileged over vision, an ethos enshrined in the title of the 1992 Madhouse compilation <u>A Basement, a Red Light, and a Feeling</u>. In those murky, atmospheric clubs, the deejay booth was often tucked away in a corner rather than placed on a stage: dancers weren't meant to be looking in one direction, they were meant to get lost in music, in the collective intimacy of the dancefloor. (Reynolds, 2012 – original underline)

Writing about an explosion of large commercially successful rave festivals in the US, Simon Reynolds (2012) notes how the DJ is set up as a spectacle, absorbing the attention of thousands of fans. He contrasts this to dancefloors where the music dominates and the DJ is heard, rather than seen. Articulated in the past tense, as a nostalgic memory of a bygone era, perhaps this cleaves DJ history too sharply into a before and after the arrival of the staged DJ, but you get the point: there is more to electronic dance music events than gazing at the DJ. Here, I wish to explore differing forms of sensory relations that can exist at a DJ-event, ranging from collective participation in which a range of subject positions are possible, to the spectacular authority of the 'stadium-DJ' (also known as an 'arena DJ'), in which context hegemonic values regarding identity hierarchies seem to be firmly embedded. At the heart of this discussion lies the notion of the spectacle, which Debord (1983, p. 3) described in 1967, as 'the present model of socially dominant life', and which Baudrillard (1988, pp. 21–2) argues is disappearing because, 'everything becomes immediately transparent, visible, exposed in the raw and inexorable light of information and communication'. In this context, during the early 1990s, the tactile-acoustic emphasis of raves and house music dance events was theorized as facilitating a disappearance from the transparency of surveillance (Jordan, 1995; Melechi, 1993; Plant, 1993; Rietveld, 1993, 1998) a Temporary Autonomous Zone or TAZ (Bey, 1991) where 'the transgressive potential of underground raves is captured most fully in the concept of communion … the sharing of common substance … an "intimate fellowship" in which traditional hierarchies are flattened' (Ott and Herman, 2003, p. 253)and in which, according to Langlois (1993), the DJ and music producer were (more or less) anonymous. Yet the electronic dance music DJ now finds professional success with a social and mobile media savvy crowd that celebrates exposure of the self. At events staged in stadium-sized venues, where the DJ is placed on a high stage, bathed in light from all directions, not only sound but also visual appearance dominates, making the DJ seem larger than life, celebrating the DJ's god-like creative Frankenstein function in bringing sound recordings to life (Middleton, 2006) in what may seem to some like a Temporary *Authoritarian* Zone (adapted from Armitage, 2008).[1]

In trying to understand the different configurations of the dance spaces and events where electronic dance music operates, it soon becomes clear that they consist of contradictory elements, in which both sonic dominance and spectacular culture intermingle to differing degrees. First, DJs present a heterogenic archival set of musical sources as an individual performance. Second, DJ-led dance events produce a fragile cohesion between friends and complete strangers on the dancefloor. Third, DJ-led events

---

[1] Armitage (2008) addresses acts of organized crime.

produce shifts in dominance and subjugation, in which the DJ makes musical decisions, yet the crowd literally vote with their feet. Fourth, during a dance event, the sensory focus can shift from looking to hearing. Here, I wish to propose that DJ-led dance events can be understood as *heterotopias,* which Foucault (2002, p. xix) describes as paradoxical categorizations that are 'disturbing, probably because they secretly undermine language, because they make it impossible to name this *and* that' (original emphasis). As part of an exercise in 'heterotopology' (Foucault, 2000, p. 179), the discussion will be illustrated by a set of interspersed vignettes, participant snap shots from the dancefloor that influenced my thinking over the past three decades regarding the role of the DJ in different phases of mediation. Although I have operated as a DJ for over 15 years, mostly in the slightly raised DJ booth of an after-hours gay club in Manchester, but also at festivals on the high-placed DJ platform, it is especially as a participant on the dancefloor that I became acutely aware of how the DJ is positioned as a communicator.

Sonic Immersion

The DJ emerged as a response to the availability of recorded music, which enabled live entertainment at lower overheads than a fully equipped band of musicians (Brewster and Broughton, 2006; Poschardt, 1998). The DJ-led dance space developed from the elite discotheque of the 1950s and 1960s to the underground disco of the 1970s. Towards the late 1960s, the disco experience became increasingly sonically immersive. Rather than music functioning as a background fill to a social meeting place, as we can still experience in bars, the dancefloor and its soundsystem became the dominant medium, while the visual field was being fragmented and subordinated to the audio experience through lighting, video and smoke effects. In a study of New York City's underground dance DJ practices, Fikentscher (2000, p. 23) confirms that the 'disco environment ... prioritizes the aural dimension at the expense of the visual ... the visual sense is lessened through the use of (relative) darkness, while auditory perception is drastically heightened, through the constant presence of music at a high volume and a wide frequency spectrum'. As a result, a tactile-acoustic experience is enhanced in which not only the ears and the hairs on one's arms, but sometimes the entire body can physically resonate with the amplified dance music, so that the perception of boundaries between inside and outside the body are blurred. This is an important element in the dance experience, as it arguably enables the dancers to let go of an alienated sense of self, melting into the sound and submitting to the beat (Hughes, 1994). Here, the DJ participates with the crowd, having 'one foot in the booth and the other on the dancefloor' (David Mancuso, cited Brewster and Broughton, 2002, p. 122). The dance DJ hereby facilitates a shared sonic journey, enabling an interactive musical dialogue with the dancers. As a participatory musical field (Turino, 2008) the dancefloor is no space for bystanders. To illustrate this notion of a sonically immersive dance experience, three participatory examples are provided next, from different DJ-led music scenes. The first example is a reggae dance club in Manchester, England, in the mid-1980s; the second a British acid house party in a squatted warehouse in the same British city at the end of the 1980s; and the third an underground dance club in New York in the early 1990s.

It's 1985 and I'm at a reggae club night in Manchester city centre, England. The small basement dancefloor is packed – maybe a hundred people, possibly less. Occasionally, light flows in from the corridor as the door opens that, via a staircase, leads up to the outside world. Apart from the shadowy outline of the DJ's body we can see only his hands, light nails against dark skin lit by a small desk lamp, selecting and playing a mix of 7-inch and 12-inch vinyl imports from Jamaica mixed in with home-grown talent, similar to the crowd's main demographics. On the dancefloor we can't really see each other but we share the tactility of the bass-heavy music that brings us together. The amplified soundwaves of reggae music like 'Bone Man Connection' by Nicodemus (1981), 'Sensimelia' by Black Uhuru (1980) and Little John ft Billy Boyo's (1982) 'What You Want to Be (Disco Jockey)' palpably vibrate the air – here, sound seems the perfect medium to reach out to and envelope our collective body. We're sharing this vibe, submitting ourselves to the groove. During the night, during the dance, we shed the visual fetishism of everyday normative racism (Bhabha, 1999) as skin colour melts into an unlit close circuit. It is difficult to apprehend what is first, the DJ or the dancing crowd – we are together at this party. The music is facilitated by the DJ (the 'selector') flanked in the booth by the MC (called the 'deejay' or toaster in Jamaican soundsystem culture) who only occasionally picks up the *mic* (microphone) to address, rather than dominate, the crowd, as part of sharing the communal experience. This is not a place for individual heroes or hierarchies; instead, we are deeply immersed into the sonic space of bass and beats – the vibe of reggae and dub. Such an ephemeral musical event, fuelled by post-colonial social marginalization, is intensely powerful in producing a sense of togetherness, as also reported in publications on soundsystem culture of Jamaican origin (Back, 1988; Stanley Niaah, 2010). In the latter context, Henriques (2011, p. xvii) introduces the important concept of 'sounding', which, 'has to be embodied as an event in a particular time and place, as distinct from being "frozen" as a text or image whose embodiment is less immediate. This is the point that Attali famously makes: "… the world is not for the beholding. It is for hearing. It is not legible, but audible".' This particular reggae club night is just one example of a dance event that is based on sonic immersion. Politically, this is significant as not only does this offer temporary relief from ocular regimes of visual culture (in this particular event informed by a northern English, a post-colonial and parochial society) but also enables the establishment of an alternative three-dimensional reality, a musical philosophy in which the very vibration of life, the vibe, is celebrated.

Only a few years later, late in the year of 1988, I'm at a different soundsystem event, an acid house party held in a nineteenth-century disused Mancunian warehouse, somewhere near the city centre, filled with excessive smoke effects, relentless strobe lights and the sound of a powerful system. The people I know appear and disappear in the extremely disorienting environment, swaying arms caught in what look like frozen snap shots. We're together, yet also isolated in thick impenetrable clouds, throbbing with white light, eyes rarely connecting, dancing and wandering around in the amorphous space. Both men and women wear amorphous androgy-nous clothes (baggy T-shirts and trousers plus trainers, anything that allows for comfortable loose movement) in non-distinct murky colours, even, at this specific event, in contrast to the rave culture that emerged almost simultaneously; as long as it feels good, the look matters little. People are here to forget about their economic and personal troubles, perhaps dabbling in the use of entactogenic and psychedelic dance drugs, rather than looking for a sexual partner (Rietveld, 1993; Melechi, 1993; Henderson, 1997). Adding to the visual disorientation is a new musical sound, acid house, electronic dance music based on the sound of the deranged Roland TB–303 Bassline, or equivalent sequencing device, splurting out wobbly bass lines that seem to defy any sense of tonality or rhythm. This sound is held together by programmed four-to-the-floor snare and bass drum beats of around 125 BPM (beats per minute). Somewhere in the corner, behind a table with turntable decks and a mixer, the DJ, a young man with dull grey skin, pulls 12-inch vinyl dance singles from a crate, mostly imported from Chicago, like Phuture's acid house classic, 'Acid Tracks' (1987), but also recordings produced in Manchester, such as the haunting techno track 'Voodoo Ray' by A Guy Called Gerald (1988). In this soundscape of the psychotic machine, the experience seemed to operate as 'a constant generator of de-individualization' (Foucault, 2004, p. xvi). Plant (1993, p. 7) observes that, 'Spectators see only the surface, but the ravers are already part of the scene, in the machinery. Beyond the spectacle lies total immersion; the end of the spectacle.'

It seems that the acid house experience borrowed some of its elements from the reggae soundsystem; in some cases, in the UK, reggae soundsystems were hired for the first acid house parties, providing the events with a similar sonic dominant experience as addressed above. The main musical inspiration for this acid house party came from Chicago and Detroit, where, in turn, electronic dance music developed as part of a musical dialogue that included electronic music from northern England (Reynolds, 1988; Sicko, 1999; Rietveld, 1998). Similar to Manchester, Chicago and Detroit are post-industrial cities that at the time offered abandoned manufacturing spaces that could be deployed for the purpose of entertainment and a cyborgian ritual of making sense of a world that is increasingly dominated by electronic communication devices (Rietveld, 2004a, 2004b). The format of electronic dance music and the beatmatching DJ techniques that helped evolve the minimalist programmed four-to-the-floor bass drum rhythm were, in turn, influenced by disco DJ techniques from New York City, so well described by Fikentscher (2000) and Lawrence (2003).

In the middle of 1992, I find myself in the small hours of the night in The Shelter, a dance club in New York City, described in a track of the same name, by Gate-ah (1992). I went there on my own and I'm dancing somewhere on the dancefloor without knowing a single person there, and without seeing many either, although I can sense the other dancers are there, all around me. Submerged in total darkness on the dancefloor, I'm embraced by the sound of a high-quality club hi-fi soundsystem, stroking my skin with bass, with beats, with synthesizer stabs. The occasional, crystal-clear vocal keeps me from getting lost, urging me to free my mind, body and spirit, to find peace of mind; everything is going to be all right. Not being able to see my fellow dancers, I let myself be transported into the velvety immersive sonic space of soulful club music, its deep bass-lines strutting at 125 BPM. Tracks like 'Follow Me' by Aly-Us (1992) or 'All Join Hands' by Ce Ce Rogers (1992) speak of hope that someday there will a world of tolerance and togetherness, without racial hatred. Although the same club space hosts other club nights at other times, in which strobes and other light effects are used with abundance, on his specific night, led by DJ Timmy Regisford, the music dominates. Now and then, what seems like once every two to five minutes, the lights flash on briefly to emphasize a peak moment in the music. As fellow dancers become visible, sometimes with a little shock of discovery, we are temporarily differentiated according to gender, sexuality, race and age, and for a moment black gay men dominate the scene in which, as a white female visitor, I'm the odd one out. Yet, the lights dim as soon as they come on, returning me to the deep sound of the dance music, selected and mixed into a DJ-led journey that caries us through the night. Before I leave, I buy an oversized Keith Haring T-shirt printed with his characteristic design of dancers – the proceeds go towards the fight against AIDS, an illness that nearly wiped out a generation of New York's gay men in their clubbing prime, causing havoc in New York's club DJ culture (see also Lawrence in this volume and Buckland, 2002). The T-shirt is the visual evidence of my presence, an object to behold.

Although engaging in varying musicscapes, these three particular examples of DJ-led dance events seem to concur to differing degrees with the concept of sonic dominance, developed by Henriques (2003, 2011), as the vibration of the sound engages dancers kinetically, while the visual field is effectively distorted, even destroyed, enabling the participants to lose themselves into the music. The DJ is an important facilitator in this relationship. Ferreira (2008, p. 19) argues that dance DJs are 'not suffering technological obliterations of their own bodies but [are] participating actively in the technical emergence of new collective dancing bodies'. In this process Jordan (1995, p. 125) shows, 'participants gradually lose subjective belief in their self and merge into a collective body'. DJ and dancer are immersed in a network of vibrating relationships that combine to produce the spatial presence of the music within the active participation of the dancers.

Inner Eye

Synaesthetic experience of music may produce visual interpretations, through lights, dance or VJ-steered images. Multi-sensory, the body movements, imagery and fluid use of light emphasize the musical experience. This point can be illustrated in events that primarily offer trance music, in particular psytrance, which developed via raves that are often offered outdoors, away from urban centres. The formation of the musical aesthetic of this genre took place during the late 1980s and early 1990s out of a music scene that gathered in Goa, an Indian province that attracted a critical mass of backpacking hippies, countercultural refugees from Western urban lifestyles. Psytrance music accompanies events that are self-consciously defined as temporary autonomous zones, similar to the heterotopias identified by St John (2001) in Australia's ConFest festival. Through its genealogy in yogic practices, the music is still associated with dance parties and festivals that may perhaps be understood as liminal religious rituals (St John, 2010) in which participants attempt to find solace from their jittery information-overloaded lives through a technologized connection with the earth and the cosmos (Rietveld, 2004a).

In 2002, in New South Wales, I'm driving inland from Byron Bay along the two-lane highway beyond Casino past hilly grassland, rain forests chopped down to make space for grazing. I'm heading for a *doof*, an Australian rave, named after the sound of the dominant four-to-the-floor kick drum that can be heard from afar. Finally, a sign indicates a gate and with my cheap little hire car I follow a pick-up truck across a bumpy field. The dirt track veers towards a eucalyptus forest and, once in there, it is an art to avoid tree trunks and potholes. We arrive at a clearing, a mini valley occupied by a sound-system and decorated with banners and three-dimensional abstract objects made of paper and cloth in bright colours – red, purple, yellow, green, orange. At a table made from a plank and trestles, that is decked out with turntables, a mixer and a CD player, the local sun-tanned DJ collective warms up for the party, including local music in the mix, like Panfandango's 'Up and Atom' (1999), which incorporates electronic interpretations of the local forest animal sounds, and A. B. Didgeridoo Oblivion's 'Liquid' (1997), an electronic trance interpretation of Australian didgeridoo music. Only half an hour after my arrival, just after six in the afternoon, the subtropical sun disappears without much warning; we are quickly steeped in darkness, illuminated only by small scattered campfires, fairy lights and the stars.

As the dark night descends, the amplified volume of music rises and there is no way back – the forest is impassable now. Far from urban habitation, we are caught together in this sonic space, mapped out by the reach of the music and the glowing lights till sunrise: one sound, one forest, one party. Watching the festive lampions dangling in the warm breeze, and the light-reflecting decorations made visible by almost non-intrusive ultraviolet light, it strikes me how visually engaging this party scene is. These patches of light guide our way to and from the dance space and participants dress in light-reflecting and lit-up accessories, preventing participants from getting lost or from falling over each other off the dancefloor. Speeding up the tempo over the evening, the music is worked by the DJ towards a 150 BPM (and over) psytrance set, mixing local tracks, such as Mik La Vage's cinematic 'Future Conduit' (2002), towards imported recordings, many Israeli – for example, the driving four-to-the-floor gallop of Infected Mushroom & Yahel's 'Electro Panic' (2002) or the Gaia-earth philosophy of Astrix's 'Life System' (2002a) framed in rapid electronic semiquaver (sixteenth) sequences that function like a jittery drone, trapping dancers in a hypnotized state that pulls them through the night. Listening to the swirling electronic sounds of psytrance, closing my eyes as I start to suffer from sleep deprivation, tracks like Astrix's 'Side Effect' (2002b) translate synaesthetically to an inner vision of a kaleido-scopic spiralling tunnel that seems to reach repetitiously into the infinite. Many of the guests seem to prefer to hang out in groups of friends by small campfires, absorbing the music as the sound waves roll up into the eucalyptus forest. During the dark cold hours of the early morning, I even manage to fall asleep for a while in the car, carried by the relentless yet meditative repetitive rhythms and washes of synth sounds.

Dawn appears, as fast as dusk, and a few hundred people come down from the higher ground to the dusty dance space. In the morning sun, the dancers face the DJ, their tired bodies swaying to the rhythm. Standing next to the DJ, behind the table at ground level, I take a blurry photograph of the tired sun-kissed faces of participants: their colourful T-shirts and sweaters contrasted against the trodden field, many keeping their hands warm in their pockets – it is a mixed crowd of locals and backpacking tourists, 20-somethings from as far as Japan, Israel and the UK. In the new daylight, the DJ slows the pace of the music, bringing down the dark energy of industrial trance beats to reconnect with the light of day, a music programming pattern that is very similar to what Davis (2004, p. 261) observed at the trance dance events that were initially developed in Goa, where 'the change of pace had a ritual function: after "destroying the ego" with hardcore sounds, "morning music" fills the void with light'. In this DJ-dancefloor context, it seems that sonic immersion that celebrates the whole body experience is not the main goal but, rather, a phase in a mental journey of self-improvement, from being emptied out in darkness towards enlightened rebirth.

Performing Producer

Electronic music is generated in the studio, which functions as a compositional tool as well as a musical instrument (Eno, 2004). In this context, the electronic dance music DJ seems to function as the living embodiment of studio-generated dance music, which Ferreira (2008) shows is further brought to live in the bodies of dancers, as 'human movements make visible what machine sounds are making audible' (p. 18), a new collectivity in a human-machine sound-movement assemblage (p. 19). During the 1980s, electronic musicians still toured with their hardware instruments, but through the 1990s the studio producer is increasingly seen on stage with a laptop with music mixing software, improvising with the recorded 'stems' of their music or, as a DJ, mixing their own recordings with related music productions. Whereas the traditional DJ is a researcher, archivist, occasional remixer and interactive performer, the producer-DJ is a composer, a technician and a (sometimes self-absorbed) performer.

The DJ can also bridge the gap between studio-producer and audience in a more direct way. For example, in London, at the CDR club night, a monthly club night held at a small basement club venue, Plastic People, any producer, professional or novice, can submit their latest track to be played by the DJ during, in the words of CDR's slogan, 'a night of ideas in the making' – as the club sports an audiophile soundsystem,[2] this club makes a good testing ground. Plastic People holds no more than 150 people, devoted to the sound of music. Some light is provided in the DJ booth, at the back of the small dancefloor, itself surrounded by four huge hi-fi speaker stacks. It is dark on the dancefloor: only a tiny emergency light shines in the middle of the dancefloor ceiling; the desk-lamp illuminates the record players; and some incidental light shines from the bar. This is a purist space that celebrates sonic dominance. In the same club, the bass-heavy FWD nights are held, with producer-DJs like Skream, Kode9 and Mala, who pioneered the sound of dubstep.

From 2002, the weekly Co-op club people congregated for several years on Sundays at Plastic People in East London, to engage with the newest broken beats, a rich mix of musical influences from deep house, UK garage and drum 'n' bass to Brazilian funk, and new jazz. Here the friendly inclusive multiethnic crowd is absorbed by the challenge of broken beats,[3] featuring DJ-producers such as IG Culture, Dego (from 4Hero), Phil Asher and the Bugz in the Attic DJ-production collective. Importantly, the Co-op DJs were also producers who brought in their test pressings, dub plates and early releases to the club night to test them out, such as Afronaught's

---

[2] Made by Funktion One. To some club audio fans, that would only be a 'showy' name drop; for others it is a sign of quality (see TAD, 2011).

[3] Broken beats, as a loosely defined music genre, is also known as the West London sound, as the music was produced in and distributed from West London, even though, confusingly, Plastic People is situated in East London.

'Transcend Me' (2001). This creates a close connection between studio musicianship and the club crowd, members of which include the musicians and singers that are heard on the recordings. During this era, the DJ booth was placed at ground level, enabling a performative creative dialogue between the musicians and the crowd. DJ crews faced the dancers, who in turn interacted with the music and the DJs, singing the music back to the DJs and having the occasional chat with members of the DJ crew. The ground-level meeting of studio producers and audience achieved an intimate sense of authenticity, as it felt as though the recordings were embodied and performed by the DJ-producer, giving the musical recordings, based on electronic studio production its aura. This, then, extends Fikentscher's definition of the club DJ as 'a pioneering force transforming the relationship between music as defined by performance and music conceptualized as authoritative text' (2003, p. 290).

The response of the dancers to the music would feed back to the production work; for example, 'Hold It Down' by 4Hero with Lady Alma (2002) is available in a version, the 'Bugz In the Attic's Co-operative Mix', that is inspired by the club night's DJ techniques and interaction with the participants on the dance-floor. Through this dialogue, a specific sonic aesthetic was shaped. Occasionally, as the vibe of the room peaked, and the crowd jumped up to the beat in unison, a participant, a fan, would take a mobile phone picture of the label that displays the discographical information in the centre of vinyl record that was played, making the physically underground club porous, globally, to the outside world. This DJ set-up enabled insider knowledge to be relayed, beyond the presence of sound, via mobile information networks, at the speed of light.[4]

It was striking, though, that despite the democratic feel of the club, the creative and reproductive gendered role-division was

---

[4] By way of illustration, when I was in Tokyo in 2002, I found the cream of new jazz and broken beat releases – for example, P'Taah Vs. Opaque 12" EP (2001), containing the powerfully deconstructed remix, 'Crossing (Evacuation of Form)' – at its cosmopolitan record shops, demonstrating that although current underground music culture can feel sonically intimate and local, it is simultaneously also visibly porous and globally distributed. The speed with which this knowledge is communicated is enhanced by the rapid development of social media and mobile phone technology.

no different than most other pioneering music assemblages: the DJs were exclusively male, an authoritative production fraternity, while the voices they captured on the recordings were mostly female or black male, emphasizing specific hegemonic power relations (Bradby, 1993). Middleton (2006, para. 12) argues in the context of identity production in DJ practices that 'recording technology, by apparently evacuating bodies from the scene of subject-production, places previous systems of both gender and race relations into crisis, a crisis which reassertions of familiar binaries will try to nullify'. Here the absence of the performing body of the recording is of importance, psychologically, as it destabilizes traditional gendered and racially coded subjectivities. By taking control over the destabilizing artefact, the recording, the authoritative DJ reinstates hegemonic binary identity differences. The gender inequality of the DJ fraternity led in the case of Co-op to the introduction of an all-female DJ collective, Ladybugs, which is still going strong. Yet, in the name choice, a gendered hierarchy is established. Although the reference to the all-male Bugz in the Attic DJ-collective can be regarded as giving one's respect to those that came before, the feminization of the team name gives the impression of a derivative reaction rather than of a bold new DJ-production group.

Spectacular DJ

From the 1970s onwards, resident DJs of some of the larger dance clubs moved their turntables from the ground-floor disco turntable desk to the a higher placed DJ booth, so the DJs could develop their role from human jukebox to that of musical director, or DJ-auteur. Yet, in this configuration, the dancers engage with each other, rather than that they singularly face the DJ. Thereby, the DJ facilitates the proceedings. For the club and party DJ, a sensory shift in performative focus occurred during the early- to mid-1990s, when electronic dance music became a significant cultural product, enhanced by the emergence of superclubs, raves, dance festivals, internationally touring DJs, an explosion of dance music compilations and a range of specialist media, including the increasing popularity of DJ magazines and, since 1995, the world wide web. As the reputations of DJs gained in authoritative cultural capital (Herman, 2006), and DJing was professionalized, DJ fees increased. Simultaneously, popular crowd-pulling DJs were placed squarely, literally, on the stage, a marketable brand in full view of the audience, as visual proof of their authentic presence. This gave rise to a new type of music star, illustrated by the title of the 1994 compilation *Journeys by Stadium DJ*, compiled by the internationally successful British DJ Paul Oakenfold for the American market, setting up the proto-sound of a globally recognizable electronic dance music style.

As the DJ becomes the visual focus of attention, dancers may be drawn from the diffused festive interaction of the collective dancefloor to look up and identify with the individual DJ. It seems that over the past 20 years or so, gazing at the DJ has gradually become the norm for DJ-led dance events, whether dance parties, raves and dance clubs. Even in small intimate participatory venues without a major stage, like Plastic People where the DJ functions as an extension of the crowd, both men and women face the performing DJ as a crucial component in participatory interaction. In their DJ skills guide, Brewster and Broughton (2002) recommend fledgling DJs to make eye contact, particularly when the crowd needs to be seduced to stay on the dancefloor, while the once leading London-based acid house DJ-promoter Rampling advises new DJs that people 'should be able to see your enthusiasm for the music' (Brophy and Frempong, 2010, p. 129).

During the economic boom of the 1990s, superclubs emerged in the UK that were marketed as global brands, with Ministry of Sound, Renaissance and Home offering a concept in night entertainment together with a roster of name DJs. However, according to Phillips (2009), this came to an end after large dance parties to celebrate the new Millennium flopped; both event promoters and successful DJs had over-estimated their earning potential and as a result charged too much, even for the most devoted fans, so that DJ-led dance parties were left half-empty. The UK party bubble burst as a consequence, during which niche magazines and some of the better known superclub brands folded. Simultaneously, though, a different type of international DJ emerged: self-disciplined, sober and with a business plan. Staged as a spectacular 'stadium DJ' or 'arena DJ', fêted as rock stars, DJs like Dutchman Armin van Buuren or Frenchman David Guetta and the electronic dance music subgenres they represent (trance, techno, EDM, hardstyle) have become examples of 'the global popular' (During, 1997). Jetting globally from party to party across time zones, an international elite of DJs appear on well-lit stages at super raves, festivals, Ibiza club residencies, private events for the global rich, and even the Olympic Games. Due to lower overheads, relentless gigging and extremely high earnings, the most successful DJs are now multi-millionaires (Warner, 2013), with Dutch DJ Tiësto (Tijs Michiel Verwest) and American DJing singer-producer Skrillex (Sonny John Moore) hitting the *Forbes* list of 'The World's Most Powerful Celebrities of 2012' (Cunningham, 2012; Tregoning, 2012).

It is important to note that the main income of DJs is derived from DJ gigs, rather than from the sales of records. In the case of DJ Tiësto, 'he's never had a crossover radio hit and his solo albums sell modestly' (Fusilini, 2011, para. 2). Despite the optimism of some independent artists (McLeod, 2005) the existence of downloadable digital files has made it a challenge to earn a viable living from the sale of music recordings (Hesmondhalgh, 2009). In response, live entertainment has re-emerged as an important way for composing musicians to make a living from their music, including studio producers, who have taken to the road to tour as producer-DJs.

The stage presence of top DJs is enhanced by adding a riser to the large stage, the wide spread of DJ-equipment across a control table, the use of large video-led screens and spectacular light shows that make these DJs appear larger than life. In the case of Deadmau5 (Joel Thomas Zimmerman), a massive cartoon-like head is worn that seems to resemble an eyeless Mickey Mouse, an image that is also consistently used as the DJ's brand logo on music artwork, an important tool in the competitive business of consumer loyalty. In some cases, it seems as if the total experience of the audio-visual show takes precedence over the improvisational interactive skills of the DJ. The pressure on famous DJs is that their reputation has already preceded their performance and audiences have high expectations of technical perfection. The size of the crowd, which in some cases can be tens of thousands, renders the improvisatory character of the DJ set futile. It may, therefore, seem tempting for some DJs to play a pre-programmed set, especially when they moved into the dance music profession as studio producers. Nevertheless, audiences continue to rate the authenticity of the improvised interactive element of the DJ set and feel cheated when a DJ is seen not to mix their music selection (see Attias in this volume), despite their undoubted pre-show efforts in the music production studio. The importance of DJ interaction with the crowd to their authenticity is further emphasized by DJ Tiësto, who claims his longstanding success is based on his ability to interact as a DJ, first and foremost, rather than as a DJing producer (Coren, 2012).

In this context, the globally marketable stadium DJ is set up in the limelight as an iconic cultural role model to fans who engage in what seems a narcissistic exposure of the unique individual self in visually dominated social media, rather than a collective disappearance into the immersive experience of sonic culture, as theorized during the early days of acid house and rave culture. Connected with 'friends' via the internet, fans come together at mega-dance-parties, super-raves and dance-festivals, to celebrate the focus of their shared 'likes', the authoritative celebrity DJ – in some cases even, just the celebrity without much experience in DJing. Fans hold up their mobile phones to spread the experience on the flat screen. Particularly in a patriarchal context, hegemonic masculinity is reconstructed (Middleton, 2006) as both competitive, with other (male) DJs, and as subordinating (the crowd).

In the case of the stadium DJ, the massive crowd is made to obey a male-constructed DJ, both sonically and visually. Although there are plenty of male fans, the popular myth-making images of top DJs and their audiences suggest an adoring, even hysterical, female crowd while the top earning DJs are currently all male (Warner, 2013). The dominant discourse is well-illustrated by a South African commercial DJ editorial:

> The richest DJs in the world fly around in private jets to exotic nightclubs where they get paid hundreds of thousands of dollars for a few hours of work. They're paid to make people have a good time and for just doing their job, DJs are worshiped like Gods. It also doesn't hurt that the nightclubs are always jam packed with the best looking women in the world including famous actresses and super models. We could (and probably should) do an entire gallery showing famous DJs hanging out with incredibly attractive women. (Editor, 2012)

In the authoritative role of the DJ, fans are compelled to look up to the male DJ, in control on stage, dominating technology and the visual spectacle in congruence with the sonic space. Although DJ-led dance events are primarily about listening, moving and musicking (see Small, 1998; Fikentscher, 2000), the visual marketing and staging of the stadium DJ emphasizes the masculinity of the DJ. This is in contrast to the increasing presence of women in the DJ profession, as shown by Gavanas and Reitsamer (in this volume), Farrugia (2012), Rodgers (2010) and Rietveld (2004a). The hierarchical ocular regime provides a spectacle of gendered difference. At first, women offered a refreshing change to the covers of trade magazines and to the look of DJ booths, leading to special events with 'female DJs' only or a separate room that specifically featured 'female DJs'. Although this gave women a foot in the door of the profession, such images and special treatment also seemed like a fascination with freaks, situating women in the DJ profession as the *Other*, 'female DJs', contrasted to normative (male) DJs.

The dominating sound and vision enhances the DJ's authoritative role (Herman, 2006) as well as their god-like function in bringing recorded music, otherwise dead as an artefact or digital file, to life (Middleton, 2006), in front of the very eyes of an audience for whom, steeped in the visual culture of the computer and television screen, seeing is believing. In a media-saturated world that is reduced to the obscene transparency of the flat screen and where there is 'no more stage' (Baudrillard, 1988, p. 21), the staged spectacle of the (masculine) DJ as the unique embodied presence of studio-produced recorded music is successfully accepted by fans as an authentic experience.

From their obscure cultural role, the hidden sonic dance scene, a internationally marketable stadium DJ emerged as an iconic global popular cultural role model to a growing mass of fans. Where the visual performance takes centre stage, we find fans massing together as atomized individuals, distracted from their sense of isolation by engaging in the spectacle of the performing DJ who demands total aural and visual focus. It is the latter that lends itself so well to global branding, marketing the star DJ as a neoliberal role model of autonomous individual success. In the context of visual differentiation, DJs slip into the hegemonic roles that precedes them, the myth of the popular hero, while women reinvent themselves as sexually desirable divas or as androgynized, even masculinized, warriors (Farrugia, 2012; see also Gavanas and Reitsamer in this volume) to develop a successful career. As the party ends and we look at each other's tired faces, ears deafened by aural aftershocks, we break off to go home, entering into a consumer mode, to purchase or download anything that will remind us of that great night out. In this, despite the participatory potential of DJ culture, the cultural industry that produces the dominant image of the DJ depends on its participants being 'enamoured of power' (Foucault, 2004, p. xvi; see also Paulsson in this volume).

Heterotopian Dance

Through a set of illustrative ethnographic examples, this chapter has explored a range of sensory relationships between the DJ and other participants, the dancers, the listeners and consumers. Clearly, this relationship is not the same on every occasion. Opening the discussion with Reynold's observation that 'EDM today has come a long way from the early days of house and techno, when sound was privileged over vision' (2012), the discussion shows that although the screen-based image of the electronic dance music DJ dominates our social media, as well as the video screens of staged DJ performances, other forms of interaction can and do exist that are less engaged with the image and more with the sonic vibe, where the dancer is lost in the sound of music, rather than entertained by the lights of the god-like stadium DJ performance. Even though the latter can also induce a loss of self, this seems more into the image of the DJ, and perhaps less into a collective musical dialogue – although, as shown in his interview with Coren (2012), DJ Tiësto would argue against the latter point.

The heterotopian qualities of DJ culture are played out at any dance event, in various contradictory configurations. Heterotopia can function as counter-spaces (Foucault, 2000), perhaps forged by necessity, rather than by choice, in the context of, for example, homophobia, racism, sexism and class division, in which the equal rights of certain individuals and social groups are undermined and even denied in everyday life. In instances of sonic dominance, as during dub reggae events, an acid house party or underground disco, the dance event may be understood as a communal celebration of togetherness in the context of social marginalization, away from the perhaps offensive differentiating daylight, a powerful celebration embodied in the shared sensuous force of the bass. Alternatively, darkness may be engaged with as an act of overcoming, in order to step, reborn, into the new break of dawn, as was illustrated by the Australian doof party. In a world that celebrates individuality, the act of temporarily dissolving our atomized selves into a collective, in submission to the amplified sounds selected and mixed by the DJ, can offer an attractive relief, an escape, and even a rite of passage. Finally, although currently the dominant image of the successful DJ may be white and male, exclusion of certain identities from what is considered to be 'normal' provides its own creative platform to claim special rights and exclusive spaces. Such configurations allow for the exploration new sets of musical aesthetics, new ways of knowing (Henriques, 2011), which the world will hear once its sound journeys out, into the light.

References

Armitage, John (2008) 'Temporary Authoritarian Zone'. *Sarai Reader*, 8: 18–19. http://www.sarai.net/publications/readers/08-fear/18–19-john-armitage.pdf [accessed 25 March 2013].

Back, Les (1988) ' "Coughing Up Fire": Sound Systems and Cultural Politics in South East London'. *New Formations*, 5(Summer): 141–52.

Baudrillard, Jean (1988) *The Ecstasy of Communication*, trans. Bernard Schutze and Caroline Schutze. New York: Semiotext(e).

Bey, Hakim (1991) *TAZ: The Temporary Autonomous Zone, Ontological Anarchy, Poetic Terrorism*. Brooklyn, NY: Autonomedia.

Bhabha, Homi K. (1999) 'The Other Question: The Stereotype and Colonial Discourse'. In Jessica Evans and Stuart Hall (eds) *Visual Culture: The Reader* (370–78). London, Thousand Oaks, CA and New Delhi: Sage.

Bradby, Barbara (1993) 'Sampling Sexuality: Gender, Technology and the Body in Dance Music'. *Popular Music*, 12(2): 155–76.

Brewster, Bill and Broughton, Frank (2002) *How to DJ Properly: The Art and Science of Playing Records*. London, New York, Toronto, Sydney and Auckland: Bantam Press.

—(2006) *Last Night a DJ Saved My Life: 100 Years of the Disc Jockey*, rev. edn. London: Headline.

Brophy, Ben and Frempong, Jerry (2010) *Everything You Need To*

Know About DJ'ing & Success: Danny Rampling Shares His 20 Years Experience at the Top. London: Aurum Press.

Buckland, Fiona (2002) *Impossible Dance: Club Culture and Queer World-making*. Middletown, CT: Wesleyan University Press.

Coren, Anna (2012) 'Tiësto x CNN International – Up Close & Personal. Xin Wang Group on *YouTube*', 6 September. http://www.youtube.com/watch?v=MTZ3UYOAOUs [accessed 22 February 2013].

Cunningham, K. (2012) 'Big Earners: The Richest DJs in the World'. *Inthemix*, 12 June. http://www.inthemix.com.au/news/53097/Big_earners_The_30_Richest_DJs_in_the_World [accessed 23 March 2013]

Davis, Erik (2004) 'Hedonic Tantra: Golden Goa's Trance Transmission'. In Graham St John (ed.) *Rave Culture and Religion* (256–72). London and New York: Routledge.

Debord, Guy (1983) *Society of the Spectacle*. Detroit, MI: Black & Red.

During, Simon (1997) 'Popular Culture on a Global Scale: A Challenge for Cultural Studies?' *Critical Inquiry*, 23(4): 808–33. http://www.jstor.org/stable/1344050 [accessed 18 March 2013].

Editor (2012) '2012 Richest DJs in the World – TOP 30 in Terms of Bookings, Royalties, Album Sale, Live Tours And Endorsements'. *SA DJ Mag*, 11 June. http://sadjmag.com/lifestyle/the-list-of-2012-top-30-millionaires/ [accessed 23 March 2013].

Eno, Brian (2004) 'The Studio as Compositional Tool'. In Christoph Cox and Daniel Warner (eds) *Audio Culture: Readings in Modern Music* (127–30). London: Continuum.

Farrugia, Rebekah (2012) *Beyond the Dancefloor: Female DJs, Technology and Electronic Dance Music Culture*. Chicago, IL and London: Intellect/University of Chicago Press.

Ferreira, Pedro Peixoto (2008) 'When Sound Meets Movement: Performance in Electronic Dance Music'. *Leonardo Music Journal*, 18: 17–20. http://www.leonardo.info/isast/journal/toclmj18.html [accessed 19 March 2013].

Fikentscher, Kai (2000) *'You Better Work!' Underground Dance Music in New York City*. Hanover, NH and London: Wesleyan University Press.

—(2003) ' "There's not a problem I can't fix, 'cause I can do it in the mix." On the Performative Technology of 12-Inch Vinyl'. In René Lysloff and Leslie Gay (eds) *Music and Technoculture* (290–315). Hanover, NH and London: Wesleyan University Press.

Foucault, Michel (2000) 'Different Spaces'. In James Fabion (ed.) *Aesthetics, Method and Epistemology: Essential Works of Foucault 1954–1984* (175–85), trans. Robert Hurley et al. London: Penguin.

—(2002) *The Order of Things: An Archaeology of the Human Sciences*, trans. Alan Sheridan-Smith. London and New York: Routledge.

—(2004) 'Preface'. In Gilles Deleuze and Félix Guattari (eds) *Anti-Oedipus: Capitalism and Schizophrenia* (xiii–xvi), trans. Robert Hurley, Mark Seem and Helen R. Lane. London and New York: Continuum.

Fusilini, Jim (2011) 'Tiësto: Electronic Music's Superstar'. *Wall Street Journal*, 30 March. http://online.wsj.com/article/SB100014240527 48704471904576229122190118978.html?mod=googlenews_wsj [accessed 23 March 2013].

Henderson, Sheila (1997) *Ecstasy: The Case Unsolved*. London: Pandora Press.

Henriques, Julian (2003) 'Sonic Dominance and the Reggae Sound System Session'. In Michael Bull and Les Back (eds) *The Auditory Culture Reader* (451–79). Oxford: Berg.

—(2011) *Sonic Bodies: Reggae Soundsystems, Performance Techniques and Ways of Knowing*. London and New York: Continuum.

Herman, Bill D. (2006) 'Scratching Out Authorship: Representations of the Electronic Music DJ at the Turn of the 21st Century'. *Popular Communication*, 4(1): 21–38.

Hesmondhalgh, David (2009) 'The Digitalisation of Music'. In Andy C. Pratt and Paul Jeffcut (eds) *Creativity and Innovation in the Cultural Economy* (57–73). Abingdon and New York: Routledge.

Hughes, Walter (1994) 'In the Empire of the Beat: Discipline and Disco'. In Andrew Ross and Tricia Rose (eds) *Microphone Fiends: Youth Music and Youth Culture* (147–57). London and New York: Routledge.

Jordan, Tim (1995) 'Collective Bodies: Raving and Politics of Gilles Deleuze and Félix Guattari'. *Body & Society*, 11(1): 125–44.

Langlois, Tony (1992) 'Can You Feel It? DJs and House Music Culture in the UK'. *Popular Music*, 11(2): 229–38.

Lawrence, Tim (2003) *Love Saves the Day: A History of American Music Culture, 1970–1979*. Durham, NC and London: Duke University Press.

McLeod, Kembrew (2005) 'MP3s are Killing Home Taping: The Rise of Internet Distribution and its Challenge to the Major Label Music Monopoly'. *Popular Music and Society*, 28(4): 521–31.

Melechi, Antonio (1993) 'The Politics of Disappearance'. In Steve Redhead (ed.) *Rave Off: Politics and Deviance in Contemporary Youth Culture* (29–40). Aldershot: Averbury.

Middleton, Richard (2006) '"Last Night a DJ Saved My Life": Avians, Cyborgs and Siren Bodies in the Era of Phonographic Technology'. *Radical Musicology*, 1 (17 May). http://www.radical-musicology.org.uk (accessed 6 May 2013).

Ott, Brian L. and Herman, Bill D. (2003) 'Mixed Messages: Resistance and Reappropriation in Rave Culture'. *Western Journal of Communication*, 67(3): 249–70.

Phillips, Dom (2009) *Superstar DJs Here We Go! The Rise and Fall of the Superstar DJ*. London: Ebury Press.

Plant, Sadie (1993) 'Building The Haçienda'. *Hybrid*, 1(February/March): 7.

Poschardt, Ulf (1998) *DJ Culture*, trans. Shaun Whiteside. London: Quartet Books.

Reynolds, Simon (1998) *Energy Flash: A Journey through Rave Music and Dance Culture*. London: Picador/Macmillan.

—(2012) 'How Rave Music Conquered America'. *The Guardian*, 2 August. http://www.guardian.co.uk/music/2012/aug/02/how-rave-music-conquered-america [accessed 25 March 2013].

Rietveld, Hillegonda C. (1993) 'Living the Dream'. In Steve Redhead (ed.) *Rave Off: Politics and Deviance in Contemporary Youth Culture* (41–78). Aldershot: Averbury.

—(1998) *This is Our House: House Music, Cultural Spaces and Technologies*. Aldershot: Ashgate.

—(2004a) 'Ephemeral Spirit: Sacrificial Cyborg and Soulful Community'. In Graham St John (ed.) *Rave Culture and Religion* (45–60). London and New York: Routledge.

—(2004b) 'House: The Haçienda Must Be Built'. In Pete Lawrence and Vicki Howard (eds) *Crossfade* (119–40). London: Serpent's Tail.

Rodgers, Tara (2010) *Pink Noises: Women on Electronic Music and Sound*. Durham, NC and London: Duke University Press.

Sicko, Dan (1999) *Techno Rebels: The Renegades of Electronic Funk*. New York: Billboard.

Small, Christopher (1998) *Musicking: The Meaning of Performance and Listening*. Hanover, NH: Wesleyan University Press.

St John, Graham (2001) 'Alternative Cultural Heterotopia and the Liminoid Body: Beyond Turner at ConFest'. *Australian Journal of Anthropology*, 12(1): 47–66.

—(2010) 'Liminal Culture and Global Movement: The Transitional World of Psytrance'. In Graham St John (ed.) *Psytrance: Local Scenes and Global Culture* (220–46). London and New York: Routledge.

Stanley Niaah, Sonjah (2010) *Dancehall: From Slave Ship to Ghetto*. Ottawa: University of Ottawa Press.

Straw, Will (1995) 'The Booth, the Floor and the Wall: Dance Music and the Fear of Falling'. In Will Straw, Stacey Johnson, Rebecca Sullivan, Rebecca and Paul Friedlander (eds) *Popular Music: Style and Identity* (249–54). Montreal: The Centre for Research on Canadian Cultural Industries and Institutions/International Association for the Study of Popular Music. http//pi.library.yorku.ca/ojs/index.php/public/article/download/30160/27715 [accessed 17 March 2013].

TAD (2011) 'Funktion 1 VS Richard Long'. *DeepHousePage.com*, 2
April. http://deephousepage.com/forums/showthread.php?t=232101
[accessed 25 March 2013].

Treoning, Jack (2012) 'Show Me the Millions: Skrillex & Tiesto Make
Forbes Power List'. *Inthemix*, 17 May. http://www.inthemix.com.au/
news/52917/Show_me_the_millions_Skrillex_Tiesto_make_Forbes_
power_list [accessed 23 March 2013].

Turino, Thomas (2008) *Music as Social Life: The Politics of
Participation*. London and Chicago, IL: University of Chicago Press.

Warner, Brian (2013) 'The 30 Richest DJs in the World'. *Celebrity
Net Worth*, 22 January. http://www.celebritynetworth.com/articles/
entertainment-articles/30-richest-djs-world [accessed 23 March 2013].

Discography

4Hero featuring Lady Alma (2002) 'Hold It Down (Bugz In the Attic's
Co-operative Mix')'. Talkin' Loud: United Kingdom, [1–0639961 /
12"].

A Guy Called Gerald (1988) *Voodoo Ray*. Rham!: United Kingdom,
[RS8804 / 12"].

A. B. Didgeridoo Oblivion (1997) 'Liquid'. *Lucid Dreaming*. Edgecore:
Australia, [Edgecore 001 / CD].

Afronaught (2001) 'Transcend Me'. Apollo: Belgium, [APOLLO 050 /
12"].

Aly-Us (1992) 'Follow Me'. Strictly Rhythm: United States, [SR1288 /
12"].

Astrix (2002a) 'Life System'. *Eye to Eye*. HOM-Mega: Israel, [HMCD
27 / CD].

—(2002b) 'Side Effect'. *Eye to Eye*. HOM-Mega: Israel, [HMCD27 /
CD].

Black Uhuru (1980) Sensimelia (Extended Mix), Taxi: Jamaica,
[TX12–003 / 12"].

Brainstorm (1978) 'Journey to the Light'. *Journey to the Light*. Tabu
Records: United States, [JZ 35327 / LP].

Ce Ce Rogers (1992) 'All Join Hands' (Essay mix by David Morales).
Atlantic: United States, [SAM 1061 / 12"].

Gate-ah (alias Kerri Chandler) (1992) 'The Shelter'. Shelter Records:
United States, [SHL–1001 / 12"].

Infected Mushroom & Yahel (2002) 'Electro Panic'. Tip World: United
Kingdom, [TIPW028 / 12"].

La Vage, Mik (2002) 'Future Conduit'. *Future Conduit*. Australia
Council for the Arts: Australia, [none / CD].

Little John ft Billy Boyo (1982) 'What You Want to Be (Disco Jockey)'. Rusty International: Jamaica, [RI003 / 12"].

Nicodemus (1981) 'Bone Man Connection'. Volcano: Jamaica, [11522 / 7"].

Oakenfold, Paul (1994) *Journeys by Stadium DJ*. Moonshine Music: United States, [MM 80008–2 / CD].

P'Taah Vs. Opaque (2001) 'Crossing (Evacuation of Form)'. *P'Taah Vs. Opaque 12* Ubiquity: United States, [UR12070 / EP].

Panfandango (1999) 'Up and Atom'. Various Artists, *Edges R Fun.* Edgecore: Australia, [Edgecore 003 / CD].

Phuture (1987) *Acid Tracks.* Trax: United States, [TX142 / 12"].

Various (1992) *A Basement, a Red Light, and a Feeling: A Madhouse Compilation.* Madhouse Records Inc.: United States, [KCLP 623 / 12"].

CHAPTER FIVE

The DJ as Electronic Deterritorializer

Mirko M. Hall and Naida Zukic[1]

In a feature article in the *New York Times* from 2010, DJ Mia Moretti is profiled as one of New York City's coolest club kids. Dutifully outfitted with turntables and a MacBook Pro with over 100 GB of dance music, Moretti has spun at some of the largest NYC parties: from the rooftop bar Le Bain to designer Prabal Gurung's after parties and Chelsea Clinton's recent wedding. She is the epitome of the superstar DJ: a self-fashioned musical auteur, who has climbed Billboard's Dance Music Charts and was named – along with her collaborator, Caitlin Moe – 'Best DJ' by *Paper* magazine in 2010 (Williams, 2010). The cultural capital invested in Moretti is perhaps not surprising for those familiar with the DJ culture of electronic dance music (EDM). In the past decade, many scholarly works of music criticism – cutting across both popular and academic venues – have argued how star and superstar DJs

[1] An earlier version of this chapter was presented at the annual convention of the National Communication Association in New Orleans in 2011. We would like to thank the editors, and especially Bernardo Attias, for their kind and critical feedback, and to librarian Richard (Dell) Morgan for his bibliographic assistance at Converse College. We are also grateful for a research grant from the consortium, South Carolina Independent Colleges and Universities, in support of this project.

are embedded within media-enhanced networks of global celebrity (Brewster and Broughton, 2006; Phillips, 2009). In discussing the cultural politics surrounding this phenomenon, our project explores how digital music technologies not only engender experiences of ecstatic pleasure, but also democratize the technical-aesthetic possibilities of DJ culture in the new millennium. By deconstructing the auratic, magically powerful, spell of the DJ as a subject of musical authenticity and authority, these digital technologies promote new 'movements of deterritorialization' – to use a celebrated phrase from noted French philosophers Gilles Deleuze and Félix Guattari (1987, p. 3). Affordable and user-friendly audio workstations and instruments continue to provide everyday listeners – through a process of democratizing technology – with the technical means to rip, mix and burn their own dancefloor soundtracks. It is our belief that these technologies can actively neutralize those networks of cultural power/knowledge that situate the DJ within the politically organized spaces of EDM.

The Refrain

The work of Deleuze and Guattari has inspired a number of scholars to explore the philosophical foundations of music and other acoustic phenomena (Bogue, 2003; Buchanan and Swiboda, 2004; Hulse and Nesbitt, 2010). These explorations are largely indebted to their idiosyncratic philosophy, which uses a poetically evocative language to describe social practices that valorize difference, heterogeneity and multiplicity. Since music has been traditionally conceived of as productive of 'meaning beyond meaning', Deleuze and Guattari's metaphorical language is uniquely suited to articulating the creative powers of music. Following several lines of thought that are posited in *A Thousand Plateaus: Capitalism and Schizophrenia* (Deleuze and Guattari, 1987), we deploy their concept of the 'refrain' to highlight how a certain synergy between DJs and digital musical technologies might resist the normalizing practices of power within EDM culture.[2] Deleuze and Guattari

---

[2] For a wide-ranging discussion of the refrain as both a philosophical and aesthetic-technical concept, see the excellent discussion in Bogue (2003, pp. 13–72). Although

famously use this concept as their starting point for analyzing music's transgressive potentialities. Although meaning 'little return' (*la ritournelle*) in the original, translator Brian Massumi chooses to render this term into English as 'refrain', because of its rich implications for sound in general. In their specific discussions about music, the refrain is always a melodic or rhythmic pattern that re-creates stable points of reference for the listener – much like the hook of a pop song. Deleuze and Guattari often use the example of birdsong to describe this process, given that birds sing to mark their territories. However, in their overall conceptual framework, the refrain assumes a much larger semantic valency. It becomes the stand-in for any discursive mechanism that mediates between moments of closure/opening, ebb/flow and deconstruction/construction.

For Deleuze and Guattari, the refrain is a 'sonor[ity] par excellence' (1987, p. 348) – a special discursive act that is capable of structuring vast soundscapes with deliberate and definitive meaning. In contrast to the specificity of the refrain, music – broadly construed – is a sonoric landscape that can never be reduced to one particular groove. But, interestingly enough, the refrain also shares with music an important and seemingly paradoxical characteristic: it is never completely static or closed off. The refrain is always a momentary event that anticipates and/or threatens to flow back into the larger musical landscape. They describe this sonoric liminality of the refrain – in its 'properly musical content' – as being both inherently repetitive and dynamic (1987, p. 299). That is to say, the refrain both constructs ('territorializes') and deconstructs ('deterritorializes') meaning in music. It is both a 'territorial assemblage' and a 'deterritorializing vector' (1987, p. 327). Deleuze and Guattari identify this dialectical movement as the 'adventure of the refrain': 'the way music lapses back into refrain ... the way it lays hold of the refrain, makes it more and more sober, reduced to a few notes, then takes it down a creative line that is so much richer, no origin or end of which is in sight' (1987, p. 302). To use Deleuzo–Guattarian parlance: The refrain is a sonoric process that continuously transforms the acoustic field through perpetual territorialization, deterritorialization and

---

we recognize the pathbreaking work of Buchanan and Swiboda's (2004) edited volume, this text consists largely of case studies in applied musicology; it forgoes close textual analyses of important Deleuzian processes like deterriorialization and the refrain.

reterritorialization. This dynamic activity of the refrain deliberately moves music toward 'planes of consistency' or places of stability and security that reproduce sonoric territories. But it also initiates energies of acoustic chaos that counteract these very tendencies. The refrain's melodic or rhythmic variations, in fact, destabilize its own sonoric milieu through this movement of semantic 'exhaustion or intrusion' (1987, p. 313). Here, the refrain is an expressive and creative movement of becoming: one in which the 'final end of music [is] the cosmic refrain of a sound machine' (Deleuze and Guattari, 1987, p. 349). As a forcefield of ever-changing sounds, it generates incessant convergences, divergences and distortions in musical meaning. These ambiguous acts of deconstruction constitute the '*labor of the refrain*' (1987, p. 302, original emphasis).

This notion of the DJ as a labouring refrain will shape the episte-mological and methodological contours of this critical discussion. It is our belief that a renewed understanding of the refrain may provide the wider EDM community with the possibility of radically transforming the figure of the DJ. In order to fully articulate this transformation, we seek to contextualize, both historically and politically, the DJ as a deterritorializer – that is as a cultural labourer, who explodes the boundaries of sonoric power/ knowledge. By explicating the medial interface between music and digital music technologies, we also investigate how this relationship functions as a 'creative, active operation' that deterritorializes the power/knowledge spaces of EDM culture (Deleuze and Guattari, 1987, p. 300). We conclude by arguing that this relationship marks a 'continuous variation of matter', which constantly transforms the aesthetic, cultural and political coordinates of the EDM DJ (Deleuze and Guattari, 1987, p. 411). Although we are unable to unpack the political contours of DJ culture in their entirety, we aim to be – like Deleuze and Guattari's project of listening awry – intentionally performative in our exploration of these movements of deterritorialization.

The DJ as Superstar

By the early 1990s, the dance club DJ had the potential to become a superstar: not only as an artist-genius, but also a late capitalist producer of seductive sonoric wares (Brewster and Broughton, 2000, 2011; Poschardt, 1997; Reynolds, 1999). In some cases, the DJ escaped (or, perhaps, deserted) the underground club scene to become a jet-setting phenomenon in constant demand at clubs and festivals around the world. DJs such as Armin van Buuren, Paul van Dyk, Paul Oakenfold, Sasha and Tiësto pushed EDM into mainstream consciousness, expanded the possibilities of the electronic dance soundscape and garnered widespread international reputations.[3] These DJs readily assumed the clichéd trappings of late capitalist musical stardom: a multi-media Wagnerian stage from which to perform and command the audience's gaze, while manipulating the latest in portable analogue and digital music technology. This new subject position involved a radical trans-formation of the aesthetic subjectivity of such DJs: they were no longer simply erudite historian-archivists, who painstakingly collected obscure vinyl records to mix new, powerful grooves, but rather happy aesthetic practitioners, who actively created original electronic compositions. Of course, DJs may produce their own music, but, as critic Simon Reynolds suggests, earlier DJ culture entailed a deliberate search for forgotten sonoric pleasures (1999, pp. 273–4). The new auratic power was enhanced by an extensive organization of co-conspirators: audiences; event promoters; clubs, raves, and house parties; record companies and the immemorial bootleg compilations.

Because of these networks of cultural power/knowledge, the superstar DJ has become not only a 'soundscape architect' (Fikentscher, 2000, p. 8), but also a significant arbiter of musical taste. By meshing together tracks in beautiful, unexpected harmony, the DJ completes the digital seduction of our ears (Gunn and Hall, 2008, pp. 141–6). The success of these DJs is not insignificant. What gives these DJs their auratic spell is not only their integration into cultural systems of power and privilege (in other words, the matrix of late capitalist production, consumption and reception),

---

[3] A non-exhaustive list of other superstar DJs might include: Dave Clarke, Norman Cook, Carl Cox, John Digweed, Laurent Garnier, David Guetta and Sven Väth. Unfortunately, DJ culture is still distinctly masculine – although we recognize that accomplished female DJs such as Mia Moretti, LaFemme, Miss Kittin and Smoking Jo do exist. For an insightful discussion of gender dynamics in EDM DJ culture, see Farrugia and Swiss (2008).

but also their uncanny ability to dissolve our fragile ego boundaries. This condition has been enhanced not only by digital music
technologies, but also pharmaceutical pleasures such as Ecstasy – a
psychoactive drug that induces a powerful state of euphoria and
intimacy. Of course, the real source of power is the music with
its ecstatic 'spiritual repetition, hedonistic flow, and antagonistic
rupture' (Rietveld, 2007, p. 98).

   In articulating the coordinates of the technical-aesthetic
and political potentialities of EDM, we view the figure of
the superstar DJ as always (already) situated within politically organized spaces. The Deleuzo–Guattarian concept of the
refrain is extremely helpful here for contextualizing these spatial
conditions of intelligibility. By passing through and labouring
within the coordinates of power, the refrain is also a rhetorical
mechanism, which transverses networks of sound that are
stabilized by precise meanings, or what Deleuze and Guattari
call 'punctual systems' – all in an effort to confront the deterritorializing configurations of power. Throughout this chapter,
we do not necessarily conceive DJs as figures of domination by
way of their late capitalist subjectivity, but rather as a kind of
'refrain' labouring within their deterritorializing potentialities
(Deleuze and Guattari, 1987, p. 300). That is to say, we posit
the figure of the DJ as a perpetually shifting interlocutor, moving
between politico-ideological closure and territorial intrusion. DJs
– now conceived as a refrain – stake out new sonoric territories
amidst musical chaos; they continuously actualize, shift, disrupt
and re-actualize the networks of acoustic power/knowledge
within EDM culture. By manipulating digital planes of musical
compositions, the DJ deterritorializes and reterritorializes the
cultural-political relations of sonoric capital.

   We want to be very clear here: every DJ has the inherent potentiality to be a deterritorializing figure. Our argument initially
concentrates on superstar DJs, because their immense global
visibility highlights the technical-aesthetic and cultural-political
power that they can wield. We are also aware that the number of
superstar DJs has always been relatively small, even at their artistic
apex around 2000 (Phillips, 2009). The DJ as an everyday music
practitioner also harnesses and actualizes the infinite possibilities
of sonoric production. The subjective contours of these DJs will be
discussed later in this chapter.

The DJ as Power/Knowledge Refrain

The refrain is rather a means of preventing music, warding it off, or forgoing it. But music exists because the refrain exists also, because music takes up the refrain, lays hold of it as a content in a form of expression, because it forms a block with it in order to take it somewhere else. (Deleuze and Guattari, 1987, p. 300)

As we suggested earlier, DJs are a 'labouring refrain', a discursive point of stability amidst a field of musical chaos and a movement toward the perpetual deterritorialization of musical variations. With this unique capacity for both repetition and transformation, they are never sequestered within the confines of their acoustic space – they are always in 'danger of breaking apart at any moment' (Deleuze and Guattari, 1987, p. 311). The DJ is, therefore, a potent politico-ideological force that facilitates the continuous production of new forms of sonoric in/stability. Similarly, the discursive territory surrounding the DJ is also encoded with aesthetic, cultural and political power. It is situated within a constant state of transcoding and transduction: a state that is punctuated by repetitive movements, where 'one milieu serves as the basis for another, or conversely is established atop another milieu, dissipates in it or is constituted in it' (Deleuze and Guattari, 1987, p. 313). The exact boundaries of these milieus are never absolutely determinable, because the movements that criss-cross the coordinates of EDM culture are never monolithic. These dynamic traversals are semantically uncontrollable, because they are infused with their very 'own ecstasies' or chaotic energies (Deleuze and Guattari, 1987, p. 313). As a powerful aesthetic force, they generate a multitude of sonoric potentialities. It is through these very traversals that we conceptualize DJs in their full ontological autonomy: as a labouring refrain that cuts across the stratified acoustic contours of EDM culture.

Because this process of deterritorialization creates new sonoric configurations by aligning itself with the forces of chaos, DJs are never the dominant figure – the territorializing refrain *par excellence* – of power in EDM culture. Rather they are (a) vibratory movement, gesture, speed and sonority; a perpetual force of deterritorialization that dismantles and reassembles 'blocks of sound' into new, hermeneutically inexhaustible assemblages. In other words, DJs are also a deterritorializing refrain. They now enter into a new politico-ideological alliance, where resistance is acutely defined by (following Deleuzo–Guattarian parlance) the rhizomatic catapulting of 'lines of flight' into the skies of sonoric chaos and out of the hyper-normalizing strata of domination. This very act of creation not only mutates these territorializing sonoric compositions, but also generates new refrains. If music is a discursive site, where acoustic power/knowledge is actively negotiated, then the DJ – as the material figuration of the refrain – offers new potentialities for the sonoric production of deterritorializing movements. These forces are the decentring systems of analogue and digital music technologies, which actualize new musical forms and modalities that have the potentiality to explode the reified power relations of EDM.

The DJ as Technological Innovator

You will be organized, you will be an organism, you will articulate your body – otherwise you're just depraved. You will be signifier and signified, interpreter and interpreted – otherwise you're just a deviant. You will be a subject, nailed down as one, a subject of enunciation recoiled into a subject of the statement – otherwise you're just a tramp. (Deleuze and Guattari, 1987, p. 159)

The development of superstar DJs and their musical ingenuity is intimately related to the availability of new music technologies and formats (vinyl records, cassette tapes, CDs, digital audiotapes [DAT] and MP3 files) over the past four decades. Prior to the digitization of music, the analogue technology of vinyl records, twin turntables and a mixer provided the only conditions of musical intelligibility for an entire generation of DJs (Butler, 2006; Fikentscher, 2000; Katz, 2010; Rietveld, 2007).

With the emergence of discothèques such as the Sanctuary, The Loft and Paradise Garage in 1970s New York City, individuals like Francis Grasso, David Mancuso and Larry Levan defined today's technical-aesthetic contours of DJing through their powerful skills of programming: in other words, their magical ability to 'work the crowd' with the right record at the right time.[4] This ability to create an electrified atmosphere on the dancefloor 'spawned a new mode of DJing and dancing that went on to become the most distinctive cultural ritual' (Lawrence, 2003, p. xi) of dance club culture. Among these practitioners, Grasso – in his active years at the Sanctuary (1969–72) – helped to create the blueprint for the modern DJ: he used two turntables with pitch control to carefully stitch together vinyl records into seamless sequences. This originary art of mixing has kept the dancefloor on fire for the last 40 years.

Almost contemporaneously, DJs working in the nascent hip-hop genre – such as Afrika Bambaataa, Grandmaster Flash and Kool DJ Herc – not only refined Grasso's technique, but began physically manipulating vinyl records to produce new exciting collages of sound in the emerging electronic dance scene. This playing and manipulation of records would later become known as 'turntablism'. The DJ as turntablist employed a variety of technical-aesthetic techniques – such as mixing, beatmatching and now scratching – to create tracks that united sounds into a 'force field of pulsating, undulating euphoria' (Reynolds, 1999, p. 5). Even if the auratic power of these DJs remained their intuitive ability to recognize the groove, their programming and technical prowess were still a defining characteristic of their musical skills.

From the late 1970s onwards, dance DJs were greatly influenced by the availability of relatively inexpensive music technology that was developed and produced in Japan. These instruments included not only the Technics SL–1200 turntable, first produced by the Panasonic Corporation in 1972, but also synthesizers, samplers, sequencers and drum machines. Sound generators – like the Roland TB–303 Bass Line, the Roland TR–808 Rhythm Composer and the Yamaha DX7 digital synthesizer – would take dance culture into new rhizomatic terrains of sound during the 1980s (Butler, 2006). The new dance DJs created new electronic soundscapes through

---

[4] In outlining the key technological innovations surrounding DJ culture, we have chosen to deliberately concentrate on those developments that are most germane to our argument. We do not attempt to reconstruct a comprehensive account of the figure of the DJ – either through aesthetic-technical or historical/sociological contexts. For a meticulously researched history of 1970s DJ culture in New York City, see Lawrence (2003). For a fascinating collection of interviews, video clips and music selections from the very same milieu, see *Maestro* (2003).

the mixing of records (from genres such as italo-disco, synthpop and electro) and through the creation of distinctive beats and synthesizer-driven grooves afforded by these new technologies.

The mating of these two technical-aesthetic techniques was not merely inspired by the infinite possibility of musical styles, but – perhaps more importantly – by the accessibility, affordability and functionality of the above equipment. DJ Juan Atkins readily acknowledges this fascination with the ability to play, mix and edit music by one's self: 'The Detroit underground has been experimenting with technology ... stretching it rather than simply using it. As the price of sequencers and synthesizers has dropped, so the experimentation has become more intense' (Barr, 2000, p. vii). These new aesthetic potentialities paved the way for the suburban teenage hipster – fighting for individuality with synthesizer in hand – to become an integral part of the modern countercultural imaginary. This 'greater aptitude for experiment' is a perfect example of a new DIY (do-it-yourself) musical ethos (May cited in Barr, 2000, p. vii) – a cultural re-orientation that has had stunning repercussions for EDM culture.

The ability of 'technologies of power' to reconstitute the figure of the EDM DJ is a *leitmotif* that underlies our thinking about the normalizing practices of acoustic power/knowledge. These technologies can be understood (literally) as the digital apparatuses themselves or (metaphorically) as those transgressive effects of labouring refrains. By flattening out the hierarchical stratifications of EDM culture, they engender endlessly non-hierarchical movements of territorialization, deterritorialization and reterritorialization. They also transform the DJ into a Deleuzian rhizome: an open-ended, destabilizing form that exists among musical planes of consistency, which are always vulnerable to systematic re-contextualizations. These movements of destabilization are – like the cultural politics of the refrain – interruptive in their rhythmic experimentations; they immanently re-activate sound's resistant potentialities. In the remainder of this essay, we seek to further theorize how these processes are deployed as instruments and effects of power. As a polyphonic nexus of deterritorialized assemblages, the figure of the DJ wields technologies of power that are infinitely greater than those of a mere territorializer. This DJ is not only the superstar, but also the everyday listener-practitioner (we and you!) of EDM.

Contemporary music technologies – most, notably, the digital audio workstation – have fundamentally changed DJing as an artistic craft. Although vinyl-based turntablism still retains a residual degree of subcultural capital (Rietveld, 2007, pp. 100, 112), the exponential growth of digital tools has enabled new networks of sonoric production and distribution. These technologies brought the precision of the recording studio, with its capabilities of recording and sequencing, to live performance through the revolutionary power of hard-disc editing and digital formats. By converting audio sound waves into a highly flexible binary code, the potential for recording, manipulating and reproducing acoustic information is endlessly multiplied. In the case of the digital synthesizer-sampler, sound can now be 'chopped up, stretched, treated, looped, and recombined' to generate never-before-heard sonorities (Reynolds, 1999, p. 41); its dynamic processes of editing, filtering, looping, morphing and phasing perpetually fashion sounds into new acoustic configurations. Likewise, the advent of MP3 technology in 1993 permitted DJs to store thousands of musical tracks on a portable player, allowing them to be both playable and aesthetically reconfigured at a moment's notice (Sterne, 2012; Taylor, 2001).

We are convinced that the mass democratization of analogue and digital equipment was a decisive factor in the emergence of contemporary DJ culture. We also believe that digitization contributed to the very *acceleration* of this democratization.[5] This event resulted in a functional transformation of *musicking* – that wonderful phrase used by musicologist Christopher Small (1998) to describe those myriad activities associated with music (such as composing, performing, listening or dancing). Nevertheless, we still want to stress that the digital medium has unique technical-aesthetic properties. Digitization allows DJs to electronically expand soundscapes in ways that would have been impossible with analogue equipment. By encoding musical information into virtually infinite combinations of binary code, sound becomes both malleable (open to constant recontextualization) and portable (open to playback on a variety of technical platforms). This process extends the aesthetic qualities of sound far beyond rectilinear spatio-temporal

---

[5] See Chris Christodoulou in this volume.

continuities (Szepanski, 1995). The digital musical instrument now becomes a '*sound machine* ... which molecularizes and atomizes, ionizes sound matter, and harnesses a cosmic energy' (Deleuze and Guattari, 1987, p. 343). That is to say, digitization provides the DJ with a toolkit that actualizes a perpetual transformation of their recording, editing (mixing, filtering, etc.) and playback capabilities.

The equipment list for the digitized DJ reveals an intimate interface between technology and creativity that includes sleek and sexy sound generators, effect processors and players. In fact, media artist Chris Salter has identified the introduction of high-powered laptops as 'perhaps the most radical technocultural shift [in] electronically created music' (2010, p. 214). Salter identifies the introduction of Apple's Macintosh PowerBook G3 in 1997 as being responsible for this shift. Although global hipsters may seem to prefer Apple laptops, DJs are equally active on both Windows and Mac OS platforms. This embrace of popular digital audio workstations (Ableton Live and Logic Studio) and mixing software (Serato Scratch Live, Traktor Pro and Virtual DJ) is now the standard repertoire not only for live performance, but also for composing, arranging and mixing songs in one's own home studio. Given the cultural capital and technical-aesthetic sensibilities of Apple Inc., it is not surprising that some superstar DJs would use and promote the company's products – electronic gear that 'sits in [your home], daring [you] to play with it, like some sort of sex toy' (Jones, 2005, p. 4). DJs Sasha and Paul van Dyk, for example, are profiled on Apple's website as key musical practitioners of Mac OS-inspired hardware and software.

Notwithstanding the seductive appeal of global celebrity, these profiles also paradoxically demystify the *musicking* process. DJs may create 'new music out of shards of reified sound', but they also have an impressive technical-aesthetic toolkit at their disposal to actualize this 'alchemical liberation of the magic trapped inside [musical objects]' (Reynolds, 1999, p. 47). In a recent interview, van Dyk describes his set-up for live performances. He uses two 17-inch MacBook Pro laptops, which hold an extensive audio library and production software like Logic Studio and Ableton Live. He complements this arrangement with a MIDI keyboard and controller for live playing. This set-up allows him to 'do some crazy stuff' (Apple.com, 2012). Such equipment also provides van Dyk with the technical-aesthetic ability to constantly remix his trance track, 'For An Angel' (a favourite of ours and one that has influenced an entire generation of EDM enthusiasts since 1994) into new lines of sonoric flight.

We must remember, however, not to fall into the trap of a naïve technological determinism that can be aptly called an 'instinctively avant-garde surrender to the "will" of technology, a "fuck art, let's dance," DJ-oriented funktionalism' (Reynolds, 1999, p. 6). Certainly the techniques of reproduction, sequencing and sampling offered by the digitization of music are capable of creating seductive grooves. Digital technologies provide the DJ with exactly the same manual control as older devices like turntables and analogue synthesizers, while providing many new and alluring options for sound regeneration. They can serve as a 'crucible for sonic alchemy – the transmutation of source material into something "new", sounds that seemingly originate from imaginary or even unimaginable instruments' (Reynolds, 1999, p. 42). Each instrument has its own different kinds of modalities and potentialities for technical-aesthetic innovation, which need to be understood and maximized by the individual user (Hall, 2010, pp. 94–100). DJs must understand their beloved equipment is only a means; their playing and programming still requires a fair amount of musical intelligence (a knack for a groovy tune) and analytical precision (technical-aesthetic know-how). As Sasha comments:

> Even though DJs are playing other people's records, it's the way you play it, the records you choose, the way you drop records, the way you program it, and your style. That's what it's about. This piece of software is allowing me to evolve that whole thing, push it forward into directions that I never thought would be possible. (Ableton.com, 2012)

The above proliferation of digital music technologies reorganizes EDM cultures into territories of momentary interruptions and ceaseless transformations. It creates new sites of sonoric praxis: 'complex, subjective territorialit[ies] of proto-enunciation', in which inventive harmonies, tones, rhythms and tempos are catapulted into unexpected 'orbits of deterritorialized sensibility' (Guattari, 1996, p. 166). This situation is affected by the technologies themselves – the musical hardware and software are the deterritorializing processes that actively transform sonorities into a variety of acoustic landscapes amidst musical chaos. These processes challenge the primacy of the EDM DJ as a sonoric territorializer. Indeed, this polyphony of technological forces transforms the cultural politics of the superstar DJ's territorializing refrain, which now remains in a perpetual state of divergence and transcoding. Deleuze and Guattari describe the inherent potentiality of the refrain as follows:

> Certain modern [musical technologies] oppose the transcendent plan(e) of organization, which is said to have dominated all of Western classical music, to the immanent sound plane, which is always given along with that to which it gives rise, brings the imperceptible to perception, and carries only differential speeds and slownesses in a kind of molecular lapping: *the work of art must mark seconds, tenths and hundredths of seconds.* (1987, p. 267)

These digital music technologies continually implode and explode the territories of EDM culture and discursively reproduce the figure of the DJ. It is the refrain's dialectical relationship to music that serves as the primary creative activity of these deterritorializing potentialities. As a result, DJs are a kind of resonance that surfs upon the sonoric waves of continuous musical variations. They negotiate not only new sonoric subjectivities and sensory affects, 'but also an active way of being [and] problematic affect' (Guattari, 1996, p. 167).

The Bedroom DJ as Everyday Listener-Practitioner

The increasing availability of digital audio workstations (as professional studio-quality recording and playback equipment) and software has had an epistemic effect on the production of EDM. If this technological change has functionally transformed the role of superstar DJs by multiplying their possibilities for pleasurable 'aesthetic engineering', then the increasing democratization of these technical means has also enabled the everyday listener to become a skilled DJ in their own right. The affordability and user-friendliness of these audio workstations provides everyone with a toolkit for learning basic DJ techniques and tapping into their own unrealized aesthetic powers.

These new conditions of musical production and consumption inaugurated the era of the so-called 'Bedroom DJ' in the mid–1990s. They are the everyday DJ enthusiasts, who make music from the informal studio of their bedroom or basement. They can buy a MacBook, use GarageBand, produce new grooves and broadcast them online through social media technologies such as Facebook, MySpace and YouTube – potentially making a name for themselves in the world of entertainment. They are now a 'DJ, a remixer, a soundscape artist, and engineer' (Taylor, 2001, p. 20). Fundamentally reduced, there is something remarkably egalitarian about this. Such a position is not entirely naïve. It is true that DJ practitioners are always embedded within the matrix of late capitalist production, consumption and reception. Because of this, individuals, who have the prerequisite financial resources and leisure time, are often better able to eclipse the 'digital divide' in music. But there are also continually evolving opportunities within this very matrix that provide important conditions for the democratization of DJing: the incessant exchange of information through online media, the subterranean acquisition of software by digital piracy, and the increasing presence of inexpensive, but highly capable computer technology.

The recent decade has also witnessed an explosion of instructional guides (like Broughton and Brewster's *How to DJ Right*, 2003), videos (like DJTutor.com) and urban-based DJ schools (like Scratch DJ Academy in the United States; the VibrA School of DJing in Germany and the international Red Bull Academy) to teach 'musical neophytes and fledgling professionals of all ages how to scratch, blend and mix music' on both analogue and digital formats (Koeppel, 2007). Because of the technical-aesthetic capabilities of contemporary technology, many of the basic DJ skills – such as beatmatching and harmonic mixing – can be quickly and almost flawlessly executed by the appropriate software, without any need for manual control. But we also realize that beginning DJs still need years of hands-on experience to familiarize themselves with all the essential music, develop advanced programming skills and create their own distinctive sound. Even if individuals need some kind of aesthetic sensibility (such as an ear for the dancefloor), it is our belief that technology can certainly help one to actualize their own potential. In the words of Small, 'every normally endowed human being, is born with the gift of music' (1998, p. 8).

Likewise, the act of sharing one's own grooves with others is another important practice at the centre of DJ culture. The revolution in digital technology not only allowed bedroom DJs to acquire professional-quality workstations, but also to access a variety of online social audio platforms. Sites such as house-mixes.com, mixcloud.com and mixlr.com allow individuals to (instantaneously) disseminate their compositions across the globe or to even interact with friends and fans in real time. These new possibilities in *musicking* resemble a kind of sonoric play that French philosopher Jacques Attali (1985) famously called 'composition'. This play produces a condition – necessarily open, polyvalent and unstable – in which everyday people make music for their very own pleasure by deliberately rejecting networks of late capitalist production and consumption. Although the internet is still ultimately embedded within the ideological coordinates of late capitalism, it still fosters powerful utopian impulses, however fragmentary and momentary. These social audio platforms are located within a musical landscape that is imbued with 'forces of music production (production technology, artistic invention, and web-based networks of music distribution) [that] have greatly exceeded the present relations of production expressed by artist/label contracts, music property rights, and traditional producer/consumer dichotomies' (Gunderson, 2004).

Conclusion

Against the background of so-called 'everyday practices' in late capitalist society (de Certeau, 1994; Lefebvre, 2008), DJ practitioners are a key component of the aesthetic processes that deterritorialize (and reterritorialize) the networks of sonoric production, dissemination and consumption in EDM culture. They deploy digital music technologies as new instances of a labouring deterritorializing refrain. This is a subversive act – laden with chaotic energies – that traverses and destabilizes the reified musical coordinates of the superstar DJ by producing new acoustic adaptations, modifications and 'variations of speed between movements in composition' (Deleuze and Guattari, 1987, p. 267). These compositional acts are the rhizome-inducing movements that trip up the differentiating effects of territorializing power and enable sonic lines of flight. They enact a movement of the refrain that is immanently circular in its self-reinforcing impulses. Such impulses destabilize the territory of the superstar DJ through the 'continuous variation of matter', where sonic absences, loops, speeds and ruptures align themselves with infinitely productive pleasures.

These Deleuzo–Guattarian variations explode the coordinates of politico-ideological power that contextualize the figure of the superstar DJ as a territorializing refrain, while simultaneously potentiating the creative agencies embodied within the everyday DJ to actualize new liberatory spaces of music. The authority of the superstar DJ as 'auteur', 'virtuoso' and 'godstar' (Reynolds, 1999, p. 275) is diminished. As Simon Frith remarked nearly 25 years ago:

> [Technology] has certainly been the necessary condition for the rise of the multinational entertainment business, for ever more sophisticated techniques of ideological manipulation, but technology has also made possible new forms of cultural democracy and new opportunities of individual and collective expression .... Each new development in recording technology enables new voices to be heard and to be heard in new ways. (2007, p. 91)

In articulating the technical-aesthetic potentialities of digital music technologies, we have conceptualized the EDM DJ as a refrain of acoustic power/knowledge that continuously traverses the highly affective, territorialized milieus of EDM culture. The DJ is a refrain that is perpetually labouring within the aesthetic, historical and cultural-political coordinates of the contemporary dance scene. Through the continuous variations of musical assemblages, the DJ negotiates the sonic lines of flight that shape the politico-ideological relationships within the power dynamics of EDM culture. We have also argued that the digitization of music is riddled with movements of deterritorialization and reterritorialization – those polyvalent sonic processes that radically transform the DJ as a figure in late capitalism. As a result, DJs are embedded within a fluctuating dialectical relationship: as super-stars, they are territorializing in their institutional authority and authenticity; yet in their everyday manifestation, they are creatively deterritorializing reified musical spaces. Our analysis valorizes the latter instance. For here, DJs – as figure – as refrain – are always in the process of non-stop actualization. They continually actualize the rhizomatic forces of territorialization, deterritorialization and reterritorialization. These are the moments that harness the new technological modalities that are forever energizing the multi-tudes of new sonoric configurations. To quote Attali, they actively materialize a condition in which 'music [is] produced by each individual for ... pleasure outside meaning, usage and exchange' (1985, p. 137).

References

Ableton.com (2012) 'Sasha A-Live'. *Abelton Artists*. http://www.ableton.com/pages/artists/sasha/ [accessed 15 June 2012].

Apple.com (2012) 'Paul van Dyk'. *Apple Pro Profiles*. http://www.apple.com/pro/profiles/paulvandyk/ [accessed 15 June 2012].

Attali, Jacques (1985) *Noise: The Political Economy of Music*, trans. Brian Massumi. Minneapolis, MN: University of Minnesota Press.

Barr, Tim (2000) *The Rough Guide to Techno*. New York: Penguin.

Bogue, Ronald (2003) *Deleuze on Music, Painting, and the Arts*. New York: Routledge.

Brewster, Bill and Broughton, Frank (2000) *Last Night a DJ Saved My Life: The History of the Disc Jockey*. New York: Grove.

—(2003) *How to DJ Right: The Art and Science of Playing Records*. New York: Grove.

—(2006) *Last Night a DJ Saved My Life: The History of the Disc Jockey*, 2nd edn. London: Headline.

—(2011) *The Record Players: DJ Revolutionaries*. New York, NY: Grove.

Buchanan, Ian and Swiboda, Marcel (2004) *Deleuze and Music*. Edinburgh: Edinburgh University Press.

Butler, Mark J. (2006) *Unlocking the Groove: Rhythm, Meter, and Musical Design in Electronic Dance Music*. Bloomington, IN: Indiana University Press.

de Certeau, Michel (1984) *The Practice of Everyday Life*, trans. Steven Rendall. Berkeley, CA: University of California Press.

Deleuze, Gilles and Guattari, Félix (1987) *A Thousand Plateaus: Capitalism and Schizophrenia*, trans. Brian Massumi. Minneapolis, MN: University of Minnesota Press.

Farrugia, Rebekah and Swiss, Thom (2008) 'Producing Producers: Women and Electronic/Dance Music'. *Current Musicology*, 86 (Fall): 79–100. http://www.music.columbia.edu/~curmus/iss/n86.html [accessed 15 June 2012].

Fikentscher, Kai (2000) *'You Better Work!' Underground Dance Music in New York City*. Hanover, NH: Wesleyan University Press.

Frith, Simon (2007) 'Art *vs* Technology: the Strange Case of Popular Music'. In *Taking Popular Music Seriously: Selected Essays* (77–122). Farnham and Burlington, VT: Ashgate.

Guattari, Pierre-Félix (1996) 'Ritornellos and Existential Affects'. In Gary Genosko (ed.) *The Guattari Reader* (158–71). Cambridge, MA: Blackwell.

Gunderson, Philip A. (2004) 'Danger Mouse's *Grey Album*, Mash-Ups, and the Age of Composition'. *Postmodern Culture*, 15(1). http://muse.jhu.edu/journals/pmc/toc/pmc15.1.html [accessed 15 June 2012].

Gunn, Joshua and Hall, Mirko M. (2008) 'Stick it in Your Ear: The Psychodynamics of iPod Enjoyment'. *Communication and Critical/Cultural Studies*, 5(2): 135–57.

Hall, Mirko M. (2010) 'Dialectical Sonority: Walter Benjamin's Acoustics of Profane Illumination'. *Telos: A Quarterly Journal of Critical Thought*, 152 (Fall): 83–102.

Hulse, Brian Clarence and Nesbitt, Nick (2010) *Sounding the Virtual: Gilles Deleuze and the Theory and Philosophy of Music*. Farnham and Burlington, VT: Ashgate.

Jones, Dylan (2005) *iPod, Therefore I Am. Thinking Inside the White Box*. New York: Bloomsbury.

Katz, Mark (2010) *Capturing Sound: How Technology Has Changed Music*, rev. edn. Berkeley, CA, Los Angeles, CA and London: University of California Press.

Koeppel, David (2007) 'Mix, Scratch and Spin: You, Too, Can Become a DJ'. *New York Times*, 3 June. http://www.nytimes.com/2007/06/03/business/yourmoney/03dj.html [accessed 15 June 2012].

Lawrence, Tim (2003) *Love Saves the Day: A History of American Dance Music Culture, 1970–1979*. Durham, NC: Duke University Press.

Lefebvre, Henri (2008) *Critique of Everyday Life*, trans. Gregory Elliott, John Moore and Michel Trebitsch, 3 vols. New York: Verso.

Maestro (2003) Josell Ramos (dir.). New York: ARTrution Productions.

Phillips, Dom (2009) *Superstar DJs Here We Go!: The Rise and Fall of the Superstar DJ*. London: Ebury.

Poschardt, Ulf (1997) *DJ-Culture: Diskjockeys und Popkultur*. Reinbek: Rowohlt.

Reynolds, Simon (1999) *Generation Ecstasy: Into the World of Techno and Rave Culture*. New York: Routledge.

Rietveld, Hillegonda C. (2007) 'The Residual Soul Sonic Force of the Vinyl 12-inch Dance Single'. In Charles R. Ackland (ed.) *Residual Media* (97–114). Minneapolis, MN: University of Minncsota Press.

Salter, Chris (2010) *Entangled: Technology and the Transformation of Performance*. Cambridge, MA: Massachusetts Institute of Technology.

Small, Christopher (1998) *Musicking: The Meaning of Performing and Listening*. Hanover, NH: Wesleyan University Press.

Sterne, Jonathan (2012) *MP3: The Meaning of a Format*. Durham, NC: Duke University Press.

Szepanski, Achim (1995) 'Heute abend findet ein Konzert statt'. *Rhizomatique*. http://edition-mille-plateaux.de/heute-abend-findet-ein-konzert-statt/ [accessed 1 July 2011].

Taylor, Timothy D. (2001) *Strange Sounds: Music, Technology, and Culture*. New York: Routledge.

Williams, Alex (2010) 'The New Club Kids'. *New York Times*, 19 November. http://www.nytimes.com/2010/11/21/fashion/21clubkids.html [accessed 15 June 2012].

Discography

van Dyk, Paul (1998) 'For An Angel', Deviant Records: United Kingdom, [DVNT24X / 12"].

CHAPTER SIX

'It's Not the Mix, It's the Selection': Music Programming in Contemporary DJ Culture

Kai Fikentscher

'You know, dance music hasn't really changed over the last 25 years. So, for a DJ like myself, programming hasn't changed either.' It's shortly after midnight, and I am interviewing Kenny Carpenter (2012) in his Berlin hotel room, located several floors above a downtown nightclub called Cookies & Cream where he is scheduled to play 'at around 3:00 a.m.'. Music programming in contemporary DJ practices, the topic of our conversation, suddenly seems to have disappeared into thin air, as I had been expecting someone with Carpenter's considerable professional experience (including a tenure at the famed Studio 54 discotheque in Manhattan during the late 1970s, the heyday of disco) to say anything but what he's just told me: that a generation after discomania ended, dance music DJs of his calibre by and large still program music the way they used to, albeit using different technologies.

The focus in this chapter is specifically on the developments that have shaped and are still shaping music programming as part of current DJ practices, at a time when DJ culture may be understood as an ever increasingly fluid field of musical sounds and associated meanings that travel globally. In particular, I wish to examine the connections between general changes in DJ culture during the last two decades, and the decisions that DJs, both professional and amateur, make when taking dancers on a musical journey. Primary data are based on participant-observation-based research in New York City, Berlin and Munich, during a roughly two-decade period, specifically from interviews, websites and web-chats with and by amateur, semi-professional and professional DJs working in and out of these and other urban centres, including Rome, Chicago, Florida's Fort Lauderdale and Balearic Palma de Mallorca. Many contacts with my consultants are longstanding and date back to my time as a researcher of underground dance music in New York City in the 1990s (Fikentscher, 2000a). Some of the interviews were informal or took place in informal settings. In all, eight DJs shared their experiences and opinions during extended interviews lasting up to an hour, while twice that many had input through various interactive platforms on the world wide web, as well as via transcripts from radio and television appearances.

There is a strong rationale to examine DJ programming, both historically and ethnographically, at the micro-level. Importantly, little follow-up research has been reported since publications such as Langlois (1992) and Hadley (1993) that connect the issue of music programming to the emergence of DJ culture proper (particularly in the UK). A considerable portion of the relevant discourse since then has tended to foreground a macro-level approach, focusing on broader themes and relationships, such as class and identity, cultural capital and gender, postmodernism and transnationalism, social networks and mediation, or the impact of digital technology on a global scale, such as in Anderson (2009), Buckland (2002), Butler (2012), Connell and Gibson (2003), Duckworth (2005), Echols (2010), St. John (2001), McCall (2001), Pini (1997), Poschardt (1998), Souvignier (2003), Thornton (1995) or Weheliye (2005). The musical decisions DJs make where the proverbial 'rubber meets the road', programming recorded music in a dynamic performance context, have received less attention in comparison. Even more than 20 years after the Pet Shop Boys helped establish the term 'DJ Culture' in the public sphere with their eponymous 1991 single, evidence suggests there is still need for further 'thick description' (Geertz, 1973), as well as detailed analyses of changes in DJ culture at the ground level where clubbers and DJs interact (Malbon, 1999). In other words, the potential of ethnographic research on DJ musicianship as the basis of a musical arena marked by a high degree of volatility and turnover of repertoire has not been fully exploited. Understandably, during the 1990s – the first fully digital decade – the techniques of mixing and beatmatching took up much space, even in discussions among DJs adjusting to newly introduced technologies, to the extent that this topic attracted more attention than music programming. At a time, however, when beatmatching and mixing can be (and often are) achieved though the push of a software sync-button, programming can be said to have returned as an important way to distinguish a DJ. Carpenter is far from the only DJ who would argue that this aspect of DJ culture, while not always acknowledged, has always been at its core.

Club DJ Programming

Within DJ culture, music programming may not only be understood as 'the essence of the DJ's art' (Reighley, 2000, p. 127) or 'the single most essential skill of DJing' (Broughton and Brewster, 2002, p. 128), but also, in more technical terms, as the strategic combination of control over tempo, pacing, selection of repertoire and sound effects, including even the manipulation of dynamics and distribution (emphasis or de-emphasis) of frequency bands. This is conceptually distinct from the technique of mixing or blending, the way a transition is accomplished from one record or track to another. In much of the early discourse on DJ culture, however, it was the DJ's mixing ability that attracted much attention, rather than his or her programming skills. This is due in part to the attention focused on DJing in rap and hip-hop performance, a context in which DJs such as Grandwizard Theodore, Grandmaster Flash and later Q-Bert provided a counter-balance to MCing and freestyling via mixing and scratching. In DJ cultures other than those defined primarily by DJ battles, turntablism and making beats (Schloss, 2004), however, programming has consistently been a more highly prioritized aspect of what constitutes quality dance DJing.

Having worked for more than a decade as a resident DJ at Club Zanzibar in Newark, New Jersey and, since 1981, as a radio jock at KISS-FM (a major urban station in New York City), DJ Tony Humphries typifies the perspective of a programming DJ in his emphatic distinction between mixing and programming:

> You wouldn't have to do so much mixing if you let the records work for themselves. There is an art to programming. The same format that works on radio also works in the club environment. It's just a different set of records... so what you do is you play a track, followed by something new and then you back it up with something that they know and like.... About every third song, you give them a well-known song. After one hour, the crowd has been exposed to ten new records … the most important thing to remember is that musical content, that is, how you program, is more important than actual mixing skills. (Humphries in Paoletta, 1991, p. 12).

Not long after, in 1992, New York DJ David DePino sounded prophetic when describing his approach to programming. Unable to predict the widespread popularity in years to follow of software that supports beatmixing, DePino made the connection between programming and the DJ's identity as performer explicit:

> Every other DJ out there mixes well … nobody can't mix. [What matters] is personal taste, what you play and when you play it … [so that] you're coming to me to hear what I like, what I'm turning you on to. So there's got to be some difference. I believe that, or else then there's no need to have more than one club in New York …. My club is open from 10 to 4, and nobody even gets there until twelve, one o'clock, and they're gone before four, [so] I've got three, four hours to really let people hear good music, my taste in music, and what they want to hear. Junior [Vasquez, DJ at Sound Factory] is open from 12 to 12, he's got 12 hours to do it. I got 4 hours … [so] I can't go through many different moods like I used to. (DePino, 1992)

Twenty years after this interview, to a professional DJ like Kenny Carpenter, quality programming still makes all the difference. Fixing us drinks from his hotel room mini-bar in Berlin, he grins: 'I still follow David Mancuso's motto: "It's not the mix, it's the selection." I may be using CD players while David still uses turntables' (Carpenter, 2012). I interject that a laptop DJ is no longer the exception to the rule. Carpenter nods and waves a warning finger.

> But on a laptop, there's too much to choose from. Besides, I don't want to play a laptop because I've seen too many DJs who do watch their computer screen more than their dance floor. Programs like Serato have made it a lot easier for young DJs, maybe too easy. More importantly, laptops break, programs crash, and that would be a nightmare for me. Playing my CDs essentially feels like playing vinyl, and the music is about 80% new music and 20 per cent old. That much music is more than enough for the 2, 3 or 4 (usually 3)-hour set I am expected to provide. At this year's Winter Music Conference in Miami, I only played for one and a half hours. Tonight, there are two opening DJs which is why we can sit here and talk. (Carpenter, 2012)

Carpenter, who since 2001 has made Rome, Italy, his base of operations, came to Berlin to DJ at the one-nighter at Cookies & Cream armed with no more than a set of headphones and a large album ('my DJ book') containing about 1,200 musical items, all on CD. For several years now, he has travelled all over Italy and Europe for similar bookings and would never carry that much music on vinyl with him, he says, even though, among DJs, vinyl was for decades the preferred sound carrier format. To a few, it still is.

Listening to Carpenter's account, I am mindful that his sets at Studio 54 and at Bond International Casino used to last ten hours every weekend. Decades later, the time to deliver a convincingly coherent music programme has shrunk while the amount of music available to a DJ has increased exponentially. The one-and-a-half hours alotted to Carpenter's set at the Miami Winter Music Conference; the three-and-a-half hours Carpenter ended up playing at Cookies & Cream that night; but also DJ Tiësto's recent comment on his 12-hour marathon set at an Amsterdam rave event that, 'to play for 12 hours straight is very tough' (cited by Coren,

2012: 7.32 minutes), are all symptomatic of changes not only in
the economy of DJ culture but of an inverse relationship between
available playing time and available music. In March 2013, Elbert
Struthers Phillips, a DJ from Chicago, waxed somewhat polemic
on his Facebook page that, 'just because you have five thousand
songs/tracks on that laptop doesn't mean you should play 'em all'
in one set. Phillips, paraphrasing the lyric from the 'The DJ', a
2008 recording by DJ Revolution featuring KRS-ONE and without
mentioning the word itself, here admonished his colleagues to pay
attention to quality programming in the face of an ever growing
and more easily available quantity of music, implying that those
who take DJing seriously might want to refocus. In his critical
stance he is not alone: opinions and arguments along this line have
for some time abounded on digital bulletin boards, blogs and other
web-based platforms that are frequented by DJs. In an exemplary
comment (one of 221) to DJ SticKem's animated YouTube clip
'A Video Message to All the Wanna Be Dj'S! (RATED R 18+)',
DJCapitalT (2012) from Fort Lauderdale echoes the sentiments of
his New York and Chicago colleagues, quoted above, stating that
laptop-based technology

> has made it easier but it definitely does NOT (sic.) make you a
> DJ. The software do(es) NOT (sic.) pick the tracks to play, it
> can't read a crowd and it definitely doesn't make you a DJ just
> because you can beatmatch. There is a little more to it than that:
> programming, flow, harmonics, reading a dancefloor, knowing
> when and where to mix the tracks etc. A DJ creates an atmos-
> phere. [It's more important to] pay attention to the end result
> rather than the medium.

Still, many DJs categorize or explain the changes in their
programming choices in relation to digital technologies,
highlighting the non-physicality of digital music, seemingly in
contrast to Carpenter's pronouncement that the principles of
music programming have not changed over the decades. To Jon
Martin, DJ and party promoter in New York, the fact that a DJ
can carry an entire collection makes for more musical individuality in the DJ booth. He adds that editing records for a specific
event is now no longer done in the recording studio but at home.
There, many so-called digital DJs use software programs such

as Ableton Live to edit or otherwise rework existing records. Having worked for many years in close proximity to several DJ-producers at a New York-based record company, Martin identifies the emergence of so-called producer packs or stems as another major change. Although these products echo the old vinyl-based DJ tools such as instrumental and acapella components of recordings, stem packs are comparatively easier available and easier to access from numerous websites that target DJ-producers: in the days of DJing with vinyl, the isolated tracks of a dance production were, if at all, always included with the fully produced version of the song. Labelled variously 'acapella', 'percapella', 'beats', 'dub version' or 'instrumental', they allowed the DJ to rearrange the song in question, enabling him or her to do his own 'edit'. This used to be done either by splicing audio-magnetic tape on an editing block or, in performance, in the DJ booth. The contemporary marketing of stems or producer-packs targets not the live DJ as much as the bedroom music producer who scans the multiplicity of options within a stem pack in the comfort of his or her home studio. Importantly, the basis for these digital sound snippets is no longer a given song or version thereof, but a niche market associated with eponymous musical subcategories of electronic dance music. On a download website such as *Producerpack* (2012) these are labelled as progressive house, minimal, deep tech, or ambient, in addition to more browseable categories such as label, format (for example, Wav Samples, Apple Loops, Ableton Live Packs), and download type (such as drum loops, MIDI piano, synth samples, vocal samples). Martin makes the connection between this industry of digitized sounds and DJ programming succinct:

> DJs-turned-home studio producers have for some time availed themselves not only to pre-existing records (sampling, editing and/or remixing them), but now use stems of both commercially released and unreleased material in ever shifting combinations. Here, the choices and timbres are in a direct relationship to the musical sub-genre, such as progressive house, dubstep, or techno. All this has made the music, the individual piece of music, more disposable. The more disposable the music has become, the less important the musical journey has become. (Martin, 2012)

The concept of a 'musical journey' is closely related, not surprisingly, to that of a programme crafted by a DJ. Not all DJs, however, evaluate the effect of a massive increase in modes of digital music manipulation in the same way. Ian Friday, a Brooklyn-based DJ/producer with years of experience of playing records to a local crowd of loyal regulars, has a somewhat tempered outlook on the effect of digital technology on programming:

> [Digital] technology certainly has had an impact on programming approach and playing style. With the advent of software programs such as Serato and Traktor for laptops, many deejays are paying more attention to a screen than to an audience in my opinion. On the other hand this technology allows for other types of creativity, for example, advanced looping and layering of music. (Friday, 2012)

Overall, there seems to be somewhat of an agreement among DJ/producers that music production has generally benefited from the transition from analogue to digital technologies. Programming skills, however, seem to have diminished in what seems reverse proportion. While the ease of access to music and creative flexibility in the digital realm have made an undeniable impact, this has been primarily in the micro-musical world of the home studio where loops and samples need to be synced in terms of fractions of a second. Yet, in the macro-world of DJ performances lasting several hours, when the musical journey becomes the essence of a DJ's set, the impact of the aforementioned changes in technology on music programming have been less profound.

While my conversations with Carpenter, Martin, Friday and others mostly focused on programming in relation changes in technology, I noticed recurrent hints at a perhaps more fundamental issue, namely the changes in employment conditions of a great number of DJs. This impact has been registered by both veteran DJs, all of whom are rooted in analogue audio, and members of the digital generation many of whom don't own or use turntables and have never edited audiomagnetic tape. In both groups, many DJs have found that if they wanted to focus their attention on the musical programme, they are often not given enough time to do so effectively. A discussion on the online Facebook page of DJ/producer Anthony Nicholson during November 2012 that focused on this issue, included dozens of responses, many from DJs who were highly critical of the tendency to book several DJs for a single dance event – the following three posts are representative of the general tenor of that discussion:

> Reggie Harell [in response to Cee White]: 'I have seen a whole lot of flyers over the years with 20+ DJ's in 2 rooms for a 5 hour event. It's sad and kind of comical watching DJ's trying to do 20–30 min sets. The truly sad thing now is a lot of the DJs out here can't really keep a crowd going after an hour of playing time.... The problem is that most promoters & club owners think that stacking DJs will bring in more people. They don't realize that the best club nights throughout history have been based on a single residency i.e. 1 DJ or 1 small group (2–4) of like-minded DJs working together. Unless the venue has multiple rooms. With the occasional guest DJ. We all need to get back to the basics.'
>
> Val de la Rosa: '[among dance party promoters] 30 minute sets are all the rage ....'
>
> Cheez Darius: 'I was just thinking about the same topic. When I see over 3 DJ's on a flyer playing in the same room for 5 hrs. I most likely won't be in attendance.'

In addition to dance events with multiple DJs on the night, the world wide web has enabled an exponential spread of DJ mixes, where the relationship between DJ and listener/dancer is perhaps at its most impersonal. Although particular discussion forums and specific DJ sites do define their audiences, both performer and audience are divorced from an instantaneously shared framework made up of time, space and culturally grounded conventions, a *schizophonic* split between sound and its associated event, comparable to recorded music and radio. One may understand these free-floating mixes as digital versions of the older promotional tool of aspiring DJs, the mix-tape. In digital form, however, they have become so widespread as to be, in the words of many a professional DJ, 'expendable'. Since most of these mixes are home-produced, rather than documenting DJ performances in an actual dance or 'clubbing' setting, it is possible to speak of these mixes as musical programmes conceived before a 'Make-Believe-Audience', in a manner similar to radio programming. Rather than responding to the local and time-specific circumstances on a given venue's dancefloor, many web-based DJs program dance music in rather short 'mini-sets', targeting a virtual audience of listeners, rather than dancers, who may be streaming live or downloading the DJ's digital programme to experience them through headphones, computer speakers or a home hi-fi, rather than immense and intense-sounding club soundsystems. Important in this comparison is not so much the narrow frequency range along which the music travels in the digital domain but the extended length of a music programme that is put together by a resident DJ in New York or Berlin, of up to 12 hours or even more, in contrast to the much shorter programme generally allotted to a web-based DJ who communicates his or her mix to an imagined audience. While there may be regulars among these digital dance music fans, as members of a *make-believe* audience they are unable to experience the embodied social bonding characteristic of the membership-only club dancefloor setting in the disco and post-disco period. Instead, DJs and their fans can meet in a more open, albeit less personal setting, as they exchange their DJ mixes on online forums, such as Hypereal 313, Dubstep Forum, Deephousepage, Netaudio, where new genres may be forged as part of the exchange and parties where DJs and dancers meet in real-world dance settings are organized and, more often, advertised.

In the post-rave era, there has been a shift towards configuring a DJ performance as a concert event. Based on the concept of a celebrity DJ, at times the music is not played for a dancing clientele, but to entertain a crowd of spectators. These concerts or showcases, while at times incorporating live singing, live choreography as well as elaborate visual effects, are markedly shorter than a DJ set at New York's Studio 54, Paradise Garage or Sound Factory used to be, 25 years ago. Programming at current 'DJ concerts' requires a different approach, one that Frankie Knuckles describes as typical of his DJ sets in Ibiza in the 1990s: 'They only give [me] an hour or two, so I have to give it my all from the very first record .... [there's] no build-up, no pacing ...' (personal communication, 1999). In other words, the musical journey is at best truncated. This was not always so, of course: Up until the end of the twentieth century, as a general rule DJs had several hours at their disposal so as to effectively pace their sets 'over several hours for the maximum entertainment of the dance crowd' (Gilbert and

Pearson, 1999, p. 126). Successful music programming was based on a larger timeframe, which in the new millennium is no longer or not always a given. To understand this relative loss of autonomy among DJs in relation to programming, it is useful to remember the formation of the dance club, or disco, DJ as a cultural force at a time when the radio DJ had lost much his (in rare cases, her) power because music programming had slipped from his control.

'Make-Believe Ballroom': Radio Music Programming

When in 1935 radio announcer Martin Block borrowed the title *The Make Believe Ballroom* from his West Coast colleague Al Jarvis for his own radio show on WNEW in New York City, he not only laid the foundation for his own career in broadcasting, in the years to follow he also became the first so-called 'celebrity disc jockey'. Passman (1971) even claims that the previously unfamiliar label 'disc jockey' was coined in the wake of the unprecedented success of Block's *Make Believe Ballroom* radio show. Structuring his first programme in New York around five hastily purchased Clyde McCoy records, while making it seem that the music was coming from a dance hall as he held imaginary conversations with McCoy, trumpeter and co-founder of *Downbeat Magazine*, Block may have originated what is known today as dance music programming or, more precisely, DJ programming. The aspect of 'Make Believe' has its origins in the convention in radio broadcasting at that time to use live musicians performing in the broadcast studio, and not recordings of performances made prior and elsewhere. In the 1930s, the appeal of radio shows such as the *Make Believe Ballroom* and Marshall Field & Company's *The Musical Clock* programme on KYW in Chicago, radio jocks such as Block and Halloween Martin (who moderated *The Musical Clock* and, like Block, selected her own music) broke with this convention. In the post-war period, broadcasting shows based on records became the norm, to the extent that live performances in broadcast studios, for example at BBC studios by the Beatles or by the Yardbirds in the 1960s, have since been regarded as non-standard to the extent that recordings of these performances have become desirable collectors' items. Even when the introduction of so-called programme directors eventually ended the radio jock's autonomy in music programming, in the context of dance music (from boogie woogie, rhythm 'n' blues and rock 'n' roll all the way up to disco, hip-hop, house and techno) the fans listening and dancing to these styles may be regarded as comparable to those listening to Martin Block's or Halloween Martin's programmes. In his account of American radio DJ careers, Passman refers to thousands of calls and letters from highly engaged listeners who often danced as much as they listened to the radio. Feedback from listeners to Miss Martin's *The Musical Clock* programme includes statements that sound almost as if they could have come from contemporary clubbers and podcast listeners: 'I dance all over the house while I comb my hair or make toast. Snappy music in the morning is so invigorating. Many times I hum all morning the last song I heard when I left the house' (Passman, 1971, pp. 53–4). Or:

> I am a musician and have been in radio in Chicago for eleven years ... this business of beginning a selection nowhere and ending it in the same place is certainly annoying to a musician. There is a feeling of being left up in the air. I do feel you can greatly improve your programs by building them intelligently, instead of throwing together some thirty records. (p. 55)

Based on this historical record, the notion of mediated dance music programming harks back several decades, even to the fields of vaudeville, music shows and their initial broadcasting on radio, and, later, TV.

As would be the case with club DJs, the success of a radio jock was linked to not just a growing audience, but also to a returning, loyal, audience, based on the approach to presenting the content of his or her programme. During the 1970s, in the context of late night-clubbing, the ingenuity, creativity, experience and techniques of individual disc jockeys drew in audiences eventually numbering in the hundreds (on a given night), and among them many became regulars due to the appeal of the musical program of their favourite DJ (Lawrence, 2003; Echols, 2010). In other words, I argue that the first concepts of the disc jockey and of music programming were formed during the early days of independently DJ-led radio shows. In relation to the successes and failures in radio (and to an extent,

TV broadcasting, such as Dick Clark's *American Bandstand*), these concepts re-emerged as essential elements of the disco DJ's rise (Goldman, 1978). Between the 1950s and 1970s, a time when the autonomously programming DJ largely disappeared from radio (with the notable exception of pirate radio), the autonomously programming club DJ emerged as an important cultural force (Fikentscher, 2000a, pp. 45–7). Both the radio jock and the disco or club DJ of yesteryear share an aspect often absent from many a DJ operating in the cyberspace of the internet; as tastemakers and trendsetters, they tailored their music to a locally and/or regionally specific clientele made up of individuals who shared distinct sets of cultural conventions, marked, for example, by dress, hairstyles, slang, or political or philosophical stance (see the chapter by Paulsson in this volume). DJs who use online social platforms, such as Boilerroom.tv or Soundcloud.com may or may not cater to specific taste groups that may or may not share a common language, age group, dress code or even vaguely defined geographic boundary. Whether the emotional intensity of experiencing a live music programme, as documented in the history of radio and club DJing, can be compared to the experience of DJ programmes on digital social platforms remains to be seen. Evidence so far suggests that 'the art of the party' is still most convincingly realized in observance of and accordance to local specificities, when the musical programme 'works' because it can be fine-tuned and customized to the moment. The optimism in the early 1990s about the ability of house music and, by extension, of techno music to act as a lingua franca of global youth culture (Gilroy, 1993) could not well foresee the limitations of DJing and of programming in cyberspace two decades later.

The Rise of the Club DJ

In the late 1970s, at the peak of discomania, New York was disco's unrivalled mecca in geographic, economic and cultural terms. After years of ignoring the increase in popularity of up-tempo rhythm 'n' blues music in urban markets in favour of rock and country music, local radio stations began broadcasting the music that was played by disc jockeys in local dance venues (Joe, 1980). Not only was the location essential, but, in an era before the Walkman or the iPod, before the internet-compatible PC or Smartphone, what mattered was easy access to specific locations where music and dance fused into what was then described as the *disco experience* (Fikentscher, 2000b). In New York City, Manhattan dance venues such as Studio 54 and the Saint employed a roster of DJs who played to the crowd's expectations. At 'Studio', as it was fondly called, the crowd depended to a large extent on the doorman's selection and therefore was marked by an intentionally monitored heterogeneity. At the Saint, the clientele consisted largely of gays and lesbians who were admitted on a membership basis. Not surprisingly, the musical programme at these two influential dance clubs differed, albeit with a good deal of overlap (see the chapter by Lawrence in this volume and Lawrence, 2011). At the time, the music program inside such a dance venue was often quite similar to urban radio programming, featuring artists such as George McCrae, Donna Summer, Chic, Andrea True Connection or the Hues Corporation. In this context, the craft of programming depended less on *what* songs to play (selection) and more on *when* and *how* to play them (sequencing, mixing). If, by contrast, a DJ had a residence on his or her own, such as Levan at Paradise Garage, the music could be selected independently of what was played on the radio. If this freedom was combined with the cultivation of a regular clientele (through membership incentives, for example), then music programming could be successfully developed into a DJ's personal style.[1]

An important example of this latter scenario was Larry Levan's pioneering and influential residence at the Paradise Garage, although similar cases can be made for Larry Patterson or Tony Humphries at Club Zanzibar, for Scott Tee or Bruce Forest at Better Days, and for Junior Vasquez at Sound Factory – with the exception of Club Zanzibar all New York City venues. At Paradise Garage, Levan based his approach to musical programming on David Mancuso's example, who played to a small group of invited friends (and friends of friends) at this own downtown residence, called The Loft. In a 1983 interview with Steven Harvey, Levan

---

[1] Compare, for example, Haden-Guest's report of Studio 54 (1997) with Lawrence's account of *the Saint* (2011) and Miezitis's summary description of New York's main dance venues at the end of the disco era (1980); see Fikentscher (2000a) for a general account of the rise of the disco and club DJ in the same city.

explains (cited in Harvey, 1983, p. 30) that, 'Nicky Siano, David Mancuso, Steve D'Aquisto and Michael Cappello, David Rodriguez from The Ginza – this is the school of DJs that I come from. David Mancuso was always very influential with his music and the mixes. He didn't play records unless they were very serious.' Club Manager Michael Brody's club concept for Paradise Garage was a combination of the musical idiosyncrasy and intimacy of The Loft with the large-scale discotheque setting of commercial New York venues such as Studio 54, Xenon or 'Bond's' (Bond International Casino). For his concept to work, Brody depended on Levan, and Levan knew about the privileged position he held during his tenure at the Paradise Garage, to the extent that he declined the invitation to the relocate to Chicago to become resident DJ at The Warehouse (the latter was seminal to the development of house music there when Levan's friend Frankie Knuckles became resident DJ in his stead) just so he could retain full control at 'the Garage' over both the musical program and the sound system he helped design (Fikentscher, 2000b; Cheren, 2000). Not surprisingly, the musical programmes by Levan at 'the Garage', by Mancuso at The Loft, as well as by Knuckles at The Warehouse in Chicago, were all quite different from urban radio programming of that time, even though radio DJ Frankie Crocker spent nights in Levan's DJ booth to learn what records might or might not be transferable to his radio show on WBLS. Similar to Mancuso and Knuckles, Levan programmed by traversing musical styles and boundaries in an almost demonstrative way: Eddy Grant, The Who, First Choice, Marianne Faithful, Manuel Göttsching, Chaka Khan, The Clash, ESG, or Inner Life featuring Jocelyn Brown, each representing musical genres that encompass a wide range of music, were just some artists whose songs might be heard at Paradise Garage in one night, perhaps even within two or three hours of non-stop dancing. This heterogeneity of style, tempo and mood was, however, always tempered by Levan's deliberate use of, and skill in, programming.

Levan explains his unique approach to programming as follows:

> Steven Harvey: When I first heard you play, I noticed you would sometimes leave spaces in between songs or create introductions for them.
> Larry Levan: That's from Nicky Siano. He believed in sets. Out of all the records you have, maybe five or six of them make

sense together. There is actually a message in the dance. The way you feel, the muscles you use, but only certain records have that. Say I was playing songs about music – 'I Love Music' by The O'Jays, 'Music' by Al Hudson and the next record is 'Weekend'. That's about getting laid, a whole other thing. If I was dancing and truly into the words and the feeling and it came on it might be a good record but it makes no sense because it doesn't have anything to do with others. So, a slight pause, a sound effect, something else to let you know it's a new paragraph rather than one continuous sentence. (cited in Harvey, 1983, pp. 29–30)

From a dancefloor perspective, Mel Cheren (2000, p. 182) observes that, 'Larry used the crossover to communicate with his crowd, his flock. It came to be known as "disco evangelism": preaching through the mix.'

While quite influential, both to local club DJs like Tony Humphries, Frankie Knuckles and Junior Vasquez, and to an inter-national cluster of fans including UK-based DJ Paul Oakenfold and DJ Mike Pickering, Levan's approach to programming has not significantly been continued by the generation of New York-based DJs who came after him. The deciding factor here has not been skill, professional drive or access to repertoire on the part of post-Levan DJs, but rather the lack of long-term DJ residencies in the New York and New Jersey area. Parties and clubs with a lifespan compa-rable to 'the Garage', such as The Shelter and 718 Sessions, while continuing to attract loyal local regulars, decreased in number, beginning in the 1990s. Due to a combination of locally changing entertainment policies and the negative impact of AIDS on much of the local underground dance clientele, New York City gradually ceased to play a leading role in the the dance music market which from the 1990s onwards expanded elsewhere, especially in Europe. After Paradise Garage and other large clubs either had closed or were under threat of being closed by city authorities, and when local independent dance labels, such as NuGroove, Strictly Rhythm or Big Beat, ceased to operate, DJ culture and by extension, diverse music programming were affected negatively in New York City. A shrinking scene, increasingly fragmented by social markers such as geography, sexual orientation, ethnic affiliation, often in combination with each other, did not offer fertile ground for a continuation of the musical bravery for which Levan had become famous and, according to some, even notorious (Terrell, 2012).The moniker *soulful house*, for example, used to advertise underground parties in New York in the 1990s, would not have made sense at dance venues such as Paradise Garage, not to the dancers, perhaps not even to Levan himself who became quite enamoured with the stripped-down Chicago house sound by the late 1980s. In the post-Garage era, soulful house in New York City became a codeword for a certain level of orthodoxy in local dance music programming, perhaps also in a reaction to the confusion in the media over the terms techno and house, including the plethora of derivatives such as acid house, deep house or trance. This confusion has continued all the way to the contemporary period, and may be illustrated by the term electro, at present a commonly used label to market a variety of EDM styles (Fikentscher, 2003b; Rietveld, 2012).

Live and Mediated Programming

In response to local licensing laws or to safeguard its clientele, many of the early discotheques exercised a rather tight control over access to the premises, using paid-for membership as the key to limiting size and type of their respective patrons. Here lies the origin of the term *dance club*, shortened to *club*, and of the associated activity, *clubbing* (Malbon, 1999). As a result, in dance venues, such as New York City's the Saint, Paradise Garage or Sound Factory, fairly close relationships between DJs and their dancefloors could develop within the limited number of dancers (members and their guests) and the equally limited number of disc jockeys working at these venues. By and large, the DJs at these and similar venues were residents, which means that they were hired to play records at one specific venue on a regular, most often weekly, basis. Patrons attending these clubs as members returned regularly or frequently and, over time, came to know and trust the DJ's choice in repertoire and their preferred mode of presentation. In turn, resident DJs became quite familiar, if not with actual names and faces, with the musical preferences of the limited clientele patronizing a particular disco or club. This constellation allowed for the rise of certain DJs to become local superstars, both within the subculture and within the music industry. Nicky Siano (at The Gallery), Tee Scott (at Better Days), Larry Levan (at Paradise Garage), Junior Vasquez (at Sound Factory) all held extended residences at New York venues that used memberships to control access. Not surprisingly, during their respective tenure, these DJs (and others like them) made forays into the practices of remixing and producing dance records in response to their dance crowds. Over time, dance music enthusiasts would speak of 'a Garage record' or 'a Better Days track', referring to the sound selections associated with certain clubs. Whether or not the record in question had been produced or remixed by the resident DJ of that venue mattered little; underlying these categorizations was the familiarity of patrons with the way an established DJ programmed his or her music.

My argument here is that DJ residences, such as the examples listed above, and the resulting effect on DJ-clientele rapport are in no small part the outcome of successful music programming. They contrast with the setting that many professional DJs and their followers increasingly found themselves in during 1990s when so-called superclubs, dance festivals and global DJ branding diminished the role of geography in the relations between DJs and dancers (Anderson, 2009; Winkler, 2012). At large-scale dance events such as Love Parade in Berlin (now defunct), Mayday in Dortmund (apart from Love Parade the largest rave festival in Germany), or inside the dance tent of Glastonbury Festival in the UK, any familiarity with a DJ's programming style or with the musical preference of a limited-size crowd may be either impossible or irrelevant. While attracting a low number of local patrons, dance clubs on the Balearic Islands Mallorca and Ibiza such as Pacha or Amnesia, for example, are defined in part by their dependence on what in the context of the Berlin EDM scene has been referred to as 'techno tourism' (Garcia, 2012). Venues of this type generally do not operate on the basis of membership. Neither do events, since the late 1990s, where thousands cram into sporting arenas to attend 'DJ concerts' by so-called 'arena DJs' or 'DJ-Superstars' (Anderson, 2009) such as Tiësto (Tijs M. Verwest), David Guetta, Paul Kalkbrenner or Deadmau5 (Joel Thomas Zimmerman). The relative anonymity of the individual dancer at events and venues of this scale is also heightened when two or more DJs are scheduled to play, which is often the case. At times, massive raves or DJ

Resident DJ	Club/City	Residence	Music Program Example
Nicky Siano	The Gallery, NYC, USA	1972–77	'A Date With the Rain' (Eddie Kendricks)
Tee Scott	Better Days, NYC, USA	1976–81	'Spank' (Jimmy 'Bo' Horne)
Larry Levan	Paradise Garage, NYC, USA	1977–87	'Time Warp' (Eddy Grant)
Frankie Knuckles	Warehouse, Chicago, USA	1977–82	'Let No Man Put Asunder' (First Choice)
Hippie Torrales	Club Zanzibar, Newark, USA	1979–82	'Do It Any Way You Wanna' (People's Choice)
Bruce Forest	Better Days, NYC, USA	1981–8	'Help Is on The Way' (Whatnauts)
Mike Pickering	Haçienda, Manchester, UK	1982–92	'Voodoo Ray' (A Guy Called Gerald)
Ron Hardy	Music Box, Chicago, USA	1983–7	'Acid Tracks' (Phuture)
Sven Väth	Omen, Frankfurt, Germany	1988–98	'Accident in Paradise' (Sven Väth)
Junior Vasquez	Sound Factory, NYC, USA	1989–95	'Just Like A Queen' (Ellis D)
Terry Francis	Fabric, London, UK	1999–2012	'Night Life' (Dark Male)
Steffi Doms	Berghain/Panorama Bar, Berlin, Germany	2008–12	'Dr. Blowfins' Black Storm Stabilizing Spheres' (Drexciya)

Table 1. Examples of DJ residences as linked to geography and example of musical programme (see full discographical information in discography).

festivals, such as global brand Ultra or Portugal's countercultural Boom Festival, feature a line-up of up to 20 or 30 DJs playing to hundreds of thousands of people in the course of several days (Mortensen, 2012).

Flow Makes the Vibe

According to psychologist Mihaly Csikszentmihalyi (1990, p. 110), '[p]urpose, resolution, and harmony unify life and give it meaning by transforming it into a seamless flow experience', concluding that '[t]hose who make the most of the potential inherent in music … have strategies for turning the experience into flow …. They plan carefully the selection to be played, and formulate specific goals for the session to come' (pp. 217–18). Although disc jockeys are not specifically mentioned in his discussion of *optimal experience,* what Csikszentmihalyi calls 'seamless flow experience' resonates uncannily with the DJ practice of programming dance music. Compare, for example, DJ pioneer of pre-disco New York, Terry Noel, describing his strategy for music programming in related terms:

> When I played a record, the record that followed would make a comment on the record that came before. At the same time, I would never lose a beat or break a rhythm. I'd throw on a Frank Sinatra record and pack the floor. I didn't want to play Frank Sinatra, but I knew I'd get them up there with Frank Sinatra. Then I'd go to the Mamas and Papas. Within ten minutes, I'd have them going crazy. I drove to a climax, just like in a play. (Goldman, 1978, p. 50)

What Noel calls 'going crazy' may be compared to what sociologist Emile Durkheim termed 'collective effervescence', a concept used by both Csikszentmihalyi and social historian Goldman to account for the pleasure induced by, respectively, *flow* in the realms of music and dance, and specifically during the disco phenomenon. Both authors stress the collective character of the experience of flow; in order to be effective, flow needs to be experienced collectively. This would exclude the experience of a DJ-authored music programme, mediated via radio or the internet to a pair of headphones or to a personal computer.

Assuming that a structural rhythm of a given musical journey is crucial to crowd response and engagement, I argue that, more so than musical technology (analogue or digital) or technical skill (the mastery of the technical apparatus), dance music programming is bound up with the identity or persona of the DJ, with the character of his or her performance over time, in other words, with his or her flow. Evidence points to a continuity in the importance of music programming. Arguably, current digital software technology seems to render virtuosity, such as beatmatching, less relevant, yet foregrounds the musical journey, the DJ's selection programme as part of an ongoing musical practice. The history of the rise of the DJ as a cultural force is then closely linked to the history of dance music programming. This close relationship applies as much to the descendants of independent American and British radio jockeys (for example, Alan Freed, Wolfman Jack or John Peel) and certainly to the first and second generation of influential New York club DJs (for example, Francis Grasso, David Mancuso, Larry Levan or Afrika Bambaataa) during the 1960s, 1970s and 1980s. These and other seminal DJ pioneers, and those they taught and influenced, tended to program their music sets specifically in relation to locally circumscribed, albeit heterogeneous, patrons and as such became influential, iconic DJ figures. However, travelling superstar DJs helped change this relationship dramatically during the 1990s, who instead of responding to the mood of the night, carefully prepared their sets in advance of their performance, much like later-day radio DJs. For example, Dutch trance DJ Tiësto was hired to play during the opening ceremony of the 2004 Summer Olympics in Athens while on 31 December 2011, American house DJ Frankie Knuckles was booked into the world-famous Opera House in Sydney, Australia, for a New Year's Eve party. Although these and similar events may signal the arrival of the DJ on the stage of 'high culture', the musical programming in Athens or Sydney in rather atypical environments on those occasions left little room for the DJ to create, establish and maintain flow.

The considerable influence of the internet within DJ culture appears to have been felt more in the modes of music production and dissemination, and perhaps less so in the realm of music programming. Arguably, this is so because the codes that govern rituals of liminality (Turner, 1974; Buckland, 2002) do not easily or quickly respond to changes in technology, even when the ritual is at best shortened or at worst rendered ineffectual because of time constraints or due to the emphasis on spectacle at the expense of content or message. David Mancuso told Lawrence (2003, pp. 85–6) of how he was influenced by Timothy Leary, who in his 1964 book *The Psychedelic Experience* had adapted concepts of liminal stages ('Bardos') from the *Tibetan Book of the Dead* (Evans-Wentz, 1968). He used the term 'bardo' to describe the structure ('journey') of the music programme at this early 'Loft' sessions:

> Leary wrote that there were three stages, or three Bardos, in a [psychedelic] trip, and I found myself using the same structure [for the music at The Loft]. The first Bardo would be very smooth, perfect, calm. The second Bardo would be like a circus. And the third Bardo was about re-entry, so people would go back into the outside world relatively smoothly.

Programming music along these distinct categories was typical not only at The Loft, but in sets by DJs influenced by Mancuso, including Nicky Siano, Larry Levan and Frankie Knuckles. Most of Mancuso's disciples were or became resident DJs and, in that capacity, could structure an entire night to manage the transition between stages and levels of various intensities and peaks. A Levan acolyte, Junior Vasquez, analysed the experience of being resident DJ at New York City's Sound Factory in the early 1990s along Leary's tri-partite bardo-structure without mentioning it by name: '... the night achieves several peaks – one at 5, another at 8, and maybe even a "fluffy-muscle-queen-peak" later on' (in Musto, 1995, p. 12). Associating the way music marks the ritualistic structure of a church service, Frankie Knuckles believes that peaking the floor at a dance club makes it feel 'like church' (in Leaphart, 1991). With the smaller number and hence lessened role of residencies in DJ culture roughly two decades later, less attention tends to be paid to the actual and potential structure and flow of a given music programme, both by DJs and dancers alike, in contradiction to Kenny Carpenter's claim during our conversation in Berlin, in 2012, as there seems to be insufficient time to structure the music effectively.

In a best-case scenario, however, if sufficient time is provided for a collective experience of a programme of music to produce flow, in Csikszentmihalyi's sense, working with a live crowd, a club DJ can respond to the moods and variables of a given time and space, manipulating them in turn through choices in music programming that shape the experience of the event. The radio DJ, by contrast, works with an imagined audience of individuals, as does the internet DJ, whether in the shape of downloadable DJ mixes or via live internet radio and video. Thus, while the dance music DJ may have inherited the tool of effective music programming from the radio DJ, the relationships of each to their respective audiences are not the same, and neither are their approaches and skills in music programming. To investigate this further, I recommend that the work of tracing and explaining the connections and disconnections between older analogue and contemporary digital scenarios (one local/global continuum among many) be accompanied by a careful examination of changes in the ways DJ work in various and often volatile settings (such as residencies, be they individual, shared or seasonal; guest spots; promotional and marketing engagements; internet radio shows; DJ-as-artist engagements etc.). Ultimately, contemporary DJs charged with programming dance music may be regarded as humanistic visionaries, presenting and performing music in recognition, reaffirmation and celebration of those qualities that are associated with happiness, meaningfulness, fulfilment, and pleasure. Music programming, then, is an aspect of DJ musicianship that may be considered both artistic and salubrious.

References

Anderson, Tammy L. (2009) *Rave Culture: The Alteration and Decline of a Philadelphia Music Scene*. Philadelphia, PA: Temple University Press.

Broughton, Frank and Brewster, Bill (2002) *How to DJ Right: The Art and Science of Playing Records*. New York: Grove Press.

Buckland, Fiona (2002) *Impossible Dance: Club Culture and Queer World-making*. Middletown, CT: Wesleyan University Press.

Butler, Mark (ed.) (2012) *Electronica, Dance and Club Music*. Farnham: Ashgate.

Cheren, Mel (2000) *Keep On Dancin: My Life and the Paradise Garage.* New York: 24 Hours For Life.

Connell, John and Gibson, Chris (2003) *Sound Tracks: Popular Music, Identity, and Place.* London and New York: Routledge.

Coren, Anna (2012) 'Tiësto x CNN International – Up Close & Personal'. Xin Wang Group on *YouTube,* 6 September. http://www.youtube.com/watch?v=MTZ3UYOAOUs [accessed 22 February 2013].

Csikszentmihalyi, Mihaly (1990) *Flow: The Psychology of Optimal Experience.* New York: Harper and Row.

DJCapitalT, Thomas (2012) Comments to DJ SticKeM, 'A Video Message To All The Wanna Be Dj'S!' (RATED R 18+), DJ SticKeM channel on *YouTube,* 7 December 2010. http://www.youtube.com/watch?v=_Kww0HUpccY [accessed 1 September 2012].

Duckworth, William (2005) *Virtual Music: How the Web Got Wired for Sound.* New York: Routledge.

Echols, Alice (2010) *Hot Stuff: Disco and the Remaking of American Culture.* New York: W. W. Norton.

Evans-Wentz, W. Y. (ed.) (1968) *Tibetan Book of the Dead: or the After-death Experiences on the Bardo Plane, According to Lā ma Kazi Dawa-Samdup's English Rendering.* Compiled by W. Y. Evans-Wentz. London: Oxford University Press.

Fikentscher, Kai (2000a) 'The Club DJ: A Brief History of a Cultural Icon'. *The UNESCO Courier*, July/August: 45–7.

—(2000b) *'You Better Work!' Underground Dance Music in New York City.* Hanover, NH: Wesleyan University Press.

—(2003a) ' "There's Not a Problem I Can't fix, 'Cause I Can Do it in the Mix": On the Performative Technology of 12-inch Vinyl'. In René Lysloff and Leslie Gay (eds) *Music and Technoculture* (290–315). Hanover, NH and London: Wesleyan University Press.

—(2003b) 'Soulful House a New York City'. *C:Cube (Cultura: Comunicazione: Consumo)*, 1(3): 16–22.

Garcia, Luis-Manuel (2012) 'Consuming Atmospheres and Social Worlds: "Techno-Tourismus" and Post-tourist Tourism in Berlin's Electronic Dance Music Scenes'. Unpublished manuscript, presented to the Society for Ethnomusicology (SEM), New Orleans, Louisiana, 3 November.

Geertz, Clifford (1973) *The Interpretation of Cultures.* New York: Basic Books.

Gilbert, Jeremy and Pearson, Ewen (1999) *Discographies: Dance Music Culture and the Politics of Sound.* New York and London: Routledge.

Gilroy, Paul (1993) 'Between Afro-centrism and Euro-centrism: Youth Culture and the Problem of Hybridity'. *YOUNG* 1(2). http://logic.itsc.cuhk.edu.hk/~b114299/young/1993-2/y932gilr.htm [accessed 22 February 2013].

Goldman, Albert (1978) *Disco*. New York: Hawthorn.

Haden-Guest, Anthony (1997) *The Last Party: Studio 54, Disco, and the Culture of the Night*. New York: William Morrow.

Hadley, Daniel (1993) ' "Ride the Rhythm": Two Approaches to DJ Practice'. *Journal of Popular Music Studies*, 5: 58–67.

Harvey, Steven (1983) 'Behind the Groove: New York City's Disco Underground'. *Collusion*, 5: 26–33.

Joe, Radcliffe A. (1980) *This Business of Disco*. New York: Billboard Books.

Langlois, Tony (1992) ' "Can You Feel It?" DJs and House Music Culture in the UK'. *Popular Music*, 11(2): 229–38.

Lawrence, Tim (2003) *Love Saves the Day: A History of American Dance Music Culture, 1970–1979*. Durham, NC and London: Duke University Press.

—(2011) 'The Forging of a White Gay Aesthetic at the Saint, 1980–84'. *Dancecult: Journal of Electronic Dance Music Culture*, 3(1): 4–27.

Leaphart, Walter F. Jr (1991) 'What is House? An Insider's Look at Dance Music (Television edit)'. Chicago: WMAQ-TV (VHS Video).

Leary, Timothy, with Metzner, Ralph and Alpert, Richard (1964) *The Psychedelic Experience*. New York: Citadel Press.

Malbon, Ben (1999) *Clubbing: Dancing, Ecstasy and Vitality*. London: Routledge.

McCall, T. (2001) *This is Not a Rave: In the Shadow of a Subculture*. New York: Thunder's Mouth Press.

Miezitis, Vita (1980) *Night Dancin'*. New York: Ballantine Books.

Mortensen, Antonia (2012) 'Electronic Dance Music: How Bedroom Beat Boys Remixed the Industry'. *CNN*, 30 March. http://edition.cnn.com/2012/03/30/showbiz/electronic-dance-music/index.html [accessed 22 February 2013].

Musto, Michael (1995) 'La Dolce Musto: The Sound Factory'. *Village Voice*, 24 January: 12.

Nicholson, Anthony (2012) *Facebook*, 1 November. http://www.facebook.com/anthony.nicholson1/posts/10151170141334118?comment_id=23577971&offset=0&total_comments=35 [accessed 17 December 2012].

Paoletta, Michael (1991) 'Tony Humphries in the Mix'. *Dance Music Report*, 15(5): 12, 46.

Passman, Joe (1971) *The Dee-jays: How the Tribal Chieftains of Radio Got to Where They're At*. New York: Macmillan.

Philips, Elbert Struthers (2013) *Facebook*. http://www.facebook.com/elbertsp1 [accessed 10 March 2013].

Pini, Maria (1997) 'Women in the Early British Rave Scene'. In Angela McRobbie (ed.) *Back to Reality? Social Experience and Cultural Studies* (152–69). Manchester: Manchester University Press.

Poschardt, Ulf (1998) *DJ Culture*. London: Quartet Books.

Producerpack.com (2012) *Editorial*. http://www.producerpack.com/ [accessed 10 March 2013].

Reighley, Kurt B. (2000) *Looking for the Perfect Beat: The Art and Culture of the DJ*. New York and London: Pocket Books.

Rietveld, Hillegonda C. (2012) 'Electro'. In David Horn and John Shepherd (eds) *The Continuum Encyclopedia of Popular Music of the World Volume 8: Genres in North America* (199–201). New York and London: Continuum.

Schloss, Joe (2004) *Making Beats: The Art of Sample-based Hip-hop*. Middletown, CT: Wesleyan University Press.

Souvignier, Todd (2003) *The World of DJs and the Turntable Culture*. Milwaukee, WI: The Hals Leonard Corp.

St John, Graham (ed.) (2001) *FreeNRG: Notes From the Edge of the Dance Floor*. Altona, VI: Common Ground Publishing.

Terrell, Angie (2012) 'Frankie Knuckles on His New Compilation, Larry Levan, and How Every Church Needs a Pastor'. *Beatport News*, 28 November. http://news.beatport.com/blog/2012/11/28/frankie-knuckles-discusses-the-release-of-his-definitive-compilation-larry-levan-and-how-every-church-needs-a-pastor/ [accessed 12/31/12].

Thornton, Sarah (1995) *Club Cultures: Music, Media, and Subcultural Capital*. Cambridge: Polity Press.

Turner, Victor (1974) *Liminal to Liminoid in Play, Flow, and Ritual: An Essay in Comparative Symbology*. New York: Rice University Studies.

Weheliye, Alexander G. (2005) *Phonographies: Grooves in Sonic Afro-Modernity*. Durham, NC: Duke University Press.

Winkler, Thomas (2012) 'Der Facharbeiter'. *Die Zeit*, 49, 29 November: 71.

Interviews

Carpenter, Kenny (2012) Interviewed by Kai Fikentscher, Berlin, 14 April.

DePino, David (1992) Interviewed by Kai Fikentscher, New York, 1 June.

Friday, Ian (2011) Interviewed by Kai Fikentscher, New York, 12 December.

Martin, Jon (2012) Interviewed by Kai Fikentscher, New York, 27 February.

Discography

A Guy Called Gerald (1988) 'Voodoo Ray', from *Voodoo Ray*. Rham!: United Kingdom, [RS8804 / 12"].

Dark Male (2002) 'Night Life – Asad's Silverlining Remix', from *Night Life*, Groovetech Records: United Kingdom, [GT 1202 / 12"].

DJ Revolution feat. KRS-ONE (2008) 'The DJ', from *King of the Decks*. Duck Down: United States [DDM LP 2085].

Drexciya (2002) 'Dr Blowfin's Black Storm Stabilizing Spheres', from *Harnessed the Storm*. Tresor: Germany, [Tresor 181 / 2 X 12"].

Ellis-D (1989) *Just Like a Queen*. XL Recordings: United Kingdom, [XLT 6 / 12"].

First Choice (1977) *Let No Man Put Asunder*. Salsoul Records: United States, [SG 397 / 12"].

Grant, Eddy (1982) *Time Warp*. Portrait: United States, [4R9–03574 / 12"].

Horne, Jimmy 'Bo' (1978) *Spank*. Sunshine Sound: United States, [SSD 205 / 12"].

People's Choice (1975) 'Do It Any Way You Wanna', from *Do It Any Way You Wanna / The Big Hurt*. Philadelphia International: United Kingdom, [S PIR 3500 / 7"].

Pet Shop Boys (1991) *DJ Culture*. Parlophone: United Kingdom, [12R 6301 / 12"].

Phuture (1987) *Acid Tracks*. Trax Records: United States, [TX142, 12"].

The Whatnauts (1981) *Help is On the Way*. Harlem International Records: United States, [H.I.R. 110, 12"].

Väth, Sven (1992) *Accident in Paradise*. Eye Q Records: Germany, [4509–91193–2, CD].

CHAPTER SEVEN

Electronic Dance Music and Technological Change: Lessons from Actor-Network Theory

Jonathan Yu

This chapter focuses on a series of responses concerning the use of new technologies from interviews with DJs and producers within various electronic dance music scenes in Melbourne.[1] The argument I put forward is that DJs and producers make certain types of technocultural[2] distinctions between what are perceived to be legitimate and illegitimate practices based on traditions and standards within their respective scenes. I further argue that there

---

[1] This chapter has been developed mainly from the first round of in-depth interviews conducted between July and August 2011 that will form part of a large case study for a PhD project concerning the impact of digitally networked technologies on music production, consumption and distribution. I thank my participants for having the patience to address and explain some of the rudimentary aspects of DJing and electronic dance music culture.

[2] I use the term 'technocultural' to refer to relationships between technology and groups of people.

are no 'natural' practices that are more legitimate than others; for example, beatmatching by ear on vinyl is no more legitimate than using the sync function on a laptop. Drawing on actor-network theory (ANT), I suggest that instead the new practices we are seeing within electronic dance music production and DJing can be regarded as the latest in a set of relations between musicians and technologies that have always been in transition.

Research Method

This chapter was developed from a small sample of seven in-depth semi-structured interviews. DJs were identified and selected through my personal contacts in a snowball sampling manner. The only criteria were that they had to be based in Melbourne. The sample consisted of five males (Jack, Vadim, Heath, Keiran and Anthony) and one female (Claire), in their early to mid-twenties and one male (Daimon) in his late thirties. There was no effort to select DJs from within a particular genre or scene, although four played mainly house music (Vadim, Heath, Keiran and Anthony). Daimon's style has changed throughout his career. Currently his music can be described as dubstep and drum 'n' bass. Jack and Claire play what Jack referred to as 'progressive pop': mainstream dance music that 'has a high level of musicianship' (Arentz, 2011). The DJs' experience ranges from being self-described amateurs to fulltime professionals. Unlike many researchers engaged with dance culture, I approach the field as an outsider in that I was not previously embedded in any of the dance music scenes in Melbourne. Although I researched the practice of DJing prior to conducting the interviews, I requested that my participants explain in their own terms, some of the basics of their musical practices and scenes they are involved in.

Three Controversies

Cheating

Cheating involves an element of deceit, achieving something through some means of deception without the necessary skills or knowledge – such as cheating in a test at school. The theme of cheating was one of the more immediately obvious in the interviews. It had been explained in mostly similar terms by different interviewees. I first heard about it from Anthony, who described himself as an amateur DJ and producer (he performs using CDJs[3] and produces using Ableton Live). He referred to cheating in passing when describing the serendipitous circumstances in which he received his first residency from a club organizer:

> He doesn't know whether I can DJ or not. I could be one that plays my laptop and cheats and auto-beat [pauses] you know, beatmatching with applications like Traktor. Doesn't matter if you miss the button, miss it by like a split second, it'll match it. A lot of people do that and cheat. That's why I think nah, they're not that good. (Batori, 2011)

Keiran, who considers himself a semi-professional DJ (he attends university but holds a few residencies and can perform using both CDJs and vinyl, though usually the former), made a similar claim: 'If you're an international DJ, you can get 10 grand to play a show. You can do your set on your computer on the plane over here, have it all ready to go for an hour and a half, plug your laptop into the mixer and just stand there' (Dole, 2011).

What is a mark of legitimacy here is the expectation that DJs manually beatmatch. It is a required skill and indicator of what could be termed embodied 'technocultural capital'[4] in their respective scenes. Cheating bypasses this necessary skill with an easier route. Vadim, a full time DJ who performs using CDJs normally (but can also handle vinyl), explicitly confirmed the expectation:

---

[3] Throughout this chapter the term CDJ will refer to the Pioneer series of CD players used by DJs; the CDJ–1000MK3 model being considered standard equipment at most clubs in Melbourne according to my interviewees.

[4] This is a term I have derived from the concept of 'cultural capital' articulated in the work of sociologist Pierre Bourdieu. The term tends to be used to describe the skills, knowledge and abilities that are associated with the higher classes in societies. I add the prefix 'techno' to steer the meaning towards relationships with technology. So the term 'technocultural capital' relates to one's skill with a particular piece of technology and the credibility and reputation one earns based on how the community perceives that ability.

... those programs that are used while playing live, they beatmatch everything for you. So you take the art of doing things with your hands and putting tracks together at the right place at the right time, that's all gone. So I can understand some people might like vinyls better, some like CDs, that's all fine. The mixing is still the same, you still have to do some sort of beatmatching to get it right. When you're using laptops and stuff like that it's totally different. That's when everything's half done for you and all you're really worried about is track selections.... I definitely think it's cheating. (Golikov, 2011)

There are a number of skills that have been associated with electronic dance music DJs. In his thoughts concerning DJ schools, van Veen (2002, p. 5) listed a few from a syllabus such as: mixer basics, beatmatching and EQing. The expectation of beatmatching as an essential skill is traceable to the early disco DJs.[5] Whilst typically associated with the laptop and sync function, the boundaries of what constitutes cheating are not limited to just these elements. Keiran explained instances of cheating concerning the properties of CDJs such as relying on the BPM counter and related functions (Dole, 2012). CDJ features that are comparable to the sync function include the CDJ–350's 'Auto BPM Lock' and the CDJ–2000's 'Quantize'. Both features use Pioneer's proprietary Rekordbox software (a database for tracks that stores, among other things, BPM information) for the automated real-time syncing of two tracks. Keiran made a point of describing these features, stating that using CDJs is no different to using a laptop to cheat (Dole, 2012). The BPM counter is a standard feature in most newer models of CDJs and allows for beatmatching through the matching up of numbers rather than purely by ear. For example, a DJ instructional YouTube clip by DJBessant (2009) outlines the steps to beatmatching without headphones using just the BPM monitor and the pitch controls – the idea being you adjust each track slowly until they reach the same BPM and then press play at the right time. Whilst clearly this involves more effort than using the sync function on a laptop, it still

---

[5] According to Brewster and Broughton's (2000) narrative, some time after 1968 the mix was pioneered by Francis Grasso who experimented with turntable speeds to create the seamless transitions via beatmatching, likely setting the standard for the following decades.

removes the skill of directly listening to the beats and for DJs such as Keiran, is considered a trick or a form of cheating (a few comments on DJBessant's video also reflect this view). Yet other DJs would not consider this 'trick' cheating at all as it still involves the manual setting of CDJ controls to achieve a seamless mix. In both cases the principle behind the accusation of cheating remained the same in that the beatmatching skill was viewed as being bypassed through some kind of automation. This also indicates that the boundaries of what constitutes cheating are fluid and contested by different DJ communities. Such boundaries would change as DJ technology and the way DJs interact with this technology changes.

The charge of cheating itself has been challenged on its assumption that manually beatmatching is a fundamental skill of contemporary DJs. Claire (a classical bassoonist turned pop musician and beginner DJ that performs irregular sets using a laptop) emphasized this point when I asked about the cheating issue:

> There's still the ability to read a crowd and to make a crowd happy and to make really musical tasteful choices and to feel what your audience wants. DJing isn't just about how you play the music, like what format you're DJing and what you're using to DJ, but you know, how you are as a DJ, like your ability to actually make people happy.... It comes down to song choice. Everybody knows when the DJ is terrible. People don't want to dance. They go get drinks, they go outside to have a cigarette or they leave the club. Like that's it, the party dies. (Rayner, 2011)

Her DJ partner Jack[6] also challenged this accusation of cheating, providing more insight from a laptop DJ perspective on the tensions with other DJs:

> [F]rom my perspective the digital formats... enable the new DJs to do way more complicated transitions and include way more complicated parts to the transitions and to their pieces. So they

---

[6] Together Claire and Jack play live sets as vocalists, guitarists and keyboardists in an electronic pop band with a sessional bass player and drummer. The DJ sets are something they have expanded into. Jack has experience as a producer working with other bands and also creating remixes.

both have their place. It's not necessarily the case of like 'I'm a new DJ. I've got a digital mixer. I push this button and then everything's great and I just do this.' It's not like that. Because the transitions that a vinyl DJ would do are not even a fucking split on what a digital DJ would do with Ableton or Traktor in terms of the technical aspect and the musicality of it. So there is that intensely deep resentment and yet it's completely unfounded. (Rayner, 2011)

Jack's comments are significant in that he recovers the creative and performative characteristic for laptop DJs and directly rejects the assumptions of the charge of cheating. There is more potential for interesting and creative mixing styles and this involves an element of skill. Therefore there is technocultural capital associated with the effective use of a laptop as an instrument and this is recognized at the very least by others who use laptops to perform. Claire's comments imply that she privileges the ability to read a crowd and make valid song selections over manually beatmatching as an essential DJ skill (a point that Jack also agreed with). This ability can also, as she rightly points out, affect a DJ's reputation among clubbers and club owners. A DJ can be excellent at beatmatching, creating perfect seamless mixes. But this matters little to their future employment if they cannot read their audience and keep partygoers from leaving the club. If the party dies, the club loses money and the DJ loses a residency or future gig. Similar sentiments can be found twenty years earlier from the DJs that Langlois (1992) spoke with. Whilst they acknowledged that careful beatmatching with BPM is important, 'the "mood" of the piece rather than its speed should take priority' (Langlois, 1992, p. 233).

Stealing

In the simplest sense, stealing is taking something that does not belong to you. This has been addressed in different ways by my interviewees. Daimon and Heath, the most established and experienced DJs and producers that I interviewed, did not see an issue here as they viewed their work as original compositions. Daimon's recordings made use of original recordings in his studio in addition to single noise samples from purchased sample packs. He summed up his approach: 'I really like the whole original thing of coming up with my own sounds and ideas and concepts and stuff. Back in the day I used to sample a few bits and pieces from other recordings but I don't really do that anymore so it's all kind of pretty much original' (Schwalger, 2011). Similarly Heath, an established professional DJ (who performs with CDJs) and producer (using Ableton Live), stated:

> Everyone's sort of lost track of what's really real anymore, you know what I mean? Like you hear a lot of songs where there's stuff that's been sampled from other songs .... I just stay away from it. I just do my own thing. Most of the stuff I write is all original anyway unless it's a licensed remix that someone's asked me to do for them. (Bain, 2011)

Keiran, who does far less producing, and Anthony, who produces remixes rather than original compositions, each discussed originality in a different way. Keiran (who performs with a partner) stated: 'I like to think that our sound that we put out there is pretty original to Melbourne. There's not a lot of people that do the same' (Dole, 2011). After detailing the structure of his remixes, Anthony expressed a similar position, 'I like to make that my trademark, whatever sound I've used, I want it to be different to everyone else' (Batori, 2011). So what defines originality in these latter instances is the creation and projection of a unique aural aesthetic through a process of 'recomposition' – using tracks and records to create a performance that is original in its arrangement of existing material (Langlois, 1992). The definition here is general enough to cover both those who compose such as Heath and Daimon and at the same time those who compile and mix set lists such as Keiran and Anthony, accounting for the skill involved in selecting the right tracks for their 'trademark' sounds. A more restrictive definition of originality could only be applied to what Heath and Daimon are attempting, with a shift towards composition and away from recomposition. This definition is from the modernist perspective that dominates discourses concerning copyright (Lobato, 2009) – the creator assembles completely original and unique works – which implies a kind of creative vacuum devoid of influences. The implication is problematic, and it has come under challenge from postmodern discourses (Lobato, 2009) in addition to a large

body of literature concerning sampling as a creative and performative practice (see, for example, McLeod, 2009; Rodgers, 2003;
Schumacher, 2004).

Stealing, as it was explained to me, fell into two different
categories. First, concerning production, it is the unauthorized use
of a sample from someone's track. When I asked Heath to explain
the issue, he expressed his disapproval of the act though acknowledged a lack of capacity to do anything about it:

> For example a song has a breakdown and it just goes to a kick
> drum and you just cut the kick drum out of that song. I don't
> agree with that sort of stuff at all … It's another one of those
> things where like there's so many people doing it now and so
> many places you can get them [samples] from, people can't keep
> up with it. You can't control it really. (Bain, 2011)

Heath has a large number of releases but is apathetic towards doing
much about the instances of stealing. This attitude can at least be
partially attributed to the fact that he earns far more revenue
performing as a DJ than he could derive from his recordings and
production work (he plays his own material as well as others'
during his sets). Heath's reputation is based on his DJing ability[7]
and I could see that this has paid off as I admired his spacious
top floor apartment in an affluent part of Melbourne during our
interview. It is also likely that due to his reputation, others may
recognize and call out potential thieves for him. Keiran is more
vocal and direct with his condemnation of stealing:

> It's a pet hate. A lot of people do it and us as DJs and producers
> notice those little intricate bits of songs. So someone will lift like
> a drum kick or a snare, clap and we'll go 'hey, that's from that
> song'. Automatically you lose respect for that person it's over,
> he's shit [pauses] you don't do that you know what I mean?
> Unless you credit their name on the remix. You know like if you
> lifted a pretty obvious sample from a song, unless you put that
> name on the remix … you're an idiot. (Dole, 2011)

---

[7] In 2010 he was voted the sixth best DJ in Australia in the annual *Inthemix* DJ
polls (*Inthemix*, 2010).

As he pointed out, experienced DJs and producers who have objectified[8] technocultural capital will be able to identify a sample that has been stolen even if it is a single unit. Their expertise is seen through the possession of an extensive collection of songs and samples that include both productions by their peers and releases that are currently in vogue within their scene. They have such a familiarity with this collection that they can identify these intricate parts of songs and how they are crafted together. The thief on the other hand does not and either assumes that the lifted parts will not be noticed or they do it anyway as a short cut. If a particular electronic dance music community was known to vilify such acts, this may also result in the loss of future employment when it becomes known in that a particular DJ has a reputation for being a thief. Various data sharing services on the internet and other new media have made it easier to acquire music and in this instance it may not only be consumed but also used in production. As Heath's statement implied, this kind of stealing is widespread. Here the boundary between acceptable and unacceptable is marked by permission for use. The permission in question can be viewed as a professional courtesy with potential social capital whereas the consequences include the possible indirect loss of economic capital and isolation from the community.

The second category of stealing is on the level of performance and is more subtle as Anthony recounted an experience with a more established DJ:

> If you happen to have a guest DJ perform live on the radio show and they've tended to use the same set, the exact same set to a *T* that you've done previously, I'm against that and we actually have heard that.... I've heard it before on Nova Nation and wasn't impressed, was *not* impressed .... It disappoints me because it's like well look at the position you're in. You've got such a high profile, everyone knows who you are, everyone listens to your music, yet you can't be original. (Batori, 2011)

---

[8] The term 'objectified' is based on one of the ways Bourdieu (1986) discussed cultural capital. In the context of this chapter it refers to the knowledge and reputation based on the ownership of objects related to electronic dance music production and DJing.

This charge of stealing is based on the more expansive definition of originality as recomposition. Vadim, who does not produce much, mentioned a similar account: 'Every now and again, you'll be out somewhere and someone will be playing exactly the same [pauses] like exactly what you were doing in a set that you've played' (Golikov, 2011). The unique aural aesthetic that was recomposed is being emulated with no reference to the one who recomposed the setlist; hence the element of deceit and fraud in passing off someone's taste – their pioneering musical sound – as your own, appropriating another's technocultural capital, which is the indicator of their labour of recomposition. In this situation, the charge of stealing is harder to prove in that the thief is not lifting anything that the recomposer can easily claim a right to. Prior to the introduction of CDJs, the ownership of physical vinyl records – especially rare records that a DJ has managed to hunt down and used to define their 'sound' – may have restricted this kind of stealing. A unique set could be maintained on the basis of the physical scarcity of the records used. However a seemingly infinite digital reproduction online has meant that a 'rare' track will not maintain its exclusivity for long. In addition, DJs define their originality not only through the songs they select, but also though the order in which they are presented and weaved together for any given performance (see Fikentscher's chapter on programming in this volume). Emulating a DJ's music programming would be considered stealing as much as using exactly the same tracks from another DJ's set.

Again the consequences of this type of stealing may be similar to the first category if caught. Nevertheless this also depends on the status of the accuser and the thief. As an established DJ, Vadim could make an accusation of stealing and assume that his peers would respect the call. Yet I suspected that part of Anthony's annoyance stemmed from the fact that as a DJ closer to the amateur end of the professional DJ spectrum, he lacked the reputation and social capital in the scene to lend credibility to his accusation, especially given the high profile of the thief. The set and its aural aesthetic became more associated with the thief who played it on a major radio show, whereas Anthony had played it to a much smaller audience in a club.

'The Kids'

Throughout the interviews, with the more established DJs in particular, I noticed a continued mentioning of 'the kids'. They were referred to with some level of hostility or antagonism at times as the constant 'other'. There was a perceived image of a young inexperienced DJ/producer, yet the interviewees who often mentioned 'the kids' were relatively young. Although age is a factor in this othering function and in the source of the term, it appears that it refers to inexperience as a DJ (a lack of technocultural capital) and inexperience in a given scene (a lack of reputation and of social capital). The first reference to 'the kids' came from the interview with Anthony: 'All these kids are trying to be DJs and you know, do research .... At the end of the day I say, if you need to be taught, don't bother' (Batori, 2011). This was in the context of a question concerning vinyl compared with digital. On the same question, Keiran was reflective on the issue:

> Well that's the argument isn't it? It's always better if it's older. It was always better. It *was* always better, you know what I mean? Everything's always *was* better. This is what happens when you're older. Like even now I'm twenty-two and I think that I've got this real hatred towards the younger kids because I just don't like them because we did it better. It's just the way it is. It's just our human mind. (Dole, 2011)

These responses suggest that it is experience, rather than age, that determines who is perceived as a 'kid'. Whilst both Keiran and Anthony are the same age, Anthony would be considered a 'kid' from Keiran's perspective due to his inexperience. Claire and Jack would also be 'kids' despite both being older than Keiran (25 and 24 respectively at the time of the interviews); both are experienced musicians but relatively inexperienced as DJs, similar to the bedroom DJ producers addressed in Whelan (2006); as such, they are exceptions to the young DJ-producers that established DJs refer to as 'the kids'.

Keiran explained his reluctance to release more of his own tracks, feeling that this would not be noticed due to 'a lot of fucking kids, they're just making rubbish and no one holds it in any high regard whatsoever' (Dole, 2011). My interviewees repeatedly highlighted the inexperience of 'the kids' with authenticated technologies (such as the vinyl and CDJs) and conventions. Describing a typical set, the lack of etiquette by 'the kids' is again mentioned by Keiran:

> You'd start off playing the back of the other DJ's set. He plays a song that you play into. I always typically like to play a single sort of genre to that; sort of lead into it. Because I don't really like it how people, kids (I say kids like the young ones tend to do it a lot) come on and just straight away out of the blocks just try to make an impression. You really notice that there's a difference in the two DJs and I don't like that. Because we're not here to compete anyway … but a lot of the kids do. (Dole, 2011)

In addition to being inexperienced, 'the kids' are also accused of the earlier charges of stealing and cheating. Heath stated that he tended to upload his songs for free because a 'lot of kids around this age that listen to this sort of stuff, a lot of them don't have credit cards and Beatport accounts so that's the only way to get it' (Bain, 2011). This could be viewed as being sympathetic towards the kids. However, when asked if he ever gave advice to people, he replied that it '[d]epends who they are [pauses] not really because it's like I said before, there's so many people doing it now. It's so hard to be different from everyone else because everything's just the same. Everyone's got the same set, the same plugins, the same software, the same samples' (Bain, 2011).

In contrast Daimon, as the oldest DJ interviewed, is more supportive when referring to 'the kids': 'I … have a lot of young, up and coming musicians come to me for advice or just [to] ask me questions about this and that so it's good to give back to the next generation rather than just taking all the information and not giving it back' (Schwalger, 2011). For those who want more, Daimon has incorporated the inexperience of 'the kids' as another revenue stream by running DJing and production workshops. Nonetheless, Heath's reluctance to give advice is understandable due to the perceived over-saturation of the local scene by 'the kids', a scene on which he depends for his primary source of revenue. This resonates with Keiran's complaint earlier. It also illustrates another interesting dynamic concerning 'the kids' – reputation and competition.

In the past, the initial costs were high, restricting DJing to the very dedicated. Now that technology has lowered the costs and the financial barriers of entry are significantly diminished, it seems as though any 'kid' is able to download a pirated version of a popular software package and begin as a 'bedroom producer'. Due to the ease of access, there is no shortage of DJs and producers, leading to more intense competition for spots at events and residencies at more amateur/semi-professional venues. In a market with an abundance of DJs, flexible technical skills such as the ability to competently play vinyl, CDJs and laptops can be beneficial. However Vadim provided an account of what, from his viewpoint, is becoming more common:

> So a lot of the times you find that promoters or people who run parties, their main thing is to get people through the door, to get people into the place. When they get approached by these young kids who go 'listen, I made a track, can I play at your party?' or something like that. They go 'what can you bring to the table?' They [the kids] go 'I can bring 10 or 15 people to your party' so straight away they go 'aw yeah, 15, 20 people, that's an extra bit of money for me' and it means the place is a bit more packed. Four, five, six years ago, the only people who stood behind the decks and were playing were actually proper DJs. (Golikov, 2011)

In this instance, 'the kids' are able to get a spot due solely to their social capital which for an event organizer means more earnings for the evening – in addition to having to pay less (or anything at all in some cases) compared with a professional. This subverts any established notion of merit and skill required to 'earn' a gig as a 'proper' DJ.

Technological Shifts

The small body of literature that addresses DJ culture and new technologies reflects the tensions within various electronic dance music scenes concerning the technological shifts addressed above. Often this tension is attributed to a disturbance of some established standard – this echoes some of the distinctions and attitudes found in the preceding pages of this chapter. According to early accounts, the emergence of laptop computers as an instrument for performance at concerts and festivals initially provoked a sense of unease and deception from audiences and critics alike (Cascone, 2002; Turner, 2003). In a proscenium setting, there was a perceived lack of presence, of aura in the performance from an audience that expected spectacle from music – the laptop was entrenched as a signifier for work in the public consciousness (Cascone, 2002). Ten years later, with the popularity of performers such as mash-up artist Girl Talk and more recently the bedroom-amateur-to-platinum-record story of Owl City, the laptop has shifted from the margins into centre stage. Nevertheless the stigma described in earlier accounts of laptop performances – the violation of established codes of music (Cascone, 2002), the lack of presence (Turner, 2003) – remains embedded at some level amongst fans and performers.

Similarly Farrugia and Swiss (2005) indicated the apprehension and hostility among some members on an electronic dance music mailing list after hearing about the (then) unreleased Final Scratch DJ tool. The antagonism exhibited was ultimately attributed to a disruption of the existing electronic dance music order caused by the new DJ technology – 'an order maintained by numerous gatekeeping practices, including the ideological enforcement of standards for discerning the value and authenticity of certain DJ practices' (Farrugia and Swiss, 2005, p. 31). The more recent provocatively titled papers by Montano (2008, 2010), 'You're Not a Real DJ Unless You Play Vinyl' and the updated version 'How Do You Know He's Not Playing Pac-Man While He's Supposed to be DJing?' indicated how the changing media environment has impacted electronic dance music culture through an ethnographic account of DJs based in Sydney, Australia. From his analysis of these discourses concerning technology and electronic dance music, Montano (2010, p. 415) concluded that 'as clubbers witness more and more DJs employing technology other than vinyl and turntables … their understandings and perceptions of what it means to be a DJ will change, and this may require a redefinition of the concept of DJing'. In the final pages of this chapter, I take this argument one step further. It is not so much that a redefinition of the concept of DJing (or the broader idea of electronic dance musicianship) is *now* required due to new media technologies. Instead I suggest that DJ/ producers are constantly redefining electronic dance musicianship through their practices and authenticating discourses; hence, there are no 'natural' practices that are intrinsically more legitimate than others.

An Actor-Network Theory Perspective

Actor-network theory (ANT) is a useful approach because it provides a foundation for this type of argument. It enables an analysis of technocultural relationships without being grounded in the essential qualities of an actor or an object. In other words ANT does not assume the technology or the cultural (i.e. human) to be the determining agent but instead the relationship is co-constitutive. Law[9] (1992, p. 386) summarized the ANT approach as:

> ... a concern with how actors and organizations mobilize, juxtapose, and hold together the bits and pieces out of which they are composed; how they are sometimes able to prevent those bits and pieces from following their own inclinations and making off; and how they manage, as a result, to conceal for a time the process of translation itself and so turn a network from a heterogeneous set of bits and pieces each with its own inclinations, into something that passes as a punctualized actor. (Law, 1992, p. 386)

A central premise of ANT is the heterogeneous network metaphor. According to Law (1992, p. 381) for ANT 'the social is nothing other than patterned networks of heterogeneous materials'. What this means is that the entities that constitute the world (individuals, technologies, media, organizations and so forth) are constructed as effects of a particular arrangement of different (heterogeneous) materials (actors). The term 'punctualize' refers to the tendency to view these network arrangements as whole entities (or black

---

[9] In this section I am drawing from the work of actor-network theorists John Law and Bruno Latour who are part of a core group credited with developing and consistently revising the ANT framework.

boxes). However part of the premise of the heterogeneous network is that its constituent actors are always in a process of change or transition – consider the contested boundaries of cheating and stealing I have described above. For ANT terms such as 'social structure' are verbs not nouns; social structures are processes of actors ordering and reordering themselves – this is what the term 'translation' refers to. This leads to a radical claim that the social involves and is shaped by both human *and* non-human actors. Law (1992) explained that we can think about this by considering our interactions with each other and all the objects that always mediate this interaction. An example could be how a DJ performance is constituted by not only the relationship between the DJ and clubbers but also the combination of non-human actors such as the devices used to perform (turntables, mixer, headphones, cables, speakers and so on) and the materials of the setting (such as those that make up the nightclub). Each actor (human or non-human) plays an equal role in the construction of the social experience of a DJ performance.

Another useful premise to draw from ANT is that it is about following controversies – moments where the heterogeneous networks that constitute a social situation are more evident. Latour (1987, p. 259) wrote, 'we study science *in action* and not ready made science or technology; to do so, we either arrive before the facts and machines are blackboxed or we follow the controversies that reopen them'. Latour's original concern was the production of scientific knowledge examined through a sociological perspective (see Latour and Woolgar, 1986). He was interested in how this knowledge was constructed not through the scientific method per se but as an effect of the interacting materials in the laboratory. Rather than investigating isolated facts of science, ANT examines the network of actors that have come together to produce scientific facts. This can be applied to any other technocultural relations, including electronic dance music culture. The previously unquestioned black boxes – be it a scientific fact or a technocultural norm in a DJ scene – are revealed to be in constructed in a particular way, an effect of networks of heterogeneous materials. This is what the preceding controversies in this chapter are really about. I have drawn from accounts where each interviewee articulated their own understanding of a set of technocultural practices that they are engaged in. Distinctions of authenticity and legitimacy are made in relation to various technologies and social protocols. The capacity to use certain technologies such as turntables, CD-Js and laptops, the capacity to read a crowd, a sense of rhythm, knowledge of an extensive or particular electronic dance music catalogue, the conventions that dictate how to source a sample, how to play into another DJ's set and so on; these are all heterogeneous materials that come together in each interviewee's articulation of a common understanding of musicianship within their particular dance community.

Returning to the initial argument, claims of particular practices being more 'natural' or 'real' than others – for example, the charge of cheating with the controversial sync function rather than manual beatmatching by ear – are useful only when the aim is to describe a set of norms within a specific dance music scene at a specific moment in time. From an ANT perspective these claims seem suspect because of their specificity – the distinctions only make sense in the context of a certain time and place. Critical discourse concerning the use of DJ software on laptops and other new media are only the most recent of a series of historical authenticating discourses and technocultural relationships in music. DJs have long been accused of being inauthentic or unoriginal by 'real' musicians. As Jack puts it:

> I think the music world is going through a really weird crisis at the moment because people are battling about technology and they're trying to read into whether it's better to do this or more credible to do that... the dudes on the vinyl turntables are pretending that like that wouldn't have been blasphemous for the people that came before. (Arentz, 2011)

When defining a term such as musicianship, there is an inherent assumption regarding the technocultural relationship between an individual and an instrument.[10] Earlier modes of musicianship involved acoustic instruments, a performative element and the discourses that legitimized and defined these modes in their specific time and place. These modes are continuously redefined albeit at

---

[10] The exception could be vocalists though an argument could be made that voice (as the manipulation or organisation of sound) in and of itself is a medium and hence falls into the category of technology.

a slow pace and hence there appear to be moments of stability concerning what defines musicianship.

The late nineteenth century saw the introduction of recorded sound. As this medium was commercially exploited to reproduce music performances and became popular, the notions of performance and musicianship were more radically redefined. In this context, Fikentscher (2003) traces the role of recording technology in restructuring the relationship between the musical performance and music as a text throughout the twentieth century, providing a historical overview of the key technologies (such as sheet music, gramophones, multi-track recorders, vinyl) and various pioneers that redefined musicianship by incorporating recorded music (music as a text) into the performance; tracing the moments where the DJ transformed a device for mere playback into an instrument for performing and composing. A more complex ANT account would acknowledge the various authenticating discourses that accompanied each innovation, revealing countless arrangements of heterogeneous materials at each historical juncture. These would be the controversies that ANT could follow –historical equivalents of the controversies in this chapter, such as questions about the virtuosity involved in 'performing' pre-recorded music compared with a 'real' instrument such as a guitar.

The authenticating discourse surrounding the CD is a useful comparison to those concerning the laptop and DJ software. Farrugia and Swiss (2005, pp. 33–4) described 'moments of resistance' to new DJ technologies and quoted one individual who posted '[p]ushing buttons has nothing to do with DJ'ing as far as I am concerned'; a comment that referred to performing with CDs. In Montano's (2010) paper, where the fieldwork was conducted in a later period (from 2002 to 2007), the discourse surrounding CDs was gaining some acceptance though the laptop was still marginalized. My own fieldwork reflects a similar dynamic. The previously marginalized CD was referred to as the standard for clubs around Melbourne and its use was less widely questioned. Instead criticism focused mainly on the laptop as the 'new' technology that was being adopted by some. DJs such as Jack and Claire recognize a burgeoning notion of musicianship with the laptop – it is not just 'pushing buttons' or clicking on icons. For both the CD and the laptop, the criticisms from established DJs imply that a certain human element involved in DJing has become automated and thus something significant has been lost in the craft. Yet, historically, the innovation of recorded music – an innovation that DJing is built on – represented seemingly an even greater loss of human agency. Prior to the phonograph, music was experienced through performance, an ephemeral 'live' moment. The act of being able to record the performance and reproduce it meant you no longer need the performer after one performance. However as Fikentscher (2003) described, the recording process became a new art form in itself with the studio as the instrument and producers such as Phil Spector as the musicians.

Similarly one only has to consider the history of DJing as a sample-based practice to be suspicious of any claims of 'stealing'. There are nuanced conditions concerning what is on the one hand classified as 'sharing' or 'sampling' and on the other hand 'stealing' – particularly in an era of digital networks, a medium that is built on sharing content. Whilst there are certain consequences of being 'called out' as a thief, Anthony's experience indicated that these accusations are also entangled in certain norms. Those who have yet to or refuse to go through a particular process of authentication are labelled 'kids' or something similar. This marginalizes their position in the community, as a 'kid' is less likely to receive support for calling out an established DJ for stealing. One can explain a set of conditions for 'sampling' but these conditions are specific to a time and place. There are precedents that have raised similar concerns and involved different processes of authentication. For some, unless you have gone out and 'discovered' or 'captured' the sound yourself, it isn't 'real' or 'authentic'. Part of the preparation work of DJ is to collect. As Farrugia and Swiss (2005, p. 34) explained, collecting 'initiates a particular subject position, allowing collectors to both see themselves as experts and demonstrate their mastery to others'. Thus collecting was viewed as a gatekeeping practice in order for DJs to claim expertise through objectified technocultural capital and firmly associated with vinyl records found in physical stores. This is bluntly illustrated by the aforementioned 'pushing buttons' poster, which continues '[i]magine the joy of finally finding that record you've been after for several years, and then compare it to downloading that track from the internet' (Farrugia and

Swiss, 2005, p. 34). In contrast, the DJ-producers I spoke with were content with the convenience of doing their preparation work online such as sourcing new tracks and acquiring samples. Their practices are no less legitimate than that of the physical collectors; rather, these activities are transposed to a different media environment.

Through an ANT approach, it is possible to note that comparative moments of authentication have a common theme. The distinctions between authentic and inauthentic practices tend to privilege the human actor over the non-human. When a loss of agency for the human actor is perceived with the adoption of a new technology, there is a sense of moving towards an inevitable moment of technological determinism where an artistic practice ceases to be artistic. This is a moment where supposedly there is no longer any skill or creativity involved in the craft, such as when button pushing replaces earlier notions of DJing. Although an ANT approach can be suspicious of such a line of argument since, first, no distinction is made between which agent engages in the act – for ANT both the human and non-human actor come together in a particular arrangement to constitute the act, be it collecting, producing, performing, beatmatching and so on. This discourse concerning technology has stemmed from a more generalized unease with new technocultural arrangements – consider the longstanding anxiety of jobs being replaced by machines. Second, the controversies concerning electronic dance music and new DJ technologies in this chapter are understood, through ANT, as part of a series of relationships between heterogeneous elements (people, technologies, practices). These manifest themselves in particular arrangements and are understood by specific actors through specific points of reference. The perspectives provided by DJ-producers during interviews should not be used to comprehensively define the relations they address. Instead, by situating these kinds of discourses in a wider history of musicianship, they can be seen as merely the most recent in a series describing continuously changing technocultural relationships. Rather than approaching each new technology within a framework of technological determinism, it is more analytically productive to examine the new creative practices and discourses that emerge and how these contribute to an ongoing redefinition of musicianship.

References

Bourdieu, Pierre (1986) 'The Forms of Capital'. In John Richardson (ed.) *Handbook of Theory and Research for the Sociology of Education* (241–58). New York: Greenwood.

Brewster, Bill and Broughton, Frank (2000) *Last Night a DJ Saved My Life: The History of the Disc Jockey*. New York: Grove.

Cascone, Kim (2002) 'Laptop Music: Counterfeiting Aura in the Age of Infinite Reproduction'. *Parachute*, 107: 52–60.

DJBessant (2009) 'Pioneer CDJ 1000 / 800 / 400 BPM Beatmatching Pitch Trick'. *YouTube* video (20 February). http://www.youtube.com/watch?v=0wIWwS3KWIM [accessed 1 August 2012].

Farrugia, Rebekah and Swiss, Thomas (2005) 'Tracking the DJs: Vinyl Records, Work, and the Debate Over New Technologies'. *Journal of Popular Music Studies*, 17(1): 30–44.

Fikentscher, Kai (2003) ' "There's Not a Problem I Can't Fix, 'Cause I Can Do it in the Mix": On the Performative Technology of 12-inch Vinyl'. In Rene Lysloff and Leslie Gay (eds) *Music and Technoculture* (290–315). Middletown, CT: Wesleyan University Press.

Inthemix (2010) 'Australia's National DJ, Festival, Clubbing & Dance Music Poll – Top 50'. http://www.inthemix.com.au/50/2010/results/djs-10-2/ [accessed 15 January 2012].

Langlois, Tony (1992) ' "Can You Feel It?" DJs and House Music Culture in the UK'. *Popular Music*, 11(2): 229–38.

Latour, Bruno (1987) *Science in Action: How to Follow Scientists and Engineers Through Society*. Cambridge, MA: Harvard University Press.

Latour, Bruno and Woolgar, Steve (1986) *Laboratory Life: The Construction of Scientific Facts*. Princeton, NJ: Princeton University Press.

Law, John (1992) 'Notes on the Theory of the Actor-Network: Ordering, Strategy and Heterogeneity'. *Systems Practice*, 5(4): 379–93.

Lobato, Ramon (2009) 'The Six Faces of Piracy: Global Media Distribution from Below'. In Robert Sickels (ed.) *The Business of Entertainment: Movies* (15–36). Westport, CT: Greenwood Press.

McLeod, Kembrew (2009) 'Crashing the Spectacle: A Forgotten History of Digital Sampling, Infringement, Copyright Liberation and the End of Recorded Music'. *Culture Machine*, 10: 114–30.

Montano, Ed (2008) ' "You're Not a Real DJ Unless You Play Vinyl" – Technology and Formats – The Progression of Dance Music and DJ Culture'. *Journal on the Art of Record Production*, 3(1). http://arpjournal.com/581/%E2%80%98you%E2%80%99re-not-a-real-dj-unless-you-play-vinyl%E2%80%99-%E2%80%93-technology-and-formats-%E2%80%93-the-progression-of-dance-music-and-dj-culture/ [accessed 15 December 2011].

—(2010) ' "How Do You Know He's Not Playing Pac-Man while He's Supposed to Be DJing?": Technology, Formats and the Digital Future of DJ Culture'. *Popular Music,* 29(3): 397–416.

Rodgers, Tara (2003) 'On the Process and Aesthetics of Sampling in Electronic Music Production'. *Organised Sound*, 8(3): 313–20.

Schumacher, Thomas (2004) ' "This is a Sampling Sport": Digital Sampling, Rap Music and the Law in Cultural Production'. In Simon Frith (ed.) *Popular Music: Critical Concepts in Media and Cultural Studies, Vol. II: The Rock Era* (169–90). London: Routledge.

Turner, Tad (2003) 'The Resonance of the Cubicle: Laptop Performance in Post-digital Musics'. *Contemporary Music Review*, 22(4): 81–92.

van Veen, tobias (2002) 'Vinyauralism: The Art and the Craft of Turntablism'. The DJ School. *Discorder*, March. http://www. quadrantcrossing.org/papers/Vinyauralism02-Discorder-tV.pdf [accessed 12 February 2012].

Whelan, Andrew (2006) 'Do U Produce? Subcultural Capital and Amateur Musicianship in Peer-to-Peer Networks'. In Michael Ayers (ed.) *Cybersounds: Essays on Virtual Music Culture* (57–81). New York: Peter Lang.

Interviews

Arentz, Jack (2011) Interviewed by Jonathan Yu, Melbourne, 20 July.

Bain, Heath (2011) Interviewed by Jonathan Yu, Melbourne, 1 August.

Batori, Anthony (2011) Interviewed by Jonathan Yu, Melbourne, 30 July.

Dole, Keiran (2011) Interviewed by Jonathan Yu, Melbourne, 1 August.

—(2012) Interview follow-up by Jonathan Yu, 1 August.

Golikov, Vadim (2011) Interviewed by Jonathan Yu, Melbourne, 1 August.

Rayner, Claire (2011) Interviewed by Jonathan Yu, Melbourne, 20 July.

Schwalger, Daimon (2011) Interviewed by Jonathan Yu, Melbourne, 15 July.

CHAPTER EIGHT

DJ Culture and the Commercial Club Scene in Sydney

Ed Montano

Drawing on a decade of ethnographic research and participant observation in the commercial Sydney club scene, this chapter explores some of the developments in the city's DJ culture since the turn of the millennium. In addition to a wider international body of work in DJ studies, including the journal *Dancecult*, there is a small body of Australian-focused and Sydney-specific research on electronic dance music, such as Brennan-Horley (2007), Brookman (2001), Chan (1999), Gibson (1999), Gibson and Pagan (2003), Luckman (2002), Murphie and Scheer (1992), and Park and Northwood (1996), which this chapter intends to complement. Grounded in interviews with some of the scene's most prominent and successful DJs, promoters, journalists and other industry personnel, it offers an analysis of the industry structures and mechanisms that have facilitated the 'mainstreaming' of dance music in the city's urban nightlife. Situated within a broader international perspective, it interrogates the tensions and conflicts that underpin the work of Sydney's DJs, who continually grapple with the forces of competition and necessity in playing alongside their international counterparts. By discussing the part played by international DJs in the local scene, it is my aim to emphasize the global flow of electronic dance music that is generated through the performances of these DJs in different parts of the world. The city's commercialization of electronic dance music culture will be situated in a framework of a global diffusion of dance music, in relation to the ways in which local DJs in Sydney seek to contest and resist the commercial dynamics of their scene through their working lives and musical practices (Gibson and McGregor, 2011, p. 207). As such, the chapter illuminates the discourses and practices that inform and sculpt a specifically local articulation of DJing, while at the same time situating this articulation in the broader global flows, or 'global pipelines' (Watson, 2008, p. 13), of information and the 'networks of commodity flow and entrepreneurial activity' (Connell and Gibson, 2003, p. 56) that circulate within contemporary urban international club culture.

Here, the terms 'global' and 'international' refer to the diffusion of music that takes place between English-speaking countries (UK/US/Australia). I acknowledge this overlooks numerous DJs and sounds from elsewhere, but it remains the case that the scene in Sydney relies significantly on tours by DJs from the US, the UK and to a lesser extent Western Europe, although there is a handful of DJs from South America, Russia and other countries that tour to Sydney. Thus, an Anglo-American, cross-Atlantic flow of DJs and music is located within my discussion of Sydney and the global diffusion of club culture. Given the global and corporate outlooks that infuse particular elements of contemporary dance music scenes (St John, 2009, p. 11), which are 'based on a globally-operated music industry dominated by a few media conglomerates' (Reitsamer, 2011, p. 31), there is a global movement of culture that affects the identity and development of local scenes, and the understandings and practices of those who are involved with these scenes. My specific focus is on the 'commercial', by which I mean the clubs and venues that attract large numbers of clubbers; that have a particularly strong presence in the local media; that typically employ DJs from both Australia and overseas; and that have an overarching commercial, profit-driven orientation embedded within 'corporate strategies' (D'Andrea, 2007, p. 95).

The chapter draws on theories of globalization and flow (Appadurai, 1996; Ho, 2003; Negus, 1996), diffusion (Kong et al., 2006) and transnationalism (Connell and Gibson, 2003). As with related concepts such as local, global and international, these concepts are defined by the specific context in which they are used, which can be a challenge. While an interrogation of these problems is beyond the scope of this chapter, their use here is intended to add to the debates of the production and consumption of music in specific locales 'in a world that has become deterritorialized, diasporic, and transnational' (Appadurai, 1996, p. 188). Contemporary music scene workers and audiences actively construct their production and consumption practices through adopting and incorporating global cultural elements into local cultural contexts. Having less hegemonic implications than 'cultural imperialism' (Negus, 1996, p. 177), the term 'globalization' has been used in reference to the cross-national and cross-cultural fusions of different styles of music in local popular culture industries (Ho, 2003, p. 144), 'at the same time as it enabled the global reach of Western popular music' (Connell and Gibson, 2003, p. 69). While the music industry remains dominated by Anglo-American multimedia corporations and their promotion of mainstream superstars with transnational appeal, this does not imply a homogenous popular music culture that only flows from the dominant to the dominated. Rather, culture of global reach and appeal is uniquely reworked and reshaped by local scene agents. This is not to dismiss the notion of cultural imperialism, for there is certainly a degree of corporate and geographical dominance in the global circulation and flow of music. Yet filtering the work of DJs in Sydney through the lens of globalization seems the most appropriate approach for interrogating the tensions that arise from their negotiations with both local and global practices.

During the time of research, between 2002 and 2012, I actively participated in Sydney's electronic dance music scene. For example, I regularly contributed to the Australian online dance music magazine *Inthemix* and won their annual contributor competition in 2011. The prize included entry to the Sydney, Melbourne and Brisbane legs of the Stereosonic festival, travel costs and, perhaps most importantly, the opportunity to interview international 'superstar' DJs Ferry Corsten, Carl Cox, Kaskade and Armin van Buuren.[1] It became evident that the appeal of these international

---

[1] My reviews of the festival can be found at these two links: www.inthemix. com.au/features/51679/Stereosonic_Festival_Reporter_Sydney_Wrapup [accessed 29 November 2011] and www.inthemix.com.au/features/51766/

DJs was not restricted by place, and that such DJs and their music easily translate across different cities. The mass appeal was clear, with a record crowd of 60,000 in Sydney. Attending the three festivals reinforced the transnationalism that underpins contemporary dance music and DJ culture. Here were DJs from various parts of the world DJing music sourced from all corners of the globe to audiences spread across Australia.

In addition to my writing contributions, between 2002 and 2005 I worked as a retail assistant on the CD counter at Central Station Records. At the time, this was Sydney's main independent dance music store, and was part of the Central Station Records group that included other stores around Australia and a record label that has had a significant role in the popularization of dance music in Australia (see Gibson and McGregor, 2011, for an insight into how the store influenced McGregor's own DJing in Dunedin, New Zealand). The industry-related benefits of working in the store allowed me to further my research into Sydney's clubbing landscape, in that I took full advantage of the opportunities for free entry into most of the city's clubs that working alongside DJs provides. All those employed to work behind the store's vinyl counter were professional DJs, and dance party promoters would often drop into the store to leave flyers or posters for their events, typically offering guest-list places or free tickets for any staff. I was thus able to form a network of contacts that proved beneficial not only when seeking out interviewees, but also when seeking entry to clubs and events.

Club Culture in Sydney

Many of the commercial dance clubs of the past decade in Sydney, between 2002 and 2012, such as Home, Sublime, Tank, Ivy, Slip Inn and Gas, were based on UK 'super clubs' such as Ministry of Sound, Renaissance and Cream, employing extensive advertising

---

Stereosonic_Festival_Reporter_Weekend_Two [accessed 9 December 2011]; the video with edited highlights of my interviews can be found here: www.inthemix.com.au/videos/51720/inthemixtv_at_Stereosonic_Sydney_2011 [accessed 1 December 2011].

campaigns, brand names and recognizable logos to promote their venues and nights. The adoption of UK clubbing brands for events in Australia, such as the Creamfields festival, demonstrates the value Australian clubbing audiences ascribe to international electronic dance music culture – in particular British versions, due to the country's historically informed political and cultural ties with the UK. This guarantees an audience for the event and reduces the work associated with marketing and developing a festival format. Park and Northwood (1996) emphasize the branded concept of the dance club as being more than just a building, describing how the super club is not only a large venue built specifically for dance music, but is also 'not restricted to its physical location', being an entity which can 'tour'. During the 1990s, the UK-based super clubs became involved in global tours, which see certain DJs tour specific locations around the world under the banner of the club brand (Connell and Gibson, 2003, p. 229). This reinforces the global character of dance club culture, while also establishing the dominance of the UK super club brands, these brands being part of what D'Andrea refers to as 'the mighty nightclub oligopoly' (2007, p. 101). This represents a specific geographical diffusion of contemporary dance music and culture that seems to follow the historical trajectories of trade and imperialism. DJs in Sydney continually negotiate this global diffusion in their local musical work. Kong et al. (2006, p. 175) note how creative industries' discourses in Asia are typically influenced by debates in the North Atlantic, whereby 'A classic diffusion model could be applied in order to trace how a particular assemblage of ideas … radiates out from centres of production elsewhere, eventually reaching Asian locations in turn.' Similar processes, with the movement of cultural formats from the centre to the margins, can be identified in electronic dance music culture. Specific globally well-connected urban locations have come to be regarded as central to dance music history. For participants in Sydney's dance music scene, its distance from what are perceived as the centres of dance music culture (Western Europe and the US) has influenced the musical direction of the scene.

Dance music history is often traced through reference to specific geographical locations that are dominated by Anglo-American voices, such as the development of house music in Chicago, techno in Detroit, acid house in Britain, trance in Goa and the Ibiza scene. However, as Connell and Gibson (2003, p. 108) point out, this is not to say different dance scenes all have similar characteristics drawn from a handful of places of significance:

> Dance music and 'techno' musical forms in the 1990s have their own histories that tend to emphasise 'authentic' origins …. Yet, experimental electronic music has been part of musical scenes across many continents, where the relatively anonymous repetitive beats and instrumental grooves of UK or American tracks are heard and enjoyed not as part of a 'passive' act of listening to overseas artists, but as the sounds and signifiers of a subculture that exists in distinct ways in each locality.

Neither does this mean that the formation of electronic dance music and its cultural forms exclusively stems from these areas, for as Kong et al. note, there are 'nuanced ways in which ideas travel, become popular and are mutated to suit local circumstances – or indeed are not absorbed' (2006, p. 176). Yet it remains the case that Australian dance music culture draws extensively on the sounds and styles of Europe and the US. Apart from the music itself being foreign in origin, much of the surrounding culture and fashion of the Australian dance music scene is also drawn from overseas (Murphie and Scheer, 1992, p. 183). It is impossible to ignore the influence that Anglo-American and European dance culture had on the formation and development of the Sydney dance scene (see Brennan-Horley, 2007, pp. 124–5; Luckman, 2001, pp. 63–4), the example of which supports Florida and Jackson's observation that major cities may not have generated particular musical innovations, but rather 'they have played a more important role in commercializing and popularizing music that may have originally emerged elsewhere' (2010, p. 311).

Local vs. International DJs

An analysis of my interviews with DJs and promoters, in addition to interview material and participant opinions within local online and print dance music media, reconfirms that the position of the local scene in relation to developments abroad is a central concern for contemporary understandings of club culture in

Sydney, demonstrating some of the key discursive themes that shape and define the scene. One main recurring issue is the value and significance of international DJs to the local scene, which is frequently addressed pejoratively – for example, international DJs are often described by clubbers and some local DJs as overrated and overpaid, yet paradoxically also as necessary for the continued commercial success of club culture in the city.

Although the suggestion is made that international DJs threaten the existence of a unique local scene and ultimately take work away from local DJs, a productive two-way exchange and flow of cultural information is generated in the dialogue between global and local experiences. This issue attracts a great deal of comment and argument but is by no means unique to Sydney; for example, Weber (1999, p. 333) observed during interviews with participants in the Toronto rave scene that '[f]amous DJs from Europe and the USA were appreciated but it was felt that many local entertainers were cheaper and equally talented. While the need to feel affiliated with the international rave scene is important, these individuals also felt that the Torontonians should be supporting their local artists.' The involvement of international DJs places the scene within a wider global framework, and demonstrates the transnationalism that informs contemporary club culture.

Putting an emphasis on international DJs, and thus by extension international dance culture, exemplifies the concept of the music and the culture diffusing from overseas locations, especially from the UK. This can be traced further back in the history of the Sydney dance scene, in that it is widely acknowledged that the dance parties and raves that were organized in the late 1980s and early 1990s were based on English models of the warehouse party (Lau, 2012, pp. 3–4), partly because they were put on by British backpackers or expats, generating the perception in Sydney of Britain as an authentic source of original rave and club culture. International DJs have a central role in the Sydney scene, their very status as visitors associated to known club brands seemingly being one of the main attractions for clubbers; Sydney DJ Trent Rackus explains that,

> The international DJs carry an expectation that they're going to offer new music and a different sound, and it's quite often the case, but obviously there are DJs who aren't worth the money

that they're charging to perform over here .... It's all about the fact that they've played at Pacha in Ibiza or somewhere like that, and people love that, because your commercial audience have all these commercial club names, such as Godskitchen, that they attach to DJs. (Rackus, 2010)

International DJs who come with associations and links to particular styles and moments in dance music history have a certain degree of promotional pulling power and marketability. Similarly, the global success of a produced track can further enhance the profile, and subsequent commercial appeal, of a DJ, 'transforming their (sub)cultural capital into a commodity' (Reitsamer, 2011, p. 37). However, as several of my interviewees were keen to point out, success in production does not necessarily translate to skilful DJing, citing numerous instances where they had witnessed talented producers displaying rudimentary DJing skills at best, with Australian DJ sets by Scottish producer Mylo in 2004 being a frequently mentioned case. Conversely, the career progression pathways of electronic dance music have also enabled many DJs to move into the field of production often via remixing, as the industry recognizes DJs for their knowledge and understanding of what works on the dancefloor, a relationship that has existed since the disco remixes that emerged in the mid-1970s (Lawrence, 2008).

The emphasis that is placed on fame and the 'star DJ' concept has resulted in a process whereby successful dance music producers can transfer on to the international DJ circuit through the popularity of their music, branding their performance identity at the forefront of global dance culture. It would appear that, with the success of dance parties that have such DJs on their line-ups, good production skills are equated with good DJing skills. This is not to say that all clubbers value skills in both of these areas, but for certain sections of the dance music community, a display of the ability to perform live, as a DJ, or the evidence of ability in music production through the release of a recording is crucial in determining the credibility and value of particular DJs. This also impacts upon the DJs' accumulation of 'symbolic and cultural capital' (Reitsamer, 2011, p. 32) within the scene. Music recording can lead to increased recognition beyond a locality, lending the producer-DJ increased commercial appeal with those who value production skills and who like the track. This concurs with the distinction Reitsamer makes between the 'first generation' and 'second, current generation' of DJs in the Viennese techno scene, the former having been able to develop an economically successful career solely around DJing, while the latter 'is required to be both a DJ and a music producer. They have to make a name for themselves not only by winning over the club audience with good DJ performances, but also by releasing recordings of international standard' (2011, p. 37). DJs have become brand names, selling not only their club performances but also music, equipment and mix compilations. For Herman, 'in a culture filled with brand names, the DJ is the ultimate brand name, the moniker under which almost everything is sold' (2006, p. 31).

Sydney DJ Alan Thompson[2] emphasizes how promoters will use the appearances of international DJs to give significance to their events and nights. He perceives this in a negative sense, drawing on his experience of being in the position of both an international DJ and a local DJ, and the tension this creates:

> The international DJ here is put on a pedestal beyond anywhere else in the world I've ever seen. Having been on both sides of that coin, i.e. being an international DJ brought into Australia for the last nine years and being treated very well, I'm now considered to be a local DJ purely because of the fact that I live here …. Certain promoters want to pay me a fee that's equivalent to someone who has just started DJing in a local bar because I live in Australia and [they] consider me to be an Australian DJ. But, on the other hand, when the flyer comes out, my name is in big writing with 'Direct from the UK'. So it's a catch-22 for me because I can't win. On one side I'm considered to be an Australian DJ because I live here, and on the other side they market me as an international. I do think, and I hear from many Australian home-grown DJs, that promoters here look down towards home-grown DJs and really do emphasise, certainly in the summer gigs, international names being brought in to pluck up their gigs. I actually think it is awful and that

---

[2] Prior to moving to Australia in 2004, Thompson lived and worked in the UK, and therefore is particularly well-placed to comment on the international scope of dance culture.

all Australian DJs should get together and do something about
it. I think it's horrendous the way Australian DJs are treated.
(Thompson, 2005)

This emphasis on international names in order to enhance the
popularity of particular events has parallels with the processes
Reitsamer discusses in her analysis of DJ careers in Vienna. In
reference to a particular club promoter, she explains how economic
success is used as a marker of quality, with DJs who are able to make
a living purely on their DJing and production work being viewed as
worthy of playing at this promoter's club nights. In turn, this limits
and restricts the opportunities available to lesser known or unknown
DJs, who 'seem to pose the "risk" that their lack of popularity would
make them attract too few music fans' (2011, p. 35).

The Educational Value and Commercial Appeal of International DJs

While there is a certain amount of negativity in some of the
opinions regarding the performances in Sydney by DJs from
overseas, it can be argued that the value of international DJs is to
be found in the new music they bring in to play during their sets.
This fulfils the DJ's role as an educator, in that he or she introduces
new music to clubbing crowds. In turn, this helps the local scene
develop, as Sydney DJ John Devecchis explains:

You have to bring internationals here. A lot of them technically
aren't that good … [but they] bring all this new and different
music. What I don't like is when promoters bring out DJs and
they've not researched them, and these DJs come out and play
all the same tracks that we've got here…. The promoters have
to be clever about who they pick, but I think internationals are
very important to Sydney. (Devecchis, 2004)

As well as this educational value of international DJs, there is also
a certain appeal for clubbers inherent in the irregularity of their
performances, with tours of the country once every two or three
years. Local DJs can be seen far more regularly. Furthermore, the

media also play a central role in establishing the values and authen-
ticities linked to specific DJs by audiences, in relation to such
things as skill, use of technology, commercial appeal and position
within the scene. At the time of our interview, Sonia Sharma was
editor of the now-defunct Sydney-based street-press dance music
magazine *3D World*, when she provided a direct acknowledgement
of the media emphasis on international DJs, while also relaying an
experience that seemed to undercut this emphasis:

> I think there is [an over-emphasis on international DJs] by,
> perhaps wrongly, the media, which does include the publication
> I work for, and by promoters. The interesting thing is we actually
> ran a signing area at Parklife[3] and at a few other events. It's
> something we've just started doing, and what it involves is having
> the international DJs come down, and meet and greet with the
> public, and the amazing thing that we found was so many punters
> coming up saying, 'Why don't you have local DJs signing?', and I
> think, for the punters, they realise … we continually get reviews
> that state, 'X' international came out to play, but 'Y' local
> support put on a much better set. I think the product in Australia,
> the DJing, is probably on par with an international level, but the
> emphasis is still on those big names. (Sharma, 2005)

Although the extent to which international DJs can provide a more
musically rewarding and pleasurable clubbing experience than
their local counterparts is questionable, their position as 'internationals' would appear to lend them an authenticity and value,
which informs the judgements and opinions of clubbers in the
scene. Sydney DJ Goodwill highlights this tension when he explains
that international DJs are often perceived as being superior to their
local counterparts, and that this is a problematic issue that arises
from the 'detached' position the Sydney scene has from the dance
music centres of the UK and the US:

> One thing that annoys me these days, and that is constantly
> reminding me that [being detached] is maybe a little bit of a

---

[3] Parklife is an annual festival that was first staged in Sydney in 2000. Since 2007
the festival has also travelled interstate to Adelaide, Brisbane, Melbourne and Perth,
playing to a combined crowd of over 100,000.

problem, is how much people look up to international DJs. Quite often it will take an international DJ to come out here and play a record for kids to think it's good … they'll play a big tune that I've been playing for three months and everyone will go, 'Oh, what's that?'…. It's just because they're from overseas people automatically assume that it's a good thing … although at the same time they pack out dance floors and turn people on to music, so there's pros and cons to it. (Goodwill, 2004)

Given there is no identifiable 'Sydney sound' in the local scene, and that local DJs play similar, if not identical, material as their international counterparts, it would seem that the tension does not reside in any attempt at musical differentiation but rather, perhaps, in notions of local and national pride and jealousy at being located on the periphery of the Anglo-American DJ circuit. In playing similar music, the local DJs position themselves stylistically within the Anglo-American flow of electronic dance music, and yet at the same time there seems to be a desire to remain separate from this flow. This is fed by the distinction made by the clubbing audience in Sydney that internationals carry a greater degree of cultural signifi-cance. Local DJs fight against this, emphasizing their own cultural and symbolic capital through markers such as career longevity and overseas gigs. Even if they do play particular tracks months before touring DJs, the locals will continually be positioned as secondary, because they are indeed local. Unless they transcend their locality and become recognized overseas (as a handful of Australian DJs such as Anthony Pappa, Phil K and Luke Chable have done), the local audience will, for the most part, situate local DJs at the lower end of the DJ hierarchy.

As can be seen in the success of club nights branded with the names of Ministry of Sound, Pacha and Hed Kandi, as well as the success of branded festivals such as Creamfields and Stereosonic, the notion of branding has come to dominate the contemporary club scene in Australia, due to club culture's increasing 'capitalist orientation as an "industry"' (D'Andrea, 2007, p. 108) and the 'definitively transnational corporate manoeuvres' (McCutcheon, 2007, p. 275) of the dance music industry. Discussing the issue of international DJs and their role in the Sydney dance scene, Sydney DJ and producer Nat Nyk emphasizes the pervasiveness of branding, suggesting that clubbers are attracted to an event not necessarily because of a specific DJ, but rather because of the event itself. He explains how certain events in Sydney have been established as prominent, regular parties with names that act as brands, being signifiers of a particular style of music, of a particular crowd and of a particular level of quality:

> I've always wondered if half the people going even know who the international DJ is …. Okay, we're not talking Carl Cox or your bigwigs here, but you see [advertised] 'John Brown from the UK' and you go, 'Who the fuck's he?' But a few people have heard of him, and so word kind of filters out he plays this kind of music, and maybe he's had a record out on a label that people know, like the Nukleuz label or the Frantic label, or something like that. So a few people know about him, and therefore the gig gets a reputation. I think it's more driven by nights. You've got Gas who bring people out, and so they might bring someone out and you don't know who it is, but it's on at Gas, so you kind of trust that it's someone worthy. It's the same with the bigger parties. You could almost argue that Utopia would still get five thousand people if they had hardly any international DJs. (Nyk, 2005)

An issue of tension in Sydney involves the performances of international DJs and how these performances impact upon the scene as a local entity. Developments in the structure of the dance party scene in Sydney, with the establishment of large, annual festival-based parties such as Field Day, Parklife, Stereosonic and Creamfields, have had an impact on the way clubbers perceive the relevance of international DJs. From a marketing perspective, these DJs serve to draw people to the parties, and within the scene this has been interpreted in two contrasting ways. One is in a positive sense, in that these DJs help to educate the scene with new music and to broaden the global perspective of the scene's participants. In contrast, there is the negative argument that suggests these DJs and the emphasis that clubbers place on them create a DJ hierarchy of skill and ability, with the local DJs being consigned to the lower reaches of this hierarchy. It is a fallacy to suggest all international DJs are more skilful and more capable DJs than their local counterparts, and yet this is a perspective that is embedded within the very fabric of the Sydney scene. This stems, I suggest, from the way the scene has its roots in imported cultural capital. With an emphasis on imported vinyl (at least prior to the development of digital distribution), on imported music, on imported sounds and on imported styles, comes an emphasis on imported DJs. This is not to suggest there is no local production activity but rather that the music played in the commercial clubs in Sydney is sourced largely from outside of the country.[4] With the centrality of the UK, Western European and US scenes to global dance music culture, it follows that the key DJs from these scenes will be elevated to positions of significance by clubbers in Australia.

The Transient Qualities of Dance Music

Dance music typically has a limited commercial lifespan in comparison to rock music. With the latter, there has been the gradual development of a 'rock canon' in which certain songs and albums are elevated to classic status by fans and journalists, and used as a measure by which to assess new releases and new bands, giving rise to rock music's 'preoccupation with a historical past' (Straw, 1988, p. 260). In contrast, dance music, while having its fair share of classic 'tunes', rests predominantly on ephemeral notions of progression and development, with scant regard given to music once its effectiveness as a floor-filler has expired. This is not to suggest DJs do not utilize old material in their sets or that DJ culture wholly rejects history (see Rietveld, 2011, for a discussion of DJing as a nomadic archival practice), but rather the accelerated cycles of commercial dance music have led to a certain disposability that contrasts markedly with other music styles. The contrasting temporal logics of dance culture and rock culture can be attributed, in part, to the relative lack of emphasis placed on the concept of authorship and on rock notions of authorial authenticity within dance culture; instead there is a preference for values such as immediacy and sensuality (Hesmondhalgh, 1998, p. 238). Today's 'big tune' can quickly become tomorrow's 'embarrassment', or rather a record that proves to be extremely popular at one point in time can, a few months later, become the focus of

---

[4] Going against the typical local media focus on international producers, Australian dance music website *Inthemix* occasionally runs features on new local production talent. See, for example, Howe (2012a, 2012b).

much derision and criticism, although, as Trent Rackus highlights, the extent to which a record may be perceived to be 'embarrassing' depends largely on the opinion of the DJ:

> There are certain DJs out there, commercial DJs, who will flog a record to death because it's an easy way to satisfy an entry level crowd ... the DJing industry revolves around new production ... it's an industry where things come and go .... From working in a record shop, I know that when you give something to someone, they turn their nose up at it if they know it's been around for a while or if they heard it on the radio. (Rackus, 2010)

Straw makes reference to this short-term sensibility, suggesting that the 12-inch dance single 'is the most disposable and ephemeral of textual forms in that its value depends entirely on the emergence of consensus', and even if this consensus initially defines the track as of value, there can just as quickly be a change in opinion, so that the single becomes culturally worthless and obsolete, and is 'dumped on the market as one of the most genuinely abject forms of cultural refuse' (1993, p. 173). As such, 'the life cycle of dance records is notoriously short-lived, as deejays and club patrons tire of them and demand novelty' (Straw, 2001, p. 169). This is an issue highlighted by Thornton when she describes how 'dance sounds are distinguished by a quick turnover of records, styles and subgenres' (1995, p. 69), and by Hadley who refers to 'the speed with which songs come and go in club culture' (1993, p. 60). Thus, dance styles and individual tracks achieve both popularity and subsequent rejection with a typically urgent rapidity. Trent Rackus suggests this quick turnover of records is grounded in the desire of DJs to remain 'fresh' in the music they play, and in expressing this he references the idea that new dance music originates within the 'underground':[5]

---

[5] The wildly varying understandings and applications of the term 'underground' make it difficult to identify exactly what constitutes underground electronic dance music in Sydney (and indeed elsewhere). The term continues to be used by those within clubbing scenes as a specific point of reference and as a way of lending shape and definition to these scenes, Thornton highlighting how clubbers apply the term to denote that which is 'more than fashionable or trendy', with 'underground' sounds and styles being '"authentic" and pitted against the mass-produced and mass-consumed' (1995, p. 117).

In dance music there's always that underground root where everything is about being fresh …. People have the opportunity to stay completely fresh with their music, and if you are doing five or six gigs a weekend, that is an important thing, because while you're doing a dream job, you don't want it to get boring, you want to remain fresh …. DJs aren't as willing to continually look at the same records in their box. They have that opportunity to go out every week and hear new records from the four corners of the world … there's a constant turnover of new music, there's always new stuff. (Rackus, 2010)

This rapid turnover in dance music (which has no doubt increased with the impact of digital distribution and the ease with which DJs can now immediately access music from around the world) is perhaps grounded more in DJ practice rather than in anything related to clubbing audiences, for, as Rackus goes on to highlight, a DJ will grow tired of a particular track far more quickly than a clubber because of the requirements of the job:

[As a DJ] you might listen to a record two or three times before you buy it, and you might do five gigs in one night and play that record three times, and by the time you get to the last gig … give it three weeks and you're over the record, but in that three weeks, someone in the audience may have only heard that every week, three times, so that's when their familiarity comes into play, and then they want to hear it because they like it, but you've played it twelve times in three weeks and are completely over it. (Rackus, 2010)

Conclusion

During the ten years of my research, various clubs, events, DJs, promoters, record stores, media and music have come and gone. The continuous evolution of Sydney's dance music scene makes it a vibrant and engaging field of research. I have been able to witness the growing mainstream profile of dance music, club culture and DJing in Sydney and elsewhere in Australia, exemplified by the array of annual festivals that currently take place around the country. This profile shows no sign of slowing down, with the 2012 launch of the first Asia-Pacific Electronic Music Conference in Sydney, demonstrating the economic and industrial significance of the scene.[6] While the list of speakers at the conference represented a broad international field, the number of local participants was testament to the current commercial prominence of DJ culture in Sydney, a culture that is 'simultaneously, a specifically *Australian*, local formation, and … an integral part of a transnational, global formation' (Maxwell, 1994, p. 123; original italics). Despite the tensions and conflicts that exist in how local Sydney DJs negotiate work alongside their international counterparts and the global diffusion of dance music, their performances ultimately lend the Sydney scene its distinct local characteristics. As Will Straw notes, 'while music styles may be cosmopolitan and circulatory in character, musical events are still very tied to place' (in Janotti, 2012, p. 6).

The DJs in Sydney work within a scene that is constrained and limited by the comparatively small population and geographical isolation of the country. This not only affects regularity of work but also dictates that dance culture in the city itself, and in Australia as a whole, lacks the sophisticated industry infrastructure that has allowed scenes in Europe, especially in the UK, and the US to develop as key sites of development in dance music. As a consequence, electronic dance music culture has developed in Australia through a reliance on the music, DJs, media and fashions of overseas dance scenes. This development can be linked to the hegemonic position of the Anglo-American music industry and the transnational promotion of its products, and to the historical ties and consequent identification Australia has with the UK in terms of language and its political and cultural relations.

As dance music culture became a mainstream phenomenon, the concept of the superstar DJ brand (Herman, 2006, pp. 30–1) helped to position the DJ at the forefront of the culture, arguably having a direct impact on the Sydney scene, at the cost of the cultural role and significance of the local DJs. The city's clubbing crowds seem to permit international DJs a greater degree of freedom in music

---

[6] See http://www.electronicmusicconference.com [accessed 26 October 2012].

selection, and thus they can take risks by focusing more on new music than the locals may. International DJs become ascribed a certain educational value by clubbers in the Sydney scene, often at the expense of the local DJs who are subsequently given the role of entertainers rather than pioneers and promoters of new music. Yet to reduce the structure of DJ culture in Sydney to such a simple dichotomy dismisses the very diversity that gives shape to the city's dance scene. There are many distinct and divergent understandings of DJing work. The DJs that are addressed here demonstrate different interpretations of the issues that shape and define their job, depending on a number of factors, including the geographical location in which they are playing; the type of club at which they are playing; the type of crowd which they are playing to; the style of music they generally play; and their status and popularity within the scene in which they are playing.

Understanding the work of particular DJs in a particular scene helps to generate a more informed and detailed understanding of that scene. Through exploring the ways in which certain DJs in Sydney interpret their work, we can see how they interpret their role as a DJ within the city's dance scene, and the way they perceive and understand this scene. Some DJs see their work as part of the mainstream, and have no qualms about describing themselves as such, while other DJs are more dubious and critical of this mainstream, preferring to see their style of DJing as more 'underground', and, similarly to D'Andrea's study of underground dancers in Ibiza and Goa, seeing their mainstream counterparts as '"crowd pleasers" pushing formulaic tunes as a means of moneymaking' (2007, p. 101). With this comes a disparity in the understanding these DJs have of educating and entertaining their audiences. Thus it would seem that DJs who are comfortable working within the mainstream are also comfortable defining their role as 'entertainers'. Those DJs who see their work as taking place outside of the mainstream identify more readily with their role as 'educators'. However, again such a binary fails to acknowledge the degree of crossover that occurs in all levels of professional DJing. A DJ who plays in 'mainstream' clubs can still incorporate a degree of education into their sets, and a DJ who plays at venues deemed as 'underground' still has to ensure they hold the attention of their audience through playing accessible music.

The Sydney scene, and indeed Australian dance culture as a whole, has long struggled with its apparent secondary position to the dance scenes of the UK, the US and Europe, in part a result of its historical (sub)cultural links to the UK; the reliance on imported vinyl; and, like many countries with relatively small populations, the dependence on an Anglo-American dance music industry infrastructure. Dance music and DJs from outside of the country still exert a certain influence over the Sydney scene, yet rather than impose on the scene a sense that it suffers from a degree of top-down cultural dominance and cultural imperialism, this influence would seem to be a component of the intrinsically global hegemonic structure of contemporary dance culture. It would be too narrow to argue that dance culture is merely imported, without taking account of Sydney's specifically local scene development and music production. I therefore agree with Kong et al. who note that 'internationalising discourses do travel effectively, but are inflected by place-specific geographies' (2006, p. 181). Yet DJs with historically hegemonic international (sub)cultural capital still exert a significant influence over the Sydney scene, and will do so for as long as the scene's participants continue to associate the global diffusion of dance music with a hierarchy of place, ultimately lending credence to Appadurai's observation that 'the task of producing locality is increasingly a struggle' (1996, p. 189).

References

Appadurai, Arjun (1996) *Modernity at Large: Cultural Dimensions of Globalization*. Minneapolis, MN: University of Minnesota Press.

Brennan-Horley, Chris (2007) 'Work and Play: Vagaries Surrounding Contemporary Cultural Production in Sydney's Dance Music Culture'. *Media International Australia*, 123: 123–37.

Brookman, Chris (2001) 'Forever Young: Consumption and Evolving Neo-tribes in the Sydney Rave Scene'. BSc Thesis, Geosciences, University of Sydney.

Chan, Sebastian (1999) 'Bubbling Acid: Sydney's Techno Underground'. In Rob White (ed.) *Australian Youth Subcultures* (65–73). Hobart: ACYS.

Connell, John and Gibson, Chris (2003) *Sound Tracks: Popular Music, Identity and Place*. London: Routledge.

D'Andrea, Anthony (2007) *Global Nomads: Techno and New Age as Transnational Countercultures in Ibiza and Goa*. London: Routledge.

Florida, Richard and Jackson, Scott (2010) 'Sonic City: The Evolving Economic Geography of the Music Industry'. *Journal of Planning Education and Research*, 29(3): 310–21.

Gibson, Chris (1999) 'Subversive Sites: Rave Culture, Spatial Politics and the Internet in Sydney, Australia'. *Area*, 31(1): 19–33.

Gibson, Chris and McGregor, Andrew (2011) 'The Shifting Spaces and Practices of Dance Music DJs in Dunedin'. In Tony Mitchell and Glenda Keam (eds) *Home, Land and Sea: Situating Music in Aotearoa New Zealand* (206–15). Rosedale, Auckland: Pearson Education.

Gibson, Chris and Pagan, Rebecca (2003) 'Rave Culture in Sydney, Australia: Mapping Youth Spaces in Media Discourse'. *Youth Sound Space* (manuscript repository). http://www.snarl.org/youth/chrispagan2.pdf [accessed 30 November 2012].

Hadley, Daniel (1993) ' "Ride the Rhythm": Two Approaches to DJ Practice'. *Journal of Popular Music Studies*, 5(1): 58–67.

Herman, Bill D. (2006) 'Scratching Out Authorship: Representations of the Electronic Music DJ at the Turn of the 21st Century'. *Popular Communication*, 4(1): 21–38.

Hesmondhalgh, David (1998) 'The British Dance Music Industry: A Case Study of Independent Cultural Production'. *British Journal of Sociology*, 49(2): 234–51.

Ho, Wai-Chung (2003) 'Between Globalisation and Localisation: A Study of Hong Kong Popular Music'. *Popular Music*, 22(2): 143–57.

Howe, Dave Ruby (2012a) 'The New Breed: 20 Local Producers You Need To Hear'. *Inthemix*, 28 May. http://www.inthemix.com.au/gallery/snap/36654/The_New_Breed_20_Local_Producers_You_Need_To_Hear [accessed 13 March 2013].

—(2012b) 'ITM's Local Producers You Need To Hear: The Sequel'. *Inthemix*, 27 June. http://www.inthemix.com.au/features/53207/ITMs_Local_Producers_You_Need_To_Hear_The_Sequel [accessed 22 March 2013].

Janotti Jr, Jeder (2012) 'Interview – Will Straw and the Importance of Music Scenes in Music and Communication Studies'. *E-Compós*, 15(2): 1–9.

Kong, Lily, Gibson, Chris, Khoo, Louisa-May and Semple, Anne-Louise (2006) 'Knowledges of the Creative Economy: Towards a Relational Geography of Diffusion and Adaptation in Asia'. *Asia Pacific Viewpoint*, 47(2): 173–94.

Lau, Stella Sai-Chun (2012) *Popular Music in Evangelical Youth Culture.* London: Routledge.

Lawrence, Tim (2008) 'Disco Madness: Walter Gibbons and the Legacy of Turntablism and Remixology'. *Journal of Popular Music Studies,* 20(3): 276–329.

Luckman, Susan (2001) 'What Are They Raving On About'? *Perfect Beat,* 5(2): 49–68.

—(2002) 'Party People: Mapping Contemporary Dance Music Cultures in Australia'. PhD thesis, University of Queensland, Australia.

Maxwell, Ian (1994) 'True to the Music: Authenticity, Articulation and Authorship in Sydney Hip Hop Culture'. *Social Semiotics,* 4(1–2): 117–37.

McCutcheon, Mark A. (2007) 'Techno, *Frakenstein* and Copyright'. *Popular Music,* 26(2): 259–80.

Murphie, Andrew and Scheer, Edward (1992) 'Dance Parties: Capital, Culture and Simulation'. In Philip Hayward (ed.) *From Pop to Punk to Postmodernism* (172–84). Sydney: Allen & Unwin.

Negus, Keith (1996) *Popular Music in Theory: An Introduction.* Cambridge: Polity Press.

Park, Michael and Northwood, Gareth (1996) 'Australian Dance Culture'. *Youth Sound Space* (manuscript repository). http://www.snarl.org/texts/features/dancecult2.htm [accessed 30 November 2012].

Reitsamer, Rosa (2011) 'The DIY Careers of Techno and Drum 'n' Bass DJs in Vienna'. *Dancecult: Journal of Electronic Dance Music Culture,* 3(1): 28–43.

Rietveld, Hillegonda C. (2011) 'Disco's Revenge: House Music's Nomadic Memory'. *Dancecult: Journal of Electronic Dance Music Culture,* 2(1): 4–23.

St John, Graham (2009) *Technomad: Global Raving Countercultures.* Equinox: London.

Straw, Will (1988) 'Music Video in its Contexts: Popular Music and Post-modernism in the 1980s'. *Popular Music,* 7(3): 247–66.

—(1993) 'The Booth, the Floor and the Wall: Dance Music and the Fear of Falling'. *Public,* 8: 169–82.

—(2001) 'Dance Music'. In Simon Frith, Will Straw and John Street (eds) *The Cambridge Companion to Pop and Rock* (158–75). Cambridge: Cambridge University Press.

Thornton, Sarah (1995) *Club Cultures: Music, Media and Subcultural Capital.* Cambridge: Polity.

Watson, Allan (2008) 'Global Music City: Knowledge and Geographical Proximity in London's Recorded Music Industry'. *Area,* 40(1): 12–23.

Weber, Timothy (1999) 'Raving in Toronto: Peace, Love, Unity and Respect in Transition'. *Journal of Youth Studies,* 2(3): 317–36.

Interviews

Devecchis, John (2004) Interviewed by Ed Montano, Sydney, 24
    September.
Goodwill (2004) Interviewed by Ed Montano, Sydney, 8 September.
Nyk, Nat (2005) Interviewed by Ed Montano, Sydney, 27 September.
Rackus, Trent (2010) Interviewed by Ed Montano, Sydney, 30
    November.
Sharma, Sonia (2005) Interviewed by Ed Montano, Sydney, 4 October.
Thompson, Alan (2005) Interviewed by Ed Montano, Sydney, 23 June.

CHAPTER NINE

DJs and the Aesthetic of Acceleration in Drum 'n' Bass

Chris Christodoulou

All musical tastes are catered for, with quick blasts from the hardest to the most liquid of styles! (Anonymous, sleeve-notes to *Fast Lane Mixed by Shy FX*, 2004)

This chapter will examine the development of drum 'n' bass and jungle as outcomes of the articulation of speed in specific DJ practices. Drum 'n' bass is an electronic dance music genre with tempos typically between 160 BPM to 180 BPM. Structurally based on short, digitally sampled breakbeats from soul and funk recordings from the 1960s and 1970s, and accelerated with the use of digital production techniques, drum 'n' bass tempos are significantly faster than the original drumming performances from which such 'breaks' are derived. Drum 'n' bass is also considerably faster than a healthy human heart at rest, beating at around 70 BPM, and even during moderate exercise, when it beats around 125 BPM (Bianco, 2007). The names of jungle and drum 'n' bass clubs and parties, such as Accelerated Culture, Set Speed and Tempo Tantrum, illustrate the importance of speed to the wider culture and discursive framework of dance events related to these electronic dance music genres (see Figures 9.1 and 9.2).[1]

Furthermore, the chapter will analyse how interactions between DJs, MCs and dancers serve to articulate clubs and raves as sites of creative performance. To this end, the genre's development will be traced through a focus on cultural participation. To investigate how speed is articulated at social dance events, performative strategies that are deployed to inscribe speed as a naturalized, ever-present experience for drum 'n' bass participants are addressed, forming the basis for the argument that such a sense of speed provides an important impulse for ritualized social interaction. Virilio's concept of dromology, which highlights the cultural impact of the increasing speed of physical and virtual communications, will be used to link this ritualization of speed to the overwhelming social and technological shifts that have occurred globally in recent decades. As a global city, London is a key site to address this issue, which has been uniquely achieved the localized formation of drum 'n' bass during the mid-1990s.

Drum 'n' Bass: Culture of Speed

In the summer of 2004, around 40 drum 'n' bass DJs and musicians gathered in London, to discuss among other issues a sense that the music's rapid tempos were bringing about a range of unwelcome aesthetic and behavioral effects among its dancefloor audiences. DJ and producer Jumping Jack Frost – one of the genre's earliest exponents – recalls that,

> It was supposed to be about the state of the scene as a whole, dealing with some issues that people were bringing up on the [internet] forums. It ended up being mainly about whether the music was getting too fast ... [Drum 'n' bass] has always been quite intense music, but the feeling was that this was affecting attitudes [on the dancefloor] ... making people violent and

---

[1] I mainly use the term 'drum 'n' bass' rather than 'jungle' – which preceded drum 'n' bass – because 'drum 'n' bass' is more frequently used by participants at the time of writing.

Figure 9.1. Promotional flyer for Set Speed, Peckham, South London.
Photo by James Burns; used with permission.

aggressive. Nowadays, some [DJ] sets force you to drink five
Red Bulls before you can dance to the music. (Jumping Jack
Frost, 2008)

Here, Jumping Jack Frost outlines three key points of discussion
that were raised at the meeting. The first point concerns the sense in

Figure 9.2. Promotional flyer for Tempo Tantrum, Brixton, South London.
Photo by James Burns; used with permission.

which acceleration seems to instigate undesirable aesthetic transformations. Participants often consider such acceleration in terms of rhythmic intricacy, where, at slower speeds, the complex patterns produced via the disassembling and reassembling of breakbeats may be processed and physically interpreted on the dancefloor with relative ease. Second, the apparent role of accelerated tempos in intensifying feelings of hostility and antagonism between dancefloor participants, whereby the acceleration of the music seems to generate an atmosphere that encourages anti-social behaviour and fighting among audiences at raves and dance clubs. The third point refers to the sense of unnatural speed produced by the music as dancers are forced to imbibe substances that increase the human heart rate, such as the caffeine-reinforced drink Red Bull.

The seemingly esoteric anxieties of a music subculture highlighted here also point to wider concerns regarding accelerated culture, which is addressed through Paul Virilio's emphasis on the significance of an encroaching regime of speed within capitalist modernity. For Virilio, acceleration constitutes a form of temporal manipulation, in which we are compelled to move at a fast pace for the purpose of economic circulation and facilitating obedience to the political state. *Dromology*, or the 'study and analysis of the impact of the increasing speed of transport and communications' (Redhead, 2004, p. 49), highlights the importance of speed in the stratification of political and economic power. Similarly, the terms *dromocracy* and *dromospheric* are introduced to emphasize changes in the perception of the world brought about by its apparent acceleration.

For Virilio (1986), *dromocracy* concerns the hierarchical structuring of society in relation to warfare and the electronic media. He explains that, etymologically, dromocracy is derived from the Greek word *dromos* (race track), a place of competition, speed and acceleration. Virilio's main argument is that the impulse to acquire speed – especially in the domains of war, transportations and communications – is entwined with cultural stratification. While provocative and broad in historical scope, Virilio's highly theoretical insights often lack concrete case studies that clearly illustrate how accelerated culture is manifested in everyday contexts, such as specific forms of leisure culture. Nevertheless, Virilio, in discussion with Sylvere Lotringer, importantly refers to music as an example of how 'real space' is replaced by 'real time' as distance

seems now less significant than the time it takes to reach a destination or goal: 'Real time reigns supreme. That's why music is the
art of reference, that is an art of time and acceleration. It's an art
of time and speed. It's even the first to have given form to speed.
It's not by chance that young people only have one art, and that's
music' (Virilio and Lotringer, 1997, p. 172). The intimacy that
Virilio highlights between music and youth culture is reinforced
by his view that 'music is more and more linked to technology',
and that, at least during the mid-1990s, the 'hottest music is
techno, industrial, synthesizing, etc.' (1997, p. 172). In this sense,
he uses electronic dance music to support his general thesis on
speed and culture. Furthermore, Virilio argues that the 'problem of
technology … is a question of rhythm', and that he is 'interested
in the proximity between speed and music'. Recognizing that there
exists a 'rhythmology for music – the whole history of instrumental
music', he also suggests that dance is an effective way to engage
directly with accelerated culture 'because, apart from musical
rhythm, there's no mediation, just the body' (1997, p. 172). Given
that Virilio has not pursued a more detailed examination of this
area, drum 'n' bass serves as a valuable site for investigating
the link between music and the cultural stratification of speed
in advanced capitalism, to which the electronic dance music DJ
producer offers a response.

   In addition, Virilio suggests that speed may be regarded as a
milieu, a *dromosphere*, both as an environment and a social force
that fundamentally transforms our behaviour and perception of
the world (Virilio, 1986, 1990; Virilio and Lotringer, 2002). In
this condition, where information is made immediately available
through instantaneous communications, a permanent 'state of
emergency' is created, in which, as was also observed on the drum
'n' bass dancefloor, speed is perceived as a type of violence: 'The
violence of speed has become both the violence and the law, the
word's destiny and its destination' (Virilio, 1986, p. 151). The idea
of speed as a milieu can be used as a starting point from which
to examine the development of drum 'n' bass within specific DJ
practices, in which speed-oriented performative strategies and
interactions with MCs and audiences have, arguably, served to
normalize the pathological effects of an accelerated culture. In the
discussion that follows, I will propose a *dromology* in which DJs
play the role of *tempo technicians*.

Tempo Technicians: DJs, Speed and Creative Performance

Drum 'n' bass music is typically performed by DJs at large-scale dance events, raves and at nightclubs located within or near metropolitan areas. A drum 'n' bass DJ performance – or 'DJ set' – lasts for around two hours; usually enough time to play approximately 30 tracks.[2] Two turntables and a mixing console, or their digital equivalents, are standard DJ tools. Using such creative technologies, the aesthetic development of drum 'n' bass in the early 1990s is intertwined with the ability of DJs to manipulate the tempos, or speeds, of music recordings. Turntables, such as the standard, but now discontinued, Technics SL–1200,[3] include a variable pitch controller, enabling the adjustment of the record's rotation speed. The 12-inch analogue[4] vinyl format seems to remain popular among drum 'n' bass DJs. The argument offered by DJs and dancers is that vinyl produces a 'warmer' sound in the lower bass frequency range when compared to digital formats such as CD and MP3. Another frequently made argument is that, despite the availability of 12-inch vinyl interface technology, such as Traktor Scratch, vinyl offers a closer sense of tactile manipulation than virtual DJ software, albeit within a relatively limited set of creative possibilities.

During the late 1980s, electronic dance music for and by DJs – specifically the house and techno genres – achieved considerable popularity with British crowds, first, for example, at Manchester's club the Haçienda or London club night Shoom and, from 1989, at large illegal rave parties held in disused warehouses and fields along the orbital route of the M25 and elsewhere in the UK

---

[2] In electronic dance music culture, the term 'track' refers to records that are largely instrumental, as opposed to songs in which lyrics are a strong feature.

[3] Various versions of Technics SL–1200 turntables were manufactured between 1972 and 2010 by Japanese company Matsushita Electric Industrial Co. Ltd, which was renamed Panasonic Corporation in 2008.

[4] In the context of electronic technologies that record and produce sound, Vincent (1999) defines 'analogue' as referring to the conversion of sound waves into electronic signals produced by variable physical quantites of voltage or spatial position; conversely, digital music technologies compress analogue sound waves into binary code of digits 0 and 1.

(Rietveld, 1998). Most of the earliest drum 'n' bass DJs such as Fabio, Grooverider and Jumping Jack Frost began their careers at such events by mixing house and techno tracks, alongside the distinctive beat patterns of American electro recordings, as favoured by hip-hop DJs and producers.

While the 4/4 beat of house and techno is often described as being based on a relentless 'four-to-the-floor' rhythm (Rietveld, 1998), hip-hop breakbeats are deconstructed, syncopated 4/4 rhythms, sampled from soul and funk recordings of the 1960s and 1970s (Butler, 2006). Technically, sampling is a process in which a continuous analogue audio signal is converted into digital information (samples), which can then be creatively manipulated by a music producer. Since the mid-1980s, samplers have been used to extend particular DJ practices, such as the use of recorded sound bites. Rhythmic breaks taken from recorded songs are an especially fruitful source of sampled material, and, once recorded into a sampler, such breakbeats can be looped to form long sequences. Samplers also enable the splicing of breaks into small components, which can be subsequently reconstructed into new patterns. An important example is the 'Amen' break, taken from a 1969

Figure 9.3. Jumping Jack Frost at Jungle Fever, with an illustration of Pan – the god of panic – in the background. London, May 2008. Photo by James Burns; used with permission.

Figure 9.4. Kenny Ken at Jungle All-Stars, London, September 2007. Photo by James Burns; used with permission.

recording by The Winstons, 'Amen Brother'. This B-side of 'Color Him Father' (1969) is a soul version of a gospel song and it is this version that was spliced by electro producer Kurtis Mantronik (of the group Mantronix) to form the basis of the driving beat of 'King of the Beats', a B-side track on the single 'Join Me Please ... (Home Boys – Make Some Noise)' (1988). During the early 1990s, DJs would accelerate versions of such breakbeats into techno and house music sets; a practice that is significant to the understanding of the formation of the rhythmic structures of the rave, jungle and, subsequently, drum 'n' bass genres.

Waugh (2000, p. 6) usefully distinguishes four-to-the-floor beats from breakbeats by arguing that 'a breakbeat is simply a rhythm, which is not in the four-to-the-floor mould'. For Waugh, breakbeats are often 'rhythmically complex', giving electronic dance music producers significant 'opportunities to create unique, exciting and individual patterns'. Although breakbeats foreground rhythm and syncopation over evenly divided beats, they nevertheless follow an overall 4/4 beat pattern; that is, a single 'break' will adhere to the regularity created by the bar structure of a four-quarter beat. In examining the rhythmic characteristics of different electronic dance music styles, Butler (2006, pp. 78–9) shows how the syncopated patterns of funk-oriented grooves differ from the metronomic on-the-beat kick and snare drum patterns of house and techno; 'breakbeat rhythms tend to de-emphasize strong beats, instead placing considerable stress on metrically weak locations'. From the listener's point of view, the effect produced by the emphasis on 'metrically weak locations' can be described as a sense that the beat is tripping over itself or that of missing a step on a flight of stairs. As such, a breakbeat could be mistaken as being a-rhythmic, since the listener must work to mentally fill-in the 'missing', unaccented, beats. Rather than lock into the dominant beat, the listener develops a shifting rhythmic perspective as a means of coping with the beats that seem to unfold around the main beat. Butler also argues that funk-oriented rhythms offer specific potential for expressive movement by dancers while helping to shape the participatory frameworks they inhabit in social dance spaces.

By mixing house and techno records with looped breakbeats, DJs were able to add rhythmic complexity to their performances. DJs Law and Jumping Jack Frost refer to a sense of 'funkiness' when they describe the seminal weekly night Rage, held at London club Heaven between 1990 and 1993: 'Around '90, Rage was one of the biggest [electronic dance music] clubs in London. Fabio and Grooverider would mix house and techno with these funky breaks. When [a break] came in, people would go crazy; screaming, climbing up the cage where the DJs were ... like it was a football match' (DJ Law, 2008). The funkiness alluded to here is more formally defined by Danielsen (2006, p. 71) in African-American funk music, as appearing 'when a layer of potential cross-rhythm is used to create small stretches in time that fall between a dominant basic pulse'. In other words, funkiness, which Danielsen identifies as being synonymous with syncopation, develops when strong 'off-beats' appear in between the main four quarter beats. Whereas house tracks largely emphasize the repetitive beat with regular kick drums, inducing what Rietveld describes as 'a sense of trance-like bliss' (1998, p. 148), breakbeats sampled from soul and funk records seem to push and pull at the dancers' sense of time by suggesting the development of new rhythmic lines. As such, their search for a regular basic pulse generates brief feelings of suspense, tension and even mild panic. The sense of panic brought about by the search for a steady beat within the syncopated rhythms derived from soul and funk is reinforced by the use of an image of Pan, the god of panic, as the insignia for the Jungle Fever rave organization (see Figure 9.3).[5] Such feelings are subsequently relieved as crowds learn to anticipate the unaccented beats due to the breakbeat's repetition at predictable points in the track's musical structure. In this context, the meaning of the word 'funk' seems to have returned, in a rhizomatic manner, to a previous meaning: in old English slang, it indicates distress, while 'funky' relates to a repulsive smell that, in jazz discourse, is transformed into its negative; a compliment that signifies the close subcultural knowledge and understanding of African-American dance music. Furthermore, the popularity of breakbeat-based house and techno tracks with London audiences seems to point to more general feelings of suspense, tension and panic, which, as Virilio (2005) argues, are produced by the density of metropolitan spaces and the rapidity of communications technologies. In the case of the London club Rage, the funkiness produced by looped breakbeats seemed to facilitate heightened levels of excitement, articulated in the 'crazy' actions – to quote DJ Law – of some of its participants. Thereby, dancing to music containing accelerated breakbeats arguably offers a means by which commonplace feelings of panic among Londoners can be temporarily managed and controlled.

During 1991, the feelings of speed produced by the use of accelerated breakbeats prompted crowds at Rage and other clubs and raves in London to yell 'Hardcore!' in a celebratory fashion (DJ Law, 2008). While rave DJ producers in the lowlands regions of Western Europe were helping to develop forms of hardcore electronic dance music that foregrounded metronomic kick drums, such as gabber-house (or 'gabba') from Rotterdam (Borthwick and Moy, 2004; Reynolds, 1998; Rietveld, 1998), the term 'hardcore' would also soon be used to define the breakbeat-based rave and techno records from the UK that the DJ sets of Fabio and Grooverider helped to inspire. In response to the demands by audiences for harder and faster rhythms, the sets of UK hardcore DJs would typically combine breakbeats, with original tempos of between 80 and 110

---

[5] In Greek mythology, Pan's angry shout after being disturbed from his afternoon naps inspired panic in distant places (*panikon deima*) (Littleton, 2005, pp. 1074–9). The musical significance of the use of Pan's image in the insignia for the Jungle Fever rave organization is supplemented by his reputation for being a lusty 'party animal' who played the rustic pan flute.

BPM, with house and techno records that are typically between 120 and 140 BPM. In the early 1990s, this was achieved by raising the pitch control of a Technics turntable containing the breakbeat-based record to a level on or near the highest +8 per cent setting, or by using the 45 RPM setting for music that was cut at 33 RPM, thereby speeding it up. Occasionally, hardcore DJs would modify their turntables to play faster than the +8 per cent limit imposed by the manufacturer. By removing the upper casing of the turntable, a blue variable transistor located on the main circuit board called 'Pot VR301' can be turned clockwise to its furthest point, allowing records to be played at speeds up to around 15 per cent faster than their originally intended rotations per minute.[6] Thereby, a breakbeat cut at 33 RPM could be played 53 per cent faster when the 45 RPM setting is combined with the modified 15 per cent pitch increase, resulting in 'chipmunk' vocals and vastly accelerated rhythms. The recontextualization of the performance technology of the turntable for the purpose of conveying feelings of speed on the dancefloor may hereby be understood as a type of *bricolage*, described by Hebdige (1979, p. 104) as the production of 'new meanings' via 'another range of commodities ... in a symbolic ensemble which serves to erase or subvert their original straight meanings'.

Formation of Drum 'n' Bass

In the later months of 1991, 'jungle techno' could be heard on the dancefloor alongside 'hardcore' at Rage to indicate the fast breakbeat-based techno, which formed the basis for the club's music policy.[7] By mid-1992, jungle techno superseded the hardcore tag as the name given to the breakbeat techno music that was mainly produced by rave DJs and producers from London, many of whom, such as Brixton-based Kenny Ken, included elements from genres associated with Jamaican soundsystem culture, specifically dub, dancehall (ragga) and reggae (see Figure 9.4). The tempos attained

---

[6] Besides invalidating the manufacturer guarantee, implementing this change makes it more difficult to accurately adjust the pitch control slider.

[7] The last Rage event at the Heaven club took place in April 1993.

by jungle techno tracks were reaching between 150 and 160 BPM, roughly double those of the Jamaican soundsystem-related forms, enabling the incorporation of powerful 'half-speed' dub-like bass-lines running at around 80 BPM, together with other idiosyncratic sounds and samples derived from Jamaican soundsystem culture, such as echoed guitar on the second and fourth beats in the bar, and MC *toasting* (MCing) typically characterized by Jamaican Patois.[8]

The first recording in the drum 'n' bass continuum to feature the word 'jungle' in its title was 'Jungle Techno' by Noise Factory, which was released on the Tottenham-based Ibiza label in October 1991. Each Ibiza record featured the word 'junglizm' on its inner sticker label, thereby giving the label a coherent sense of identity, while also serving as a memorable term for audiences to categorize similar music that was played at dance events such as Jungle Book and Jungle Fever. The increasing presence of black British audiences at early jungle clubs such as Sunday Roast at the SW1 Club in Vauxhall, South London, initiated a morphing of breakbeat hardcore from a style bought in considerable numbers by both rave audiences and the wider record-buying public in the UK, to a local scene focused on multi-ethnic, inner city London and the suburbs of south-east England.

By 1993, the genre name 'drum 'n' bass', which initially emerged as an alternative name for Jamaican instrumental dub tracks in the 1970s (Bradley, 2000), was increasingly used alongside 'jungle' to describe records that placed particular emphasis on the drum 'n' bass elements. While popular at clubs and raves in inner city raves in and around London, Bristol, and metropolitan regions of the Midlands, jungle initially found little support in the British mass media until 1995, when 'drum 'n' bass' emerged as the genre's main denominator (James, 1997). Although the terms continue to be interchanged, drum 'n' bass is preferred by some producers to jungle, and vice versa, presumably on the basis of the latter's ethno-centric connotations.

---

[8] In his study of reggae sound-systems in South London, Les Back (1988) designates the term 'Mic (microphone) Chanter' to the acronym 'MC', although 'Master of Ceremonies' is more widely applied to a performer who introduces or verbally directs other performers and the audience. In this regard, both definitions are applicable to the practices of the drum 'n' bass MC. 'MC' also functions as a verb, as in 'to perform as an MC'.

MCs and Dancefloor Activity

Durant (1984) argues that the practice of dancing articulates the workings of cultural discourse on the body and subjectivity:

> There is in the history of dancing an overlay of body and society emphatically contrary to conceptions of the body simply speaking itself in a natural expression (sic), which is prior to cultural constraints. As gesture and mobility, bodily movements are subject to socially and historically variant conventions and divisions, according to which terms of address and effect are established over and beyond physical resources and restrictions. (p. 95)

Durant suggests that while certain kinds of music may seem to facilitate body movements as instinctual responses, the participation and pleasure in action connected to dancing can articulate the conditions of power in and through which dance forms and practices develop. Thereby, the centrality of the dancefloor as a site for the construction of a *junglist* identity – permeated by an impulse to galvanize a sense of working-class consciousness in the rapidly changing social and material environments of inner city London – points to a desire to manage the perceived destructive aspects of accelerated culture through dance.

On the drum 'n' bass dancefloor, the desire to acquire a sense of control over one's accelerated social environment is signified by specific kinds of slow, controlled movements that seem to be in sharp contrast to the music's up-tempo rhythms. The majority of London's participants jab and parry with their arms as if shadow-boxing or performing the Chinese martial art form T'ai Chi. Latin-influenced drum 'n' bass is often played at the club Swerve, where some participants perform gestures reminiscent of Capoeira: an Afro-Brazilian martial art and dance form defined by graceful and disciplined bodily movements, usually taking the form of simulated combat between two people. The presence of Capoeira-style dancing at London drum 'n' bass clubs can be framed by Gilroy's view that the bodily discipline inspired by martial arts has shaped various forms of African-Caribbean-influenced music and cultural practice (2002, p. 309): 'In black cultures, the themes of bodily control and care emerge most strongly in relation to dance and the martial arts.' While distinct social and peer groups are identifiable on the dancefloor, most participants seem to avoid visual or physical contact, even couples. This apparent social and emotional disconnectedness is generally only broken during a moment of peak excitement, typically when the bass dramatically reappears at the end of a crescendo or after a relatively quiet moment in the music. One such moment at early to mid-1990s club night A.W.O.L. (A Way Of Life) is marked by MC GQ remarking 'Time to drop the bomb', after which dancers respond to the high volume 'bass-bomb' by bobbing and weaving as if evading an airborne attack while in a warzone. Combined with a non-stop drum 'n' bass soundtrack, spectacular light effects, and booming, bass-heavy soundsystem, such dancefloor movements suggest the creation of an attritional, speed-based milieu where the *dromosphere* seems to attack social and subjective structures, in which a sense of self seems to be constantly under threat of dissolution. Participants learn to show coolness under the pressure of explosive bass lines and rapid, machine gun-like breakbeats through bodily discipline and a calm demeanour. Complex rhythms are typically negotiated through an emphasis on every first and third beat in the bar, whereby dancers raise and dip their upper bodies in time with these downbeats. Pleasure is thereby achieved out of showing control in challenging and chaotic conditions. At the same time, the presence of powerful bass frequencies in this context of subjective and shared embattlement seems to generate a sense of re-embodiment via what Goodman calls the 'bass materialism' that can be found in music that is strongly influenced by Jamaican soundsystem culture and where a 'rearrangement of the senses' is an effect of the collective 'processing of vibration' on the dance-floor (2010, p. 28). The role of the drum 'n' bass DJ here is to provide a continuous soundscape that conveys a sense of the urban jungle as a battlefield of accelerated culture in which only the most competently adapted to the challenging conditions of life in a post-industrial inner city can survive.

According to Les Back, in the context of reggae sound-systems (1988, p. 142), an MC is a 'Master of Ceremonies' or 'Microphone Chanter' who 'is in contact with the crowd, not just introducing the music, but performing to and directing the dance'. Typically standing alongside the drum 'n' bass DJ, the MC resembles the second-in-command of a combat regiment by coordinating crowd behaviour as if instructing troops, pointing to a form of 'sonic warfare', Goodman's phrase for musical idioms which employ 'Jamaican pop musical concepts and methods as a prototype', and that 'operate using competitive sound clashing' (2010, p. 28). Drum 'n' bass MCs – who are often second- and third-generation descendants of West Indian families – use speech patterns associated with reggae soundsystem MCing in a rapid manner to both support the high tempos of the music and compete with other MCs. For example, almost every drum 'n' bass MC adopts a short chant that can be delivered spontaneously and repeated quickly. At A.W.O.L. MC Fearless would say, 'When I say "More", you say "Fire!"' Anticipating the audience's reply, 'Fire!', the DJ would reduce the volume of the record being played in order to emphasize the audience's collective response, which also includes members raising their cigarette lighters in the air – the 'fire' referred to being the lighter's flame. In addition, specific kinds of material experience are articulated through the tempo, pitch and tone of the MC's voice. Fast rhyming, turns-of-phrase, and verbal dexterity (displayed in the deployment of alliteration, onomatopoeia, the slurring and rolling of 'r's, the stuttering of consonants) articulate the value of speed and rhythm in a performative setting, while fragmentary allusions to particular events or forms of behaviour associated with urban everyday life convey the necessity of adaptability as a mode of survival in difficult cultural and material conditions. In this sense, the largely rhetorical flow of MC chat articulates one's ability to negotiate the sensory overload threatened by travelling 'in the fast lane' of urban life, which can be both thrilling and exhausting. The terms and phrases the MC employs, together the rapid verbal techniques used to deliver them, are distinctive features of situated activities in which articulations of social membership in drum 'n' bass culture are embedded.

Metropolitan Acceleration

The early popularity of hardcore rave DJ sets with urban and mainly working-class electronic dance music audiences in the UK led to the increased production of rave-oriented music that incorporated both four-to-the-floor beats and electro-style break-beats. By late 1992, particular hardcore rave DJ producers from London and other parts of southern England increasingly omitted the four-to-the-floor rhythm in favour of breakbeats that were accelerated to around 160 BPM. According to DJ Chef, from East London pirate radio station Kool FM, this preference for break-beats was shaped by a fondness for hip-hop, held by multiethnic rave audiences in London:

> More people who went to hardcore raves in places like Hackney and Tottenham were brought up on hip-hop, so the tunes that got the biggest reactions were the ones with the breaks in them. In the end, you got certain DJs who would just play the breakbeat tracks, and forget the house stuff completely. That didn't go down well at certain raves, but the London crowds wanted more of it. (DJ Chef, 2008)

The increasing absence of the four-to-the-floor rhythm at hardcore raves seemed to polarize UK rave audiences. While crowds in metro-politan regions of the Midlands and southern England favoured the accelerated funk, soul and hip-hop grooves of breakbeat hardcore, in the north of England and Scotland, the fast, yet bouncy on-the-beat rhythms of happy hardcore were generally preferred. This regional difference can be examined by linking Lefebvre's (2004) view that rhythm can be used as an analytical tool for examining the interaction of time and space in the city to a dromological analysis of drum 'n' bass. For Lefebvre, a 'rhythmanalyst' is 'capable of listening to a house, a street, a town, as one listens to a symphony, an opera' (2004, p. 87). Lefebvre's interest in correlating bodily rhythms, machine rhythms and urban spaces as a way of understanding social relationships can be applied to the inner city conditions that influenced the development of breakbeat hardcore and its offshoot, drum 'n' bass. This regional difference can be examined by linking Konečni's view that music listeners are 'engaged in a constant exchange with the social and non-social environment, of which the acoustic stimuli are a part' (1982, p. 501). Thereby, it becomes possible to link the preference for fast and rhythmically complex breakbeats among urban audiences to the desire to produce predictable cycles out of the feelings of speed and unpredictability linked to metropolitan life. Since the early 2000s, the rate of acceleration in drum 'n' bass has slowed, with most tracks containing tempos of around 170 BPM. However, framed by an extreme focus on speed as a medium or instrument of violence and aggression, drum 'n' bass-influenced hardcore dance music sub- and micro-genres formed in the early twenty-first century like breakcore and speedcore regularly attain speeds of between 250 and 300 BPM.

The role played by the rhythmic character of London and the musical rhythms and tempos of drum 'n' bass may be considered in light of research conducted by Richard Wiseman in collaboration with the British Council (2006). Wiseman timed the walking speeds of pedestrians to measure the pace of life in London and other cities around the world. The research concluded that urban life has accelerated by an average of 10 per cent since the early 1990s. Additionally, the research linked an increasing pace of life with the increasing pace of change in the physical and social environments of cities, highlighting transformations brought about by globalization and new information and communications technologies (ICTs). In this context, the development of drum 'n' bass may be closely linked to the development in the 1990s of what Castells calls a 'network society' (2000, p. 17) in which the increasing speed of communications is entwined with the growing importance of 'informationalism' as the main source of economic productivity. In turn, the role of London as a global nodal point for accelerated flows of commerce, information and migration, is arguably inscribed in the varying social and economic prospects of specific parts of the city during the period in which the shift to the network society has occurred. In addition, Kevin Robins and Frank Webster argue that a transition to fragmented post-Fordist production practices, have been brought about by 'global expansion and integration of economic and financial activities … greater penetration of market relationships into everyday life, increased flexibility of production and consumption, changed work patterns, as well as an acceleration of the pace of change itself' (1999, p. 169). Such arguments illustrate the shift from an industrial society – based on economic productivity within relatively stable social and employment structures – to a society that has become dependent on informational speed.

The development of new DJ mix practices attests to the continuing relationship between the creative formation of drum 'n' bass and the cultural prevalence of informational speed in a metropolitan context. One such practice is the 'double-drop', which involves maintaining a continuous mix between two different drum 'n' bass recordings in order for both to 'drop in' at the same time; that is, where the main climactic moments of each track – usually where bass-lines are re-introduced alongside the drums – are mixed to sound synchronously. In electronic dance music, beatmatching (the ability to perform a continuous mix where tracks with varying BPM rates are modified to play at the same tempo) is one of the key skills of an accomplished DJ. With the widespread use of virtual DJ software that can automatically detect and 'sync' track BPMs, the performance of double-drops has added another means by which a drum 'n' bass DJ can demonstrate skill via the ability to make creative decisions quickly and spontaneously. DJs who can perform double-drops using only CDs and vinyl records are given particular acclaim. Popularized in 2003 and 2004 by East London-based Andy C, the double-drop technique requires the DJ to have especially fast reactions in order to rapidly sync the tempo of a new record in his or her headphones before the drop occurs in the track that is already playing. For example, a DJ mix CD by Andy C, released by Resist in 2007 to commemorate ten years of the *Drum 'n' Bass Arena* website (www.breakbeat.co.uk), features 29 tracks in 63 minutes and 45 seconds. Played in their entirety, most drum 'n' bass tracks are between six and eight minutes long. However, only eight of the tracks in Andy C's set go unmixed for more than one minute. The double-drop mixing style is now widely practiced and highlights the continued significance of the drum 'n' bass DJ as a creative performer who actively restructures music recordings in a dromological context, where rapid reactions are celebrated.

In the *Here-and-Now*: Dancefloor Demographics and the 'Present-Time'

If it had a label on it, it would be 'London, UK'. It's the home of drum 'n' bass, no question. It feels like urban London life; the constant pressure; the constant rush, rush, rush. (Nicole 'Raggo Twin', 2008)

Inner city life ... Inner city pressure ... (Metalheadz, 'Inner City Life', 1994)

The desire for accelerated music may be understood in the context of the demographics of dance club and rave audiences in London during the early 1990s, at clubs that are seminal to drum 'n' bass, like Rage, Speed, Jungle Book, A.W.O.L., Sunday Roast and the long-running club night Jungle Fever (see Figure 9.5). A number of sociologists, such as Giddens (2006), Lockwood (1982) and Roberts (2001) address the decline of traditional working-class occupations in heavy industry and the rise of a new type of working class in these regions: routine non-manual jobs in the service sector, such as clerical and administrative work; skilled manual jobs or crafts which require apprenticeships or university qualifications; unskilled manual workers, such as security guards, cleaners and retail staff. These sociological accounts suggest that feelings of belonging to a distinct working-class community have changed considerably with the development of a post-industrial society. A key outcome of the acceleration of (change in) British culture in the 1990s was the transformation of the kinds of jobs undertaken by British working-class males from skilled and long-term manual work in heavy industry to less-secure jobs in the service sector where ICTs are an increasing feature (Castells, 2000). Thereby, the engagement with the technologized sound of acceleration is specifically pertinent for male participants in drum 'n' bass, whose experience of the acceleration of the pace of change in a post-industrial society especially unsettling. For example, Lockwood (1982) claims that the post-industrial working-class attitude to life is fatalistic; individuals often feel they can do little to change their everyday situations, and improvements in their circumstances are largely down to luck or fate. This attitude is summarized by everyday phrases like 'take life as it comes' and 'live for today because tomorrow may never come'.

For Londoners without sufficient cultural, social and economic capital in the fast-changing post-industrial contexts of the 1990s, familiarization with accelerated change through listening and dancing to drum 'n' bass is arguably a means of managing this bewildering experience. The combination of accelerated techno tracks with sampled breakbeats can facilitate a sense of getting 'up-to-speed' with rapid cultural transformations. The desire to

Figure 9.5. The entrance queue at Jungle Fever, London, May 2008.
Photo by James Burns; used with permission.

attain a condition of speed is thereby connected to a need or impulse to adapt to changes over which one has little or no control; a need that may be further frustrated by the absence of formal education or valuable employment opportunities. While speed is associated with a form of power that is based on the acquisition of mobility in both the social and spatial senses, the experience of slowness and inertia involve being immobilized into micro-territories and the limiting of life opportunities and career chances. As such, the desire for speed inscribed in, and embodied by, the music's accelerated breakbeats seems to develop out of a need to connect the breaks and ruptures of everyday life. In this context, the repetitive, cyclical, looped and accelerated breakbeats contained in drum 'n' bass tracks seem to articulate an attitude of living from day to day and in the here-and-now, rejecting long-term planning in favour of a frantic 'present-time orientation' (Lockwood, 1982, p. 363). An emphasis is thereby placed on immediate gratification so that pleasures of the moment are not sacrificed for uncertain future rewards. The frantic and rapid quality of drum 'n' bass breakbeats thereby befits the experience of London as a city of permanent and uncontrollable acceleration for many of its working-class inhabitants.

Conclusion

This chapter shows, through a rhythm-analytical model, how the preference for fast and rhythmically complex breakbeats among audiences in English towns and cities influenced the desire to produce predictable cycles and rhythms out of everyday experiences of speed, volatility and panic in a post-industrial context. In this way, a dromology of drum 'n' bass has been produced, examining ways in which experiences of speed framed the creative practices of this DJ-driven genre of electronic dance music during its formation in the early 1990s. The discussion showed how the use of accelerated breakbeats by DJ-producers occurred in response to club and rave audience demands for increased speed. These DJ-producers, who were mostly based in London, played a crucial role in developing drum 'n' bass music by manipulating and modifying record turntables to accelerate the breakbeats that were originally sampled from hip-hop recordings. Accelerating breakbeat rhythms that were initially sampled by electro DJ-producers from 1960s and 1970s African-American soul and funk records attests to the speed-centred logic or impulse of early drum 'n' bass DJ practices and accentuated the quality of *funkiness*.

In brief, then, drum 'n' bass may be regarded as a response to sometimes bewildering social and technological shifts that have occurred during the last few decades, blended through the specific ethnic and class-based demographic mix of London. While tempos of drum 'n' bass tracks have steadied since the early 2000s, indicating a stabilization of the initial shock produced by the UK's transformation into a post-industrial society, the continued emphasis on DJs as creative producers in the genre suggests that DJs will continue to play a key role in shaping its aesthetics of acceleration.

References

Back, Les (1988) 'Coughing Up Fire: Sound-systems in South-east London'. *New Formations*, 5: 203–18.

Bianco, Ted (2007) 'The Beating Heart: Same Song, Different Rhythm'. In Julian Peto (ed.) *The Heart* (181–92). New Haven, CT and London: Yale University Press.

Borthwick, Stuart and Moy, Ron (2004) *Popular Music Genres: An Introduction.* Edinburgh: Edinburgh University Press.

Bradley, Lloyd (2000) *Bass Culture: When Reggae Was King.* London: Penguin.

Butler, Mark J. (2006) *Unlocking the Groove: Rhythm, Meter, and Musical Design in Electronic Dance Music.* Bloomington, IN: Indiana University Press.

Castells, Manuel (2000) *The Rise of the Network Society: The Information Age; Economy, Society, and Culture.* Oxford: Blackwell.

Danielsen, Anne (2006) *Presence and Pleasure: The Funk Grooves of James Brown and Parliament.* Middletown, CT: Wesleyan University Press.

Durant, Alan (1984) *Conditions of Music.* London: Macmillan.

Giddens, Anthony (2006) *Sociology.* Cambridge: Polity.

Gilroy, Paul (2002) *There Ain't No Black in the Union Jack.* London: Routledge.

Goodman, Steve (2010) *Sonic Warfare: Sound, Affect, and the Ecology of Fear.* Cambridge, MA: Massachusetts Institute of Technology Press.

Hebdige, Dick (1979) *Subculture: The Meaning of Style.* London: Routledge.

James, Martin (1997) *State of Bass: Jungle, the Story So Far.* Basingstoke: Boxtree.

Konečni, Vladimir J. (1982), 'Social Interaction and Musical Preference'. In D. Deutsch (ed.) *The Psychology of Music* (497–516). London: Academic Press.

Lefebvre, Henri (2004) *Rhythmanalysis: Space, Time, and Everyday Life,* trans. Stuart Elden and Gerald Moore. London: Continuum.

Littleton, C. Scott (2005) *Gods, Goddesses and Mythology.* New York: Marshall Cavendish.

Lockwood, David (1982) 'Sources of Variation in Working-class Images of Society'. In Anthony Giddens and David Held (eds) *Classes, Power, and Conflict: Classical and Contemporary Debates* (359–72). London: Macmillan.

Reynolds, Simon (1998) *Energy Flash: A Journey Through Rave Music and Dance Culture.* London: Picador.

Rietveld, Hillegonda C. (1998) *This is Our House: House Music, Cultural Spaces and Technologies.* Aldershot: Ashgate.

Roberts, Ken (2001) *Class in Modern Britain.* Palgrave: Basingstoke.

Robins, Kevin and Webster, Frank (1999) *Times of the Technoculture: From the Information Age to the Virtual Life.* London: Routledge.

Virilio, Paul (1986) *Speed and Politics.* New York: Semiotext(e).

—(1990) *Popular Defense and Ecological Struggles.* New York: Semiotext(e).

—(1999) *Negative Horizon*. London: Continuum.
—(2005) *City of Panic*. Oxford: Berg.
Virilio, Paul and Lotringer, Sylvere (1997) *Pure War*. New York: Semiotext(e).
—(2002a) *Crepuscular Dawn*. New York: Semiotext(e).
—(2002b) *The Accident of Art*. New York: Semiotext(e).
Vincent, Robin (1999) *PC Music*. London: PC Publishing.
Wiseman, Richard (2006) *Pace of Life Project*. http://www.richardwiseman.com/quirkology/pace_home.htm [accessed 5 August 2012].
Waugh, Ian (2000) *Quick Guide to Dance Music*. London: PC Publishing.

Interviews

DJ Chef (2008) Interviewed by Chris Christodoulou, Shoreditch, East London, 21 April.
DJ Law (2008) Interviewed by Chris Christodoulou, Tooting, South London, 16 May.
Jumping Jack Frost (2008) Interviewed by Chris Christodoulou, Tooting, South London, 16 May.
Nicole 'Raggo Twin' (2008) Interviewed by Chris Christodoulou, Tooting, South London, 16 May.

Discography

Andy C and Grooverider. (2007), *Drum & Bass Arena*, Resist Music: United Kingdom, [RESISTCD87 / CD].
Goldie presents Metalheadz (1994) 'Inner City' Life. FFRR Records: United Kingdom, [FX 251 / 12"].
Mantronix (1988) 'Join Me Please … (Home Boys – Make Some Noise)'. Capitol: United States, [V–15386 / 12"].
Noise Factory (1991) 'Jungle Techno'. Ibiza Records: United Kingdom, [IR008 / 12"].
The Winstons (1969) *Color Him Father / Amen, Brother*. Metromedia: United States, [MMS–117 / 7"].
Various (2004), *Fast Lane Mixed by Shy FX*. Trouble on Vinyl: United Kingdom, [TOVLP05CD / CD].

CHAPTER TEN

The Forging of a White Gay Aesthetic at the Saint, 1980–4

Tim Lawrence[1]

Attracting an affluent white gay crowd of 4,000-plus on peak nights, the Saint was probably the most prolific employer of DJs in New York City between 1980 and 1988, when it closed before opening for a much briefer run. Only the Paradise Garage, another private party that pulled in a predominantly ethnic gay crowd of 3,000-plus on peak weekend nights, rivalled the reach of the Saint during its 1977–87 run. Yet whereas historians of dance culture have hailed the Garage's Larry Levan to be the most influential DJ in the city during the 1980s, the shifting roster of selectors who worked at the Saint have merited barely a single mention – an unlikely scenario given that privileged white groups often receive more attention than disadvantaged subaltern groups.[2] Based on

---

[1] This chapter was previously published as 'The Forging of a White Gay Aesthetic at the Saint, 1980–84'; see Lawrence (2011).

[2] See Bill Brewster and Frank Broughton (1999), Fiona Buckland (2002), Matthew Collin with John Godfrey (1997), Kai Fikentscher (2000), Sheryl Garratt (1998), Ulf Postchardt (1998), Simon Reynolds (1998) and Peter Shapiro (2005). Brewster and Broughton, Buckland and Shapiro devote some space to the Saint, but restrict their account of the DJs to a paragraph at most. The historians of US gay culture, Clendinen and Nagourney (1999), provide a rare reference to the Saint (1999,

numerous interviews with key protagonists, documentary material held in the Saint's archive, and recordings of DJ sets from the Saint, this article will redress the imbalance by outlining the contributions of Jim Burgess, Alan Dodd and Roy Thode, the Saint's principle DJs during the opening 1980–1 season, as well as Shaun Buchanan, George Cadenas, Michael Fierman, Michael Jorba, Robbie Leslie, Howard Merritt, Chuck Parsons, Terry Sherman and Sharon White, who appeared regularly in subsequent seasons.[3] Thanks to their numerousness, none could come close to controlling the turntables at the Saint as the singular Levan did at the Garage, but their collective impact was considerable, even if their very collectivity also meant that each was ultimately disposable.

This chapter positions the Saint DJs not as isolated artists who developed their style in privacy before performing in front of a crowd, but instead as mediators of a taste culture who combined an expertise in music with a recognition of the need to satisfy the often complex and potentially contradictory desires of the Saint crowd. If that need ran through 1970s dance culture in general, and has also defined many subsequent scenes, it took on a particularly acute character at the Saint, where a significant number of dancers came to express their opinions with unusual force thanks to the rise of an individualized consumer-is-right mentality that accompanied the high cost of entry, as well as the enormous value

pp. 446–7) yet focus on the club's infrastructure and membership regulations. Charles Kaiser (1997, p. 283) references the Saint (but not its DJs) in passing. I chart Larry Levan's playing career in detail in my first monograph, *Love Saves the Day: A History of American Dance Music Culture, 1970–79* (Lawrence, 2003). I pick up the story in my third monograph, which is provisionally titled *Life and Death on the New York Dance Floor, 1980–83* (Lawrence, forthcoming). See also Mel Cheren's (2000) *Keep On Dancin': My Life and the Paradise Garage* for a personal recollection of Levan's life.

[3] Although not all are quoted directly, I am grateful to Brian Chin, Michael Fesco, John Giove, Stuart Lee, Jorge La Torre, Robbie Leslie, Howard Merritt, Mann Parrish, Terry Sherman, Marsha Stern and Sharon White for agreeing to be interviewed, some of them several times over. I'd also like to thank Stephen Pevner of the Saint-at-Large for providing access to the Saint archive's collection of posters, DJ schedules, in-house journals and digital files of DJ sets by Shaun Buchanan, Jim Burgess, Robbie Leslie, Howard Merritt, Terry Sherman and Roy Thode, which informed much of this article. I'm also grateful to Marsha Stern for providing additional recordings of Roy Thode's DJ sets, and to Conor Lynch for providing additional information on his own collection of recorded DJ sets from the Saint.

a certain cadre of gay men started to place on the enjoyability of their Saturday night. Convinced of the superiority of their own taste, these dancers practised a form of critical connoisseurship that strengthened their own elite status while establishing distance between the Saint and parallel scenes that were framed as being less discerning. In particular, dissatisfied dancers started to write letters of complaint to the management, and in so doing reframed the dancer as an individual consumer rather than a participant in a collective practice. Pressured by the management, the venue's DJs were compelled to respond, often by selecting more conservative records, and in an ironic twist the Saint began to relinquish its cutting-edge cachet as a result.

Paying attention to the historical juncture, which witnessed the emergence of neoliberal economics, the intensification of identity politics and the onset of the AIDS epidemic, the article also traces the various ways the Saint DJs sought to please the crowd, as well as the related circumstances that led to the emergence and entrenchment of a white gay male aesthetic during the first four seasons of the venue's run. The chapter also notes that although Saint DJs were nearly unanimous in their rejection of house music across the 1985–8 period, they helped pioneer an aesthetic that emphasized smooth blending and the matching of texturally similar tracks across an extended period of time, and therefore anticipated the sensibility that would later inform a significant proportion of DJ mixing in clubs that supported EDM. Indeed once they acclimatized to the rougher, harder textures of early house, ex-Saint dancers were able to make a smooth transition to the Sound Factory, where Junior Vasquez, who declared Levan to be his primary influence, developed a trance-oriented repetitive style from 1989 onwards.

Opened by theatre designer and St Mark's Baths owner Bruce Mailman at 150 Second Avenue on the site of the old Fillmore East, the Saint surpassed the architectural ambitions of private party venues that had attracted a near-homogeneous white gay crowd. Whereas the Tenth Floor and Flamingo added minimal design touches to the ex-industrial buildings in which they were located, the Saint's architectural aesthetic was rigorously futuristic and featured a hi-tech electronic coat-check system, while the interior of the downstairs lounge area and the stairs that led up to the dance-floor and the third-floor balcony area were built out of concrete and steel. Lacking angles, the circular floor encouraged dancers to lose their bearings and open themselves to the unfamiliar. Above, a vast planetarium hood dominated the venue's stunning infrastructure, with the lighting operator able to draw on a vast array of effects that could transport dancers into different virtual environments.

Although the Saint was located in the heart of the multicul-tural East Village, the vast majority of its members were white, gay men who were comparatively well-off, which they had to be, because members paid $125 for their cards and then $10 per party, while guests had to be invited by a member and pay $18 per party.[4] The nucleus of the group formed first on Fire Island when revellers congregated at the Sandpiper, a discotheque located in the upmarket Pines, and they reconvened in Manhattan at the Tenth Floor, where the limited capacity led members to refer to themselves as 'the 500', or the 500 most desirable (creative, stylish, attractive, successful, etc.) gay men in New York. After the sheer stress of managing the door contributed to the closure of the Tenth Floor, the growing contingent switched its allegiance to Michael Fesco's Flamingo, where they came to number more than a thousand and began to refer to themselves as 'the A-list'. Mailman then courted the group in the summer of 1980, and closed his membership list of 2,000 before opening night on 20 September. Flamingo regulars would recount that they had no choice but to switches allegiances when the new venue rose like a mirage.

The crowd might have been as racially homogeneous as any in New York. 'The Saint was 95 per cent white gay men', notes Sharon White, a DJ at the Pavilion on Fire Island as well as the Saint, and one of the tiny number of female members. 'Everything else fell into the remaining 5 per cent, whether it be women, blacks or Latinos.' The absence of black, Latin and Asian men was in fact less pronounced than it had been at the Tenth Floor and Flamingo. Sherman, who struck up a strong friendship with Mailman, notes that a black friend of his called Duane was 'one of Bruce's regular dancing partners', and adds that he had three black boyfriends during the period, and all of them would head to the Saint, irrespective of whether he was DJing that night or not. 'It was a

---

[4] According to InflationData.com, inflation from October 1980 to October 2010 totals 157.91 per cent, so the $125 membership would rise to $322.38, the $10 entry for members would rise to $25.79, and the $18 charge for non-members would rise to $46.42.

bigger club, so there was more room, so of course you saw more blacks', says the Peruvian-born Jorge La Torre, a regular at the Tenth Floor and Flamingo before he defected to the Saint. 'I think black men also felt more welcome, and you began to see white men with black lovers. But if you saw a handful of black people that was a lot' (2009).

If the low turnout indicates that many black men still didn't feel welcome, it remained the case that to a significant extent the Saint and the Garage subdivided according to a combination of sexual attraction and musical preference (with black and Latino gay men heading to the Garage if their sexual preference was for black and Latino men, etc.). Moreover, the hierarchies that kept poorer black and Latino dancers out of the Saint can in part be attributed to what Sherman (2009) calls 'societal racism', and not Mailman's need to introduce a business model that would enable him to repay the approximate $3–6 million cost of opening the venue.[5] 'Should Bruce have initiated an affirmative action policy like "White Males $10, African-Americans Free" and put on chartered buses from 125th Street, Bed Stuy [Bedford-Stuyvesant, Brooklyn] and the Bronx to the Lower East Side?' asks Sherman. 'Maybe. But Bruce didn't care who came and there was no racial profiling [or membership policy that excluded black and Latino men] specific to the Saint.'

There was, however, sex profiling, with women excluded on the grounds that they would compromise the gay male dance ritual if they were allowed to occupy anything more than the very outer margins of the venue. According to Leslie (2008), who previously DJed at 12 West, a comparatively mixed gay private party, located underneath Westbound Highway on West 12th Street, the policy grew out of Mailman's belief that 'gay men danced well together' and that women would disrupt this collective energy because they used their bodies differently. In contrast to the plurality of expressive styles that could be witnessed at the Loft and the Paradise Garage, the resulting dance dynamic forged a form of locked-in conformity that evokes Walter Hughes' description of the depersonalized white gay disco dancer as 'becoming an extension of the machine that generates the beat' (Hughes, 1994, p. 151).

[5] A range of figures are quoted in Claudia Cohen and Cyndi Stivers (1980), Nathan Fain (1980) and Jan Hodenfield (1980).

'The Saint seemed almost synchronized', comments La Torre. 'If someone was doing a certain move, the others would start to follow. They would go along with whatever it was that was going on' (La Torre, 2009). Creating an interconnected, amoeba-like organism that mutated in barely perceptible ways, dancers moved within constrictions set not only by the disciplinary injunctions of the beat, as suggested by Hughes, but also within a general social code that discouraged men who came from a white, Anglo-Saxon, Protestant background from expressing themselves physically, irrespective of their sexuality. Added to that, Saint dancers also contended with a more specific macho code that gained currency in New York in the late 1970s that led gay men to rein in the way they would use their bodies. 'The goal was the moment of unity, the moment when everything disappeared, when time and space disappeared', explains La Torre (2009), who would also head to the Garage on a fairly regular basis, and notes that dancers there were significantly more expressive. 'It was just pure energy. It was extremely welcoming, and extremely powerful. Within it everything seemed possible.'[6]

Whereas David Mancuso was inseparable from the Loft because the party was situated in his own home, and Larry Levan was all but inextricably tied to the Paradise Garage because Michael Brody built the venue around his appeal, Mailman insured that no single DJ figure (or musical host, as Mancuso preferred to think of himself) become so heavily identified with the Saint. Mailman recognized that the affectively and emotionally charged environment of the dancefloor could encourage DJs to behave temperamentally, and concluded that it made better business sense for him to encourage his dancers to form an attachment to the venue rather than any single DJ. As a result, he introduced a revolving roster of DJs from the outset, and established a broader framework that positioned DJs as hired entertainers whose primary function was to serve the community and the setting. The break with previous employment practice, in which DJs would seek out residencies where they would play on a regular basis until they fell out of favour with the dancers or the management, was marked, with Mailman instituting

---

[6] Although her focus isn't the dancefloor dynamic, Fiona Buckland (2002) provides a useful account of the Saint as a space of queer affirmation through an interview with a member called Tito.

a framework in which they could expect to play once or twice a month if they were lucky. As such, their status as freelancers was embedded ahead of the more general shift towards one-off, flexible contracts – a shift that would become one of the hallmarks of market-driven neoliberalism. 'After Flamingo closed things really changed', comments Merritt (2009), a Flamingo resident who went on to play regularly at the Saint. 'None of the big clubs had an in-house disc jockey. You had your calendar and you'd get called by the clubs, and gradually you would fill in the nights.'

If the development threatened to undermine the ability of the Saint roster to form a deep bond with the dancefloor, that possible consequence was countered by the fact that Mailman's DJs played 10-hour-plus sets that encouraged emotive ties to be formed. While Mailman also believed that the huge cost of his venture required him to institute a system that guaranteed his dancers wouldn't become bored by a single in-house DJ, he also drew regularly on a delineated pool of principal DJs, as well as a secondary pool of up-and-coming selectors to perform on weekdays and sometimes on Sundays, which were less busy. For their part, the DJs acquired the aura of orchestra conductors; their names would be advertised in advance, and it became established practice for a spinner to pause at around six o'clock in the morning, at the peak of the night, in order to receive applause from an audience that was largely familiar with the ovation rituals of New York's theatres and concert halls. After that, the DJ got to stretch out during an extended encore that would often last for four hours or more. Within the core group, a consensus emerged that the Saint wasn't necessarily the nicest or warmest environment in which they could work, but performing there nevertheless marked a career pinnacle, and also bestowed them with the kind of cachet that could lead to further job offers elsewhere.

Of the principal DJs who played the opening season – all three were members of Judy Weinstein's For the Record, the most prestigious record pool in the city – Dodd was the smoothest, and 'could play a whole night like glass', says Leslie (2008). For his part, Thode was a busier, trickier mixer who liked to cut back and forth between two back-beated copies of the same record to generate an echo effect, execute extended mixes using two separate recordings, introduce reverb effects, and so on. 'Roy could take a part and restructure it better than anyone', comments Marsha Stern (2008), a close friend of Thode's and one of the few women to hold a Saint membership card. 'We would tease him and say he was getting too knobby, but the rearranging was part of the art form. He had an innate sense of magic-making, and a real rapport with the crowd. People would come up to the booth and say, "It's just a wonderful party."' Burgess, a prolific studio hand who mixed records such as 'I Love the Nightlife (Disco 'Round)' by Alicia Bridges (1978), 'A Lover's Holiday' by Change (1980), 'Runaway Love' by Linda Clifford (1978), 'Secret Love Affair' by Madleen Kane (1979), 'The Beat Goes On and On' by Ripple (1977), and 'Da' Ya' Think I'm Sexy' by Rod Stewart (1980), was more mercurial than Dodd and Thode. 'Jim Burgess was probably the most talented mixologist', comments Leslie (2008). 'Sometimes he was on and sometimes not. But when he asserted himself nobody could touch him for technique.'

Signalling his retirement in advance, Burgess played his last party on 31 January 1981, yet instead of letting the night run its regular course, he walked out of the booth in high style at 6.00 a.m. with the crowd in a state of rapture and nowhere else to go. Near the booth at the time, White was called on to step in, and after grabbing some records from the on-site apartment of the principal lighting designer and operator Mark Ackerman, she approached the booth like a boxer moving through a parting crowd, and proceeded to rescue the party. Her performance vindicated the earlier decision of Ackerman (a close friend) to schedule her to play in March; Mailman had opposed the move, but backed down when Ackerman, a hugely influential figure, told him he would resign if he overruled the booking. Proud of her ability to play 'outside of the box', White joined a roster that included Leslie, a consummate professional and hugely popular figure whose style emphasized smoothness and tonality, as well as Parsons, who favoured a harder, faster aesthetic. 'Chuck [Parsons] was never a favourite with the crowd, but Bruce loved what he played and he got almost all of the big parties from 1982 to 1986', comments Sherman (2009). 'It also helped that he was a brilliant technician and almost never had a bad mix.'[7]

---

[7] Sherman notes that Parsons was regularly asked to play big parties including 'Opening Night', 'Halloween', 'New Year's Eve', the 'Black Party' and 'Closing Night'. Leslie was the regular DJ at the 'White Party'. A range of DJs would step in for 'Night People', 'Christmas', 'Land of Make Believe', 'Disco Day', 'Summer Opening', 'Summer Closing' and the Memorial Day party, which took on different titles.

All of the Saint DJs replicated an established arc that resembled the affective flows enjoyed in other clubs, yet was more precisely calibrated in terms of tempo and energy in Mailman's setting. Often beginning with an orchestral recording, which would enable them to 'tune' the room while making a statement about their sophistication and tastefulness, they would go on to play bright mid-tempo songs to invite people onto the floor and set a positive tone. From there the DJs would build to the peak period that ran between about 2.00 and 6.00 a.m., and involved them selecting higher-tempo tracks that scampered along at 125 BPM upwards. 'There would be a series of peaks', comments Fierman, who got his break through the Hot New Talent Night, which Mailman inaugurated on 12 May 1982, and went on to become one of the venue's most influential spinners. 'But you couldn't play 100 hits in a row, each one an increment better than the other, so to build the excitement one had to pull back to get to another peak' (Dupre, n.d.). At around 6.00 a.m., in a ritual that was not replicated in other venues, the DJ would let the final record of the peak set fade, accept the applause of the crowd, and acknowledge the work of the light person and the generosity of the crowd (if indeed the applause was enthusiastic, which wasn't always the case). After that, the DJ would take the tempo right down and play a set that was commonly referred to as 'sleaze' or 'morning music'.

More than other crowds, Saint dancers demanded that their DJs generate 'a very smooth flow' (in the words of Leslie, 2008) as well as turn to certain records during peak of the night. 'It's not like the DJs were clones of each other, but we were expected to play the things that were popular with the crowd at that particular moment', comments White. 'I used to say that we all played the same records, but in a different order.' While the taste of some Saint DJs might have coincided seamlessly with what the crowd wanted to hear, White maintains that the crowd's preference would take precedence when there was a discrepancy, and she felt compelled to play 'filler' tracks that were beyond her 'scope of appreciation' between the hours of 2.00 and 6.00 a.m. Evoked as being equal when Leslie (2008) talked about the existence of a 'third-person consciousness' in a 1983 interview (Park, 1983, p. 37), the dancing crowd was in fact more powerful than the DJ during the middle part of the night, after which the initiative reverted back to the DJ during the elongated 'sleaze' or 'morning' session, because the crowd had been satiated by then. 'You were expected to take a left turn because you'd given them all they expected', adds White (2009). 'We shined as individuals after 6.00 a.m. Before that, anybody could have been playing.'

Saint DJs also had to operate in the conditions that characterized the post-'disco sucks' era. As has been described in detail elsewhere, a combination of the overproduction of disco music in the aftermath of the success of *Saturday Night Fever* combined with the onset of a deep recession that enabled right-wingers to link the perceived decline of the United States with the advances made by the countercultural coalition of the late 1960s led to a homophobic, racist and sexist backlash against disco that positioned the culture as the overdetermined source of the crisis facing white straight men.[8] Felt most keenly in suburban areas and the boardrooms of major record companies, where executives were demographically inclined to favour rock above disco, the backlash resulted in the 'disco' nomenclature falling into disuse and the dramatic cutting back of production. But in urban centres such as New York and San Francisco public clubs and private parties continued to attract significant numbers of dancers, and this vibrant network provided independent record companies with a core market that was focused, enthusiastic and (as is often the case with dance crowds) hungry for innovation. Along with venues such as Bond's and Danceteria, the Saint opened shortly after the majors (with the partial exception of Warner Brothers) decided to withdraw from the disco market. As a result, its DJs turned with renewed interest to the release schedules of New York and San Francisco's independent sector, as well as the import recordings that could be found in specialist stores such as Vinyl Mania.

The Saint DJs played US synth pop tracks such as 'Gloria' by Laura Branigan (1982) and 'Stormy Weather' by Viola Wills (1982). They drew on the rich seam of high-energy music that was being released by West Coast labels such as Megatone and Moby Dick, many of them recorded by Sylvester with Patrick Cowley (1982) and the Weather Girls, with 'Do You Wanna Funk' and 'It's

---

[8] The most detailed analytical account of the 'disco sucks' movement can still be found in my own *Love Saves the Day*, especially pages 363–401. Published two years later, Shapiro (2005, pp. 226–32) also provides a substantial account of the moment in *Turn the Beat Around*.

Raining Men' two of the most popular. (At one point during 1982, Brian Chin [1982, p. 48], the dance columnist for *Billboard*, went so far as to wonder if Eurodisco had 'emigrated' to San Francisco.) They turned to up-tempo R&B-oriented tracks including Sharon Redd's 'Can You Handle It?' They looked towards Europe and Canada (where the backlash against disco was less severe) and integrated cuts from Abba's album *The Visitors* (1981) as well as recordings such as 'Hit 'N Run Lover' by Carol Jiani (1981), 'Step by Step' by Peter Griffin (1981), 'Feels Like I'm in Love' by Kelly Marie (1980), 'Don't Stop the Train' by Phyllis Nelson (1980), 'Hot Leather' by the Passengers (1979) and 'Hills of Katmandu' by Tantra (1979). Conscious that they were the progeny of the white gay DJs and dancers who helped popularize disco, they also continued to play a significant proportion of disco and late disco classics, including Cut Glass's 'Without Your Love' (1979), Jimmy Ruffin's 'Hold On to My Love' (1980), Marlena Shaw's 'Touch Me in the Morning' (1979) and Voyage's 'Souvenirs' (1983) among the most popular.

The mix grew out of the matrix of 1970s New York dance, which foregrounded sonically polycultural sounds, even in settings that were tightly defined demographically. That applied to the Tenth Floor, where the light-skinned black DJ Ray Yeates drew on cuts by outfits such as the Equals and the Staple Singers, and also Flamingo, where Michael Fesco employed the Puerto Rican Richie Rivera to offset Howard Merritt's sweeter, more melodic selections with rumbling rhythm sections, esoteric jazz progressions, and angular synthesizer workouts. At the Saint, White, along with Steve Williams, maintained an ethnic presence in the booth – they were joined by the alternate lighting operator Richard Tucker, who was also black – and along with Burgess, Dodd and Thode, White drew liberally on music recorded by African-American musicians. Thode was particularly notable for his embrace of jazz- and R&B-oriented selections, and in his personalized notepad of favourite records, titled 'The BPM (Beats per Minute) Bible', listed groups such as Donald Byrd, Chic, Manu Dibango, Earth, Wind & Fire, First Choice, Aretha Franklin, Instant Funk, Taana Gardner, Gwen Guthrie, Isaac Hayes, Herbie Hancock, Nona Hendrix, Loleatta Holloway, Grace Jones, Chaka Khan, Gladys Knight, Kool & the Gang, Stefanie Mills, Northend, the Pointer Sisters, Sharon Redd, Sister Sledge, and Sparque, along with more obvious choices such as Donna Summer, Sylvester and Two Tons of Fun. All of these groups were just as likely to be heard in an ethnically mixed venue.[9] The tastes of the DJs were related to their cultural experiences, and Thode along with White shaped their taste in the heart of the disco era, when R&B and funk were dominant influences, and when clubs and sounds were more likely to be both racially and sexually mixed than would prove to be the case in the more sedimented decade of the 1980s. At the annual Black Party (effectively a leather party) held in early 1981, Thode demonstrated that his taste remained rooted in the ethos of the 1970s when he opened his set with records such as Ozo's mystical percussion-chant 'Anambra' (1976), Taana Gardner's heavy R&B groove 'Heartbeat' and Sharon Redd's optimistic R&B workout 'Can You Handle It?' (1980) which he juxtaposed with 'Passion' by Rod Stewart (1980) and 'Magic' by Olivia Newton-John (1980). Maintaining the mix throughout the night, Thode opened the fourth hour of his set with a rapped version of 'Walk the Night' (Bent Boys, 1984), the Talking Heads' Africanist 'I Zimbra' (1979), and Karen Young's R&B disco anthem 'Hot Shot' (1978), which he followed with the playful, bubbly 'Feels Like I'm In Love' by Kelly Marie (1980).[10] Brief as they are, Buckland's (2002, p. 68) and Shapiro's (2005, pp. 74–6) account of the Saint's soundtrack as consisting of Hi-NRG and new wave tracks along with Brewster and Broughton's (1999, p. 312) argument that the Saint DJs 'favoured a very particular sound, playing melody-soaked songs with a heavy kick-drum, richly orchestrated strings and sentimental lyrics' fail to consider the extent to which Thode's selections overlapped with those of Levan and Mancuso.

Dramatic shifts in the makeup of the Saint roster nevertheless augured an increased emphasis on the sounds of Eurodisco, new wave and Hi-NRG, which were associated with the historically contingent preferences of a subsection of white musicians and listeners. First, shockingly, Thode died of a drug overdose in May 1982, and while nobody can be sure if he committed suicide, he had attempted to take his life previously and was feeling particularly

---

[9] Marsha Stern holds the original copy of Roy Thode's *The BPM (Beats per Minute) Bible*.

[10] Roy Thode set at the Black Party, the Saint, held in early 1981. MP3 recording provided by Marsha Stern.

low shortly before the incident. Thode's close friend Marsha Stern, very possibly the last person to see him alive, notes that the DJ had had a major argument with his boyfriend shortly before the overdose, and confirms the opinion of some of Thode's DJ peers that he was also highly sensitive to the opinions of dancers. (He revealed this in an article he published [Thode, 1982] in the first edition of *Stardust*, the Saint's in-house journal.) 'Being the DJ made him the butt of everyone's comments', comments Stern (2008). 'He might have played brilliantly, but if the guy writing the editorial page in a magazine happened to have a lousy time, maybe because he had some bad drugs, he could be quick to hand out a lashing. There were also some nasty-ass queens who would write letters. Roy even received hate mail. These people are nuts, but if you're a little too sensitive, you can let that get to you.'

Mailman organized a tribute party, and then appears to have told Leslie and White separately that he expected them to assume Thode's mantle as the main attraction at the Saint (meaning the DJ who would draw in the biggest crowds, and also provide the venue with a sense of aesthetic direction). Both DJs were given prominent roles when the club opened for its third season in the autumn, but the equilibrium was short-lived: Leslie was handed a contract that secured his commitment to the Saint, while White was told that her services were no longer required around the spring of 1983. 'Bruce just didn't feel that I was doing my best', she recalls (2009). 'I don't know whether it was because I was playing what I wanted to play, or whether he thought I was lazy. He just fired me.' She adds: 'The responsibility got to be too large for the reward. It got to be a pain in the ass. So I was more than willing to say, "Whatever"' (2009).

The pressure was intense, not simply because of the size of the crowd, but also because individuals and clusters of individuals became increasingly ready to criticize specific DJ performances by writing to Mailman, or if they were part of the core group that knew Mailman personally and were the first to sign up to his membership scheme, speaking with him directly. 'People measured success by how satisfied they were at the end of the night', comments La Torre (2009). 'Had they had a peak experience? If they had, they went home happy. If they didn't then they blamed the DJ. I am not certain people actually meant it; they were not critical enough or observant enough of why sometimes it happened and why sometimes it didn't. But I heard it from everybody. It was just

the thing to say.' Mailman respected his DJs, but depended financially on the financial support of his heavily mythologized A-list
membership, and having benefited from the critical judgement that
the Saint was superior to Flamingo, he began to present letters of
complaint to DJs who were perceived to have had an off-night and
asked for an explanation in order to protect his venue's status.

As long as the Saint came out 'smelling like a rose', Mailman
would back the DJ, comments White (2009). But repeated
complaints could lead to a DJ being struck off the roster, and before
Mailman sacked White he asked her to monitor Wayne Scott, who
was judged to be unpredictable; at the end of his final set, Scott
played the resonant 'Town Without Pity' by Gene Pitney (1961).
George Cadenas experienced an even more abrupt ending when he
played 'White Rabbit' by the Great Society and Grace Slick (1968)
at the peak of the Saint's white party in early 1983, and witnessed
the record to fall flat. 'It didn't happen, and that was the end of
him', recalls Merritt (2009). Merritt concluded that playing to the
best of his ability was no longer sufficient, and took to calling up
drug dealers to find out what had been selling in the run-up to the
weekend so he could tailor his selections accordingly. 'If you had
a bad night you never got asked back', remarks Merritt (2009).
'One disc jockey might play two Saturdays, and if the second night
wasn't so good, the inner circle would go to Bruce, and the DJ
wouldn't be booked the next month.'

Leslie and Sherman insist that Mailman didn't want his DJs to
play a narrower and safer range of records, and, although Merritt
perceived him to be clamping down on artistic freedom when
he asked them to start preparing playlists in advance, the owner
apparently believed the strategy would encourage the introduction
of a broader range of sounds than might have been the case if
DJs responded only to the immediate demands of the crowd. The
favour shown to someone like Buchanan supports Leslie's position,
as do off-the-record conversations in which the owner would rally
against the relative conservatism of some of his DJs. Nevertheless,
the value attributed to the letters of complaint unquestionably
led DJs to frame their risks within a specific horizon, and the
unceremonious sacking of Cadenas, Scott and White increased the
impression that performances were being surveilled. The precise
relationship between Thode's death and the letters of complaint
must remain unknown, yet during 1983 and 1984 DJs tailored

their selections with increasing precision to the expectations of a crowd, which hankered for an arc of seamless intensification, and favoured sounds that were heavily electronic, rhythmically monosyllabic, harmonically adventurous and high tempo because those elements enhanced their perceived journey into a collective parallel consciousness.

'After Roy, new DJs came in with new flavours', notes Stern (2008). 'Michael Fierman didn't have as much of an R&B flavour to his music, and nor did Michael Jorba. Michael would play OMD, more rockish stuff, more heady stuff, and so there was a different complexion to the music.' She adds: 'Alan Dodd, Howard Merritt, Robbie [Leslie] and to a certain extent Jim Burgess were known for being more white-sounding compared to Richie Rivera and Roy [Thode]. But all of those DJs played a lot more R&B than some of the newer DJs.' According to Sherman, Buchanan and Parsons pioneered the playing of ultra-fast dance tracks that were rock rather than disco-tinged, including 'That's Good' by Devo (1982), 'White Wedding' by Billy Idol (1982), 'Now You're Mine' by Giorgio Moroder with Helen Terry (1984), 'Twist of Fate' by Olivia Newton-John (1983), 'City of Night' by Rational Youth (1982), 'Dancing in the Dark' by Bruce Springsteen (1984), 'Jump' by Van Halen (1983) and 'Holding Out for a Hero' by Bonnie Tyler (1984), along with new wave tracks by the Associates, Blancmange, China Crisis, the Comateens, A Flock of Seagulls, the Lotus Easters, Orchestral Manoeuvres in the Dark, and Spandau Ballet. Other popular import tracks included 'The Night (La Noche)' by Azul Y Negro (1982) and 'Come and Get Your Love' by Lime (1982). From 1983 onwards, Saint DJs also started to play European Hi-NRG tracks such as 'So Many Men, So Little Time' by Miquel Brown (1983) and 'High Energy' by Evelyn Thomas (1984), the death of Patrick Cowley from AIDS in 1982 having slowed the output on the West Coast.

The point wasn't that these records were 'white' so much as they weren't counter-balanced by records that suggested a complementary set of cultural allegiances, and during 1983 and 1984 Saint DJs played very few if any records that could be heard at the Garage. If that also confirms that the DJs at these venues selected equally few tracks that could be heard at the Saint, the Garage was nevertheless less isolated than its Second Avenue counterpart because Levan's taste-making role extended beyond the black gay network, whereas Saint spinners didn't appeal beyond the white gay scene. In fact elements of the narrowing Saint aesthetic could be heard outside of the white gay network, and English new wave was played heavily at spots such as Danceteria, which were inappropriately labelled rock-dance clubs. However, DJs such as Mark Kamins (perhaps the most influential selector at Danceteria) weren't taking their cues from the Saint, and they also steered clear of the high tempo selections that Saint DJs would play between 2.00 and 6.00 a.m.

An increasingly prominent figure during 1983, Fierman maintains the 'unification of the room' was his 'main goal', and along with other spinners he would maintain a steady energy until, usually around two or three in the morning, he would introduce the first of a series of anthems that would generate a mini-surge from the basement and the peripheral areas onto the floor. After that, he would punctuate his selections with additional 'anthems' that would generate 'evanescent convergences' in which everyone would 'feel connected'.[11] Barry Walters, a Mudd Club and Danceteria regular who went to the Saint as well as the Paradise Garage for the first time in 1983, was struck by the uniformity of the aesthetic. 'Larry and Mark Kamins and Justin Strauss and Anita Sarko didn't mix smoothly and they also brought a lot of different styles into the mix', he recalls (Walters, 2009). 'At the Saint the mixes were much smoother and the variations between the records were almost infinitesimal. It was the first time I encountered a style of DJing where one record was only slightly different from the record I'd just heard.' La Torre was keenly aware of the reason for the manicured smoothness of the style. 'Even though the records might sound repetitive, that was just because the DJ wanted to make the moment last', comments the dancer (La Torre, 2009). 'The DJs would drag the same beat for what seemed like a very long time, just to maintain that feeling, that peak experience.' However, La Torre adds that by 1986 the sound had become 'so white' and 'defined' it began to turn him off. 'I was not pleased with the music, and the vibe was becoming just a little too chemical', he recalls. 'It was not really soulful and it didn't have that Latin or black beat.

---

[11] Michael Fierman interview with Dupre for an unfinished documentary about the Saint, undated. The original transcript is held by Stephen Pevner. A copy of the transcript is held by the author.

They had distilled it so much the sound became boring by 1986' (2009).

The distillation process assumed its shape across 1983 and 1984, and when Mario Z (1984) interviewed Leslie for the *New York Native* in March 1984, the DJ acknowledged that the Saint sound had indeed started to congeal. 'Music has evolved but New York's gay market has faithfully held on to the romantic period of disco, which was 1978 through 1980', he commented. 'While we've all been dancing to that, we haven't noticed that there are a lot of records being produced that over the past couple of years we've ignored because they haven't fit into the mould that the audience has demanded' (1984, pp. 21, 24). By this point Leslie had emerged as the venue's pre-eminent draw, and in a June 1983 interview with the spinner the Saint cashier Jan Carl Park (1983, p. 36) made much of his preeminent appeal. Yet strangely reticent in his interview with Z, Leslie emphasized the need for aesthetic renewal and, although some members resented his 'pushing ahead', he insisted he couldn't 'remain stationary', because if he did 'everyone is going to wake up and find that they're terribly bored'.

Having started to play at the Saint during the 1983–4 season, Sherman drew on records that were deemed to be funky, including 'Padlock' by Gwen Guthrie (1983), 'Clouds' by Chaka Khan (1980), 'Square Biz' by Tina Marie (1981), 'White Lines' by Grandmaster & Melle Mel (1983), 'You Don't Know' by Serious Intention (1984) and 'No Favors' by Tempers (1984), and he also pitched down anything that ran at 136 beats-per-minute-plus because 'it made some of the records that were *really* bad sound a bit less cheesy'. 'It's sort of a myth that all anybody wanted to hear were things like "Heaven Must Have Sent You" by Bonnie Pointer [1978] or "Trippin' on The Moon" by Cerrone [1981]', he argues (Sherman, 2010). Then again, Sherman notes that he owed his position to the fact that Mailman 'liked the fact I was not afraid to play "unusual things", even though some of the crowd might not like them'. Leslie, meanwhile, sought to renew the Saint's aesthetic by introducing new wave tracks alongside the more refined end of Hi-NRG and Italian dance imports, which he continued to pepper with classic disco. But looking back, he notes: 'Overall we were walking on a cliff edge musically at the Saint and product was running scarcer by the week. I felt a feeling of imminent disaster' (Leslie, 2009).

The shift towards a white-identified aesthetic coincided with wider shifts in identity politics, which proposed that marginalized citizens should act not as self-interested individuals but instead within like-minded groups. Growing out of the countercultural movements of the 1960s, and refined when the black lesbian feminist group the Combahee River Collective (1977) published a statement of aims that reflected on their common material experiences and objectives in 1977, identity politics challenged the idea that history should be driven by internally cohesive nations. Immanuel Wallerstein (1983, p. 159) drew attention to the shift when he remarked on the way people were beginning to seek the protection of groups that were deemed to be both equal in status yet also particular in composition, and his argument shed light on the Saint. After all, the poster for the opening night party featured a cyborg-like figure of St Sebastian with lasers shooting out of his fingertips and eyes, and therefore figured the Saint dancer as a figure of persecution, righteousness and beauty who could experience redemption and transcendence through the assertion of his homosexual identity on the dancefloor (and this before AIDS was reported in the media). Following the turbulence of the 1982–3 season, the 1983–4 season might have marked the moment when the membership acquired a settled sense of itself. And over time, the infrastructure of the venue also might have exerted a cumulative influence on the contours of the music, with DJs increasingly tuned to the ease with which smooth, shiny, futuristic sounds complemented the contours of the building. Dancers and spinners proceeded to coalesce around a sound that was so distinctive it couldn't be heard in any parallel dance milieu.

The marked acceleration of consumer culture during the 1980s – which culminated in 'hyperconsumption' (Ritzer, 1999) – also enabled people who enjoyed relatively easy access to cash or credit to experience and shape their identity through the practice of buying objects or experiences in a way that was historically unprecedented. This articulation of consumer-identity was particularly marked at the Saint, where the enormous investment that went into the development necessitated high entry prices. The Saint was therefore characteristic of what Arjun Appadurai (1996, p. 115) describes as the 1980s rupture with the preceding decade, inasmuch as Mailman's venue embodied a dramatic break in terms of scope, expense, ambition, infrastructure and price with Flamingo and 12

West. Consequently the Saint suggested an at least partial shift in the framework of the dancefloor experience from one of participation to one of consumption, for while venues needed to charge some sort of money at the entrance and/or the bar to cover costs, the much higher entry price at the Saint brought this relationship to the fore. The dance experience shifted accordingly from being a communal activity that relied on a necessary financial contribution to one that raised a series of customer expectations. When those expectations were not met – because, perhaps, a DJ didn't play the right record at the right moment – complaints were raised in the register of the consumer who believes that money should be able to purchase an object or experience that is of equivalent value, and that some form of redress should follow disappointment. In response, Mailman introduced a range of strategies that, whether intended or not, had the effect of defining the Saint product more rigorously.

The fragmentation and commodification of the wider music scene in New York accentuated the uniqueness-bordering-on-isolation of Mailman's venue. Across the period Saint spinners received fewer and fewer offers to play in alternative spots, and Leslie expressed his regret at this development in his interview with the *New York Native* (Park, 1983, p. 37) in June 1983. 'Gay music is a very specialized sound, and once you become fluent with it you lose contact with all the other things that are going on musically', he noted. 'You tend to get a little too narrow. That is the benefit of playing at a black club or a straight club: broadening yourself.'[12] Convinced that the Garage was a much more promising place to test new music, and also that Hi-NRG would never sell domestically, record company promoters who had besieged Flamingo and 12 West during the 1970s also disengaged with the Saint. In turn, *Billboard* calculated that Hi-NRG didn't deserve a great deal of coverage, and dance chart compiler and reporter Brian Chin proceeded to take his cues from 'black DJs' and a 'token representation of Fire Island gay DJs' because the latter group was 'playing to no discernible effect to the rest of the industry'. He adds: 'I had a very retrograde attitude of Saint music, and I was wrong

---

[12] Leslie posits 'gay music' as being separate from 'black' and 'straight' music without explaining why. In the process, the whiteness of the gay music he describes is rendered invisible.

not to recognize it. But I was fighting to create a context in which club music still had a place in the music industry' (Chin, 1982). The foreign location of the record companies that were releasing Hi-NRG music also meant that in contrast to DJ-remixers such as Jim Burgess and Tom Savarese, who stamped their imprint on an array of high-profile domestic disco releases during the 1970s, and also Junior Vasquez, who would go on to become an influential house remixer in the early 1990s, Leslie and his peers weren't able to establish an equivalent studio foothold from which they could reshape the sound of music.

The acceleration of the AIDS epidemic during the early 1980s entrenched the Saint crowd's sense of its own specificity and isolation still further. First identified in 1981, named in 1982, identified tentatively as an epidemic in 1983, and linked to the virus that would later be known as HIV in 1984, AIDS hit the Saint more intensely than any other dance venue because a high proportion of its dancers engaged in unprotected promiscuous sex. The promiscuity had even been allowed if not encouraged by the Saint, where dancers would elope to an unpoliced upstairs balcony to engage in sex. AIDS was even nicknamed 'Saint's disease' (Shilts, 1987, p. 149) early on because of the marked proliferation of the disease among Mailman's membership. Initially the Saint crowd carried on as if the disease was an unpleasant mutation of other pernicious but usually non-fatal sexually transmitted diseases that had circulated in the gay male community with increasing preponderance across the 1970s, and an early fundraiser held at the venue was criticized for directing the bulk of the proceeds to the cost of staging the event. But during the 1983–4 season the threat of the disease became better understood and dancers began to change their habits, and a siege mentality began to take hold when gay campaigners criticized the governmental response to the crisis for being too slow while attempting to deflect the rise in homophobic hate on the part of moral majority representatives.[13] Within this context, the pre-AIDS sound of disco came to embody a nostalgic

---

[13] See, for example, Larry Kramer's article '1,112 and Counting' (1983). While some AIDS activists in the Gay Men's Health Crisis deemed Kramer too contentious, in part because of his repeated critique of what he perceived to be excessive gay hedonism, the article is also seen as a key moment in the raising of AIDS awareness.

moment in which unprotected sex didn't carry the threat of death, even if its intensified recycling added force to the argument that the Saint was trapped in time.

For these and other reasons, music industry reps might have disengaged even more than they would have done in other circumstances. 'Because all the early victims of AIDS were gay, white males, it was no longer considered "cool" by straight people in the domestic record industry to dance in gay, white clubs', argues Sherman. 'It was definitely homophobia, although perfectly understandable since nobody knew what it was, where it came from, or how you could "catch" it, and there was a bit of reverse-racism thrown in for good measure. Hanging with white gay males was definitely not sexy by 1983.' If the white gay community's disengagement from the concerns of other groups in the countercultural coalition left it more isolated politically than would have been the case if those early affiliations had been maintained, responsibility for the drift also lies elsewhere, for while white gay men might have been slow to engage with civil rights and concerns of black gay men across the 1970s, the leaders of the African-American community were also reluctant to address the problem of black homophobia along with the wider need to campaign for gay civil rights. The Saint remained the most homogeneous of all of New York's clubbing communities of the early 1980s, and the venue's lack of engagement with sonic and social diversity in the post-1983 period left its membership more vulnerable and stranded than it might have been when the AIDS crisis spiralled into an epidemic.

Several factors led to the weakening of the demographic and aesthetic convergence around whiteness, gayness and masculinity across the 1983–4 season. First, the decimation of his membership by AIDS across the second half of the 1980s prompted Mailman to reduce the cost of entry in order to boost numbers, and as a result a younger, less economically privileged group of dancers who had less of an affinity with classic disco and were more open to new sounds, converged on the venue. Second, Mailman closed the Saint in 1988 not because it had become impossible to fill the floor, but because inflation in the real estate market (which paralleled the rise of the stock market) meant that this was the best way for him to make money out of the venture. Third, the diminution of the crowd along with the added cost of opening a new venue prompted future owners to develop less expensive, less tightly controlled clubs, which in turn undermined the likelihood the remainder of the 'A-list' would find an equivalent home. Finally, Saint DJs (aside from Sherman) had ignored the flow of house music from Chicago to New York across 1985–8 because they judged the sound to be 'too black', but during those four years the sound established itself as the irrefutable successor-genre to disco in New York as well as many European cities, and when Junior Vasquez championed a hard, tribal variation of house at the Sound Factory between 1989 and 1995, he carried a significant proportion of the surviving Saint membership with him.

The shifting contours of the white gay dance milieu during the post–1988 period shouldn't be allowed to obscure the originality, power and influence of the Saint. Moreover, while house music would go on to become the dominant sound of dance in many countries during the 1990s, the genre failed to break out of the club milieu with anything like the force of 1970s disco in the US, whereas the Hi-NRG sound popularized at the Saint was picked up much more readily. The commercial success of Hi-NRG might have weakened the cultural capital of the Saint, yet the popularity of the sound remains an indicator of the venue's capacity to, if not generate new trends, then at least align itself with their emergence. In addition, while the infrastructure of Mailman's venue was effectively irreproducible, the Saint attracted notable numbers of dancers from other states in the US as well as Europe, and Ian Levine (to quote one example) has gone on to recount (Brewster, 1999) how he attempted to replicate the Saint's musical agenda at Heaven, which was arguably the leading gay nightspot in London during the 1980s and 1990s. (In a tangential move, the owners of the Ministry of Sound would model their venue on the Paradise Garage.)

More broadly, Saint DJs were among the first to prioritize a style of DJing that emphasized the seamless linking of tracks that differed only slightly in terms of their aesthetic content, and this style would become the dominant practice in house culture, in which DJs broke with the practice of Levan and Mancuso, as well as figures such as Afrika Bambaataa (the Roxy) and Jellybean Benitez (the Funhouse), who developed a pluralistic style that could lead them to juxtaposition contrasting tracks. Even if the Saint DJs didn't directly inspire the broader shift to the infinite aesthetic of 'house music all night long' – and their early disengagement from house indicates that they didn't – their forging of a milieu that brought together sonic repetition, smooth mixing and drug consumption was anticipatory if not visionary. That the Saint helped establish an early version of the kind of trance-oriented seamlessness that would become so popular in club and rave circuits also indicates that the assumed influence of Levan on contemporary dance culture requires a more nuanced analysis. As it is, the Saint DJs have for the most part drifted into historical anonymity, with the part exception of Robbie Leslie. If their profile might have been higher had they matched Levan's partial embrace of house, the coincidence of a complex range of contingent circumstances explains why such a move was always unlikely.

References

Appadurai, Arjun (1996) *Modernity at Large: Cultural Dimensions of Globalization*. Minneapolis, MN: University of Minnesota Press.

Brewster, Bill (1999) 'Ian Levine'. 2 March, Interview with Ian Levine http://www.djhistory.com/interviews/ian-levine [accessed 21 July 2009].

Brewster, Bill and Broughton, Frank (1999) *Last Night a DJ Saved My Life: The History of the Disc Jockey*. London: Headline.

Buckland, Fiona (2002) *Impossible Dance: Club Culture and Queer World-making*. Middletown, CT: Wesleyan University Press.

Cheren, Mel (2000) *Keep On Dancin': My Life and the Paradise Garage*. New York: 24 Hours for Life.

Chin, Brian (1982) 'Dance Trax'. *Billboard*, 19 June: 48.

Clendinen, Dudley and Nagourney, Adam (1999) *Out for Good: The Struggle to Build a Gay Rights Movement in America*. New York: Simon & Schuster.

Cohen, Claudia and Stivers, Cyndi (1980) 'I, Claudia'. *New York Daily News*, 15 September.

Collin, Matthew with contributions by Godfrey, John (1997) *Altered State: The Story of Ecstasy Culture and Acid House*, London: Serpent's Tail.

Combahee River Collective (1977) 'The Combahee River Collective Statement'. http://circuitous.org/scraps/combahee.html [accessed 20 November 2010].

Fain, Nathan (1980) 'The New Boogie Merchants'. *After Dark*, September: 47–51.

Fikentscher, Kai (2000) *'You Better Work!' Underground Dance Music in New York City*. Hanover, NH and London: Wesleyan University Press.

Garratt, Sheryl (1998) *Adventures in Wonderland: A Decade of Club Culture*. London: Headline.

Hodenfield, Jan (1980) 'A Gay Disco on a Grand Scale'. *New York Daily News*, 17 November: 11.

Hughes, Walter (1994) 'In the Empire of the Beat – Discipline and Disco'. In Andrew Ross and Tricia Rose (eds) *Microphone Fiends: Youth Music and Youth Culture* (147–54). London: Routledge.

Kaiser, Charles (1997) *The Gay Metropolis, 1940–1996*. London: Weidenfeld and Nicolson.

Kramer, Larry (1983) '1,112 and Counting'. *New York Native*, 14 March. http://la.indymedia.org/news/2003/05/58757.php [accessed 20 October 2010].

Lawrence, Tim (2003) *Love Saves the Day: A History of American Dance Music Culture, 1970–79*. Durham, NC and London: Duke University Press.

—(2009) *Hold on to your Dreams: Arthur Russell and the Downtown Music Scene, 1973–92*. Duke University Press.

—(2011) 'The Forging of a White Gay Aesthetic at the Saint, 1980–83'. *Dancecult: Journal of Electronic Dance Music*, 3(1): 4–27.

—(forthcoming) *Life and Death on the New York Dance Floor: A History, 1980–84*. Durham, NC: Duke University Press.

Park, Jan Carl (1983) 'The A-Gay's Disc Jockey: Robbie Leslie and the Politics of the Turntable'. *New York Native*, 20 June: 36–7.

Postchardt, Ulf (1998) *DJ-Culture*, trans. Shaun Whiteside. London: Quartet Books.

Reynolds, Simon (1998) *Energy Flash: A Journey Through Rave Music and Dance Culture*. London: Picador.

Ritzer, George (1999) *Enchanting a Disenchanted World: Revolutionising the Means of Consumption*. Thousand Oaks, CA, London and New Delhi: Pine Forge Press.

Shapiro, Peter (2005) *Turn the Beat Around: The Secret History of Disco*. London: Faber and Faber.

Shilts, Randy (1987) *And the Band Played On: Politics, People, and the AIDS Epidemic*. New York: St. Martin's Press.

Thode, Roy (n.d.) *The BPM (Beats per Minute) Bible*, unpublished notepad (original copy held by Marsha Stern).

Thode, Roy (1982) 'A Letter From a DJ'. *Star Dust*, Spring: 2.

Wallerstein, Immanuel (1983) *Historical Capitalism*. New York: Verso.

Z, Mario (1984) 'Robbie Leslie: The Pat Boone of DJs'. *New York Native*, 12 March: 21, 24.

Interviews

Dupre, Jeff (n.d.) Interview with Michael Fierman (courtesy of Stephen Pevner, minor edits introduced).

La Torre, Jorge (2009) Interviewed by Tim Lawrence, New York, 18 February.

Leslie, Robbie (2008) Interviewed on the telephone by Tim Lawrence, 23 October.

Leslie, Robbie (2009) Interviewed by Tim Lawrence, email, 7 April.

Merritt, Howard (2009) Interviewed on the telephone by Tim Lawrence, 21 January.

Sherman, Terry (2009) Interviewed by Tim Lawrence, email, 20 April.

—(2010) Interviewed by Tim Lawrence, email, 4 December.

Stern, Marsha (2008) Interviewed on the telephone by Tim Lawrence, 19 November.

White, Sharon (2009) Interviewed on the telephone by Tim Lawrence, 30 April.

Discography

Abba (1981) *The Visitors*. Polar: Sweden, [POLS 342 / LP].

Azul Y Negro (1982) 'The Night (La Noche)'. Mercury: Spain, [64 00 749 / 12"].

Bent Boys (1984) 'Walk the Night. Matra', J.C. Records: Canada, [JC12–024 / 12"].

Branigan, Laura (1982) 'Gloria'. Atlantic: United States, [DM 4835 / 12"].

Bridges, Alicia (1978) 'I Love the Nightlife (Disco 'Round)'. Polydor: Canada, [PD 14483 / 7"].

Brown, Miquel (1983) 'So Many Men, So Little Time'. TSR Records: United States, [TSR 828 / 12"].

Cerrone (1981) 'Trippin' on the Moon'. Malligator: France, [ZC 8757 / 12"].

Change (1980) 'A Lover's Holiday'. WEA: United Kingdom, [K 79141, 7"].

Clifford, Linda (1978) 'Runaway Love'. Curtom: United States, [PRO-A–731, 12"].

Cut Glass (1979) 'Without Your Love'. Earhole Records: United States, [EH 1001 / 12"].

Devo (1982) 'That's Good, from *Oh No! It's Devo*'. Warner Bros. Records: United States, [9 23741–1 / LP].

Gardner, Taana (1981) 'Heartbeat'. West End Records: United States, [WES–22132 / 12"].

Grandmaster & Melle Mel (1983) 'White Lines'. Sugar Hill Records:
    United States, [SH–465 / 12"].
Griffin, Peter (1981) 'Step by Step'. Electrola: Germany, [1C 052–46 249
    YZ / 12"].
Guthrie, Gwen (1983) 'Padlock'. Garage Records: United States, [ITG
    72001 / 7"].
Idol, Billy (1982) 'White Wedding', from *Billy Idol*. Chrysalis: United
    States, [CHR 1377 / LP].
Jiani, Carol (1981) 'Hit 'n' Run Lover'. Matra: Canada, [W–12044 / 12"].
Kane, Madleen (1979) 'Secret Love Affair'. Pye International: United
    Kingdom, [12P 5007 / 12"].
Khan, Chaka (1980) 'Clouds'. Warner Bros. Records: United States,
    [WBS49216 / 7"].
Lime (1982) 'Come and Get Your Love'. Prism: United States, [PDS
    440 / 12"].
Marie, Kelly (1980) 'Feels Like I'm in Love'. Calibre + Plus! United
    Kingdom, [PLUSL 1 / 12"].
Marie, Tina (1981) 'Square Biz'. Motown (vinyl): 12TMG 1236, US.
    http://www.discogs.com/Teena-Marie-Square-Biz/release/211302
    [accessed 3 May 2013].
Moroder, Giorgio with Terry, Helen (1984) 'Now You're Mine'. Virgin:
    United Kingdom, [VS 710–12 / 12"].
Nelson, Phyllis (1980) 'Don't Stop the Train'. Carrere: France, [8.091 /
    12"].
Newton-John, Olivia (1980) 'Magic'. MCA Records: Canada,
    [MCA–41247 / 7"].
—(1983) 'Twist of Fate'. MCA Records: United States, [MCA–52284 / 7"].
Ozo (1976) 'Anambra'. DJM Records: United Kingdom, [DJT 10764 / 12"].
Passengers (1979) 'Hot Leather'. RCA Victor: Spain, [SPBO–7234 / 7"].
Pitney, Gene (1961) 'Town Without Pity'. Musicor Records: United
    States, [MU 1009 / 7"].
Pointer, Bonnie (1978) 'Heaven Must Have Sent You'. Motown: United
    States, [M 1459F / 7"].
Rational Youth (1982) 'City of Night'. Yul Records: Canada, [12 YUL
    3 / 12"].
Redd, Sharon (1980) 'Can You Handle It'? Epic: United Kingdom, [EPC
    9572 / 7"].
Ripple (1977) 'The Beat Goes On and On'. Salsoul Records: United
    States, [S7 2057 / 7"].
Ruffin, Jimmy (1980) 'Hold On to My Love'. RSO Records Inc.: United
    Kingdom, [RSO 57 / 7"].
Serious Intention (1984) 'You Don't Know'. Easy Street Records: United
    States, [EZS–7512 / 12"].

Shaw, Marlena (1979) 'Touch Me in the Morning'. Columbia: United States, [AS 678 / 12"].

Springsteen, Bruce (1984) 'Dancing in the Dark'. Columbia: United States, [38–04463 / 7"].

Stewart, Rod (1978) 'Da' Ya' Think I'm Sexy'. Riva Records: United Kingdom, [SAM 92 / 12"].

—(1980) 'Passion'. Warner Bros. Records: United States, [WBS 49617 / 7"].

Sylvester with Patrick Cowley (1982) 'Do You Wanna Funk'. Megatone Records (vinyl): MT 102. http://www.discogs.com/Patrick-Cowley-Featuring-Sylvester-Do-Ya-Wanna-Funk/release/2190101 [accessed 4 May 2013].

Talking Heads (1979) 'I Zimbra'. Sire: United States, [PRO-A–846 / 12"].

Tantra (1979) 'Hills of Katmandu', Philips: Italy, [9198 334 / 12"].

Tempers (1984) 'No Favors'. MCA Records: United States, [MCA–23506 / 12"].

The Great Society with Grace Slick (1968) 'White Rabbit', from *Conspicuous Only In Its Absence*. Columbia: United States, [CS 9624 / LP].

Thomas, Evelyn (1984) 'High Energy'. Record Shack Records: United Kingdom, [SOHOT 18 / 12"].

Tyler, Bonnie (1984) 'Holding Out for a Hero'. CBS: United Kingdom, [TA 4251 / 12"].

Van Halen (1983) 'Jump', from *1984*. Warner Bros. Records: United States, [1–23985 / LP].

Voyage (1983) 'Souvenirs'. Power Records: Canada, [PXD 002 / 12"].

Weather Girls (1982) 'It's Raining Men'. Columbia: United States, [44–03181].

Wills, Viola (1982) 'Stormy Weather'. Sunergy: United States, [SNG–0001 / 12"].

Young, Karen (1978) 'Hot Shot'. West End Records: United States, [WES 12111 / 12"].

CHAPTER ELEVEN

DJs as Cultural Mediators: The Mixing Work of São Paulo's Peripheral DJs

Ivan Paolo de Paris Fontanari[1]

Utilizing a local perspective, this chapter aims to contribute to the mapping and understanding of forms, roles and meanings the DJ can take around the world. It examines the experience and performance of electronic dance music in a 'Do It Yourself' (DIY) techno and drum 'n' bass scene found in 2005 in poor working-class districts of São Paulo, depicting particular understandings of what it means to be a DJ and what practical roles this implies for the mostly non-white, working-class youth who run this scene. For Seeger (2004, p. xiii), 'musical anthropology looks at the way musical performances create many aspects of culture and social life'. Seeger's approach is followed here in assuming that 'music

[1] This article is based on research conducted for the preparation of my doctoral dissertation presented to the Graduate Program of Social Anthropology at the Federal University of Rio Grande do Sul, Brazil. The research was advised by Dr Elizabeth Lucas and fully financed by the National Council for the Scientific and Technological Development – CNPq, Brazil, which included one year as 'visiting scholar' under the supervision of Dr Anthony Seeger at the Department of Ethnomusicology at UCLA.

is part of the very construction and interpretation of social and conceptual relationships and processes' (p. xiv).

Mixing records is one of the most distinctive of DJs' musical practices; it defines and structures the DJ's musical and professional identity. Drawing from Seeger's approach, this chapter argues that the principles underlying mix practices transcend music by building a locally paradoxical identity. Among their audiences, DJs fulfil a continuous and multi-layered process of cultural mediation by manipulating and negotiating between familiar and unfamiliar references in order to build up a local identity based on difference. In describing these references anthropologically as familiar and unfamiliar, I discuss the roles DJs play as they diffuse techno and drum 'n' bass in the face of local, dominant sensibilities shaped by Brazilian working-class mainstream music genres.

Additionally, performance theory will help shed light on the agency of concrete individuals acting in processes of cultural mediation as well as on the importance of cultural performances in these processes. This 'performative approach' allows a fresh perspective, away from mainstream studies of cultural mediation, which focus on large-scale political, ideological, semantic and symbolic structures in friction and neglect the importance of cultural performances and mediators in cultural mediation processes (e.g., Burke, 1978; Mazzarella, 2004; Montero, 2006). Peripheral DJs in São Paulo illustrate how cultural mediation is achieved by particular *flesh-and-blood-plus-machine* agents through cultural performances, a process in which subjective dimensions are intertwined with large-scale processes that involve traditional values, class divisions and globalization.

Performance theorist Richard Schechner (1985, p. 4) remarks that the 'transformation of being and/or consciousness' is one of the main features of cultural performances. As an example, he remembers wondering whether the figure he watched dancing the deer dance in the Arizona Yaqui in 1981 was a man and a deer simultaneously. He suggested that, while putting on the deer mask, the man was neither a man nor a deer, but 'somewhere in between'. Despite dealing mainly with non-mediated cultural performances, Schechner offers us an interpretive key to understand the role of DJs as cultural mediators, enabling a conceptual decentring of the figure of the DJ: no longer an essentialized figure but instead a character who can be incorporated into one's life trajectory. As social subjects, DJs practise a role that is ontologically enabled by the instruments they manipulate, making them DJs. Just as the deer mask makes the man a kind of deer, the mixer is not just a part of the DJs' costume: it has a physical function and makes the person a kind of mixer. Just as the deer dancer incarnates his character, becoming another being, the youth in São Paulo incarnate the character of the DJ as they play that role while manipulating their equipment, their machines. DJs thus could be thought of as cyborgs in Haraway's sense, 'hybrid creature[s] ... compounded of special kinds of machines and special kinds of organisms appropriate to the late twentieth century' (Haraway, 1991, p. 1).

From this perspective, DJs are not just music selectors and mixers, but also technologically improved social subjects. Living on the outskirts of the Brazilian metropolis, São Paulo, they personify a transnational character. DJ equipment, techniques and music were developed and initially disseminated in places far away from this local scene. Locally, they are exotic, techno-social apparatuses brought by older generations from such global power centres as London and New York. Therefore, I conceptualize DJs as transnational characters embodied by locals in order to symbolically manage their local world and to produce themselves as social subjects. Armed with 'subcultural capital' (Thornton, 1995), the DJ is thus an upgraded version of the everyday locals. Thus, while mixing records, DJs re/mix themselves, becoming translocal subjects of the mixes they make. In order to illustrate these propositions, I contextualize the emergence of this particular dance music scene in São Paulo and situate it aesthetically and socio-culturally in its urban setting. After that I describe and discuss the roles played by DJs among their audiences and the paradoxical nature of the identity they build.

Approaching the Scene

The argument of this chapter is based on nine months of ethnographic fieldwork conducted in 2005 in the metropolitan region of São Paulo. The research focuses on parties run in the sub-standard infrastructure districts of the east side of the city. São Paulo is the largest Brazilian city, with 11 million people; its less developed districts, where my fieldwork was conducted, are locally identified as 'periphery', which reflects both geographical location and the fact that districts become less developed as one leaves the city's central region. 'Periphery' also includes the unplanned districts, inhabited by poor working classes in self-built dwellings or in all-the-same-basic-pattern buildings built by government housing programmes.[2] In contrast, the central region concentrates public administration buildings, hospitals, parks, monuments, works of famous architects, financial and cultural institutions, fancy night-clubs, shopping centres, and the best schools and universities, as well as the houses and buildings where the cosmopolitan middle class and elite live. It is the region most tourists get to know when passing through São Paulo. 'Centre' and 'periphery' do not refer to homogeneous, hermetic and separated worlds; nonetheless, these categories are crucial to understanding electronic dance music in São Paulo. Each of the worlds they refer to has its own specific scene, although eventually they do communicate with the other.

During my fieldwork I formally interviewed 22 DJs in different stages of their careers, one promoter and one record-store owner. Most of them were also party organizers. The interviews were always conducted in daylight, either in the interviewees' homes or their workplaces. Only one of the DJs interviewed was female. She and her female promoter formed the sole all-female crew acting in this scene – by the way, the most successful in party promotion at the time I was in the field. Except for a female promoter in one crew, the other nine crews were formed exclusively by male DJs. The male–female ratio among interviewees strongly reflected the gendered disproportion of DJs in this scene as well as gender inequalities in the labour market among Brazilian poor working classes (Fontoura and Bonetti, 2011).[3]

---

[2] By using the term 'poor working classes' I assume its ethnic-racial connotation. A considerable part of the people included in this category are non-white, mostly of mixed African, indigenous and Iberian origin. In Brazil, social class corresponds to ethnicity/race in the sense that the lower the income in any region is, the bigger the non-white proportion of the population will be (Telles, 2004). Therefore, the proportion of non-whites is bigger in the poorer districts.

[3] By counting the names of the DJs in the flyers of parties I attended in east São Paulo and metropolitan region between May and December 2005, I reached 136 DJs. Of these, 126 were male; that is, 92 per cent. It is noteworthy that only about 20 per cent of the 136 performed regularly and were active in organizing events.

I attended 27 night events, including those in small farms close to urban areas, small clubs in central urban areas of east side districts, and underground clubs in decadent areas in downtown São Paulo. Additionally, at least once a week I would go to places of daylight sociability in historic downtown São Paulo, such as record and clothing stores where DJs and DJs-to-be met to socialize and talk about music, the scene, to set up contacts, and to spread out flyers and plan events.

I first heard about techno and drum 'n' bass parties in the peripheral districts of São Paulo while talking to a local raver during a short trip to that city in my previous research (Fontanari, 2003). The local mainstream media's silence about this scene echoed the invisibility of the poor population and their cultural expressions to middle- and upper-class Brazilians. As a world created for their own enjoyment, little of it spread beyond its socio-cultural circumstances. That silence contrasted with mainstream and underground, local, middle-class electronic dance music clubs and raves, which were eventually covered negatively or positively in national mainstream media, as well as promoted by websites supported by professional promoters, journalists and designers.

Although I have done previous fieldwork in a different electronic dance music scene in Brazil and have taken a course in DJ techniques some years before, during this research project I was an outsider both to the DJs' world and to the periphery of São Paulo. I was born and raised in the central region of a much smaller capital, Porto Alegre, the southern-most Brazilian capital, with 1.4 million inhabitants; I came from a white, lower middle-class family. In addition to studying social sciences and anthropology, I trained as an electric guitar player in the rock tradition and studied Western music theory. Despite having immersed myself in the field as ethnographer, to the interviewees and participants of the scene I studied I was still an odd, big and white creature 'from the South'. This perspective, however, nurtured a curiosity that permeated our interactions: 'What are you really looking for, living alone for months in São Paulo, expending your time and money going to our parties and interviewing unknown DJs and partygoers?' a DJ once asked me after we developed mutual confidence. That question revealed their stigma as poor young people as well as the low credibility of their music to their parents, relatives and neighbours and the low investment in DJ careers by club owners in their social milieu. Their cultural agency, though achieved in a quite visceral way, did not seem worth the attention of an outsider even for DJs themselves.

Techno and Drum 'n' Bass among São Paulo's Poor Working Classes

In order to situate this particular techno and drum 'n' bass scene historically, it must be framed within a larger process achieved by other local generations of DJs. This scene is the unfolding of a larger dance music scene achieved in São Paulo's mid-east quarters by large commercial clubs in previous decades. In these clubs DJs gradually introduced poor working-class young people to a wide variety of dance music genres brought from the United States and Europe. These genres included disco, house music and, later on, hardcore, techno and jungle. In their performances, these genres were interlocked with an already more familiar repertoire of Brazilian mainstream, popular genres, like samba, *pagode*, *axé* music, and Brazilian rock, as well as international rap, R&B, dance pop and electronic rock. In the late 1980s, the dissemination of dance club music was motivated by the release of remixes of Brazilian pop rock hits atop disco and house music rhythmic textures by Brazilian national music industry (Assef, 2003, pp. 126–8). It was part of a strategy to widen the market for Brazilian pop rock and rock artists that prepared large audience's sensibility to the later reception of genres with a more synthetic sound.

In the early 1990s, DJs at Toco (1972–97), the first and biggest club ever set up in São Paulo's mid-east quarters, were beginning to specialize in techno and hardcore/jungle, but they had a marginal status in the face of a huge variety of mainstream dance music genres. The establishment of electronic dance music clubs, such as Sound Factory (1991–7) and Overnight (1988–2004), represented an increasingly specialized audience. However, as these large clubs in the mid-east quarters broke up, there were no electronic dance music parties for many beginner DJs and partygoers. The only way out was to run their own parties, for which there was already an audience.

These techno and drum 'n' bass performances in clubs allowed the emergence of a 'clubber' identity, which sheltered thousands of poor working-class youth.[4] These large club parties engendered the creation of a spontaneous and wide network of acquaintances and friendships around the taste for techno and drum 'n' bass among youth living all over the poor districts of the São Paulo metropolitan region. This network was also nurtured by private gatherings such as birthday parties, where electronic dance music and its scene identity was disseminated among friends, neighbours and relatives, as well as by the attendance at mass dance events such as the *Mercado Mundo Mix* (World Mix Market) and the *Parada da Paz* (Peace Parade), a soundsystem parade that began in 1997. It processed through the main avenues of São Paulo, becoming more visible every year as the number of followers increased, reaching many thousands. Supported by radio stations, gyms, dance clubs and LGBT (lesbian, gay, bisexual and transsexual) associations, *Parada da Paz* was organized by the same people that hold the itinerant, alternative/LGBT culture fair *Mercado Mundo Mix*. This fair started in 1994, making designer clothing, recorded DJs' sets, drag queen shows and LGBT culture easily accessible to a wide public for the first time in São Paulo (Assef, 2003, p. 224). Among this public were many working-class youth.

Promoter Thelles is said to be the first to organize autonomous electronic dance music events in the east side of São Paulo. One such example is the project called Descolada, which took place in São Miguel from the mid-1990s up to early 2000s, and which gathered a house, techno and drum 'n' bass audience formed by previous clubs and public events on a more regular basis. In the early 2000s, *projetos* (party organizations) such as E.Vision, Fever, Tendence, Circuit of Love and Contrattack began to organize parties. These *projetos* were formed on the basis of friendship and residential closeness in the east side. The parties they ran tried to appeal to the public gathered by Descolada. All these events were

---

[4] In this context, 'clubber' is a somewhat loose term for a youth identity, self-attributed by those who used to attend electronic dance music parties mainly as audience members. A female promoter once told me that, in order to be a clubber, one has to follow a clothing standard by using a mix of stylized colourful clothes, which are usually accompanied by piercings on different parts of the face and body and a stylish hairstyle. This 'clubber style' is loosely inspired by the way The Prodigy and Altern8 members built their characters in their 1991–2 videos (Assef, 2003 p. 223).

relevant to the formation of an autonomous and exclusive techno and drum 'n' bass scene in the far-east quarters of São Paulo.

Although it is the richest Brazilian city, São Paulo has a high level of social inequality and the way electronic dance music is experienced there seems a direct reflection of such inequality. We can situate this peripheral techno and drum 'n' bass scene as an intersection of class-marked performative music genres. In terms of social class, this scene contrasted with the transnationally inspired, legal, commercially minded club and rave events attended by the white middle-classes that were taking place in São Paulo's central region and nearby rural areas. 'Clubs' and 'raves' were terms that referred locally to electronic dance music events following middle-class, cosmopolitan standards known around the world. Yet in the urban peripheries where this scene took place, it contrasted aesthetically with a wide variety of forms of sociability associated with working-class entertainment aimed at the young. These forms of sociability are epitomized by genres that mark different ways of being a working-class Brazilian, like samba, *pagode*, *axé* music, rap, *sertanejo* and *forró*. Techno and drum 'n' bass, however, evoked cultural referents quite distant from their urban experience as Brazilian working-class youth, although the way these genres were experienced reflected a mix of international and local elements.

A survey ordered by São Paulo's municipal administration in 2003 and aimed at building a profile of the contemporary local youth is quite revealing about the minority status of techno and drum 'n' bass among poor youth. Among a sample population of 2,259 people between 15 and 24 years old, selected proportionally according to different regions of the city, five 'homogeneous zones' (HZs) were defined into which all the city districts were classified. These HZs were defined based on criteria for youth social inclusion, with HZ1 being the one for the most included and HZ5 for the least. Samba, *pagode* and *axé* music were, in this order, the three most preferred genres among HZs 4 and 5 – that is, the HZs embracing the less socially included youth. HZ3 differed from HZ4 and HZ5 only for axé music being replaced by 'rock' as the third most preferred genre. Among the 11 genres considered (samba, rock, *pagode*, *axé*, reggae, rap, *forró*, MPB, pop, funk and techno), techno was the only category to refer to a wide variety of electronic dance music genres. It was the least preferred among the three lower HZs, the area within which the absolute majority of the participants of this scene fit. According to this survey, techno and drum 'n' bass were the preference of a minority among poor youth in São Paulo city, whereas samba, *pagode* and *axé*, genres strongly associated with poor working-class Brazilians, were symbols for a dominant sensibility among local youth (Prefeitura Municipal de São Paulo, 2003).

Putting together techno, drum 'n' bass and Brazilian poor working-class youth, these peripheral parties were a critical mix not only for the dominant relationships established locally between music and social class, but also for the active involvement of working-class youth within transnational culture flux. They shared symbols, meanings and practices from different places, including local and international working- and middle-class scenes, although they redefined them in a uniquely expressive manner.

Offstage Roles of DJs

DJs acting in this 'peripheral' scene, like any other DJs, were not just music performers; they did all the pre-performance work such as searching for music and information, shopping for vinyl in stores and online, listening to tracks and rehearsing mixes. In contrast with the minority of professional DJs acting in local clubs and raves, who concentrated on their roles as music performers, producers and networkers, the amateur DJs in the east-side scene had to deal with all the logistical and administrative work necessary to run parties and mobilize social networks both in-person and online. Further, they did this work in addition to their regular jobs.

In contrast to the Vienna techno and drum 'n' bass scene that Reitsamer (2011) describes, the DJs on the east side of São Paulo did not pursue individual, do-it-yourself career models. Besides playing records, Reitsamer's DJs incorporated multiple roles as performers, producers, nightclub organizers, network entrepreneurs and self-promoters. Although DJs acting in the peripheral districts of São Paulo performed multiple roles, they acted in a way appropriate both to their own way of achieving things in general and to the expectations of their audiences. Rather than individual careers, they developed collective ones, acting together in *projetos*. As I noted elsewhere (Fontanari, 2008), this pattern of organization changed when some DJs of poor, working-class origin tried to upgrade their careers by reaching the middle-class, commercial clubs, of São Paulo's central region.

These *projetos* were based on personal loyalties, housing proximity, and exchanges of work, money, knowledge and equipment (turntables, amplifiers, etc.). If organizing *projetos* was a way to overcome their financial obstacles, it was also the socially acceptable way to work things out in periphery. It allowed low-income, poorly educated, working-class youth to acquire the necessary equipment and knowledge to take on the international *dramatis personae* of the DJ and to become specialized in a locally uncommon transnational musical language. These multiple *projetos*, which ran parties on alternating weekends, formed the social basis of this electronic dance music scene.

In 2005, most of the people taking part in techno and drum 'n' bass dissemination among São Paulo poor working-class youth, including DJs themselves, were just beginning to use the internet as a source of information about music, both as a place to buy/import vinyl records and as a way to build and enhance social networks. In contrast, most of the Brazilian middle classes had already been familiar with the internet since the mid-1990s. Access to information about electronic dance music depended so strongly on physical social interaction that this was an important source of power for some DJs. Back then, this reinforced DJs' roles for their audiences in the face of the growing transnational presence in their everyday, local lives. Limited competence in English reading and understanding, as well as the social hierarchies, urban segregation, class and ethnic/racial prejudice, made personal interactions with DJs the best way of exchanging information about electronic dance music.

However, Escuro, a drum 'n' bass DJ socialized in this setting, once commented that his audience also had limited proficiency in reading and understanding Portuguese, their native language. This conversation revealed that DJs perceived themselves as doing a kind of educational work in talking to and performing for young people with scarce resources who attended their parties. 'We have to pass on something to them', they often told me. Since both DJs and their audiences shared low living standards and lack of access to good quality education, such a transnational musical language had a crucial role in promoting and stimulating a dislocation from their original place of belonging to the construction of a place to shelter an identity based on a critical way of self-construction among poor working classes.

The roles played by these committed DJs among their socially disadvantaged audience resembles the roles of Jamaican DJs. During the 1950s, as Jamaican radio stations were quite conservative, soundsystem 'deejays', or 'toasters' (comparable to rappers, who appeared later in the US), used to spread community news like radio DJs, while the selector (the DJ) played the latest American rhythm 'n' blues hits on specialized soundsystems (Brewster and Broughton, 1999). The soundsystems thus fulfilled an important public role, symbolically connecting local people to other places as well as providing events of intense musical involvement that reinforced local identity. Later on, in the 1960s and 1970s, when Jamaican migrants took them to London, these soundsystems were regarded as a medium to pass on important messages for people. In this way, music could have educational, informative and historicizing roles for the community, as well as work for the building of a black consciousness against oppression (St John, 2009, p. 30). This educational and informational role of the Jamaican soundsystems involves the transmission of information 'about sound', but also, as Henriques (2011) points out, 'through sound'; a bi-dimensional process of spreading information also shared by São Paulo's peripheral DJs.[5]

The parties held in São Paulo's periphery were nomadic: they were held in a different district every time, since each *projeto* was rooted in a different locality and tended to rent nearby places. They thus dodged locally dominant, mainstream, working-class cultural patterns of interaction in nightclub events. Such trajectory made DJs and partygoers regularly travel to unexplored regions of town, which reinforced a local cosmopolitan ethos among them. By building a sense of community and belonging for regular party-goers, DJs fulfilled a role similar to that of the 'DJ as cultural hero', which Williams (1986) attributes to Chicago's black disc jockeys

---

[5] Through the notion of 'sonic bodies' Henriques (2011) develops an approach which focuses on sonic and corporeal ways of knowing put into play by Jamaican soundsystems, as opposed to mental, visual and representational ones. To him, the soundsystems' crewmembers embody a 'sonic logos' and by performing music to their audiences they put into play a process of 'knowing and thinking through sound'.

of the 1940s and 1950s. Back then, by talking in familiar language patterns and broadcasting jazz, blues and rhythm 'n' blues songs from early morning till late night, disc jockeys built a sense of community for black migrants from the rural south who experienced a clash of rural and urban worlds. For these migrants, DJs were important personalities with whom the audiences identified and whom they followed as models.

Although not openly negotiating ethnic identities, the peripheral techno and drum 'n' bass DJs in São Paulo embodied similar roles. Through musical performances these DJs built a way of belonging based on a 'transnational, cosmopolitan perspective' for their audiences. DJs thus created a way of belonging that engaged the local urban experience with mediated cosmopolitan sounds, characters, places and perspectives from around the world, built on niche and micro exchanges of information, even though almost none of the DJs acting in this scene had been abroad. Through the embodied and sensorial experience of music and dance, local and global connections were embedded in the mix.

Techno and Drum 'n' Bass Parties as a Cultural Mix

The particular principles that DJs follow in the elimination of difference between two tracks through the manipulation of low-, medium- and high-frequency controls of the mixer are productive for understanding the socio-cultural roles of DJs in disseminating electronic dance music among their young poor working-class audiences in São Paulo.[6] From the early 1990s, DJs had had to deal with people unfamiliar with electronic dance genres, reacting against them in ways that expressed a clear resistance to otherness. Following Stokes (1994), music has the power to evoke and arrange things beyond itself (such as collective memories or moral and

---

[6] Overall, dance DJs who use a mixer can, at least potentially, use it to layer or to crosscut two different tracks at some point during their performances. By contrast, experienced DJs and dancers can easily identify two different tracks a DJ is using in a mix, although lay people on the dancefloor often do not notice the mix, but nevertheless enjoy the outcome of the mix as a single track.

political order) and musical performances put into play imagined ethnicities and identities; therefore, these reactions seem consistent with the challenge that techno and drum 'n' bass represented to socio-cultural identities of local audiences. These were notions of time, space and place, and self-conceptions of ethnicity, gender, class and generation. DJs initially introduced specific electronic dance genres by mixing them with Brazilian mainstream popular genres and thus by mediating familiar and unfamiliar worlds. If DJs did not change the notions and values that structured local, familiar worlds, at least they challenged their limits and created a cultural space in which to be different.

In the 1970s and 1980s, in the socio-cultural movement called *bailes black* (black dances) (Assef, 2003; Vianna, 1997), DJs disseminated American funk and fed the development of Brazilian black identity. In the same period, discotheques were set up in the east side of São Paulo and disseminated disco-club repertoire. Both developments formed important background for the later introduction of house music in the late 1980s and techno and jungle (later drum 'n' bass) in the early 1990s among working-class young people. However, in the mid-2000s electronic dance music DJs still struggled to disseminate their music among their social peers, for whom Brazilian popular mainstream genres as samba, *pagode*, *axé* music and *sertanejo* were the most appealing.[7]

A DJ who specialized in jungle, revealed to me that in the mid-1990s DJs had to perform a wide variety of genres to be praised by their audiences in the large clubs on the east side.[8] These genres included the ones supported by national and international music industry, radio and television. If DJs tried to move a bit further from this pattern, playing something 'exotic' such as jungle, people on the dancefloor laughed at them, he said. Ermelino recalled the case of Marky, the most successful Brazilian drum 'n' bass DJ. In the early 1990s, when Marky, a resident DJ at Toco,

---

[7] It is remarkable that, since the 1970s, Brazil has been one of the few countries in the world where the consumption of national popular music exceeds the consumption of music from abroad (Bastos, 2007). That reveals a strong preference for mainstream popular Brazilian genres.

[8] In order to preserve their anonymity, the nicknames used by direct contributors during fieldwork were changed respecting the same logics of the originals. For the purpose of historical record, however, the names of things and places were kept.

began to introduce hardcore and jungle among his set composed mainly of mainstream Brazilian popular music genres, he used to receive notes with offensive messages from the audience demanding that he switched the repertoire. That changed, however, when DJs and organizers created particular spaces for poor working-class youth where the new electronic dance music genres, such as jungle and techno, were played; these venues included Sound Factory, the rave Descolada and the Parada da Paz. Therefore, DJs not only mixed tracks, but also made room for minority musical sensibilities. A particular setting where that process could be observed was the party that DJs Randy Jay, from *projeto* E.Vision, and promoter Lilica, from Circuit of Love, held in a poor district of Guarulhos, a satellite city of São Paulo.

Randy Jay, who specialized in techno, gave me a flyer for a benefit party called Electronic Solidarity, which he was going to run along with *projeto* Circuit of Love at the end of October 2005. According to the flyer, the party would last from noon to 11.00 p.m. on Sunday. I left my place at 3 p.m., caught a bus to the subway, transferred twice and took another bus to the party's location, where I arrived almost three hours later. As I had not met anybody dressing as a 'clubber' on the same bus, and as I had no idea where I was going, I asked the bus fare collector if he had seen any party near the end of the line. 'Only a Church party', he told me. It surprised me, but the only thing I could do was to wait and check it out. After about an hour the bus arrived at the district where the party was taking place.

It was – I later came to know – the 264th celebration of the traditional, Catholic popular festival of Nossa Senhora do Bonsucesso, which began in 1741. According to official information, the celebration was one of the older ones in Guarulhos and consisted of pilgrimages, processions, singing, Masses and fairs. Besides religious activities, the city administration supported 'cultural events' for the general public, which were aimed at the 'strengthening of traditional culture'. These cultural events thus supported presentations of traditional music and dance by artists from São Paulo's state countryside.

There were thousands of people of varied ages walking around the district: parents with small children, groups of single youth, the elderly. Groups of policemen watched the movement at some distance. Sellers sold food and drinks in stands with loudspeakers playing mainstream Brazilian popular music. I stepped out of the bus and walked up the first street I could find, looking for Randy's party. Through that street I arrived at a public square where a Mass was being celebrated. I kept on walking through a larger street, trying to distinguish techno or drum 'n' bass beats among a mixture of sounds coming from multiple sources. I passed by an amusement park and finally arrived at Randy's party. It was being held in a street corner ice-cream store, in a marginal area almost outside the area circumscribed to the religious party. All the attendants arriving from this side of the religious party had to pass by the ice-cream store.

Space was limited. With the DJ equipment, loudspeakers and the ice-cream bar, no more than 50 people would fit. The most motivated stayed inside; the others remained outside. Some came from São Paulo. Others were locals. Even though the latter seemed outsiders to the techno and drum 'n' bass scene, they enjoyed dancing. When I was using my camcorder, one of the guys from São Paulo told me to be careful because, for him, I was putting myself at risk by displaying that equipment in this neighbourhood.[9] On the other side of the street there was a bar and restaurant attended almost exclusively by men who drank together; they were chatting and listening to a man singing *sertanejo* (Brazilian country music) and playing acoustic guitar. Positioning myself in the middle of the street I could listen to techno and *sertanejo*, as well as see an amusement park on my left. On my right, a little further up, people gathered in the religious celebrations that were, by that time, nearing their end. After sunset, the stroboscopic white light flashing through the ice-cream store doors made the party look (from afar) like an extraterrestrial spaceship landed in Guarulhos's outskirts. Nevertheless, it was not seen as strange by the local public, for whom it could have been just an updated attraction of the bicentennial celebration of Nossa Senhora do Bonsucesso.

Lilica acknowledged that techno and drum 'n' bass did not correspond to the dominant musical preferences of Guarulhos residents,

---

[9] Back then, before the commercial explosion of a wide variety of electronic devices for communication in Brazil, such devices as multi-functional mobile phones, mini-DV camcorders and digital cameras were still a novelty even for the middle-classes. I bought mine thanks to the funds I obtained from the cultural branch of a private bank, Itaú Cultural, as an academic prize for my Master's thesis project.

although she insisted on promoting it. There, people identified more with mainstream, popular Brazilian genres. As Lilica later confided to me in an interview (2005), she talked to people who ran small businesses in the district, looking for financial support, but many declined, saying nobody there would enjoy her music. She said she would bring people from São Paulo, which did not convince them. The ice-cream storeowner appreciated the idea and offered the place, certainly thinking of the chance to increase his sales. Since she had no funds to rent a bigger place, she took it. In fact, the middle-aged men drinking beer and listening to a *sertanejo* singer across the street stayed there while the ice-cream store party developed. Only local young people, particularly men, joined the clubbers, who, like me, came from other metropolitan regions.

By bringing a techno and drum 'n' bass party to a traditional religious celebration, as well as by setting it in an ice-cream store, Lilica was acting as a cultural 'mixer', giving a new frame to the electronic dance music experience. This experience was not unusual for the regular techno and drum 'n' bass working-class fans. In this scene, young working-class DJs and their parties were much closer to Brazilian working-class, mainstream, popular culture than any other kind of dance DJs and events in São Paulo, such as the middle-class dance clubs and raves. Sometimes, as in this religious celebration, electronic dance music parties were enmeshed in working-class, Brazilian popular culture, forming a new mix in which it became difficult or even meaningless to demarcate Brazilian working-class, traditionally-influenced culture, since these events made sense to their participants as a whole. That identity may be described as a hybrid, a product of the meeting of cultural referents brought from distant places. Middle-class dance club events in the highly urbanized central regions of São Paulo were framed by an already cosmopolitan, middle-class ethos, whereas in peripheral regions the DJs were responsible for introducing that cosmopolitan experience.

Room for Difference

On a small farm called Sítio Elo, located in a district called Parque do Carmo on the east side of São Paulo, where the best parties attracted about a thousand people, I attended three dance events in 2005. There, *projetos* used to set up two dancefloors, one indoors, in a wide party room and the other outdoors, under the trees. Next to the party room there was a swimming pool, where people used to jump in and later walk among the crowd in wet clothes and bare feet. Eventually, heterosexual couples had sexual intercourse among a small crowd playing around in the water. Other couples, more discreet, seemed to prefer the darkness among the trees. I saw boys walking around in bare chests and sometimes bare feet. Rather than a sexualized posturing, they behaved in a relaxed manner, as if they were at home, without reason to care about formality. In contrast, DJs were less informal, even stiff, in their public behaviour and personal presentation.

The exotic aesthetic of techno and drum 'n' bass music and its implied openness to difference, reinforced by flyer distribution in LGBT beauty salons and parties, opened up room for the presence of gay couples and a small number of drag queens and transgender people in the peripheral east-side parties, though there were none at the Electronic Solidarity party described above, in Guarulhos. Even at those parties that included LGBT people, however, the majority of partygoers displayed heterosexual inclinations, and gender inequality was still remarkable, as the disproportion of male to female DJs demonstrates. The general ethos of the parties I attended in São Paulo's east zone nevertheless differed sharply from that of other working-class nighttime entertainment. The more typical working-class entertainment was marked by explicit male domination, intolerance not only of gender diversity but of any kind of unusual behaviour; profit-making practices, unofficial local power hierarchies, heterosexual flirting and male invasive behaviour as they sought women to spend the party with. On that issue, this scene mixed the heterosexual-but-non-sexualized ethos of middle-class clubs and raves, where the search for romantic partners could be considered outsider behaviour; the homo-sexualized ethos of LGBT clubs; and the hegemonic patri-archal standards of mainstream working-class clubs – all in the same event.

Techno and drum 'n' bass DJs promoting this scene, as well as their regular audience, thus operated in a confluence of paradoxes through which they struggled to manage their identity as a type of liberal, cosmopolitan, poor working-class youth. For their promoters and participants, these parties were ambiguous experiences, both mundane and otherworldly, distancing them from their social and urban place of belonging yet also allowing them to approach it. The places were on the periphery; the equipment and infrastructure were far from state of the art. Like a great variety of commercial activities and cultural practices in the periphery, the events were not licensed. However, the ethos driving the sociability and musical experience, as well as body ornaments and the whole mix of references taking place, were quite unfamiliar by local standards.

This kind of experience was not possible in events that were structured around the most common Brazilian mainstream, working-class, popular music genres, such as samba, *pagode*, *axé* music, *sertanejo* and *forró*, that catered to the dominant sensibility of the DJs' social peers. The musical, performative and interactional referents of these events were rooted in Brazilian traditional social dance standards, which assume established, normative ways to use the body; to present the self publicly; to interact with people of the same and opposite sex in mixed settings. At such parties, these standards were often reinforced by hegemonic, macho, Catholic-influenced moral judgements, which were eventually publicly expressed through verbal or physical assault against whoever transgressed the established norms.[10] The security staff were ready to act on anyone who went beyond such behavioural norms. Contact between clubbers and staff and organizers was usually cold, impersonal and driven by an explicit interest in profit.

These features were also reinforced by a highly normative musical structure, which adapts a dance music genre to the pop song format, which consists of an introduction followed by verses and chorus, which repeats until the song arrives at a climax. It lasts less than four minutes. The elements guiding the audience's identification with the music are basically the rhythm and the lyrics, which articulate the traditional body and moral normativity, and which frame those elements in a catchy melody. By drawing on Seeger's (2004) argument that musical performances create many aspects of

---

[10] It is remarkable that even in the most culturally liberal, cosmopolitan, central region of São Paulo, around the end of Paulista Avenue, where are set many middle-class, underground and LGBT clubs, there are often cases of physical assaults against, and even murdering of, men who 'look gay'. So far, this exemplifies the reactions partygoers, especially those who use public transportation, were subjected to.

culture and social life as well as on Stokes's (1994) assertion that music has the power to evoke and arrange extra-musical processes (such as collective memories or moral and political order) and that musical performances put into play imagined ethnicities and identities, I argue here that such normative features are reinforced (through symbols and social interaction, social hierarchies of class, gender, ethnicity, race and generation), while they also stimulate a *hyperconsciousness*, an always vigilant state of mind. Thereby free expressions of whatever may challenge hegemonic values are effectively inhibited.

The São Paulo peripheral techno and drum 'n' bass scene created space to be different from the dominant standards of Brazilian popular, working-class mainstream culture, although it did not allow one to be totally different. DJs and partygoers resisted normative frameworks, showing their clear dissatisfaction with dominant cultural trends in their social milieu and seeking new trends to identify themselves with. In this sense, this is not a resistance against cultural normativity pervasive in society as a whole, but rather against dominant trends relevant to their milieu and for their generation. These subcultural features resonate with the notion of 'autonomous zones' that Graham St John (2009) and Rietveld (1998) associate with underground raves, particularly in Europe and the US, where raves have suffered a systematic repression by public authorities. Underground raves, as St John (2009) presents them, are structured through practices and values resistant to structuring principles of modernity, such as the individual, rationality, state control and repression, private property and for-profit exchange. By contrast, on the fringes of this Brazilian peripheral metropolis, where modernity and globalization are experienced in a quite distinctive way, electronic dance music culture enables a *way to be different*. Although this peripheral scene can be considered an 'autonomous zone', its autonomy is equivalent to the DJ's ability to construct a hybrid identity by mixing familiar and unfamiliar referents. In this sense, the cultural space that DJs build to be different does not need to be totally autonomous. The conditions for the existence of this space depend on the ability of DJs and promoters to mediate difference. Through the DJ's work, the social situation historically experienced by excluded populations may transform zones of self-exclusion into strategies for inclusion and self-transformation.

Final Mix

In this chapter I have presented and discussed the role that techno and drum 'n' bass DJs in São Paulo's periphery play among their audiences from the angle of cultural mediation. Assuming the importance of DJ mixing as a structuring musical practice for the scene they achieve and drawing on the idea that 'musical performances create many aspects of culture and social life' (Seeger, 2004, p. xiii), I have demonstrated the extra-musical power of the DJ mix to understand the socio-cultural roles of DJs among their audiences. In doing so, I presented two further levels in which DJ mixing may help to conceptualize the mobilization, visions and practices of electronic dance music scenes: first, the introduction of electronic dance music genres and, second, the hybrid identity of the cultural performance, extending to DJs and their audiences as social subjects, mixing local conditions and global influences.

These DJs are experts in the process of making exotic elements locally meaningful by including them in familiar frames of sensibility and practice. DJs use the mixer to crossfade, EQ and segue sequences of different tracks without necessarily allowing the audience to notice the points of connection. On a different but related level, global, new music genres and repertoire are translated and introduced by being gradually interlocked with genres that are already known. These genres are blended according to the same principles DJs use to join together different tracks by means of the mixer. Complementarily, DJs temporarily create a relatively autonomous zone to experience their 'strange' music.

Due to their generic aesthetic differences from hegemonic local aesthetics among the working-class, techno and drum 'n' bass offer practical effectiveness on the dancefloor and are more meaningful as dance music genres than other music to DJs and their audiences. In this way, techno and drum 'n' bass genres operate as metaphor for the peripheral youth's disappointment with Brazilian popular mainstream music genres and the values of the world they represent. The connections between music and people are not given; instead, they are objects DJs mix as cultural mediators through music, dance and verbal means.

As I have demonstrated, the role performed by São Paulo's peripheral DJs, and the way they define themselves as DJs in practice, depends not just on the multiple functions they have beyond playing music, but also on the socio-cultural settings from which they emerge as social actors and in which they are enmeshed. In contrast to other electronic dance music scenes, the success achieved by these peripheral DJs does not depend exclusively on their individual subcultural capital, but rather on their capacity to work collectively and to attend to the symbolic and identitary needs of audiences. I identified the lack of a cultural space to be different as a main need in their social milieu. This sense of being different can take many forms, such as differences of gender, generation, aesthetic preferences and perceptions of place. The electronic dance music scene that local DJs have built is a collective mixing of cultural referents from different and quite distant origins. Thus, the roles of DJs among their audiences should be understood not only through the DJ's musical mix, but also through the kind of cultural performances they achieve and their relationship with the socio-cultural circumstances from which they emerge.

References

Assef, Cláudia (2003) *Todo DJ já Sambou: a História do Disc-Jockey no Brasil*. São Paulo: Conrad.

Bastos, Rafael José de Menezes (2007) *As Contribuições da Música Popular Brasileira às Músicas Populares do Mundo: Diálogos Transatlânticos Brasil/Europa/África, Primeira Parte, Antropologia em Primeira Mão*. Florianópolis: UFSC.

Brewster, Bill and Broughton, Frank (1999) *Last Night a DJ Saved My Life: The History of Disc Jockey*. New York: Grove Press.

Burke, Peter (1978) *Popular Culture in Early Modern Europe, 1500–1800*. Burlington, VT: Ashgate.

Fontanari, Ivan Paolo de Paris (2003) 'Rave à Margem do Guaíba: Música e Identidade Jovem na Cena Eletrônica de Porto Alegre'. Master's thesis, Universidade Federal do Rio Grande do Sul, Porto Alegre. http://hdl.handle.net/10183/3703 [accessed 7 February 2013].

—(2008) 'Os DJs da Perifa: Música Eletrônica, Mediação, Globalização e Performance entre Grupos Populares em São Paulo'. PhD diss., Universidade Federal do Rio Grande do Sul, Porto Alegre. http://hdl.handle.net/10183/14398 [accessed 7 February 2013].

Fontoura, Natalia and Bonetti, Alinne (2011) 'Trabalho Doméstico Remunerado e as Desigualdades de Gênero e Raça no Brasil

Contemporâneo'. In Jorge A. de Castro and Fábio M. Vaz (eds) *Situação Social Brasileira: Monitoramento e Condições de Vida* (245–62). Brasília: IPEA.

Haraway, Donna J. (1991) *Simians, Cyborgs, and Women: the Reinvention of Nature*. New York: Routledge.

Henriques, Julian (2011) *Sonic Bodies: Reggae Sound Systems, Performance Techniques, and Ways of Knowing*. New York and London: Continuum.

Mazzarella, William (2004) 'Culture, Globalization, Mediation'. *Annual Review of Anthropology*, 33: 345–67.

Montero, Paula (2006) 'Índios e Missionários no Brasil: Para uma Teoria da Mediação Cultural'. In Paula Montero (ed.) *Deus na Aldeia: Missionários, Índios e Mediação Cultural* (31–66). São Paulo: Globo.

Prefeitura Municipal de São Paulo (2003) *Mapa da Juventude: Perfil e Comportamento do Jovem de São Paulo*. Institutional report.

Reitsamer, Rosa (2011) 'The DIY Careers of Techno and Drum 'n Bass DJs in Vienna'. *Dancecult: Journal of Electronic Dance Music Culture*, 3(1): 28–43.

Rietveld, Hillegonda C. (1998) *This is Our House: House Music, Cultural Spaces and Technology*. Aldershot: Ashgate.

Seeger, Anthony (2004) *Why Suyá Sing: A Musical Anthropology of an Amazonian People*. Urbana, IL: University of Illinois Press.

Schechner, Richard (1985) *Between Theater and Anthropology*. Philadelphia, PA: University of Pennsylvania Press.

St John, Graham (2009) *Technomad: Global Raving Countercultures*. London: Equinox.

Stokes, Martin (1994) *Ethnicity, Identity and Music: The Musical Construction of Place*. Oxford: Berg Publishers.

Telles, Edward E. (2004) *Race in Another America: The Significance of Skin Color in Brazil*. Princeton, NJ: Princeton University Press.

Thornton, Sarah (1995) *Club Cultures: Music, Media, and Subcultural Capital*. Hanover, NH: Wesleyan University Press.

Vianna, Hermano (1997) *O Mundo Funk Carioca*. Rio de Janeiro: Jorge Zahar.

Williams, Gilbert A. (1986) 'The Black Disc Jockey as a Cultural Hero'. *Popular Music and Society*, 10(3): 79–90.

Interview

Lilica (2005) Interviewed by Ivan Paolo de Paris Fontanari, Periphery of Guarulhos, 28 September.

CHAPTER TWELVE

War on the Dancefloor: *Synthscenen*'s Military Power Games

Johanna Paulsson

Introduction

This chapter investigates the role of the DJ in relation to military aesthetics and the political economy of sexuality mainly within *synthscenen* ('the synth scene'), a Swedish umbrella term (derived from the word synthesizer) describing a stylistically diverse club scene and subculture (Rahm, 2012) that primarily engages with synthpop, electronic body music (EBM), electro-industrial music and similar subgenres, and has its roots in the 1980s. The idea of 'War on the Dancefloor' is inspired by a song by the Austrian solo project Nachtmahr (2009), which metaphorically explores the role of the DJ as commander and thereby illuminates the power relation between the DJ and the crowd, and how it interrelates with the militaristic aesthetics in European EBM, industrial music and related DJ culture.[1] DJs in the scene participate in the creation

---

[1] This idea has previously been explored by the author in Paulsson (2011).

of a playground that both imitates and subverts hegemonic power relations, turning the dancefloor into a symbolical battlefield on several different levels. Contrary to Rodgers (2010, p. 9) I argue that the rhetoric of 'combat and domination' can be used to highlight structures of power not only when addressing the history of electronic music but also in terms of the DJ's social status and the transmission of sound. Within *synthscenen* you sometimes find club-goers wearing vintage military uniforms, fetish style side caps and corsets or even military hats with totalitarian insignia among the usual black-clad crowd. Incorporating the ambiguous aesthetics of European EBM and industrial music, *synthscenen* and its international equivalents has been criticized for flirting with political symbols, especially imagery with Nazi and fascist implications. However, this fascist fascination refers to an abstraction of power on a symbolical level rather than to a political perspective. In addition, technological features of club culture in general, such as the vocoder (an electronic special effect that robotizes the voice, popular during the formation of electronic disco) and loudspeakers, either originate from or are also employed as military devices (Goodman, 2010; Pieslak, 2009; Tompkins, 2010); for example, Tompkins (2010, p. 20) notes that the 1970s 'would finally catch the vocoder in its double life: secret masking agent for the military and studio tool for the musician'. Similarly, loudspeakers and sound have been employed since World War II as part of psychological tactics in warfare in order to deceive the enemy (Goodman, 2010, p. 41; Pieslak, 2009, p. 80; Tompkins, 2010, p. 63). This means that although often less openly displayed or explicitly referred to within other genres not associated with *synthscenen*, certain aspects or offsprings of war and propaganda machinery are present on all dancefloors, making a discussion of the DJ in the position of a commander pertinent to DJ culture in general – regardless of genre or club scene. The notion of a consensual power exchange that will outline this discussion refers to the similarities between sadomasochism (SM)[2] as a play-like behaviour, where, according to Weinberg (2006, p. 33), 'the ritualization of dominance and submission' is the essence, and the aesthetics that

---

[2] The subject of SM and fetish clubs will not be explored further in this chapter, but will rather be used as a metaphorical framework for my discussion on the role of the DJ.

define *synthscenen*. Although the term SM is somewhat simpli-
fying, I will generally use it in the chapter, referring to Dancer et
al.'s (2006, p. 83) notion that all SM relationships are consensual;
'both partners agree to the general power differential framework
of the relationship'. Within this framework, this chapter examines
how power and pleasure are reproduced in the DJ culture that
relates to *synthscenen* in Sweden and associated international club
scenes in terms of club/subcultural hierarchies (Thornton, 1995;
Hutton, 2006). In order to illuminate these structures of power I
conceptualize the dancefloor as a metaphorical combat zone.

The research for this chapter was achieved through interviews
with Swedish DJs and international artists in combination with
participant observation among dance crowds in Sweden (Stockholm
and Malmö) as well as in Germany (Berlin and Cologne). A total
of 15 email interviews and three face-to-face interviews have
been conducted with DJs and artists between 2010 and 2012.[3]
Additionally, less formal correspondence and conversations with
participants at clubs and festivals were collected during this time.
Among these are informants from Sweden, France, Germany and
Greece, who attend international events such as the Amphi Festival
– a gothic gathering similar to the larger predecessor Wave-Gotik-
Treffen in Leipzig – that brings together 16,000 black-clad visitors
from countries worldwide and is held at the culture and leisure
park Tanzbrunnen on the bank of the River Rhine in Cologne,
Germany. Working as freelance journalist and music critic for one
of the major newspapers in Sweden, my connection with this scene
is both personal and professional. Although the mainstream media
coverage of this scene is scarce, I have occasionally covered events
within *synthscenen* as a journalist and tend to be associated with
this role by many of my interviewees. Since my personal music
preference resides in this scene, I usually spend my leisure time at
such club nights, while my holidays are devoted to gothic gatherings
such as the Amphi Festival. My own insider experiences provide
the necessary understanding for the specific logic of this subculture,
but on the other hand may result in difficulties in gaining analytical
distance. Thus, my own observations and the interviewees' general
descriptions and views on the aesthetics, politics and ambivalence

---

[3] DJ interviews were conducted in Swedish and translated to English by the author.

within the scene, will be analysed with reference to feminist media studies and critical literature in the fields of technology, warfare and electronic dance music culture (EDMC). While focusing on the role of the DJ, this chapter extends into aesthetic aspects that are integral to this particular DJ culture, such as clothes, artwork, lyrics and other attributes that contribute to the production of the dancefloor ambience. The DJ interviews started out as quite simple questionnaires and in some cases evolved into deeper, more personal conversations. My aim has not been to investigate political views as such but rather to examine how, in particular, Swedish DJs in this club scene address sometimes controversial musical and visual aesthetics of its dancefloor. Furthermore, DJs have been asked to describe their own experience of the power relations between themselves and the dance crowd within *synthscenen*. The face-to-face interviews with named electronic music artists – former Kraftwerk member Wolfgang Flür (who presents DJ/VJ shows under the alias Musik Soldat), DAF (Deutsch Amerikanische Freundschaft) and Nachtmahr – will add to the framework either as artists who have had a seminal impact on the aesthetics of this scene, or as popular/controversial representatives of the different subgenres that constitute *synthscenen* at the time of writing; each have employed references to warfare and/or totalitarianism in one way or another and provide insight in the specific aspects of their work. *Synthscenen* is a quite small community in Sweden and in order not to affect their reputation, and thereby their possibilities to get gigs, all other DJ interviewees and informants will be referred to anonymously. For the same reason the names of specific clubs and festivals will be omitted, apart from the international Amphi Festival in Germany.

My main interviewees are both male and female DJs who are active at clubs in Stockholm, Gothenburg and Malmö – the three largest cities in Sweden. Since the possibilities to make a living as a professional DJ within this scene in a small country such as Sweden is more or less non-existent, the majority work as DJs in addition to other jobs or studies. Some of the DJs are part of my personal and professional network, while others have been recruited through snowball sampling. Several of them – both veterans and newcomers – are also club organizers or event promoters, and are in some cases also active as DJs in other contexts, for instance at indie music clubs or fetish clubs. Within the context of *synthscenen*, these DJs play a variety of synthesizer-based music genres, from synthpop to electro-industrial music – characterized by futuristic and 'inhuman' features such as vocodered or distorted (male) vocals and layered textures – and the hard-hitting beats of 'old-school' EBM, with often shouted yet undistorted vocals. Many of the DJs also play a selection of contemporary subgenres such as futurepop – a trance music infused relative to synthpop and EBM – and aggrotech, featuring faster tempos, aggressive/pessimistic lyrics and distorted (male) vocals. Although music styles have diversified under the banner of EBM and industrial music (originally, in the mid-1970s, a style of experimental music featuring transgressive and provocative themes) since the early 1980s, these genres still share similar aesthetics. Even synthpop bands with a much 'softer' sound (melodic music with clear vocals) may share SM related or military inspired stylistics such as white (or red) shirt with black tie, and early representatives of the genre have played an important role in creating both the visual and textual repertoire of this scene; an example can be found in Depeche Mode's song 'Master and Servant' (1984). As one Stockholm-based male DJ notes, the Swedish scene is 'wide and fragmented musically', but comparatively small considering the number of people buying records and attending events. Some clubs are specialized, for instance focusing solely on EBM, while others present a wider selection of music, attracting a more diverse audience. Internationally, the EBM/electro/industrial faction might also be considered a 'substream' (Brill, 2008, p. 5) of the gothic scene – a dark and dramatic post-punk subculture, which features theatrical dress styles that refer to vampire imagery. Although there are local variations and, according to Brill, EBM would not be regarded a proper part of the gothic subculture, 'Goths and Electroheads' often share the same spaces at clubs and festivals as well as the same music (Brill, 2008, p. 5).

DJs within the scene sometimes produce music as members of a band, but rarely in their position as a DJ. *Synthscenen* is essentially a dance music scene where followers, in a rockist manner, tend to focus more on the album-based careers of single artists rather than the anonymously produced releases that in many other club scenes make the DJ the focal point of the fans. Thus, live acts are almost as important as DJs for the dancefloor. Although far from every club-goer and follower of *synthscenen* would dress up, stylistic features are essentially what distinguish this club scene from other club cultures; the interest in uniforms and military attire such as combat boots, in particular, construct social roles and group identity and affect the relationship between the DJ and the crowd. These transgressive characteristics of *synthscenen* and the international EBM/electro/industrial faction draw attention to order, discipline and authority, not least from a gender perspective. As Hutton (2006, p. 8) points out: 'Club scenes are sites of multiple struggles in terms of women asserting themselves within these spaces.' This aspect will be analysed through the performance of masculinity and the gendering of sound.

The DJ in a Consensual Power Exchange

The fascist fascination is not unique for *synthscenen*, but is rather constantly present in the postmodern desire for large-scale arena events, from football games to concerts or even DJ events in a much more commercial context. As Koepnick (1999, p. 1) points out: 'Deeply engrossed in the power of the visual, the postmodern imagination remains haunted by the operatic extravaganzas of Nazi culture and aesthetics.' Yet Susan Sontag's classic description of fascist aesthetics in 'Fascinating Fascism' (1975) does not only bring to mind a large-scale arena concert with a rock star at the centre of attention. Although DJs have a central position primarily within club culture (Gavanas, 2009, p. 78), Sontag's (1975) words could almost be mistaken for an account of a dancefloor, where the DJ takes on the role of 'an all-powerful, hypnotic leader figure or force' and at the same time awakens a similar theme of domination and enslavement. This notion has perhaps become more relevant in the 2010s when commercial club music producers and DJs finally seem to have caught up with the traditional rock star in popularity: in the summer of 2012 the Swedish DJ trio Swedish House Mafia, for instance, announced their break-up and managed to sell out three concerts in a row at a Swedish arena with a capacity of 35,000 people each night. However, Sontag's (1975) depiction of 'the orgiastic transaction between mighty forces and their puppets', particularly resembles the Nachtmahr song 'Unbeugsam' (2010) where Thomas Rainer sings about conquering the world and letting *die Puppen* (the puppets) dance as it pleases him. Although, in reality, not necessarily typical for DJ practices within *synthscenen*, the ritualization of dominance and submission humorously described by Nachtmahr is possible to apply on, at least, some DJ events: when asked to describe his interaction with the audience during his DJ and VJ shows under the name of Musik Soldat, Wolfgang Flür (2012) would in fact refer to himself as '*Der Rattenfänger von Hameln*' ('The Ratcatcher of Hamelin'), while explaining that it does not take long before the crowd on the dancefloor imitates his movements. However, Flür is the focal point and in possession of this status as 'commander' because of his past in Kraftwerk (one of the seminal artists of synthpop and electronic dance music). Thus, his DJ performances seem to have much in common with DJ practices of other electronic dance music cultures, as confirmed by one of my DJ interviewees:

> In the realm of house and techno, where DJs often perform fixed sets, people do not request songs to the same extent as they do in *synthscenen*. I enjoy the feeling of not knowing exactly what to play during the evening and I try to listen to people's requests, and, if possible, fit them into the set. But it must not be too much. I am not a jukebox. (DJ, male, Stockholm)

Although some DJs within *synthscenen* may put a lot of effort into planning the music selection for the evening, most of them would emphasize the need of being responsive, of respecting the audience and of trying to fit requested songs into their sets. When asked to describe their role as a DJ, many of my interviewees referred to themselves as entertainers or even used the expression 'people's pleaser', and simultaneously emphasized their ambition to introduce new music. Even a Gothenburg-based female DJ, who explicitly complained about the audience's tendency to treat the DJ like a 'jukebox', stressed the importance of letting the dance crowd feel included in the choice of music. On the other hand, for practical reasons, this may not always possible:

> For instance, if I am in the middle of a set of heavy EBM, it is often difficult to fit a cheerful synthpop tune into the mix smoothly, and not everyone wants to understand that. Actually I have sometimes been planning a night quite carefully; analyzing BPM [beats per minute], melodies and lyrics of different songs,

thinking about which of them to play in order to make the songs fit together in a neat and clever way, to achieve a flow, and then it is difficult to throw in a song request. (DJ, male, Malmö)

The DJ decides what to play, and within these decisions lies the ultimate power. When stating that in reality, she has the power to play what she likes and not to play what she does not like, one Stockholm-based female DJ sums up the typical notion of the DJ as a gatekeeper (Gavanas, 2009, p. 95). Or as another interviewee (DJ, male, Stockholm) puts it: 'I never play music that I personally do not like or understand. I see myself as a "filter" and a surety for that good music is played on the dancefloor.' The authority of the DJ as tastemaker, illustrated by the above statements, ought to be understood in the context of 'a commitment to a taste community' (Frith, 1996, p. 89) – in this case *synthscenen*. One male DJ from Stockholm use the word 'missionary', whereas others, in a similar sense, express an ambition to promote new music of *synthscenen* and attract new audiences.

Most of the DJs describes a quite democratic and symbiotic relationship between the DJ and the crowd, yet – for some – at 'arm's length distance'. A Stockholm-based male DJ mentions both the feeling of affinity and the sense of getting a kick out of being the person who makes people happy for the moment. Furthermore, it is possible to detect a sense of responsibility or duty; the DJ has both the power and the pressure to please the people. Or as one Stockholm-based male DJ puts it: 'A DJ has the power, but an unanimous audience can dismiss him/her.' Similarly, a Stockholm-based female DJ mentions the impact of social media, such as Facebook and Twitter, which according to her means that 'every club goer is a potential critic'. This suggests that the crowd in reality has a certain power, not only immediately on the dance-floor, but also regarding public reputation. The DJ can make the crowd 'happy, he can make them sad, he can make them sweat, he can make them relax. He has the power over the emotional situation of this group of people for the night', as Thomas Rainer (2010) concludes. It is striking that Rainer (2010) also states that people 'empower' the DJ 'to lead them through the night', implying that this still is a commission of trust that is built on consent and cannot be conquered by force. Within electronic dance music, where the spiritual and ritual dimension (Gavanas, 2009, p. 79) is often emphasized, the collective experience of the dancefloor would be referred to in terms of 'the vibe' (St John, 2009) and, as we have seen, the DJs within *synthscenen* sometimes even tend to become servants rather than masters. While having the authority to decide what music to play and consequently 'commanding' people to dance, the role of the DJ is not dictatorial. Similarly to SM scenes, the power relation between the DJ and the dance crowd could rather be described as 'both consensual and collaboratively produced' (Weinberg, 2006, p. 33).

The Militarization of the Dancefloor

The techno-influenced industrial project Nachtmahr evolved out of Thomas Rainer's (2010) background as a DJ, and the military image of the one-man band was inspired by his previous experience in the army: 'I found the similarities very appealing so I said: "Why not use this imagery to present ourselves as soldiers of – warriors of – sound, who shoot with bass drums instead of machineguns?"' With its aggressive, hard-hitting beat, the Nachtmahr song 'War on the Dancefloor' (2009) explores the role of the DJ in the lyrics on a metaphorical level: On the dancefloor, the people are the soldiers and the DJ is the commander, according to Rainer (2010), 'because he [the DJ] can steer the people in the direction he wants'. Other anthems give straight orders, for instance the song 'Tanz Zwo Drei Vier' by Faderhead (2010a), and the club setting, with uniforms, black combat boots and cyberpunk/rave-influenced cybergoths with goggles and gas-masks, emphasize the similarities between war and the EBM/electro/industrial dancefloor. What Tompkins (2010, p. 63) in the context of warfare calls 'the illusion of conflict' is not only a psychological tactic featuring 'electronically generated ghost armies' but also an aesthetic aspect of genres within *synthscenen*. As Brill (2008, p. 152) notes, many EBM/electro/industrial artists 'invoke scenarios of battle and war in their lyrics and their choice of sounds and samples'. In the Faderhead song 'Noisebastardz' (2010b) the club correspondingly becomes a 'bunker', where the DJ is the 'beatmaster' and where the girls on the dancefloor are not only wearing 'latex skirts' but also 'masks like there's a bomb alert'. These accounts within the song lyrics symbolically position the DJ as a dance dictator, and challenge the quite common position of the DJ as a spiritual or religious leader, which has been proposed in the context of other areas of electronic dance music culture (Gavanas, 2009; Till, 2010).

Goodman (2010, p. 33) notes that for a number of thinkers, from the Italian futurists to Virilio and Kittler, 'war has come to mean much more than battles between nation-states; rather, it expresses an ontological condition'. Thus, the concept of war has been used as 'an attempt to describe a low-intensity warfare that reconstitutes the most mundane aspects of everyday existence through psycho-social torque and sensory overload' (Goodman, 2010, p. 33). Therefore, placing the DJ in the powerful position of a commander – although in reality, the DJ might sometimes be more of a servant than a master – is an effective way of highlighting not only the gatekeeper function of the DJ, but also the hierarchies within club culture. As in Goodman's (2010) discussion on 'the subpolitics of frequency' – a term explored in terms of the militarization of the audiosphere and acoustic weaponry for crowd control, as well as sonic forces within Jamaican soundsystem practices – it is easy to object that part of the argumentation here lies on a purely linguistic level; a military terminology applied to music. Yet it might help identify specific structures of power that might otherwise be less obvious. Pieslak (2009, p. 172) states that, 'one person's musical pleasure is another's intense pain'; when, for example, recordings like Metallica's 'Enter Sandman', in addition to children's songs, hip-hop and pop songs were played at cacophonous levels by American soldiers to torture prisoners in Iraq and at Guantánamo Bay, this was done at locations ironically referred to as 'The Disco' (Bayoumi, 2005). Thus the metaphor seems to be working both ways between war and dance settings. I do not argue that dancefloors are dangerous places, yet we do need to pay attention to the aspect of power embedded into the transmission of sound, as is also well-documented by Henriques (2011) in the context of Jamaican soundsystem practices, developed from political PA rallies (Stolzoff, 2000, p. 42). Kittler's notion that 'popular sonic media entail the "misuse" of military technologies' (Goodman, 2010, p. 43) is particularly relevant in understanding the dance-floor. According to Wolfgang Flür (2012) the first machine, which Florian Schneider of Kraftwerk found was taken from a military device: 'It was a real vocoder, one of the first.' The use of the vocodered voice has spread into popular music; the idea behind a speech encryption device with military origins (Goodman, 2010, pp. xix–xx), once used for confusing the enemy, is now employed to 'confuse' the listener of synthpop, electro-industrial music and the like or simply to seduce the audience in a number of commercially oriented genres, not associated with *synthscenen*, such as disco, hip-hop, and contemporary house music. Similarly, war imagery and uniforms are part of the mainstream culture, where militaristic aesthetics are infused in everything from video games to the latest high street fashion. In 'Wargasm: Military Imagery in Pop Music' Simon Reynolds (1998) explores militaristic imagery in hip-hop as well as jungle and gabba, tracing jungle's militarism back to the early days of hardcore rave in 1991–2 and drug abuse, while noting that gabba – 'an aural blitzkrieg of stormtrooper beats' – is even more explicit about its 'militaristic fantasies'. Correspondingly many EBM/electro/industrial acts deliberately seek parallels between music and warfare, often referring to the transmission of sound in the lyrics, but there is a crucial difference: DJs and followers of this scene often have to deal with militaristic and totalitarian aesthetics taken to its extremes as a means of creating self-reflective and intellectual provocation – for example, politically problematic allusions and contradictory messages are deliberately employed to make the audience 'think twice about the imagery', as Rainer (2010) of Nachtmahr confirms.

'Love Music, Hate Politics' – Ambivalent Dancefloor Aesthetics

Within the EBM/electro/industrial faction it could be said that the theme of power and pleasure resides not only in the lyrics or verbal samples, but also in the non-verbal elements of the sound. It is dance music that communicates with both the body and the brains; rather than escaping from reality this music is often debating reality, and the history of Europe still operates as some kind of unifying theme. Since VJs and video projections are not common features within *synthscenen*, the visual repertoire on the dancefloor is displayed by the dancefloor participants and live acts. Yet, the interest in Soviet communist and Nazi aesthetics is above all about the totalitarianism of the imagery (Kingsepp, 2008, p. 247); even without using predefined symbols, a powerful aesthetic design can induce a range of powerful connotations. As Hanley (2004, p. 174) notes: 'These symbols still resonate with the atrocities carried out during World War II, and it is very hard to disassociate the images from their original signification.' The fans of Nachtmahr, for instance, are wearing military side caps and armbands with the letter N as in Nachtmahr, which also could refer to Napoleon or National Socialism. Third Reich military paraphernalia is still highly taboo – especially in Germany – and what is taboo is always provocative. It is exactly the context dependent aspect of provocation that is central here. As one male DJ from Stockholm reflects: 'Of course, there are people who perceive four-on-the-floor [beats] as authoritative if there are German vocals on top, but that highlights the listeners' own prejudices about people and culture rather than the standpoint of the musicians.' While saying that people in Germany are eager to distance themselves from right-wing extremism, a Stockholm-based female DJ states that Swedish EBM fans have a relatively relaxed relationship to politics, with 'listeners from all across the political spectrum'. The idea of 'what you see is *not* (necessarily) what you get' often serves as a way of separating this subculture from the outside world, even though the ambivalent aesthetics sometimes pose certain difficulties for DJs in their position as gatekeepers; in the words of one Stockholm-based male DJ, 'It is a balancing act. I would never play right-wing extremist, racist or sexist music as far as I am aware of it. But at the same time, I love provocative, stupid and challenging music. "Der Mussolini" [a 1980s underground hit by DAF (1981a)] probably sounds like a Nazi song to someone who is not in the know.'

While one male DJ from Stockholm simply says that so far he has not encountered anything he would not play, apart from 'bad music', a Malmö-based male DJ states that neither values nor messages have ever prevented him from playing the songs he wanted to play; yet he carefully selects his music and tries to avoid misconceptions regarding the samples used in certain songs by ensuring that they – for instance Leæther Strip's 'The White Disgrace' (1993) – are only played within a specific context – *synthscenen* – where he believes that the audience is aware of the artist's intention, in this case, of an 'anti-racist message'. Within the EBM/electro/industrial faction, the use of offensive imagery is often regarded as a means to describe and criticize things considered wrong in society – such in-scene inversion is typical of subcultural capital, conferring 'status on its owner in the eyes of the relevant beholder' (Thornton, 1995, p. 11). As one of my interviewees points out:

> Some harsher bands within *synthscenen* tend to have somewhat sexist lyrics, and whether their records should be played or not can always be questioned. In interviews these bands explain that it is just a way for them to express their dislike to how wrong things are in the world, so to say. If that is the case, the whole thing turns out to be a form of aggressive parody, which I think is quite all right. Then everyone might not be aware of that fact and misinterpret the message, like they do with so many other things. (DJ, female, Malmö)

The notion of 'aggressive parody' similarly applies to the ironic use of totalitarian insignia and military aesthetics. In her dissertation about the representation of Nazi Germany in popular culture, Eva Kingsepp (2008, p. 292) not only discusses the dimension of humour, but also a ritualistic strategy to protect oneself against Nazi symbolism: 'Here, the discharging of the fetischistic [sic.] power inherent in the symbols turns out to be important. By having acquired an unusual amount of "objective" knowledge about the historical context the individual has, so to speak, become immune to the dangers otherwise present.' As Hanley (2004, p. 164) points out, 'Industrial music in general makes use of shock tactics on a regular basis as a form of protest. Bands attempt to shock their listeners with the horrors of something negative, instead of telling them the positive alternatives.' Consequently, some of the more controversial acts provide a second layer of information to their provocative image by adding anti-war quotes, crossed out swastikas or the like to record sleeves or stage performances. Since the rise of neo-Nazism in the 1990s Germany, bands such as Die Krupps have been careful to explicitly distance themselves from right-wing extremism, by labelling their records with the slogan 'Love music, hate fascism'. Nachtmahr – often a target for critical debate regarding sexism and Nazism – has extended this message to 'Love music, hate politics', but if it is possible to separate one from the other obviously depends on how the word politics is defined. Yet, a male DJ based in Gothenburg makes a similar statement: 'We are dealing with music, not politics. And of course anyone who has symbols implying xenophobia and the like will be dismissed. They have to find another forum. At [club name omitted] there should be an open-minded atmosphere, good music and good beer.' With this in mind, it should be taken into consideration that musicologists Susan McClary and Robert Walser have stated in more general terms, regarding rock music and the often distrusted dimensions of art that appeal to the senses, that 'pleasure frequently *is* the politics of music' (1990, p. 287). Within electronic dance music, the politics of pleasure (Gavanas, 2009, p. 78) is perhaps more associated with marginalized groups (for instance gay or black communities) claiming spaces (Buckland, 2002; Gavanas, 2009, p. 80), and therefore, less evident in the primarily white, heterosexual, middle-class context of *synthscenen*. Similar to the discotheques described by Thornton (1995, p. 65) and gothic gatherings like the Amphi Festival, this dancing crowd embraces the 'spectacle', where '[w]atching and being seen are key pleasures'. Furthermore, Monroe (2005, p. 203) explores the parallels between Attali's work and the Slovenian industrial music group Laibach, noting that both 'identify pop culture as a site of micro- and macro-political struggle, and seek to illuminate hidden links between music and power'. As Attali (1985) argues, politics are an integral part of music – therefore, the notion of underlying power structures is not unique for the EBM/electro/industrial dancefloor. Till (2010, p. 141) explores whether functions formerly served within society by religions are now being addressed by cults of popular music and observes that a feature common to electronic dance music culture 'is its separation from mainstream culture. Clubs are a place of escape, of transgression, of release.' This perception is not very far from Bakhtin's (1984, p. 10) ideas about carnival as a 'temporary liberation from the prevailing truth and from established order'. In the context of *synthscenen*, most of my informants and inter-viewees display dominant social moral virtues, which in effect are turned upside down in a carnivalesque manner. However, as Brill (2008, p. 168) suggests, the transgression of cultural norms is not necessarily positive; it 'can even be reactionary, especially if these norms – like anti-racist or anti-sexist taboos – are progressive'. In particular, the upside down version of hegemonic values does not offer a new alternative, only the negative image of what already is and thereby offers a temporary retreat only.

Subcultural Capital, Style and Gendered Sounds

Power relations are not only reproduced between DJs and dancefloors, but also between DJs in terms of gender politics. My DJ interviewees are born between the late 1960s and the late 1980s, revealing that there is a generation difference, which, for instance, might affect musical preferences; while some veterans refer to newer genres such as aggrotech in a negative sense, a female DJ based in Gothenburg explicitly expresses an ambition to promote 'new bands that a younger audience might listen to'. Although the actual audience of *synthscenen* is not homosocial, dominant aesthetic preferences may also be affected by the hegemonic association of commercialism with femininity and of authenticity with masculinity (Ganetz et al., 2009, p. 14) – for example Brill (2008, p. 154) notes that, 'Although there are quite a few female Goths with a liking for harsher styles of music, it is commonly held that genres like EBM and Industrial are a male domain, while softer styles with more mass appeal (e.g. Synth Pop) are regarded and sometimes ridiculed as "music for girls"'. Similarly, technology tends to be associated with masculinity (Gavanas, 2009, p. 84), which may partly explain the lack of female artists and DJs within the EBM/electro/industrial faction. Noting that *synthscenen* traditionally have attracted 'computer nerds and others interested in technology – a group which consisted mainly of men', one female DJ observes that this is starting to change:

> At least, there are more and more women in the DJ booths and among the club organizers. As organizer I am also trying to make the division as equal as possible, but it is difficult. Within old school EBM, in particular, there are not so many female band members. Another reason why there are fewer women than men working as DJs, organizing and playing in bands, I think, has to do with role models. It is a rather laddish atmosphere and there are not so many women to identify with. As a woman you have to be quite persistent in order to show what you can do, that you are interested and that you are there on your own merits. (DJ, female, Stockholm)

The hegemonic male dominance behind the DJ turntables and on stage within *synthscenen* seems to represent the social networks of the (mostly male) club organizers themselves. My DJ interviewees often refer to presumed 'typical' gender roles regarding technology and the notion that women make heavier demands on themselves in terms of technical skill and musical knowledge than their male colleagues, or comment that, although not superior in DJ skills, male DJs are better at promoting themselves. As Reitsamer (2011, p. 32) notes, scene networks and self-marketing are important for getting access to DJ performances at nightclubs and making a name as a DJ. However, the female DJs of *synthscenen* often emphasize that the male club organizers do want them to play at their clubs. But, similarly to the female techno and drum 'n' bass DJs in Vienna interviewed by Reitsamer (2011, pp. 33–4), many of my female DJ interviewees have obtained a certain amount of 'symbolic capital' by also being club organizers. Yet, gaining a position as DJ is not only dependent on symbolic capital but also on subcultural capital:

> Then it is also the case that in order to be able to DJ you do not only have to believe in yourself but also perform. You need to have knowledge about the bands, have a feeling for which songs to play when and where, keep track of both new and old bands, be aware of which songs that are worn out and which are not, and so on. Thus, it takes a certain experience, namely age; and the scene still suffers from the fact that there were fewer girls active in the past. (DJ, female, Gothenburg)

Role models are important, but also access to skill development – primarily regarding the selection of music. The above quote further confirms the fact that subcultural capital is linked to long-term experience of the scene. As in the gothic subculture, 'productive involvement' (being a DJ, promoter or club organizer) and 'sheer length of affiliation to the subculture' are the main 'status criteria', regardless of gender (Brill, 2008, p. 108). One Stockholm-based female DJ states that she is 'relatively unique' in her role as a female DJ within *synthscenen*, and explains that she no longer feels treated differently but that she did so at first, being assigned less favourable timeslots and compensation. However, she is not sure if this treatment was gender related or just had to do with the fact that she was a novice at the time.

Clubs are often described as somewhat hedonistic spaces, detached from the hegemonic culture of the outside world, but this perspective often ignores what Thornton (1995, p. 163) calls 'the micro-structures of power entailed in the cultural disagreements and debates that go on between more closely associated social groups'. The web of internal hierarchies within *synthscenen* becomes evident in both outfits and music selections. Thus, a discussion about military aesthetics often reveals a distance between DJs and the crowd. While some DJs disclose that they do not understand the charm of militarism at all and find uniforms ridiculous, others find the military style attractive and even use a DJ alias that deliberately flirts with the notion of the DJ as commander. Even to those DJs interested in military style, dressing up seems to be less important in their professional role, where they pay more attention to the music instead, but may also have practical reasons, as one Stockholm-based female DJ points out: 'When DJing I want to concentrate on the music, not on if the tie knot is proper or on that I am feeling too warm in my woollen uniform.' There are reasons to believe that gaining subcultural capital through appearance is less important to DJs, as they are already in a position of power. However, outfits on the dancefloor may influence music selection, as one Malmö-based male DJ comments, 'If there are a lot of people in uniforms and the like I will probably play more EBM, automatically assuming that this is what they prefer.' Furthermore, a Stockholm-based male DJ admits that military aesthetics has an impact, especially when he composes a DJ set of 'slightly march-influenced tunes', mentioning songs such as Laibach's 'Tanz mit Laibach' (2003), 'Muskel' by DAF (1981b) and the band Parzival. In terms of gender politics, the same DJ notes that claiming space is more natural to men, due to 'patriarchal norms and structures' and that the EBM scene has 'some traits of machoism, while also being clearly homoerotic'. Thus, it is worth noting that hypermasculinity is not only a typical ideal for many EBM bands and their (mainly) male followers but also a theme or type of behaviour that can be found in SM encounters (Weinberg, 2006, p. 22). As, Brill (2008, p. 10) notes there is 'a significant overlap' between the Gothic and fetish/SM scenes regarding 'style codes and imagery'; when, for instance, German EBM duo DAF started adopting an aesthetic of black leather and military paraphernalia in the early 1980s, they were inspired by the male gay SM scene, which according to the singer Gabriel 'Gabi' Delgado-López (2010) is interested in displaying powerful masculine images, namely 'policemen, construction worker ... let's say the Village People'. This means that the appearance of hypermasculinity does not necessarily represent machismo ideology but is rather part of a role.

Conclusion

In this chapter, the role of the DJ has been explored in relation to subcultural capital and to the aspect of power embedded into both the transmission of sound and the politics of music selection. Similarly to SM scenes, the relationship between the DJ and the crowd within *synthscenen* is perhaps best described as a consensual power exchange. Yet, drawing on the notion that the EBM/electro/ industrial faction metaphorically positions the DJ in the role of a commander is an effective way of highlighting not only the gatekeeper function of the DJ, but also the hierarchies within club cultures themselves. The EBM/electro/industrial faction, in particular, abuses both totalitarian aesthetics and military technology, and as shown, the transgressive nature of these genres draws attention to different aspects of order, discipline and authority. These are all properties of power that – often in a much less conscious way – also permeate other music genres and mainstream culture. According to Rodgers (2010, p. 6) '[t]he tools for making electronic music are not innocent: true sound "mediums", they are an interface to ghosts of technoscientific projects past'. Nevertheless, the tolerant atmosphere regarding provocative aesthetics should be subject to deeper scrutiny within the music scene, of which the DJ culture of *synthscenen* is a case study. Although both totalitarian and sexist imagery occasionally is subject for debate within the scene, many followers tend to dismiss criticism, marking it as a typical expression of the uninitiated outsiders' lack of knowledge, while ignoring that the artist's intention is not necessarily the same as audience reception. According to Till (2010, p. 132): 'Within EDMC there is no one author. The club is the text, and both the experience of it and its substance are different for each clubber.' Thus, it is problematic that the audience within club and subcultures such as *synthscenen* tend to see themselves as immune of hegemonic values. Structures of power are put into work as soon as we, regardless of genre, march out into the night, heading for the more or less military fashion show on the dancefloor, dictated by a DJ 'commander'. DJs and the dance crowds they serve – especially in a commercial context – are never innocent in terms of power relations. Whether we see the dancefloor as a battlefield or not, the struggle continues, not least from a gender perspective.

References

Attali, Jacques (1985) *Noise: The Political Economy of Music*, trans. Brian Massumi. Minneapolis, MN and London: University of Minnesota Press.

Bakhtin, Mikhail (1984) *Rabelais and His World*, trans. Hélène Iswolsky. Bloomington, IN: Indiana University Press.

Bayoumi, Moustafa (2005) 'Disco Inferno'. *The Nation*, 7 December. http://www.thenation.com/article/disco-inferno [accessed 7 March 2013].

Brill, Dunja (2008) *Goth Culture: Gender, Sexuality and Style*. Oxford and New York: Berg.

Buckland, Fiona (2002) *Impossible Dance: Club Culture and Queer World-making*. Middletown, CT: Wesleyan University Press.

Dancer, Peter L., Kleinplatz, Peggy J. and Moser, Charles (2006) '24/7 SM Slavery'. In Peggy J. Kleinplatz and Charles Moser (eds) *Sadomasochism: Powerful Pleasures* (81–101). Binghamton, NY: Harrington Park Press.

Frith, Simon (1996) *Performing Rites: On the Value of Popular Music*. Cambridge, MA: Harvard University Press.

Ganetz, Hillevi, Gavanas, Anna, Huss, Hasse and Werner, Ann (eds) (2009) *Rundgång: Genus och populärmusik*. Stockholm: Makadam.

Gavanas, Anna (2009) ' "You Better Be Listening to My Fucking Music You Bastard!" Teknologi, Genusifiering och Andlighet Bland DJs på Elektroniska Dansmusikscener i Berlin, London och Stockholm'. In Hillevi Ganetz, Anna Gavanas, Hasse Huss and Ann Werner (eds) *Rundgång: Genus och populärmusik* (77–120). Stockholm: Makadam.

Goodman, Steve (2010) *Sonic Warfare: Sound, Affect, and the Ecology of Fear*. Cambridge, MA and London: MIT Press.

Hanley, Jason J. (2004) ' "The Land of Rape and Honey": The Use of World War II Propaganda in the Music Videos of Ministry and Laibach'. *American Music*, 22(1): 158–75. http://www.jstor.org/stable/3592974 [accessed 7 March 2013].

Henriques, Julian (2011) *Sonic Bodies: Reggae Sound Systems, Performance Techniques, and Ways of Knowing*. London and New York, NY: Continuum.

Hutton, Fiona (2006) *Risky Pleasures? Club Cultures and Feminine Identities*. Burlington, VT and Aldershot: Ashgate.

Kingsepp, Eva (2008) 'Nazityskland i populärkulturen: Minne, myt, medier'. PhD diss., Stockholm University. http://su.diva-portal.org/smash/get/diva2:199724/FULLTEXT01 [accessed 7 March 2013].

Koepnick, Lutz (1999) *Walter Benjamin and the Aesthetics of Power*. Lincoln, NE and London: University of Nebraska Press.

McClary, Susan and Walser, Robert (1990) 'Start Making Sense! Musicology Wrestles with Rock'. In Simon Frith and Andrew Goodwin (eds) *On Record: Rock, Pop, and the Written Word* (277–92). London and New York, NY: Routledge.

Monroe, Alexei (2005) *Interrogation Machine: Laibach and NSK*. Cambridge, MA: MIT Press.

Paulsson, Johanna (2011) ' "War on the Dancefloor": The Reproduction of Power and Pleasure at the Amphi Festival in Cologne'. *Dancecult: Journal of Electronic Dance Music Culture*, 3(1). http://dj.dancecult.net/index.php/journal/article/view/81 [accessed 7 March 2013].

Pieslak, Jonathan (2009) *Sound Targets: American Soldiers and Music in the Iraq War*. Bloomington and Indianapolis, IN: Indiana University Press.

Rahm, Bengt (2012) *Den svenska synthen*. Stockholm: Kalla Kulor Förlag.

Reitsamer, Rosa (2011) 'The DIY Careers of Techno and Drum 'n' Bass DJs in Vienna'. *Dancecult: Journal of Electronic Dance Music Culture*, 3(1): 28–43. http://dj.dancecult.net/index.php/journal/article/view/77/12 [accessed 7 March 2013].

Reynolds, Simon (1998) 'Wargasm: Military Imagery in Pop Music'. *The Red Feather Journal of Postmodern Criminology*, 6. http://critcrim.org/redfeather/journal-pomocrim/vol-6-virtual/wargasm.html [accessed 7 March 2013].

Rodgers, Tara (2010) *Pink Noises: Women on Electronic Music and Sound*. Durham, NC: Duke University Press.

Sontag, Susan (1975) 'Fascinating Fascism'. *The New York Review of Books*, 6 February. http://www.nybooks.com/articles/archives/1975/feb/06/fascinating-fascism/ [accessed 7 September 2013].

St John, Graham (2009) *Technomad: Global Raving Countercultures*. London and Oakville, CT: Equinox.

Stolzoff, Norman C. (2000) *Wake the Town and Tell the People: Dancehall Culture in Jamaica*. Durham, NC: Duke University Press.

Thornton, Sarah (1995) *Club Cultures. Music, Media and Subcultural Capital*. Cambridge: Polity Press.

Till, Rupert (2010) *Pop Cult: Religion and Popular Music*. London and New York: Continuum.

Tompkins, Dave (2010) *How to Wreck a Nice Beach. The Vocoder from World War II to Hip-Hop. The Machine Speaks*. Chicago, IL and Brooklyn, NY: Stop Smiling Books and Melville House Publishing.

Weinberg, Thomas S. (2006) 'Sadomasochism and the Social Sciences: A Review of the Sociological and Social Psychological Literature'. In Peggy J. Kleinplatz and Charles Moser (eds) *Sadomasochism: Powerful Pleasures* (17–40). Binghamton, NY: Harrington Park Press.

Interviews

Delgado-López, Gabriel 'Gabi' (DAF) (2010) Interviewed by Johanna Paulsson, Hornstull Strand, Stockholm, 5 June.

Flür, Wolfgang (2012) Interviewed by Johanna Paulsson, Goethe-Institut Schweden, Stockholm, 8 June.

Rainer, Thomas (Nachtmahr) (2010) Interviewed by Johanna Paulsson, Amphi Festival, Cologne, 25 July.

Discography

DAF (Deutsch Amerikanische Freundschaft) (1981a) 'Der Mussolini'. Virgin: United Kingdom, [vs418–12 / 12"].

—(1981b) 'Muskel', from *Gold und Liebe*. Virgin: Germany, [204 165 / LP].

Depeche Mode (1984) 'Master and Servant', from *Some Great Reward*. Mute: United Kingdom, [CD STUMM 19 / CD].

Faderhead (2010a) 'Tanz Zwo Drei Vier', from *Trilogy*. L-Tracks: Germany, [none / CD].

—(2010b) 'Noisebastardz', from *Trilogy*. L-Tracks: Germany, [none / CD].

Laibach (2003) 'Tanz mit Laibach'. Mute: United Kingdom, [CDMUTE241 / CD].

Leæther Strip (1993) 'The White Disgrace', from *Underneath the Laughter*. Zoth Ommog: Germany, [CD ZOT 103 / CD].

Nachtmahr (2009) 'War on the Dancefloor', from *Alle Lust will Ewigkeit*. Trisol: Germany, [TRI 367CD / CD].

—(2010) 'Unbeugsam', from *Semper Fidelis*. Trisol: Germany, [TRI 409 CD / CD].

CHAPTER THIRTEEN

DJ-driven Literature: A Linguistic Remix

Simon A. Morrison

> I used to do loads of clubbing and that's what I wanted to capture
> – to get that perpetual movement into my writing, the beats and
> rhythms of the language (Irvine Welsh, interview, 2001)

The Second Summer of Love in 1988 formed the perfect storm
of cultural, political and pharmaceutical effects. Imported house
music, DJ-driven music productions defined by a minimalist
electronic four-to-the-floor beat, fused with a new dance drug
– MDMA or ecstasy (famously shortened to 'E') – to create
a so-called 'Chemical Generation' (Champion, 1997) of young
people disenfranchised by the hard-edged politics of Thatcherism.
Margaret Thatcher, the UK's prime minister at the time, infamously
claimed in a *Woman's Own* article, published on 31 October 1987
(Keay, 1987), that there was 'no such thing as society'. Whilst
this may have been perceived to be true within the UK's everyday
hegemonic life, on the dance fields and in the party warehouses
and nightclubs of the UK, young adults found their sense of society
on the DJ-driven dancefloor. As the sociopolitical impact of the
nascent rave scene became clear, this new subculture came onto the
radar of journalists, filmmakers and authors, who were all keen to

use society's cultural preoccupations as source material for their output. This chapter offers a focus on how British *DJ-driven literature*, penned by writers such as Irvine Welsh, Pat W. Hendersen and Jeff Noon, describes and mediates the activities of DJs and their interactions with club-goers within this subcultural scene.

By detaching the construct of the DJ from the broader subcultural context of electronic dance music culture, the DJ is examined here as focus of literary exploration. Having identified both fictional and real-world literary representations of DJs, it is possible to consider their role in such works. For instance, does the DJ stand as charismatic godhead of the dancefloor or as its artisan servant? A character of transformative significance or merely supplier of the soundtrack within the musical text? Do we learn about the techniques of the DJ? In short, what does the DJ actually represent, what does the DJ bring to this literary party? After mapping this discussion, the chapter will offer an examination of how these fictional representations of the DJ archetype may have added to the ongoing, broader understanding of the practices within DJ cultures to a possibly non-participatory readership outside dance culture, creating what Calcutt and Shephard (1998, p. iv) describe with reference to cult fiction as 'an alternative and radical path to the recognized canon of high literature'.

To respond to these issues, I draw on literary texts – particularly male, British works of the past 15 years – each inspired by the rave scene but concerned with post-rave club culture and the role of DJ as auteur within that context. Textual analysis in itself reveals, I believe, a great deal about the role the DJ plays within the unfolding narrative. However, these texts are also held up against theoretical readings drawn from key commentators Sarah Thornton, Steve Redhead and Stan Beeler, supported by the work on subculture by academic sociologists Dick Hebdige and David Muggleton, to investigate discursive articulations of the musical and cultural setting, in the literature which reports it. I further draw on interviews with Irvine Welsh and Pat W. Hendersen – two authors in this genre, whose fictional works are under consideration in this chapter. In a deliberate resistance to the structuralist idea that the literary text speaks in its own right, I begin from a position where the intentions, motivations and preoccupations of these authors are considered of great significance to their work, beyond the black and white limitations of what the text may itself discursively produce. The chapter further considers the interplay of music, drug consumption and behavioural patterns, each contributing to the context within which the DJ resides. The DJ's work, after all, is about judicious selection and the resulting 'mix'. However where, in fact, does the DJ fit into this interplay of power relations, into this mix?

The marrying of the cultural spheres of electronic dance music and cult fiction, defined by Calcutt and Shephard as 'literature from the margins and extremes' (1998, p. x), sits within a growing academic discipline that considers the intersection between music and literature. Whether Jack Kerouac's writing about bebop jazz during the 1950s, or Hunter S. Thompson bringing rock music into his 1960s gonzo prose, there has long been a synergy between these forms.[1] In her introduction to the 1997 collection of club fiction, *Disco Biscuits*, editor Sarah Champion takes up this very point:

> It was perhaps inevitable that this culture would finally influence literature too. In the fifties and sixties, jazz and psychedelia inspired writing from Jack Kerouac's *On The Road* to Allen Ginsberg's *Howl* and Tom Wolfe's *Electric Kool Aid Acid Test*. In the nineties, we have Irvine Welsh's *Trainspotting*, the book, the film and the attitude. (1997, p. xiv)

This subcultural rave terrain itself became a literary locus. Redhead (2000, p. xii) reports how book readings became 'gigs'; for example, Jeff Noon's 1995 novel, *Pollen*, was launched at the Haçienda, Manchester's flagship nightclub at the time, while the Arthrob parties featured readings by Irvine Welsh, combined with DJ sets by Andy Weatherall and Richard Fearless. Irvine Welsh is himself a DJ and the production, design and marketing of his books are evidently rooted within dance culture; according to Calcutt and Shephard (1998), a 1997 edition of the novel *Ecstasy* (Welsh, 1996b) was even released with a dance music CD.

However, although there have been many academic studies of the history of electronic dance music and the subcultural implications

---

[1] As defined by Doulas Brinkley in *Fear and Loathing in America* (Thompson, 2000), gonzo journalism 'requires virtually no rewriting: the reporter and his quest for information are central to the story, told via a fusion of bedrock reality and stark fantasy in a way that is meant to amuse both the author and the reader' (p. xiv).

of the rave scene, there has been little consideration of its wider cultural implications. Beeler's 2007 work *Dance, Drugs and Escape* is a welcome attempt to address this gap but is descriptive, without a penetrative critical analysis. As partial remedy, in arguing for a subset of DJ-driven literature, this chapter offers a closer examination of the ongoing and persistent role of electronic dance music culture within literary discourse, which is understood here as 'the dialectic relationship between the phenomenon and its artistic representations' (Beeler, 2007, p. 182). It is my contention that this DJ-driven literature, as well as representations in film and both the mass and niche news media, contributed hugely to the permeation of electronic dance music culture into the broader cultural consciousness, while the notion of the DJ itself became a literary meme.[2] As, for example, Collin (2009) and Garratt (1998) have shown, rave culture began very much as a scene for a cognisant 1980s in-crowd; any broader understanding of the role of the DJ within that scene was limited, almost exclusively, by the parameters of the dancefloor and the walls of the warehouses that fast became the marginalized, post-industrial leisure spaces in which to party, and thereby escape, the UK's restrictive licensing practices. By the end of the twentieth century, however, house music had become the soundtrack to British adverts for multinational companies such as Playstation and Guinness (Phillips, 2009), whilst the techniques and modes of the DJ were well understood by UK audiences.

Thornton (1995, p. 34) argues that this was enabled by a process of *enculturation,* the cultural mechanism by which an artefact, such as a music recording, moves from 'the private to the public sphere'. Similarly, club fictions reproduce the landscape of the nightclub, the habits of casual and recreational drug consumption and the hitherto secret, almost magical machinations of the DJ. Thus, it can be argued that electronic dance music culture, and repetitive beat literature (Redhead, 2000) has enabled the cultural coronation of the DJ by elevating him (the male DJ is usually foregrounded in such representations) beyond the real-world nightclub and into a text-based fictional world. Within this world, they are not merely

---

[2] By niche media, here I refer to the specific media relating to electronic dance music culture, including magazines such as *DJ, Mixmag, i-DJ* and *Jockey Slut*, as well as fanzines such as *Boys Own*.

celebrated by an exclusive realm of participant clubbers but can reach beyond dance culture to embrace a wider circle of readers.

It is only now, with the benefits of hindsight and an expanding academic and literary scholarship, that serious attempts can be made to understand the rave scene, the cultural underground's last stand in the twentieth century, broadly taking place between the Second Summer of Love in 1988 and the change of the millennium. Here I will take issue with post-subcultural theorists, such as Muggleton (1998), who argue that our inexorable drift into postmodernism has created a mutable, fluid set of conditions that no longer allow for homogenous subcultural formation. From both my own reading, and from a basis of participant observation, I prefer to contend that electronic dance music culture, in its nascent rave format, was the last of what Hebdige (1983, p. 97) calls 'spectacular subcultures'. In purely visual terms, rave culture may well have ducked the linear glare of daylight, preferring to bathe in the fragmented flash of the nightclub strobe but if we read 'spectacular' to mean *impressive* or *astonishing*, then, I argue, this subculture successfully integrated both spectacular and countercultural impulses, to weave a locally coherent homology defined by music, fashion and drug practices. Equally, it contained a political agenda more evolved than that acknowledged by, for example, music journalist Simon Reynolds who argues, reductively, against the scene's 'sensations rather than truths, fascination rather than meaning' (1998, p. 91).

In locating the concept 'culture', Hebdige notes that 'as a scientific term, it refers to both a process (artificial development of microscopic organisms) and a product (organisms so produced)' (1983, p. 4). In this sense, club culture seems more akin to a low cultural product on a laboratory petri dish than a serious high-cultural artistic endeavour worthy of serious consideration, as 'high culture is generally conceived in terms of aesthetic values, hierarchies and canons, while popular culture is portrayed as a curiously flat folk culture' (Thornton, 1995, p. 8). If club fiction, as cult fiction, falls squarely in the category of low and mass culture, as opposed to high art, it would be my contention that we learn more about our society from an appreciation of such 'curiously flat folk culture'. Further, I propose that it should be elevated to higher ground, the abject rendered sacred, even, where club fiction can truly be 'something that could be talked about with the reverence traditionally reserved for all things classical' (Calcutt and Shephard, 1998, p. iv). Authors working within electronic dance music culture choose deliberately, perhaps provocatively, to bathe in the metaphorical slime of the petri dish, to revel in what Tom Wolfe (2009) usefully describes as the *nostalgie de la boue*, a love and longing for the mud, proudly using it to charge their quills. Welsh, in particular, celebrates the sanctity of the *quotidian* (everyday) abject, eulogizing excrement and sexual fluids as though fine champagne.

It is here, therefore, in this profane cultural mix of myth and mire that the DJ of the literature under discussion resides. Notably, Barthes (2009) shows that the hegemonic production of myth is not a matter of a lie or confession but, rather, of *inflection*, a subtle change in meaning of words; through *mythmaking*, therefore, one might elevate oneself from this mire. A nightclub and rave dancefloor is itself a space of escape. In her essay 'Living The Dream', an early study of acid house parties and clubs in Manchester, England, Rietveld (1993) argues that, 'the rave offered a release from day to day realities, a temporary escapist disappearance like the weekend or holiday' (1993, p. 58). Although I would not concur with the idea that such escape is *all* that electronic dance music culture is about, participants do indeed talk of 'living the dream' and Reynolds notes, 'Rave's relentlessly utopian imagery – events/promoters called Living Dream, Fantazia, Rezerection, Utopia, even' (1998, p. 90). Nightclubs and raves are fabrications of both architectural and anthropological form; the dancefloor is a dreamscape and the DJ, through sound, is the weaver of that dream. If this fits within a postmodern sense of reinvention and obfuscation then, I argue, that concept also extends to the DJs themselves, who change their names to fabricate identities and conceal themselves behind banks of equipment, separating themselves from their audience and, arguably, from the usually prosaic ramifications of authenticity, preferring instead to play to specific notions of myth inherent in subcultures, as Hebdige (1983) has shown: mud deployed as camouflage.

DJs as Fiction

DJs spin their own myths about their genesis, their musical influences, their careers, perfectly encapsulated in the fact that so many change their names in an attempt to 'escape the principle of identity' (Breton, cited in Hebdige, 1983, p. 165) and even, in the case of successful DJ producers Daft Punk and Deadmau5, concealing their faces behind masks and headwear. Nevertheless, social identities are not entirely escapable; following Barthes' notion of *myth* (2009), for example, male DJs tend to exaggerate their image according to gendered notions of the pioneering hero (Farrugia, 2012). Real-world DJs, therefore, are already constructs – characters, even caricatures – eulogized as larger than life, their hero status happily reinforced by various niche media. In this context, Frith and Savage (1998, p. 12) introduce Umberto Eco's concept of *media squared*, 'a PR-led agenda in place of reportage, soap opera treated as reality, reality treated as soap opera'. Importantly, then, whether we read fiction or non-fiction, they are both mediated versions of reality and, I argue, as such they are equally valid. Journalist Hunter S. Thompson, drawing on William Faulkner, famously observes that 'the best fiction is far more *true* than any kind of journalism – and the best journalists have always known this' (Thompson, 1979, jacket cover). Redhead brings this slippery idea to club culture in asking novelist Alan Warner if fiction is 'a way of telling contemporary history better' (2000, p. 128). Here I will contend that there is indeed a way to understand the experience, and even reality, of electronic dance music culture, through fiction; identity, mythology, built from words.

In a semantic approach to cultural studies, Collin (2009, p. 340) identifies references to 'sub' cultures where behaviour is 'sur'-real within a 'mythologized underground', which Hebdige (1983, p. 54) distinguishes from the superficiality of surfaces. Having located the DJ in this, metaphorically speaking, darkened cultural basement, let us now identify literary representations of DJs in this context. It was Irvine Welsh's first novel, *Trainspotting*, published in 1994, that arguably opened the cellar doors and brought light to this underground world, leading quickly to a ubiquity of rave novels that Collin refers to as 'pulp fiction drugsploitation', alongside independent books, published like 'do-it-yourself white labels from bedroom techno producers' (2009, p. 301). In *Cult Fiction*, Calcutt and Shephard (1998, p. xv) ask, as a direct consequence: 'How many books are now aimed squarely and cynically at club culture, with jacket-designers taking their brief from DJ flyers and other "yoof" accessories?' Champion's 1997 collection *Disco Biscuits*, the title referring to the local name for a dance drug tablet, also provides a rich seam for subterranean cultural miners, in which Martin Millar's (1997) contribution introduces us to Sunshine Star-Traveller – a DJ (although not a very good one); while Michael River's short story 'Electrovoodoo' contains a DJ called The Undergod. Elsewhere, other texts contain famous, unknown or fictional DJs. An example for the first is Keoki, who features in *Disco Bloodbath*, James St James' (1999) recollection of the Club Kids (famous club personalities in New York City), and also in Frank Owen's (2004) depiction of the same, *Clubland Confidential*; the second might include the unknown DJ and son of the anonymous author of 'Confessions of a Middle-aged Ecstasy Eater' (2001); while the third could include Jody, providing an immersive soundtrack, 'Scorched Out For Love' in Jeff Noon's novel *Needle In the Groove* (2001).

Noon's Powerful Cyborg Magicians

We may locate some of the principal creators of these DJ characters in Steve Redhead's collection *Repetitive Beat Generation* (2000), a title that itself plays on the beat generation literary scene of the 1950s, as well as on the UK's Criminal Justice and Disorder Act, 1994 (UK Government, 1994), which in section 63 (1b) describes music played at raves as 'sounds wholly or predominantly characterised by the emission of a succession of repetitive beats'. Among those authors interviewed by Redhead are Nicholas Blincoe and Alan Warner, alongside Irvine Welsh, who will be considered in more depth later in this chapter. Also included is Manchester writer Jeff Noon, who often places DJs within his cyberculture prose – for instance DJNA, a fictional outlaw DJ, in his contribution of the same name to Champion's collection *Disco Biscuits* (1997). In this short story, participants in a futuristic dance music culture are presented as a social underclass and DJs operate as free radicals, pursued by authorities keen to mechanize the music process. Elsewhere, in his 1993 novel *Vurt*, Noon uses a local club scene not only on the grounds of verisimilitude, but exigency:

> I was looking round Manchester and thinking what have we got here, we've got these young people on the streets, we've got the

drugs, we've got the music, we've got the guns .... I was writing a book about Manchester and it had to have that in it .... What I noticed is that there are certain correlations between what say the cyberpunk of William Gibson introduced into science fiction with what the record producers and DJs were doing with the equipment. (Noon, cited in Redhead, 2000, p. 113)

Noon is especially relevant because he incorporates actual DJ techniques and practices into his literary output. There are several examples of this musical sensibility within his collection of short stories, *Pixel Juice* (2000b). For instance, in his interview with Redhead (2000, pp. 110–18) Noon refers to the short story 'Metaphorazine' as one of his 'greatest hits' and to 'Homo Karaoke' as 'a kind of weird DJ story', before discussing doing a 'dub' of it, stripping it to its beats and pieces, which he also does with several stories within that collection. 'Homo Karaoke' is built around the DJ sound clash, a soundsystem battle made popular in the reggae scene. In this narrative, DJs do battle from trenches formed of soundsystems, using records as their missiles. Here, music is literally a weapon and DJ ability means the better skill to wield that weapon. The environment is therefore identifiable; the DJ's desire to build reputation, to produce myth, understandable. Noon takes the DJ battle to its ultimate end, with DJs Perfume Sword and Skinvader strapped into machines. Perfume Sword tells us: 'It's dark in the booth, and the world closes in' (Noon, 2000b, p. 91) as he proceeds to actually get *inside* the music. There are details of his set, the 'wavelength' (2000b, p. 92) that breaks across the floor as Perfume Sword explains his moves: 'Now I become the Lizard Ninja Tongue; antique Led Zep drum loop, hip hop scatter-shot maniac' (2000b, p. 92).

Even more compelling than the subject matter, I argue, is the way Noon then uses the very next short story in the *Pixel Juice* collection to construct a linguistic dub of 'Homo Karaoke', a 'Dub Karaoke', subtitled 'electric haiku remix' (2000b, p. 97):

needleburst skullfire
mutating beats-per-minute
operating heartache

In a similar mapping of musical devices upon the linguistic, elsewhere in the collection, the short story 'Orgmentations (in the mix)', segues into 'Hands of the DJ'. Noon's story 'Orgmentations' ends as follows (2000b, p. 309):

> (Hands of the DJ move around.) Oh, dear sweet reader, you really should have been there!
> \\\\\\\\\ FRACTAL SCRATCH //////////
> \\\\\\\\\\V//////////
> \\\\V/////
> \V/

This typographical interpretation of a vinyl scratch segues into the actual story 'Hands of the DJ', where 'dark gossip was told of DJ Pixel Juice, so fast, so deep, were the ranges of her landscape of scratch' (Noon, 2000b, p. 310).

The titular character Pixel Juice is an especially striking example of the DJ archetype, not least because she represents a rare female appearance in what seems a male-dominated occupation. Returning to Eco's notion of *media squared* and the nebulous, perhaps nefarious, role of the media in constructing versions of reality, Noon makes a very deliberate point about the PR management of reputation:

> The thing about the DJ, she was never one for hanging out. She didn't give interviews. Never turned up to accept awards. No known vices, which pissed off the marketing boys no end. (2000b, p. 311)

As she is gay in a patriarchal context, she does not stand out as a feminine threat or as visual object of desire, a gender issue expanded upon in Farrugia's (2012) study of DJs and gender politics. As such, there is still no attraction for the media: 'No fucking story! Sniff, sniff' (Noon, 2000b, p. 312). An extremely skilled DJ, 'her hands moved around at sonic boom, making ghosts of themselves in the stage lights' (p. 310). Working this linguistic cross-fade by echoing words, Noon adds that, 'Vinyl went wet to the traces, held sway in time to rapid-fire fingertronics; etch-plate aesthetics, fractal scratches (really should have been there) out on the limits of the human edit' (p. 310). Noon then provides the readers with their own ticket to his fictional Magnetic Field Weekender, and they should feel privileged as 'Half the known universe got turned away' (p. 310). At this festival, Noon deconstructs the DJ process – a useful guide to the reader, as literary tourist in this strange sonic world:

> She turned up the volume a touch, and then, slowly, lingering, let her left hand rest exactly one millimetre above the spinning vinyl. She was waiting, poised like a cat for the beat. Now! She brought the hand down, added some black bass of her own. (2000b, p. 314)

The conclusion of 'Hands of the DJ' in *Pixel Juice* introduces a 16-year-old 'wannabe' DJ who plays on the rock 'n' roll myths that surround the supposed dark arts of DJing, and also the gloves Pixel Juice wears. We discover that one of her hands is robotic, the other is made of butterflies – a very deliberate counterpointing, as a DJ's hands do indeed mark the interface between human and machine – organic flesh and electronic circuit board. As a science fiction author, Noon is central to the literary exploration of the DJ archetype as cyborg, firmly outlining in these two stories, 'Orgmentations' and 'Hands of the DJ', that the ability to DJ is, firstly, a cultural weapon that can be wielded, and, secondly, that DJing is a dark art, a magical gift that can be coveted; that it signifies both power and mystery. In a sense then, this DJ-driven literature offers a melding of two worlds: the arguably more stable nature of the printed word upon the page, set against the fluid movement of the dancefloor. Although literature has previously addressed such subcultural areas, DJ-driven literature deliberately sets out to appropriate such a murky underworld as its context, to wrestle narrative order upon this muddy milieu.

Hendersen: Real DJs

Let us now turn to the work of Pat W. Hendersen. Although less well known than Welsh and Noon, Hendersen is the author of three novels that, I argue, fall perfectly within the DJ-driven literary canon – *Decade* (2009), *Want* (2010), and *Club* (2012). It is the third of these that will be considered here.[3] *Club* is worthy of

---

[3] Hendersen's novel *Club* was published by lulu.com on 26 November 2012. However, in preparing this chapter the author first relied on a pre-publication proof copy.

investigation because of the archetypal way it positions the heroic male DJ within the narrative. Here, we witness the mixed interplay of music, fashion, drug consumption and behavioural patterns, the homology that contributes to the DJ's practices: 'The right people. The right drugs. The right music' (Hendersen, 2012, p. 350). In this sense, Hendersen works the 'invisible seam between language, experience and reality' (Hebdige, 1983, p. 10) to create a natural-istic presentation of a club environment, undoubtedly bolstered by placing *real DJs* within that context. Although this strategy may be understood almost as a type of product placement, it allows a cognizant readership immediate grasp of the DJ-character through *a priori* understanding gleaned from, for instance, media represen-tations. DJs referred to within the story include Zammo, Graeme Park, Paul Wain, Justin Robertson and Dave Seaman. They ply their art within real-world club environments, with real-world music, to a crowd fuelled on real-world drugs that enhance an otherworldly virtual experience of the club's sonic architecture. In conversation, Hendersen remarks: 'I wanted to be realistic and these people were playing just such venues as Shake during the period so in a way it was necessary scene building. Just like describing the enclosed geography of the club's location (Hendersen, 2012).

The narrative of *Club* unravels in the immured locus of this fictional club, Shake – a stage upon which Hendersen places both clubber and DJ, co-conspirators in a weekend revolution, with the DJ as cultural, sonic instigator, in an environment where 'Bohemian creatives mixed with rich socialites, mixed with working class heroes and the only stand out rank system among the masses were the DJs and the dealers .... The dealers did their dealing and the DJs practiced their art to ensure that once Friday arrived, everything came together to ensure that chaos could reign' (2012, pp. 5–6). The implication here is that for a nightclub to function there must necessarily be a balanced homology woven by DJ and dealer, in interaction with the clubber, what Thornton calls the 'the buzz of energy which results from the interaction of records, DJs and crowd' (1995, p. 27). For Hendersen, the role of the DJ in this process is more like that of first among equals; or, in this case, perhaps two among equals, along with the nightclub dealer. Beeler remarks, 'The DJ can still be a star, but the individuals at the event do not passively take in the show; they dance' (2007, p. 145), which supports the notion that here, although elevated upon the stage, the DJ ostensibly remains *part* of the party. Hendersen goes further, in making the apparently reductive decision to pull back the curtain to reveal the DJ in their more mundane métier: Graeme Park playing cards before his set; backstage conversations with Justin Robertson; Dave Seaman's walk to the DJ booth; the reader even witnesses DJs taking drugs. At one point the principal character, Colin, approaches what the text refers to as the 'DJ Console' and says of Justin Robertson that 'Justin looked to be concentrating hard on what he was doing. Couldn't have been easy but he was producing the goods. How the hell could he play music like this when he's feeling the same way?' (Hendersen, 2012, p. 187). Here, 'the same way' indicates the DJ is under the influence of drugs. Whether a living DJ might mind being 'outed' as drug user, even in fiction, is a morally ambiguous question. Perhaps it is for the detectives within the novel's narrative to investigate.

Hendersen is very clear, in a pivotal scene from his first novel, *Decade* (2009), in this naturalistic strive for authenticity, in placing recalled details almost as pointillism upon the canvas: the club – this time a real night, The Rhumba Club at Citrus in Edinburgh – is a 'Little P-shaped dungeon' (2009, p. 239); the drugs are snowballs – 'Mate, these little bitches are the future, ah'm tellin' ya' (p. 238); and the DJ is Alastair Cooke, a real-world DJ playing a real-world set. The narrative is rooted in such specifics, moored by detail, set against the broader wash of the soundtrack, which is diegetic, in the sense that Cooke's set is audible within the discourse and made clear to us, as reader, as the narrative takes us through the rising drama of the track, and its sampled Martin Luther King vocal. Furthermore, it becomes meta-diegetic when we, as reader, share the muffled tones of the beat perceived subjectively by a character, mediated through a sound-system, through the pharmaceutical filter of drug consumption. At first the music is described as 'the standard low bass thump of underground dance music, loud and immediate with the size of the club' (2009, p. 239) before 'The reggae now had a tingly electronic tune segueing into it that matched the sensations all through Colin's body' (p. 240). In this scene, therefore, we not only share Colin's point of view, but also his auditory equipment.

My particular interest lies in how a writer renders the DJ process, that production of sound, in the printed word. In order to assist our understanding of the moment of a record's impact, it will be helpful to defer to a DJ, in this case Dave Haslam (1998, p. 160), who states that, 'The important chemistry is the reaction between the music and the crowd; and the DJ is somewhere at the centre of it all, a catalyst.' Elsewhere, Beeler (2007, p. 121) explains: 'A good rave or club DJ controls the emotions of the crowd, bringing them up to an ecstatic frenzy and down to a cool, rather contemplative state through judicious selection of music', whilst Thornton identifies 'the figure of the DJ with his finger on the pulse of the crowd' (1995, p. 85) – all DJ-driven emotive connections rendered in literary form by Hendersen. To achieve this, many of the club writers addressed here strive for that most loaded, problematic and elastic of concepts: authenticity. Through the verisimilitude of detail, through the articulation of DJ technique and interaction, and through a naturalistic presentation that is common in much popular fiction, an author can sketch what seems an authentic, yet mythological, representation of the DJ – both their technique within the DJ booth, and life beyond it – creating a believable hegemonic fictional environment within which, and against which, the DJ might play their music. In terms of narrative strategy, Hendersen pays more attention to sketching in the background, the backstory, than to blindly celebrating the ready-made super-DJ, remarking in interview (2012) that, 'I'm happy to leave writing about them like they're some sort of super being to someone else.' That someone else might well be Irvine Welsh.

Naturalism in Welsh

Irvine Welsh is an author who, Collin (2009, p. 302) argues, is 'the most extraordinary literary phenomenon of Ecstasy culture' becoming 'its icon and its bard' (2009, p. 303); the author Beeler calls 'the most prominent writer of the Chemical Generation' (2007, p. 56). A nightclub is a cauldron of colour and energy. It takes an author like Welsh – confident in their embedded experience of club culture, and their ability to capture that intangible magic – to transcribe it into the written word.

In Welsh's 2002 novel *Glue*, the character Carl Ewart stands as a symbol of the transformative potential of the DJ, the carefully described parabolic arc of his journey into DJ N-SIGN elevating the individual above the sociopolitical mire; important not for what he does, but what he *represents*. For Welsh, there exists a bridge of experience and understanding between creator and reader of words, a bridge constructed from bricks of cultural resonance, without the artifice of an obvious literary construct. This connection between his characters and the reader seems like a private, unmediated, conversation. According to Welsh, 'it's almost like you're stuck in a room with them ... and sometimes they're not the sort of person you want to be stuck in a room with. But at least you can put the book down. You can't shut those fuckers up' (2012). There is therefore a level of assumption on the part of Welsh that to have even opened the book we are 'in the know' and the author can therefore employ the short-hand argot of the dance-floor, the syntax of the DJ, to work that connection and to keep it seemingly direct, allowing what Saussure describes as language that 'blends with the life of society' (cited in Hebdige, 1983, p. 90).

We will first consider the subject matter within the text of *Glue*, before further addressing Welsh's literary style. In describing the lower echelons of urban Scotland's Edinburgh society, Welsh might be considered a social-realist in the literary tradition of Dickens and Orwell. In documenting society's underclass, his work is certainly in keeping with both Hunter S. Thompson's earlier contention that fiction can be 'truer' than journalism, as well as with the characteristics of naturalism, defined by Drabble (2000, p. 713) as 'the authenticity and accuracy of detail, thus investing the novel with the value of social history'. Accuracy is key; as Welsh reports to Redhead:

I still hold to the idea that it's pretentious not to write about drugs. To me they're just an unremarkable part of the scheme of things. When I see a novel that hasn't got any drugs in it I think to myself 'well, what kind of social life is this supposed to be depicting?' It's a subculture they're writing about. (2000, p. 148)

Thornton (1995) introduces the concept of 'subcultural capital', in which hipness is a signifer of (sub)cultural credibility, whereby 'the DJ became a guarantor of subcultural authenticity' (p. 60). In turn, subcultural capital can enable the accumulation of *actual* economic capital, as shown by Phillips (2009) and his account of the rise of the *superstar DJ*. Using Welsh's *Glue* (2002) as an example of such cultural and economic hierarchies, we witness the rise of

Carl Ewart through such structures during his transformation into a significant DJ, N-SIGN. Here, to be a DJ is to enjoy economic, geographic and social escape – a life reboot. Welsh hereby places the DJ firmly atop this hierarchal structure, in which the DJ gains the largest amount of both subcultural and economic capital.

Welsh's novel is a four-ball piece built around Edinburgh friends. Through the passage of the novel, two characters slide downwards – one goes to prison and dies from AIDS, the other becomes a bloated caricature of his former self. The remaining two are awarded different degrees of escape, by virtue of their accumulation of subcultural capital – one, Billy Birrell, through success in boxing, and Carl in DJing. Early on in the novel, the role music plays in the Ewart family home provides backdrop and context to a more loving domestic environment than that experienced by the other friends. Carl's father encourages his interest in music and early forays into DJing, which immediately sets him apart from the interests of his peers. As Billy observes, 'Still it's his tunes and he's daein awright. Getting noticed, getting respect. Goin roond the shoaps wi him, the clubs, n ye kin see it's no two schemies anymair, it's N-SIGN the DJ and Business Birrell, the boxer' (Welsh, 2002, p. 192).

Carl's interest in music becomes a point of resistance. On a trip to Munich, Carl is more interested in the interior of the city's record shops than its pubs, and this begins to open up cultural differences, as well as fresh conversational possibilities with new friends, on the basis of music:

> The truth ay it is, and ah feel a bit guilty aboot it, but this is what ah like the maist now, crackin on wi some heads about sounds, checkin oot what cunts are listening tae, sussin oot what's gaun doon. Apart fae bein oan the decks, this is the highest form ay enjoyment for me. (Welsh, 2002, p. 276)

Success as a DJ signifies separation – cultural, economic, geographic (and, it might be argued, moral) separation – as Carl moves first to London, then Paris, Berlin and ultimately Australia, in an apparent contravention of Reynolds' assertion that club culture is 'the cult of acceleration without destination' (1998, p. 86). It is no accident that N-SIGN's album is called *Departures*. As he sheds the skin of his socio-economic upbringing, Welsh's 'self-mythologising process' (Welsh, 2000, p. 148) builds:

They didnae like Carl Ewart, white-trash schemie. But they liked N-SIGN. N-SIGN's played at warehoose perties in London, raised funds for anti-racist groups, aw sorts ay deserving community organisations. They love N-SIGN. They'll never, ever get thir heads roond the fact that the only difference between Carl Ewart and N-SIGN is that one worked liftin boxes in a warehoose for nae money while the other played records in one fir tons ay it. (Welsh, 2002, p. 332)

The ability to DJ affords Carl the opportunity to travel, to explore. Like the Beat Generation hitting the road, to travel, to tour, is to escape the quicksand of the quotidian, fulfilling the belief that 'DJs have to some extent replaced the role of the band or the performer' (Brown, 1998, p. 78). In his extensive reference notes at the end of *Subculture: The Meaning of Style*, Hebdige refers to Susan Sontag's concept of the 'métier of the adventurer as a spiritual vocation' (1983, p. 168). It is Carl's ability to play music that carves out this escape route, in the peripatetic possibilities inherent in the DJ lifestyle. Similarly, Beeler draws on Malbon to explain this cultural and geographic expansion: 'The explosion in [international] clubbing cultures over the last ten years has thus been accompanied by – and undoubtedly further fuelled through – the ever widening horizons of some of the clubbers themselves' (2007, p. 74). As Beeler explains: 'Superstar DJs now fill places in the cultural industries that parallel those held by rock stars' (2007, p. 4).

If the subject matter of *Glue* is of relevance in showing the transformative potential of the DJ in literature, then the style of presentation is, as with Noon, equally key. With reference to Middleton's (1997) conceptual framework, one of its 'signifying structures' (p. 10) is undoubtedly language, and Welsh is very deliberate in constructing his text in the language of the dancefloor, the syntax of the nightclub. As I have identified, the key aspiration of most DJ-driven literature is *authenticity* and that is dictated, and constructed, by specific constructions of meaning. Hebdige (1983) addresses subcultural use of, and resistance to, the 'language of the Master', in a post-colonialist context. Welsh deliberately subverts the 'language of the Master', in this case the English linguistic dominance of Britain, by choosing to write not only in Scots dialect but in a particular vernacular of the Leith area of Edinburgh, which in itself offers stylistic challenges. Hebdige points out that, 'Any elision, truncation or convergence of prevailing linguistic and ideological categories can have profoundly disorienting effects' (1983, p. 91) and this is further illustrated by Welsh when he states that, 'To me, acid house is in your fucking DNA. That's why I wrote in the Scottish vernacular – not because I wanted to make a point like James Kelman or Alasdair Gray – but because I just liked the beat, the 4/4 beat. The English language is weights and measures – controlling, imperialistic – and I don't want to be controlled' (2012).

The following passage from *Glue* suggests how Welsh expects this level of understanding on the part of his reader:

> Ah head oaf back tae the decks tae check oot the sounds situ. Ah'm gled ah bought some records n eftir borrowin some fae Rolf ah've goat enough tae dea a good forty-five minutes quality mixin. Ah get ready tae hit the decks. The mixer looks a bit unfamiliar or maybe it's just the pills, but fuck it, jist git in thaire. (2002, p. 327)

As well as an understanding regarding dialect, Welsh presumes a level of understanding of the mechanics of the DJ process and the music involved, in order to step across the bridge described earlier and join him on the other side of the localized subcultural divide. At one stage, as Carl begins to DJ, his set list forms almost a club review: 'I'm mixing UK acid-house rave tracks like *Beat This* and *We Call It Acieed* in with old Chicago house anthems like *Love Can't Turn Around* and taking it right back up through Belgium hardcore, like this track *Inssomniak*' (2002, p. 328). Again, notions of verisimilitude come to the fore, in confidently describing the techniques and musical ammunition of the DJ, in order to achieve an authentic experience, in the process establishing a joint account of subcultural capital to which both author and reader have access.

As well as subverting the language of the Master in a dialectical sense, Welsh determinedly subverts it in terms of graphology. Throughout his novels he plays with the shape of text, providing a means to depict the affective characteristics of sonic gesture. The 1996 short story 'The Undefeated, for instance, includes what seem like sticky notes upon the page and shopping lists, even boxes (pp. 248–9). To keep the beat of the writing, a sense of movement,

Welsh banishes restrictive speech marks, preferring to keep the pace flowing with dashes, reminiscent of Kerouac's fictional work. Far from enabling a disconnection between the literal and the literary, this graphological approach smoothes the process of recognition and association on the part of a cognizant readership. Consider the following passage from *Glue* (2002, p. 399) by Welsh, which details N-SIGN's drug-affected state-of-mind as he gets ready to DJ:

> The bass begins to synchronise with my heartbeat and I feel my brain expand beyond the confines of skull and grey matter.
> wwwWOOOOOSSSSHHH

Welsh thereby employs the language of the rave to engender a mutual level of understanding between author and interpreter. Welsh is the master at the literary 'tell' – the linguistic nod, the semiotic wink – as good, perhaps, as a physical hug between writer and reader on the dancefloor, or across the page, a secret mythologizing code that Thornton refers to as 'cryptic shorthand, innuendo and careful omission' (1995, p. 146).

The career development of DJ N-SIGN demonstrates considerable mythmaking in the construction of his public image. Welsh even refers to actual British DJ trade magazines, such as *DJ* and *Mixmag* to confirm the media are complicit in the fabrication of reputation: 'N-SIGN cunts it up in Ibiza. N-SIGN top caner. Fuckin shite. All the dance press: fuckin mythologising shite' (2002, p. 473).[4] Welsh's vernacular and argot work to bring the reader closer to the text – and even further – stepping past the liminal red rope of the dance club, Welsh inviting the reader to join him in the inner sanctum, the VIP room of Haslam's 'disco text' (Haslam, 1998a, p. 157), where sonic dreams are spun from words. The transformative process that sees Carl Ewart become N-SIGN is a fascinating literary evocation of the heroic male DJ archetype. Whilst *Glue* might be ostensibly written for an 'in-crowd' readership, the high

---

[4] Interestingly, DJ and club culture magazine *Mixmag* threatened to 'out' the identity of the real Carl Ewart in the feature 'Top 12 Fictional DJs' in their November 2011 issue. I pressed Welsh on this in an interview at Molly Malone's pub (Glasgow) and he conceded the DJ character was indeed based on a real DJ but wouldn't reveal his identity (2012).

profile of Welsh, and commensurate sales, suggest he has crossed over to a broader audience. I agree with Beeler (2007, p. 62) that the novel works equally for the club culture cognoscenti and subcultural tourist, for the scene insider and voyeuristic non-partic-ipant. All are invited to check their preconceptions with their coat, to step onto a dancefloor made of words.

Rolling in the Mud

The purpose of this chapter is not to assess the literary quality of the work of Noon, Hendersen or Welsh. Instead, it set out to identify the existence of DJs within literature and to consider what the narrative construction of the role of the DJ might be, in terms of the known, unknown and fictional DJ characters illus-trated within the work. Further, by bringing together these texts for the first time under the banner of DJ-driven literature, we might consider how they collectively serve to mediate the myth of the heroic DJ; produce and reproduce the social identities and behaviour associated with a cohesive subculture and manufacture the requisite mud in which these characters might roll and revel.

Nostalgie de la boue, as Wolfe (2009) puts it – the longing for the mud – demonstrates an attraction to the abject. I argue here that the almost fetishistic interest in this abject, the *other*, arises because it affords the non-cognate a look at 'the edge'. As well as a core participant readership, already immersed in this earthly mud, Calcutt and Shephard (1998, p. xi) further locate this non-participant readership 'enjoying the experience of extremes vicariously without having to leave [their] mundane mainstream experience'. Thus, under the cover of darkness, behind the covers of a book, such cult fiction texts provide a literary dancefloor for the DJ-author to work their dark arts – a voyeuristic glimpse at the abject, without having to get one's own body muddy and dirty with sweat. DJ-driven writers such as Irvine Welsh and Jeff Noon therefore sit within a lineage of cult fiction writers who each had to draw on specific literary techniques and representational modes in order to authentically capture the spirit and energy of their particular subcultural environment – 'gatekeepers and holy dealers of particular fictional worlds' (Calcutt and Shephard, 1998, p.

xiii). Whether Jack Kerouac on jazz, Hunter S. Thompson on rock or Irvine Welsh on acid house, when writing about music – from trumpet players to guitar gods to masters of the turntables – these writers had to reach for a kind of artistic synesthesia to find a voice with which to describe the musical magic in words, as well as the techniques of the DJ interactions with the dancefloor.

Champion recollects how someone once told her, 'surely people who go clubbing don't read' (Champion, 2000, p. 18), compounded by the assertion within the UK's 'style bible' magazine *The Face* that 'the novel form is peculiarly unsuited to tales of club culture' (cited by Redhead, 2000, p. xxii). The emergence of DJ-driven authors disproves that perspective. In terms of the processes of enculturation, it is important to acknowledge and articulate the different levels on which these novels work, from the niche productions of Hendersen to the high street distribution channels enjoyed by Welsh. However, as cult fiction products, the texts under consideration can speak to both a cognate and non-cognate readership. Whether Noon's detailing of DJ technique; Hendersen's naturalistic rendering of the life of the DJ; or the genuine trans-formative dynamic of the DJ in Welsh, it may further be argued that the archetype of the DJ has passed into mainstream under-standing via the process of its cultural representation. These DJ-driven writers understood that there was beauty to be found in the mud, in bringing to life the slime of the petri dish. They saw how, with the addition of only one letter, the urban could be made urbane. And that that letter was E.

References

Anonymous (2001) 'Confessions of a Middle-aged Ecstasy Eater'. *Granta: The Magazine of New Writing*, 74, Summer: 7–34.

Barthes, Roland (2009) *Mythologies*. London: Vintage.

Beeler, Stan (2007) *Dance, Drugs and Escape: The Club Scene in Literature, Film and Television Since the Late 1980s*. Jefferson, NC: McFarland & Co.

Brown, Adam (1998) 'Let's All Have A Disco? Football, Popular Music and Democratization'. In Steve Redhead, Derek Wynne and Justin O'Connor (eds) *The Clubcultures Reader: Readings in Popular Cultural Studies* (61–83). Oxford: Blackwell.

Calcutt, Andrew and Shephard, Richard (1998) *Cult Fiction: A Reader's Guide*. London: Prion.

Champion, Sarah (ed.) (1997) *Disco Biscuits: New Fiction from the Chemical Generation*. London: Hodder & Stoughton.

—(2000) 'Generation E'. In Steve Redhead (ed.) *Repetitive Beat Generation* (13–23). Edinburgh: Canongate.

Collin, Matthew (2009) *Altered State: The Story of Ecstasy Culture and Acid House*. London: Serpent's Tail.

Drabble, Margaret (2000) *The Oxford Companion to English Literature*. Oxford: Oxford University Press.

Farrugia, Rebekah (2012) *Beyond the Dance Floor: Female DJs, Technology and Electronic Dance Music Culture*. Bristol: Intellect.

Frith, Simon and Savage, Jon (1998) 'Pearls and Swine: Intellectuals and the Mass Media'. In Steve Redhead, Derek Wynne and Justin O'Connor (eds) *The Clubcultures Reader: Readings in Popular Cultural Studies* (7–17). Oxford: Blackwell.

Garratt, Sheryl (1998) *Adventures in Wonderland: A Decade in Club Culture*. London: Headline.

Haslam, Dave (1998) 'DJ Culture'. In Steve Redhead, Derek Wynne and Justin O'Connor (eds) *The Clubcultures Reader: Readings in Popular Cultural Studies* (150–61). Oxford: Blackwell.

Hebdige, Dick (1983) *Subculture: The Meaning of Style*. London: Methuen.

Hendersen, Pat W. (2009) *Decade*. London: Phoenix Publishing.

—(2010) *Want*. Raleigh, NC: lulu.com.

—(2012) *Club*. Raleigh, NC: lulu.com.

Keay, D. (1987) 'Aids, Education and the Year 2000'. *Woman's Own*, 31 October: 8–10.

Middleton, Richard (1997) *Studying Popular Music*. Milton Keynes, Philadelphia, PA: Open University Press.

Millar, Martin (1997) 'How Sunshine Star-traveller Lost His Girlfriend'. In Sarah Champion (ed.) *Disco Biscuits: New Fiction from the Chemical Generation*. London: Hodder & Stoughton.

Muggleton, David (1998) 'The Post-subculturalist'. In Steve Redhead, Derek Wynne and Justin O'Connor (eds) *The Clubcultures Reader: Readings in Popular Cultural Studies* (167–85). Oxford: Blackwell.

Noon, Jeff (1993) *Vurt*. London: Pan Books.

—(1995) *Pollen*. Manchester: Ringpull.

—(1997) 'DJNA'. In Sarah Champion (ed.) *Disco Biscuits: New Fiction from the Chemical Generation* (171–87). London: Hodder & Stoughton.

—(2000a) 'Dub Fiction'. In Steve Redhead (ed.) *Repetitive Beat Generation* (111–18). Edinburgh: Canongate.

—(2000b) *Pixel Juice*. London: Anchor.

—(2001) *Needle In the Groove*. London: Black Swan.

Owen, Frank (2004) *Clubland Confidential*. London: Ebury Press.

Phillips, Dom (2009) *Superstar DJs Here We Go!: The Incredible Rise of Clubland's Finest*. London: Ebury Press.

Redhead, Steve (ed.) (2000) *Repetitive Beat Generation*. Edinburgh: Canongate.

Reynolds, Simon (1998) 'Rave Culture: Living Dream or Living Death?' In Steve Redhead, Derek Wynne and Justin O'Connor (eds) *The Clubcultures Reader: Readings in Popular Cultural Studies* (84–93). Oxford: Blackwell.

Rietveld, Hillegonda C. (1993) 'Living the Dream'. In Steve Redhead (ed.) *Rave Off: Politics and Deviance in Contemporary Youth Culture* (41–78). Aldershot: Avebury.

River, Michael (1997) 'Electrovoodoo'. In Sarah Champion (ed.) *Disco Biscuits: New Fiction from the Chemical Generation* (97–107). London: Hodder & Stoughton.

St James, James (1999) *Disco Bloodbath*. London: Sceptre.

Thompson, Hunter S. (1979) *The Great Shark Hunt*. New York: Summit Books.

—(2000) *Fear and Loathing in America – The Brutal Odyssey of an Outlaw Journalist 1968–1976*. London: Bloomsbury.

—(2009) *Ancient Gonzo Wisdom*. Cambridge, MA: Da Capo Press.

Thornton, Sarah (1995) *Club Cultures: Music, Media and Subcultural Capital*. Cambridge: Polity.

UK Government (1994) Criminal Justice and Disorder Act. http://www.legislation.gov.uk/ukpga/1994/33/section/63 [accessed 29 December 2012].

Warner, Alan (2000) 'Celtic Trails'. In Steve Redhead (ed.) *Repetitive Beat Generation* (127–34). Edinburgh: Canongate.

Weinzierl, Rupert and Muggleton, David (2003) 'What is "Post-subcultural Studies" Anyway?' In David Muggleton and Rupert Weinzierl (eds) *The Post-Subcultures Reader* (3–23). Oxford: Berg.

Welsh, Irvine (1994) *Trainspotting*. London: Minerva.

—(1996a) *Ecstasy*. London: Jonathan Cape.

—(1996b) 'The Undefeated'. In Irvine Welsh (ed.) *Ecstasy: Three Tales of Chemical Romance* (151–276). London: Jonathan Cape.

—(2000) 'Post-Punk Junk'. In Steve Redhead (ed.) *Repetitive Beat Generation* (137–50). Edinburgh: Canongate.

—(2002) *Glue*. London: Vintage.

Wolfe, Tom (2009) *Radical Chic and Mau-mauing the Flak Catchers*. London: Picador.

Interviews

Hendersen, Pat W. (2012) Interviewed by Simon Morrison, via phone, 4 February.

Welsh, Irvine (2001) Interviewed by Simon Morrison.

—(2012) Interviewed by Simon Morrison, Glasgow, 19–23 February.

CONTRIBUTORS

Bernardo Alexander Attias is Professor and Chair of Communication Studies at California State University Northridge, USA. His research is at the intersections of communication, technology and media, from the perspectives of rhetoric and cultural studies. Alongside Anna Gavanas, he guest-edited the special issue of *Dancecult* devoted to DJ culture. He has over 20 years of DJ experience, spinning eclectic sets incorporating house, hip-hop, and drum 'n' bass as well as funk, jazz, blues and swing.

Chris Christodoulou is a Lecturer in Contemporary Media Practice at the University of Westminster in London. He completed his PhD on speed and cultural practice in drum 'n' bass, undertaken at London South Bank University, in 2009. His article, 'Rumble in the Jungle: City, Place and Uncanny Bass', appeared in *Dancecult*'s special issue on DJ Culture (2011, 3(1)).

Kai Fikentscher is a performer-scholar with a background in jazz performance and ethnomusicology. His multi-disciplinary research into music, dance, technology and culture has been published in several languages, in various edited volumes and journals, and in his award-winning book *'You Better Work!' Underground Dance Music in New York City* (Wesleyan University Press, 2000). He has lectured and performed (on electric guitar and turntables) in the US and Germany.

Ivan Paolo de Paris Fontanari received his doctoral degree in Social Anthropology from Federal University of Rio Grande do Sul, Brazil. He has conducted ethnographic research and published in Portuguese and English about middle- and working-class electronic dance music scenes in Brazil on issues as identity, globalization, cultural mediation and social trajectories. He is author of *Os DJs* *da Perifa: Música Eletrônica, Trajetórias e Mediações Culturais em São Paulo* (Editora Sulina, 2013).

Anna Gavanas, Docent, holds PhD in Social Anthropology from Linköping University, Sweden. Her publications on electronic music focus on technological change, authenticity and gender. In 2011 she was a Guest Editor of a special issue on DJ cultures for the international journal *Dancecult*. A vinyl DJ since the late 1990s, she is music producer and label manager at Meerkat Recordings, making electronic music as Gavana and as a member of Bass Trolls.

Mirko M. Hall is the Germanist at Converse College, a liberal arts college for women in South Carolina. His research in the field of Sound Studies explores how musical practices offer listeners strategies for actively participating in cultural creativity, critique and resistance. He is completing *Musicking Against the Grain: German Musical Discourses, 1800–1980*, a book that explores the nexus of music and critical theory in modernity.

Tim Lawrence is professor in Cultural Studies at the University of East London. He is the author of *Love Saves the Day: A History of American Dance Music Culture, 1970–79* (Duke University Press, 2003), *Hold On to Your Dreams: Arthur Russell and the Downtown Music Scene, 1973–92* (Duke University Press, 2009), and the forthcoming *Life and Death on the New York Dance Floor, 1980–83*. He is a founding member of Lucky Cloud Sound System, which has been staging parties with David Mancuso in London since 2003, and also of the Centre for Cultural Studies Research at the University of East London.

Ed Montano is a lecturer in Music Industry at RMIT University, and writes for the Australian dance music website *Inthemix* (inthemix.com.au). His research focuses on commercial club culture in Australia. Ed is Reviews Editor and Operations Director for *Dancecult: Journal of Electronic Dance Music Culture*, and is on the executive committee of the International Association for the Study of Popular Music.

Simon A. Morrison is currently researching a PhD at Leeds University, considering the intersection of club culture and literature. He also teaches at both Leeds and Manchester Metropolitan universities. During the last 18 years, he has reported on global club cultures, editing Ministry of Sound's *Ibiza* magazine and writing for magazines such as *DJ* and *Mixmag*, culminating in the book *Discombobulated* (Headpress, 2010).

Johanna Paulsson is an independent writer and music journalist. She has a BA with a major in Musicology from Stockholm University and is currently a music critic for the Swedish newspaper *Dagens Nyheter*. As a freelance journalist she covers everything from opera to electronic dance music culture and is particularly interested in the relationship between music and politics.

Rosa Reitsamer is an Assistant Professor at the Department of Music Sociology at the University of Music and Performing Arts in Vienna, Austria. In 2013 she published her monograph *Die Do-it-yourself-Karrieren der DJs: Über die Arbeit in elektronischen Musikszenen* (Transcript Verlag, 2013) and various articles on how agency is achieved in popular music scenes and how gender, ethnicity and locality are negotiated by cultural producers.

Hillegonda C. Rietveld is Reader in Music Culture at London South Bank University and Editor of *IASPM@Journal*. She has published extensively in the field of electronic dance music culture; DJed in dives, clubs and festival tents; and produced her first electronic dance music recording in 1982, as member of Quando Quango, for Factory Records.

Jonathan Yu is a doctoral candidate in the School of Culture and Communication at the University of Melbourne. His research is on the impact of new digital technologies on the consumption, production and distribution of music.

Naida Zukic is a New York-based, Bosnian-born Communication and Performance Studies scholar and Butoh artist. Her research critiques photographic representations of violence and formulates new theories of subjectivity, ethics and responsibility. Zukic's digital performances, which evoke the ethico-aesthetics of photography, memory and movement, have been screened internationally. She has published on these topics in *Digital Icons*, *Liminalities* and *Text and Performance Quarterly*.

INDEX

The letter f after an entry denotes figure

A-list, the 222
A Way Of Life (A.W.O.L.) (club)
    208–9
Ableton 21, 27, 156 *see also*
    software
accelerated culture 198–9, 207–8
    see also speed
acceleration *see* speed
acid house 83–4 *see also* Welsh,
    Irvine
Ackerman, Mark 226
acoustics 104–6, 113
ACS Crossroads conference 5
actor-network theory (ANT)
    165–70
African-Caribbean culture 208–9
Afrika Bambaataa 111, 240
aggressive parody 281
aggrotech 273
AIDS 85, 238–9
Albini, Steve 30
'Amen' break 201–2
Amphi Festival 271
analogue sound 24, 31–3, 37, 110,
    130, 200 *see also* vinyl
Andrews, Tony 34
Andy C. 212
Apple Inc. 114
arena DJs *see* stadium DJs
Arthrob (parties) 293
Asia-Pacific Electronic Music
    Conference 189

Attali, Jacques 118
audience
    expectation 93
    participation 89–90
    reading the 156
    virtual 131–2
aura 36, 38
authenticity 17, 30–6, 38–9,
    169–70 *see also* originality
    audiences and 94
    creative dialogue and 90
'autonomous zones' 265 *see also*
    TAZ

bailes black (black dances) 259
Bakhtin, Mikhail 282
'bardo' 144
'bass materialism' 208
Baudrillard, Jean 80
beatmatching 21, 23–5
    double-drops and 212
    laptops and 26–8
    legitimacy and 153–5
    trainwrecking and 28–9
bedroom DJs 116–18
    music programming and 128–9
Beeler, Stan
    Dance, Drugs and Escape 294
Bell, Alexander Graham 18
Bell, Chichester A. 18
Benjamin, Walter 6, 36
Berger, Jonathan 35

Big Black
  Songs About Fucking 30
Billboard 237
Block, Martin 133–4
  Make Believe Ballroom, The
    133
Born in the USA (Springsteen,
    Bruce) 15
Bourdieu, Pierre 53
BPM counters 24, 154
branding 92–3, 95, 177, 179–81,
    184–5
Brazil *see* São Paulo
breakbeats 3, 202–5, 210
bricolage 205
Brody, Michael 137
broken beats 89n. 3
Buchanan, Shaun 233
'burden of representation' 61–2
Burgess, Jim 220, 226, 233,
    238
'buttonistas' 29 *see also* 'sync'
    button

Cadenas, George 232
Calcutt, Andrew
  Cult Fiction 297
Capoeira (dance) 207
carnival 282
Carpenter, Kenny 123, 127
CD players 24–5
CDs (compact discs) 15–16, 168–9
  see also digital sound
  beatmatching and 24–5
  music programming and 127
  relationship with sound 36–7
  sound quality and 30–3
CDJs 24–8, 153–5
celebrity DJs 94, 132–3
Central Station Records (Sydney)
    176
Champion, Sarah
  Disco Biscuits 293, 297–8

cheating 152–6
'Chemical Generation' 291
Chicago, Illinois 84, 177
  DJs 257–8
Chin, Brian 237
class 213–14
  São Paulo and 251, 252–4,
    260, 262–3
Club (Henderson, Pat W.) 301–3
club culture 295, 306 *see also*
    synthscenen
  female DJs and 62–4 *see also*
    gender imbalance
  Sydney and 176–9
club fiction 294–6 *see also*
    literature
clubbing 139
Clubland Confidential (Owen,
    Frank) 298
clubs 285
  New York City and 85, 126,
    132, 142, 144 *see also*
    discotheques; Saint, the
  São Paulo and 254
  Sydney and 174, 176–80
collecting 169–70
collective activism 70–1
'collective effervescence' 142
collective participation 80, 82–3,
    86, 97
Combahee River Collective 236
compact discs *see* CDs
competition 162–3
compositions 6, 118–19 *see also*
    recomposition
computer software *see* software
concert events 132 *see also* events
'Confessions of a Middle-aged
    Ecstasy Eater' (Anon.) 298
consumer culture 236–7
'controllerists' 16, 27–9
Cook, Alice Clark 20
Crocker, Frankie 137

cult fiction 293, 295, 310–11 *see also* literature
Cult Fiction (Calcutt, Andrew and Shephard, Richard) 297
culture 295–6
cyborgs 8, 249
cylinders 17–19

dance clubs 139–40 *see also* discotheques
Dance, Drugs and Escape (Beeler, Stan) 294
dance music
history 177–8
lifespan 186–8
Dancecult: Journal of Electronic Dance Music Culture (Special Issue on the DJ) 5
dancers 90
Saint, the and 220–1, 223–4, 227, 236
sexual orientation and 223–4
Danceteria (club) 234
dancing 207–9
Deadmau5 21–4, 93, 140
Decade (Hendersen, Pat W.) 301
Deleuze, Gilles 40–1, 104–6, 108
Thousand Plateaus: Capitalism and Schizophrenia, A 104
democratization 104, 113 *see also* bedroom DJs
Depeche Mode
'Master and Servant' 273
DePino, David 126
'Der Mussolini' (DAF) 280
Descolada 253
deterritorialization 104–6, 108–10, 118–19
technology and 115–16
Detroit, Michigan 84, 177
Deutsch Amerikanische Freundschaft (DAF) 272, 285–6

'Der Mussolini' 280
Die Krupps 281
digital audio workstations 113–14 *see also* technology
digital sound 30–7 *see also* digitization
downloading and 93
gender and 57
Digital Vinyl System (DVS) 16, 25–6
digitization 113–15, 119–20 *see also* technology
'Disco, The' 278
Disco Biscuits (Champion, Sarah) 293, 297–8
Disco Bloodbath (St James, James) 298
disco music 228–9
discotheques 81, 110–11, 135–9
membership and 139–40
DJ-auteur 91
'DJ Culture' (Pet Shop Boys) 125
DJ-driven literature 294–5 *see also* literature
DJ Forums 22
DJ Law 203–4
DJ mixes 131–2
DJ schools 154 *see also* education
DJ Tech Tools 22, 35
DJs 6, 7
Dodd, Alan 220, 225, 233
doof 86
double-drops 212
dromocracy 198–9
dromology 196, 198, 215
dromosphere 199, 208
drugs 108, 291, 305
drum machines 39–40
drum 'n' bass 195
class and 213–14
dancing and 207–9
DJs 200–5, 208, 212, 256–9, 263
double-drops and 212

formation of 205–6
London and 211–15
performances 200–5, 207–9
regional differences and 210–11
São Paulo and 252–5, 266
speed and 195–9, 204–5,
    210–15
dub 83, 129, 205–6, 299
dubstep 89
DVS see Digital Vinyl System

earnings see fees
Ecstasy 108, 291
Ecstasy (Welsh, Irvine) 293
Edison, Thomas Alva 17–18
education 117 see also DJ schools
international DJs and 182
Electric Kool Aid Acid Test
    (Wolfe, Tom) 293
electro 139
Electroheads 273
electro-industrial music 273–4,
    277, 279–86
electronic body music (EBM)
    273–4, 277, 279–86
electronic dance music (EDM) 2,
    39–40
as genre 2–3
events 80–1, 83–5
tactile-acoustic experiences and
    82
user-groups 2n1
electronic pop-dance 2
Electronic Solidarity 260–2
electronica 2
'Electrovoodoo' (River, Michael)
    298
employment conditions 130–3,
    224–5
enculturation 294
Encyclopedia of Record Producers,
    The (Olsen/Verna/Wolff) 54
ethnicity 68–9 see also race

etiquette 162
Eurodisco 229–30
European DJ cultures 51–2 see
    also gender imbalance
events 132, 140
experience 118 see also
    inexperience
eye contact 92

Fabio 201, 203–4
Face, The 311
Faderhead
    'Noisebastardz' 277–8
    'Tanz Zwo Drei Vier' 277
Farrugia, Rebekah 8
fascism 270, 274, 279–81
'feedback loop' 28–9
fees 92–3
female underrepresentation 51–4
    see also gender imbalance;
    sexualization
cultural processes and 56–9
guitars and 54
networking strategies for 69–74
reasons for 54–60
technology and 54–7, 59, 73
femininity 60–9, 73, 283 see also
    female underrepresentation
'feminist-queer politics' strategy 72
Ferreira, Pedro 40–1
festivals 140 see also events and
    raves
fiction 297–8
'fidelity' 31
Fierman, Michael 227, 233–4
Final Scratch 164
500, the 222
Flamingo (club) 221–2, 225, 229
flow 142, 173–4
Flür, Wolfgang 272, 275
'For an Angel' (van Dyk, Paul)
    114–15
format theory 17

formatism 17
formats 15–17, 30–6
  early format wars and 17–21
  relationship with sound and
    36–9
Foucault, Michel 81 *see also*
  heterotopia
'four-to-the-floor' disco beats 3,
    84, 201, 280
Friday, Ian 130
funk 40, 202–4, 215, 235, 259
Funktion One 34
futurepop 273

gabba 204, 279
gay scene, the 221, 236 *see also*
  AIDS; homophobia; sexual
  orientation
gender imbalance 7–9, 51–3,
    90–1, 283–4 *see also* female
    underrepresentation; male
    domination
  Brazil and 250
  commercialization and 60
  DJs and 90–1, 94–6
  gatekeeping practices and 56–8
  profiling 223
  strategies for 71–2
  technology and 59
  visual culture and 95
geographic locations 177–8
Gill, Rosalind 60–1
Ginsberg, Allen
  Howl 293
Girl Talk 164
globalization 2, 90, 173–5
  bedroom DJs and 118
  club culture and 177–8
  speed and 211
  stadium DJs and 93–4
Glue (Welsh, Irvine) 304–10
Goa, India 86, 88, 177
Goodman, Steve 208–9, 278–9

Goths 273
Grandmaster Flash 111
graphology 308–9
Grasso, Francis 111
Gristleism (Throbbing Gristle) 16
Groove (magazine) 71
Grooverider 201, 203–4
Guattari, Félix 104–6, 108
  *Thousand Plateaus: Capitalism
    and Schizophrenia, A* 104
Guetta, David 23, 92–3, 140
Guitar Player 30
guitars 54

Hacienda (club) 293
Halloween Martin 133–4
  Musical Clock, The 133
'Hands of the DJ' (Noon, Jeff)
    300
hardcore 204, 210
Hawtin, Richie 25
heartbeat 2–3
Heaven (club) 240
Hebdige, Dick 295
  *Subculture: The Meaning of
    Style* 307
Hendersen, Pat W. 301
  Club 301–3
  Decade 301
  Want 301
Henriques, Julian 83, 85
heterogeneous networks 165–7
heterotopia 81, 96
Hilton, Paris 23
Hi-NRG 230, 237–8, 240
hip-hop 111, 201, 210
history 177–8
'Homo Karaoke' (Noon, Jeff) 299
homophobia 239
house music 79–80, 135–9, 200–5,
    210, 240
  enculturation and 294
  Saint, the and 221, 240–1

São Paulo, Brazil and 259
Second Summer of Love and 291
Vasquez, Junior and 238, 240
'How Do You Know He's Not Playing Pac-Man?' (Montano, Ed) 164
Howl (Ginsberg, Allen) 293
Humphries, Tony 126
'hyperconsumption' 236
hypersonic frequencies 32n. 12

Ibiza (record label) 206
Ibiza, Spain 140, 177
identity 22, 91, 263, 296–7
    branding and 180–1
    clubber 252–3
    consumer culture and 236
    formats and 17, 38
    gender 56, 59, 67, 91
    hybrid 262, 265
    mixing and 248–9
    programming and 126, 142–3
identity politics 236
immersion 81–6, 88
industrial music 269–70, 281–2
    see also electro-industrial music; *synthscenen*
inexperience 161–3 *see also* 'kids'
'inner groove distortion' 19
international DJs 174–5, 178–86
internet, the 118, 131–2, 143 *see also* social media; websites
    authenticity and 169–70
    Brazil and 256
    gender and 53, 57, 59–60, 71–2
    stealing and 159
internet DJs 145
Inthemix (publication) 175

Jamaica 3 *see also* Jamaican soundsystem culture

Jamaican soundsystem culture 83, 205–6, 208–9, 257, 278
Jarvis, Al 133
Jay, Randy 260–1
Jellybean Benitez 240
Jorba, Michael 233
Journeys by Stadium DJ (Paul Oakenfield) 92
Jumping Jack Frost 196–7, 201, 201f, 203
jungle 205–6, 279 *see also* drum 'n' bass
'Jungle Techno' (Noise Factory) 206

Kalkbrenner, Paul 140
Kamins, Mark 234
Kenny Ken 202f, 205
Kerouac, Jack 293
    On the Road 293
'kids' 161–3, 169
Kirn, Peter 22
Knuckles, Frankie 132, 137, 143, 144
Kool DJ Herc 111
Kraftwerk 55, 275, 278

labouring refrain 106, 108–9, 118–19 *see also* refrain
Laibach 282
laptops 16, 25–7, 114
    legitimacy and 153–6
    music programming and 127–8
    stigma and 164, 168–70
Latour, Bruno 166
Leary, Timothy 144
    Psychedelic Experience, The 144
Lefebvre, Henri 210
legitimacy 151–6
Leslie, Robbie 223, 226, 231, 233, 235

Levan, Larry 136–9, 219, 224,
    233, 241
Lilica (promoter) 260, 261–2
liminality 105, 143–4
literature 292, 310–11
    DJ characters 298–301
    DJ-driven literature 294–8
    Hendersen, Pat W. 301–4
    music and 293–4, 303–4, 311
    Noon, Jeff 298–301
    Real DJs in 301–4
    Welsh, Irvine 304–10
live performance see performance
'Living The Dream' (Rietveld,
    Hillegonda C.) 296
Loft, The 136–7, 144
London, England 211–15
Looptroop 15
loudspeaker 270

'machinism' 40
Mailman, Bruce 221–6, 231–2,
    237 see also Saint, the
mainstreaming 22–3
Make Believe Ballroom, The (radio
    show) 133
male domination 51–3 see
    also gender imbalance;
    masculinity
Manchester, England 83–4
Mancuso, David 136–7, 144–5, 224
Mantronik, Kurtis 202
Marky (DJ) 259–60
Martin, Jon 128–9
masculinity 55, 73–4, 283 see also
    male domination
    cultural processes and 56–9
    hypermasculinity 285–6
    records and 56–7
    stadium DJs and 94–5
    technology and 53–7, 59, 283
'Master and Servant' (Depeche
    Mode) 273

'Master of Ceremonies' 208–9
McRobbie, Angela 60
MCs 208–9
MDMA see Ecstasy
mechanical in music, the 20, 25,
    29–30, 36
    authenticity and 170
    DJ culture and 38–42, 249
    gender and 54–5, 57
    media squared 297
mediation 248
Melbourne, Australia 152, 157–8
membership 139–40
Mercado Mundo Mix (World Mix
    Market) 253
Merritt, Howard 225, 229, 232,
    233
'Metaphorazine' (Noon, Jeff) 299
'Microphone Chanters' 208–9
MIDI 27, 114
'Militant Vinylists' 15
military aesthetics 269–70, 273,
    277–9
Millar, Martin 298
Milner, Greg 15–16
mixes 131–2
Modulations: Cinema for the Ear
    54
Montano, Ed 164
    'How Do You Know He's Not
        Playing Pac-Man?' 164
    'You're Not a Real DJ Unless
        You Play Vinyl' 164
Moretti, Mia 103
MP3s 17, 33–5
    relationship with sound 37,
        38–9
Mr.C 22
Muggleton, David 295
multiple DJs 131
'music appreciation' 20
music programming 123–5
    club DJs and 125–33, 135

digital technology and 128–30
discotheques and 136–40
DJ identity and 143
flow and 142–5
home studios and 128–30
internet, the and 143
quality/quantity 127–8
radio 133–5
research and 145
resident DJs and 139–41
time and 130–3
music studio, the 6, 88–9
Musical Clock, The (radio show) 133–4
musical journey 130–2, 142–4
musical language 256–7
musicianship 167–8
musicking 113–14
myth 296–7

Nachtmahr 272, 277, 280, 281
   'Unbeugsam' 274–5
   'War on the Dancefloor' 269, 277
Nazi symbolism 270, 279–81 *see also* fascism
Needle in the Groove (Noon, Jeff) 298
neoliberalism 60, 95, 221, 225
network society 211
networks 69–73
New York City 84–5, 135–9, 219–22, 228 *see also* Saint, the
New York Native 235, 237
New York Times 23
Noel, Terry 142
Noise Factory
   'Jungle Techno' 206
'Noisebastardz' (Faderhead) 277–8
Noon, Jeff 298
   'Hands of the DJ' 300
   'Homo Karaoke' 299

'Metaphorazine' 299
'Orgmentations' 299–300
Needle in the Groove 298
Pixel Juice 299–301
Pollen 293
Vurt 298
normative music structure 264–5
Nossa Senhora do Bonsucesso 260–1
nostalgia 41, 79, 238
nostalgie de la boue 296, 310
Nyquist-Shannon sampling theorum 32n. 12

Oakenfield, Paul
   Journeys by Stadium DJ 92
occupations 213
Olsen, Eric
   Encyclopedia of Record Producers, The 54
On the Road (Kerouac, Jack) 293
'open work' 6
optimal experience 142
'Orgmentations' (Noon, Jeff) 299–300
originality 156–60, 167
Owen, Frank
   Clubland Confidential 298
Owl City 164

Panasonic Technics SL–1200 24, 111, 200 *see also* Technics turntables
panic 203–4
Parada da Paz (Peace Parade) 253
Paradise Garage 136–8, 219, 223–4, 233–4
Parsons, Chuck 226, 233
Paulsson, Johanna 271
Pauly D 23
performances 7, 40, 113, 169, 132
   actor-network theory and 166, 168

authenticity in 93–4
branding and 180–1
failure and 24, 28–9
gender and 59–60, 95–6
international 182, 185
laptop 164
musicianship and 168
performance theory 247–9,
264–5
speed and 200–5
stealing and 159–60
technology and 114
Pet Shop Boys 124–5
'DJ Culture' 125
Phillips, Elbert Struthers 128
phonograph, the 17–21
Pioneer CD players 24–5, 28,
153n. 3, 154 see also CDJs
Pioneer CDJ–1000 24–5
Pioneer CDJ–2000 Nexus 28
Pioneer Rekordbox 154 see also
software
Pixel Juice (Noon, Jeff) 299–301
Plastic People 89, 92
playback 24–5
pleasure 104, 107–8, 142, 208,
282
politics 270, 279–82
Pollen (Noon, Jeff) 293
Porte Alegre 251
postfeminism 60–1
post-rave 132, 292
power relationships 269–71,
274–8, 282
pre-performance work 255, 275–6
pre-programming 94–5
producer DJs 89–90, 93, 180–1
producer packs 129
'programmatic politics' strategy
71–2
programming see music
programming
projetos 253

Psychedelic Experience, The
(Leary, Timothy) 144
psytrance 86–7

queer 67, 72

race 222–4, 233, 239, 258 see also
ethnicity
Rackus, Trent 187–8
radio DJs 126, 133–5, 137, 143–5,
257
radio shows 133–5
Rage (club) 203–4
Rainer, Thomas 274–5, 276–7
raves 86–7, 200–1, 209–10, 298
see also events; festivals
culture and 294–6
literature and 293
novels and 297
São Paulo and 254
underground 265
'recomposition' 157–60
record collecting 56–7, 133–4,
169–70
recording 31–2, 36–7, 169
technology 168 see also
technology
records 19 see also vinyl
record stores 56–7
Red Bull 197–8
Redhead, Steve
Repetitive Beat Generation 298
refrain, the 104–6, 108–10 see also
labouring refrain
technology and 116, 119
reggae 82–4, 209, 299, 303
regional differences 210–11
Regisford, Timmy 85
Reitsamer, Rosa 181, 182, 255, 284
remixes 157–8, 180
Repetitive Beat Generation
(Redhead, Steve) 298
resident DJs 139–41

Reynolds, Simon 79
  'Wargasm: Military Imagery in
    Pop Music' 279
  'rhythmanalysts' 210
rhythmical structures 3
Rietveld, Hillegonda C. 265
  'Living The Dream' 296
River, Michael
  'Electrovoodoo' 298
Rivera, Richie 229, 233
rock music 186
Rodgers, Tara 52–3
Roland TB–303 Bass Line 84, 111
    see also synthesizers
Roland TR–808 Rhythm
    Composer 40, 111 *see also*
    synthesizers
Rolling Stone 21
Ryle, Gilbert 40

sadomasochism (SM) 270–1
Saint, the (club) 136, 219–21
  AIDS and 238–9
  architecture of 221–2
  closure of 239–40
  consumer culture and 236–7
  criticism of 231–2, 234–5
  dancers and 220–1, 223–4,
    227, 236, 239
  DJs at 224–35, 237, 240–1
  gay members of 219–24, 234,
    236
  influence of 240
  race and 222–4, 233
sampler 39, 113, 201–2
sampling 156–9, 169, 201–2
San Francisco 228
Sandpiper (discotheque) 222
São Paulo, Brazil 249–51
  'autonomous zones' and 265
  class and 251, 252–6, 260,
    262–3
  cultural mix in 258–62, 267

DJs and 255–62, 266–7
  education and 256
  homogeneous zones and
    254–5
  internet, the and 256
  music scene/events in 252–5,
    259–65
  normative music structure and
    264–5
  peripheries of 250, 254–5
  projetos and 253, 255–6, 257
  reaction to EDM 258–60
  sexual orientation and 263–4
Sasha 114–15
Savarese, Tom 238
Schechner, Richard 248
Schneider, Florian 278
Schulman, Jacob 22
Scott, Wayne 232
  'seamless flow experience' 142
Second Summer of Love 291
Seeger, Anthony 247–8, 264–5
Serato 127, 130 *see also* software
  Itch 27
  Scratch Live 26
sex *see* gender imbalance
sexual orientation 68, 72 *see also*
    homophobia
  Saint, the and 219–24, 234,
    236
  São Paulo and 263
sexualisation 60–9 *see also* female
    underrepresentation
Sharma, Sonia 183
Shelter, The 85
Shephard, Richard
  Cult Fiction 297
Sherman, Terry 222–3, 235
Skrillex 23, 93
SM (sadomasochism) 270–1
social audio platforms 118 *see also*
    social media
social interaction 256–7

social media 94, 117–18, 131–2,
135, 276 *see also* internet,
the; websites
gender and 59, 63, 71–2
social structures 166
'societal racism' 223
society 291–2
software 26–8, 114–17, 128–30,
154, 200, 212
Songs About Fucking (Big Black)
30
sonic dominance 85, 96–7
sonic immersion 81–6, 88
'sonic warfare' 209
soulful house 138–9
Sound Factory 221
sound quality 30–6
'sounding' 83
Sousa, John Philip 19–20
spectacle, the 79–80
speed 195–6
class and 213–14
drum 'n' bass and 195–9,
204–5, 210–15
London and 211–15
network society and 211
urban life and 211
violence and 196–8, 199
Springsteen, Bruce
Born in the USA 15
St James, James
Disco Bloodbath 298
St John, Graham 5, 86, 265
stadium DJs 80, 91–6 *see also*
superstar DJs
stealing 156–60, 169
stem packs 129
Sterne, Jonathan 17
Stokes, Martin 258, 265
Straw, Will 57, 187
studio, the 6, 88–9
Studio 54 136
subcultural capital 249, 305

Subculture: The Meaning of Style
(Hebdige, Dick) 307
subjectivity 36–41
super clubs 92, 176–7
superstar DJs 106–8, 110–12, 305,
307 *see also* stadium DJs
clubs and 139–40
deterritorialization and 118–20
music programming and 143
territorialisation and 118–20
Swedish House Mafia 274
Swerve (club) 207
Sydney, Australia 173
Central Station Records 176
commercial club culture in
173–4, 176–8, 184–6
DJ culture in 173, 188–90
flow and 173–4
globalization and 173–8, 191
international DJs and 174–6,
178–86, 189–90
local DJs 178–86, 189–90
transnationalism and 176
synaesthesia 86–8
'sync' button 23, 27–9
synthpop bands 273
synthesizers 39, 111–12 *see also*
technology
synthesizer-sampler 113
synthscenen (the synth scene) 269,
272
carnival and 282
clothing 270, 273–4, 277, 285
DJs 272–8, 284, 286
experience and 284
gender and 283–4
military aesthetics and 269–70,
273, 277–8, 279–81, 285
musical genres within 272–3
offensive imagery in 280–1, 286
politics and 270, 279–82
power relationships and
269–71, 274–8, 285, 286–7

sadomasochism and 270–1,
    273, 285
technology and 270

tactile-acoustic experiences 82 *see
    also* sonic immersion
Tainter, Charles Sumner 18
talent, lack of 23
'Tanz Zwo Drei Vier' (Faderhead)
    277
techne 29
Technics SL–1200 24, 111, 200 *see
    also* Technics turntables
Technics turntables 24, 111, 200,
    205
techno 40, 79–80, 135, 178, 200–6
    São Paulo and 252–5, 266
    Vienna and 181
'techno tourism' 140
technocultural capital 153, 156
technologies of power 112
technology 29, 110–19 *see also*
    formats
    bedroom DJs and 116–18
    change and 163–5, 170
    digitization and 113–15
    experimenting with 112
    gender equality and 59, 73
    Japanese 111
    live performance and 113
    masculinity and 53–6, 59, 283
    synthscenen and 270
    technocultural distinctions and
        151
tempo 2–3
Temporary *Authoritarian* Zone 80
Temporary Autonomous Zone
    (TAZ) 80, 86
Tenth Floor (club) 221–2, 229
terratorialization 105–6 *see also*
    deterritorialization
technology and 116
Thatcher, Margaret 291

Thode, Roy 220, 225–6, 229–33
Thompson, Hunter S. 293, 297
Thornton, Sarah 294
*Thousand Plateaus: Capitalism
    and Schizophrenia, A*
    (Deleuze and Guattari) 104
3D World 183
Throbbing Gristle
    Gristleism 16
Tiësto 93–4, 96, 127, 140, 143
Toco (club) 252, 259
tokenism 62–3
torture 278
Trainspotting (Welsh, Irvine) 293,
    297
'trainwrecking' 28–9
Traktor 130, 153, 156 *see also*
    software
DJ 27
    Scratch 26, 200
trance 3, 86, 88
transnationalism 176, 249
Tucker, Richard 229
turntables 6, 23–6, 110–1, 200,
    205 *see also* vinyl
'turntablism' 111
12 West (club) 223

Umfunktionierung 6
'Unbeugsam' (Nachtmahr) 274–5
'Undefeated, The' (Welsh, Irvine)
    308
'underground' 187–8
'unification of the room' 234

van Buuren, Armin 92–3
van Dyk, Paul 114–15
    'For an Angel' 115
van Veen, Tobias 24, 28
Vasquez, Junior 144, 221, 238, 240
Verna, Paul
    *Encyclopedia of Record
        Producers, The* 54

vibe 83, 90, 96, 277
Vienna, Austria 181–2, 255
vinyl 16–17, 29, 129 *see also*
    Digital Vinyl System
    beatmatching and 24–5
    relationship with sound 36–7
    sound quality and 32–3, 35–6
    turntables and 6, 23–6, 110–11,
        200, 205
Virilio, Paul 196, 198–9
Virtual DJ 27
virtuosity 17, 21–30
    human component and 24
visual dimension 81, 85–7, 93–4
    see also spectacle
    gender and 95
vocoder 270, 279
Vurt (Noon, Jeff) 298–9

Wall Street Journal 22
Walters, Barry 234
Want (Hendersen, Pat W.) 301
war 278
'War on the Dancefloor'
    (Nachtmahr) 269
Warehouse, the (club) 137
'Wargasm: Military Imagery in
    Pop Music' (Reynolds,
    Simon) 279
websites 22–3, 63, 129, 131–2
    see also internet, the; social
    media

Drum 'n' Bass Arena 212
Welsh, Irvine 293, 304–5
    Ecstasy 293
    Glue 304–10
    graphology and 308–9
    language and 307–9
    Trainspotting 293, 297
    'Undefeated, The' 308
West, Richard 22
White, Sharon 226, 229, 231–2
white gay community *see* gay
    scene; race
whiteness 69
Wiseman, Richard 211
Wolfe, Tom
    Electric Kool Aid Acid Test
        293
Wolff, Carlo
    *Encyclopedia of Record
        Producers, The* 54
Women's Own 291

Yamaha DX7 111 *see also*
    synthesizers
Yeates, Ray 229
Young, Neil 30–1
'You're Not a Real DJ Unless You
    Play Vinyl' (Montano, Ed)
    164

Zimmerman, Joel Thomas 21–2
    see also Deadmau5